Turner Classic Movies British Film Guides
General Editor: Jeffrey Richards

Cinema and Society Series
General Editor: Jeffrey Richards

PAST AND PRESENT
National Identity and the British Historical Film

James Chapman

I.B. TAURIS

LONDON · NEW YORK

Published in 2005 by I.B. Tauris & Co Ltd
6 Salem Road, London W2 4BU

In the United States of America and Canada distributed by Palgrave
Macmillan, a division of St. Martin's Press,
175 Fifth Avenue, New York NY 10010
www.ibtauris.com

ISBN 1 85043 807 2 (hardback)
EAN 978 1 85043 807 6 (hardback)
ISBN 1 85043 808 0 (paperback)
EAN 978 1 85043 808 3 (paperback)

A full CIP record for this book is available from the British Library
A full CIP record for this book is available from the Library of Congress

Library of Congress catalog card: available

Project management by M&M Publishing Services
Typeset by FiSH Books, London
Printed and bound in Great Britain by MPG Books Ltd, Bodmin

For Einor Day

Contents

List of Illustrations

General Editor's Introduction

DURING the course of the nineteenth century a permanent split developed between academic and popular history. The latter, a heady amalgam of popular painting, poetry, novels, plays and films, is more enduring and influential than almost any academic history. Labour MP and film buff Sir Gerald Kaufman spoke for many when he wrote in his memoir *My Life in the Silver Screen*: 'In my youngest years all my history lessons were taught me via the cinema screen.' Popular history centres largely on the colourful and the arresting, on battles and boudoirs. This tendency is firmly borne out by James Chapman's choice of the 13 British history films for analysis in his superb study of the genre: half of them are concerned wholly or in part with the private lives of royalty and five feature episodes from Britain's wars.

It has long been argued, however, that historical films tell us more about the period in which they were made than about the period in which they were set. Chapman sets out to test that proposition through a systematic, in-depth examination of a series of key films dating from the 1930s to the 1990s. Not only does he provide insightful analyses of the individual films in all their aspects – writing, acting, direction and visuals – but he locates them in their historical and cinematic contexts. He explains the intentions of the film-makers, the reaction of the critics, the success or otherwise of the films at the box office and the responses of audiences both domestic and foreign. He also demonstrates how the films comment on Britain's contemporary foreign policy, on the role and nature of the British monarchy and the

British Empire, and on changing attitudes to class, gender and national identity. Extensively researched, elegantly written, cogently argued and immensely readable, this book is a major contribution to our understanding of the role and influence of popular culture.

Jeffrey Richards

Acknowledgements

THIS book has been a long time in the making. I began thinking about a study of the British historical film in 1996 while writing my first book, *The British at War*, which dealt with the organisation and content of film propaganda in Britain during the Second World War. At the time the only major study of the genre was Sue Harper's magnificent *Picturing the Past: The Rise and Fall of the British Costume Film*, mapping both the production trends and the shifts in popular taste from 1930 to 1950. My own project was different: case studies of selected films from the 1930s to the present. As it happened, *Past and Present* then sat on the shelf for several years. It was twice postponed when irresistible opportunities arose to write books on the James Bond films (*Licence To Thrill*) and then on the British adventure series of the 1960s (*Saints and Avengers*). In the meantime, a number of books have added to the scholarly literature on the historical film, including Andrew Higson's *English Heritage, English Cinema: Costume Drama Since 1980* and Claire Monk and Amy Sargeant's edited volume *British Historical Cinema*, while no less than three titles in the I.B. Tauris 'British Film Guides' series were films I had always intended to include in this study (*The Private Life of Henry VIII*, *A Night to Remember* and *The Charge of the Light Brigade*). Given the long gestation period of the book, I should, therefore, record my thanks in the first instance both to Professor Jeffrey Richards, general editor of the 'Cinema and Society' series, and to Philippa Brewster, my commissioning editor at I.B. Tauris, for their faith in a project that has taken the best part of a decade to come to fruition.

As with any archivally based research project, I owe an enormous debt of gratitude to those unsung archivists and librarians who make the historian's job so much easier than it would be otherwise. The staff of the National Library of the British Film Institute, the British Library at St Pancras, the British Newspaper Library at Colindale and the Public Records Office (now the National Archives) at Kew have provided unstinting assistance that is entirely characteristic but rarely acknowledged. For their special help, I would like to acknowledge the invaluable assistance provided by Janet Moat and Victoria Hedley of the BFI Special Collections Unit. And I am particularly indebted to Kathryn Johnson, Curator of the Modern Drama Collection at the British Library, who kindly arranged for me to consult papers from the Laurence Olivier Archive that had yet to be added to the main collection.

Numerous friends and colleagues have provided advice, assistance and comments in the preparation of this book. My thanks are due in particular to Dr Anthony Aldgate, Dr Mark Connelly, Mr Michael Coyne, Mrs Sally Dux, Dr Jo Fox, Dr Mark Glancy, Dr Sheldon Hall, Professor Sue Harper, Dr Matthew Hilton, Professor Arthur Marwick, Professor Vincent Porter, Dr Amy Sargeant, Professor Pierre Sorlin, Dr Andrew Spicer and Mr Philip Timothy. In the course of my research, furthermore, I have benefited enormously from the opportunity of presenting research papers at the University of East Anglia ('Cinema, History, Identity: An International Conference on British Cinema', July 1998), the Jagiellonian University, Krakow ('British Cinema Pasts', April 2001) and the Institute of Historical Research ('Issues in Film History' seminar group, February 2004). I would like to extend my thanks to the participants in those conferences and seminars who have commented helpfully on my work in progress.

Most of this book was written during a year's study leave from The Open University, and I would be remiss indeed if I did not acknowledge the generosity of my colleagues in the History Department who covered my usual teaching and administrative duties. I should like to record especially my gratitude to Dr Annika Mombauer, who kindly deputised for me on the Taught MA in History while I put my feet up to watch films! The costs of travel and archive work were partially offset by the Arts Faculty Research Committee, which provided additional funding to enable me to complete the book.

The illustrations in this book were provided by BFI Stills, Posters and Designs. They appear by courtesy of Carlton International Media

Ltd, Paramount Home Entertainment (UK) Ltd, PolyGram Filmed Entertainment and Twentieth Century-Fox Film Corporation. They are reproduced here for the purpose of critical analysis.

As ever, I would like to record my thanks to my parents, Colin and Anne Chapman, whose encouragement and support remain invaluable.

This book is dedicated to my late school history master, Einor Day, an inspiring teacher and a true gentleman.

Abbreviations

ABPC Associated British Picture Corporation
AKS   Army Kinematograph Service
ATP   Associated Talking Pictures
BBC   British Broadcasting Corporation
BBFC British Board of Film Censors
B&D   British & Dominions Film Corporation
BFI   British Film Institute
BFM   British Film Makers
BFPA British Film Producers Association
BIP   British International Pictures
CEA   Cinematograph Exhibitors Association
GBPC Gaumont-British Picture Corporation
GCFC General Cinema Finance Corporation
GFD   General Film Distributors
GPO   General Post Office
LFP   London Film Productions
MGM   Metro-Goldwyn-Mayer
MOI   Ministry of Information
NFFC National Film Finance Corporation
PEP   Political and Economic Planning
PFE   PolyGram Filmed Entertainment

Introduction

I think the only reason to make films that are a reflection on history is to talk about the present.

Ken Loach[1]

IT is a truth universally acknowledged – amongst historians at least – that a historical feature film will often have as much to say about the present in which it was made as about the past in which it was set. The idea that films 'reflect' the societies and cultures in which they are produced and consumed is far from being a revelation: it has informed theoretical discourses around film ever since Siegfried Kracauer posited the notion that films provided insights into the collective unconscious of their audiences.[2] A film does not necessarily have to be set in a contemporary idiom to be understood in this way, as Mark C. Carnes recognises in the introduction to his book *Past Imperfect*: 'Even some explicitly "historical" films are chiefly important for what they say about the era in which they were made.'[3] In totalitarian regimes such as Nazi Germany and the Soviet Union, propaganda films used historical stories to make explicit parallels with the present: *Jew Süss* and *Alexander Nevsky*, for example, were consciously allegorical films whose meanings were apparent to audiences at the time.[4] Elsewhere the meanings have often been implicit: it has become commonplace, for example, to relate the ideological themes of the Hollywood western to the social and political concerns of twentieth-century America.[5]

This book is a study of different ways in which the British historical film has used the past as a means of 'talking about' the present. It comprises a series of case studies of historical feature films produced in Britain between the 1930s and the 1990s. The criteria for inclusion I will explain in a moment. First, however, it is necessary to define the terms of this study, in particular the question of what and what does not constitute a historical film. The genre label 'historical film' is one of several – others include 'costume film', 'period film' and 'heritage film' – used to describe films whose narrative is set wholly or partly in the past. Although the precise meaning of these terms is contested, particularly 'heritage film' which is a critical label rather than one that has wide currency in the film industry itself, there is a broad consensus among most, though not all, scholars that a historical film is one that is based, however loosely, on actual historical events or real historical persons. Thus it is that the historical film is a narrower category than the costume or the period film, both of which are terms that denote narratives set in the past but that are not necessarily in themselves 'historical'.[6]

This definition presupposes that there is a difference between 'history' and 'the past'. In this book I am taking history to mean 'the recorded past' or 'the past that we know'.[7] As not everything about the past is or can be known, then it follows that history is an incomplete record of the past. It also follows that a historical film is one that is based on the recorded past. The historical film thus includes films based on historical events such as *The Charge of the Light Brigade*, *Zulu* (the Battle of Rorke's Drift) and *A Night to Remember* (the sinking of the *Titanic*).[8] It also includes biopics (film industry shorthand for 'biographical pictures') about real historical persons. In British cinema most biopics have tended to be about either monarchs (*The Private Life of Henry VIII*, *Tudor Rose*, *Victoria the Great*, *Alfred the Great*, *Mary, Queen of Scots*, *Lady Jane*, *Mrs Brown*, *Elizabeth*) or other famous national figures such as statesmen, generals and adventurers (*The Life Story of David Lloyd George*, *Nelson*, *The Iron Duke*, *Drake of England*, *Rhodes of Africa*, *The Prime Minister*, *The Young Mr Pitt*, *Scott of the Antarctic*, *Lawrence of Arabia*, *Becket*, *Cromwell*, *Young Winston*). However, the historical film in this definition does not include films that happen to be set in the past but are predominantly fictional narratives. Thus it excludes the cycle of Gainsborough costume melodramas of the mid-1940s (*The Man in Grey*, *Fanny by Gaslight*, *Madonna of the Seven Moons*, *The Wicked*

Lady, Jassy) and the acclaimed literary adaptations by film-makers such as David Lean (*Great Expectations, Oliver Twist, A Passage to India*) and Merchant-Ivory (*A Room With A View, Maurice, Howards End, The Remains of the Day*).

It should immediately be apparent that the historical film is an imprecise genre whose boundaries are difficult to define. *Henry V*, for example, could be classed both as a historical film (chronicling Henry's campaign in France culminating in the Battle of Agincourt) and as a Shakespearean adaptation. What about fictional films that include real historical characters (*The Scarlet Pimpernel, Shakespeare in Love*) or that are set against a background of real historical events (*A Tale of Two Cities, Hope and Glory*)? The difficulty of assessing the relative balance of fictional and historical elements in a narrative is exemplified by looking at a film such as *Fire Over England* (dir. William K. Howard, 1937). This was one of a cycle of expensively mounted historical and/or costume films produced by Alexander Korda in the wake of his success with *The Private Life of Henry VIII* in 1933. It was based on a historical novel by A.E.W. Mason set at the time of the Spanish Armada in 1588. The film is a mixture of fact and fiction. The principal protagonist, naval lieutenant Michael Ingolby (Laurence Olivier), is an invented character, and his mission to rescue his father from the Spanish Inquisition is a fictional adventure story rather than one that is based on any recorded events. However, the film also features real historical characters in major roles, especially Queen Elizabeth I (Flora Robson), the Earl of Leicester (Leslie Banks) and King Philip II of Spain (Raymond Massey), and its climax is the defeat of the Armada. The Historical Association, which took a keen interest in the representation of history on film during the 1930s, commissioned a review of *Fire Over England* from two historians which was published in the British Film Institute's educational journal *Sight and Sound*. Professors Hearnshaw and Neale accepted that the main narrative of the film was 'avowedly fiction and must be judged by standards similar to those we apply to historical novels'. While they felt that 'the historical setting in which the fictional adventure story is shown is fairly sound', they objected to the story itself on the grounds that 'history is once more violated for the sake of melodrama'. 'From an educational point of view,' they averred, 'it seems regrettable and even dangerous to link a famous incident in English history with a purely fictitious character.' The one aspect of the film they did admire, however, was Robson's performance as Elizabeth I, which they considered to be historically and psychologically accurate: 'No one will go far wrong who takes his idea of the historical Queen Elizabeth from Flora Robson. Her interpretation, even her words, ring true; and indeed sometimes, as in the supreme moment at Tilbury, her words are the very words spoken by Elizabeth.'[9]

As the historical film cannot always easily be defined simply in terms of its narrative, therefore, other features of the genre must be taken into account. A common characteristic of the historical film, for instance, is its tendency to assert its own status 'as history' through the use of devices such as voice overs and title captions to establish the historical context of the narrative (date, place, events and so forth). There is also a tendency, in British examples of the genre, to assert the historical authenticity of the film. This is evident at several different levels: in the production and promotional discourses around the films (statements by the film-makers, publicity materials and so forth) and in their *mise-en-scène* (especially sets, dressings and costumes). The historical film often quotes from historical sources: thus *Zulu* uses army dispatches and *Scott of the Antarctic* includes quotations from the journals of Captain Scott. This quotation extends to the visuals, in that individual shots are often composed to resemble visual records of the past: Holbein's portraits of Henry VIII (*The Private Life of Henry VIII*), Nicholas Hilliard's of Elizabeth I (*Elizabeth*), G.W. Joy's painting of 'General Gordon's Last Stand' (*Khartoum*) and photographs of Captain Scott and his party (*Scott of the Antarctic*). The historical film thus deploys visual style to create a sense of historical verisimilitude. This verisimilitude (meaning 'the appearance of being real') contrasts with non-historical costume films such as the Gainsborough melodramas which made no pretence of historical authenticity and which displayed signifiers of the past in a highly eclectic way.[10]

Professional historians, of course, are rarely satisfied with the results of film-makers' efforts to represent the past. For a long time, indeed, many historians had little time for the historical feature film and were interested only in actuality and documentary film that had more obvious 'use value' as primary sources. In the 1930s, when the Historical Association sponsored an investigation of the use of films for the teaching of history, it was mainly concerned with educational films for showing in the classroom. It did, however, reserve some barbed asides for 'the historical entertainment film', declaring that 'history is being exploited by the type of historical film shown in the cinemas' and that the result was 'a sin against truth'. It urged that film producers 'should not sacrifice great historical happenings to the imaginary needs of "telling a sequence", nor pervert history for the sake of box office returns. The liberty of the artist to present scenes beautifully and dramatically does not carry with it a licence for falsification.' It recommended, furthermore, 'that a competent historian be called in for consultation before production, in order to give an opinion whether the general impression produced by the film was likely to be reasonably accurate'.[11] The charge that historical feature films misrepresent history in the interests of telling a story has persisted ever since. *Chariots of Fire* (dir. Hugh Hudson, 1981) was criticised for numerous examples of dramatic licence in its account of British athletes competing at the 1924 Olympic Games. 'I understand the needs of movie producers to make a good film', one historian remarked. 'But there were too many historical inaccuracies. The poetic licence was overdone.'[12]

The points of contention between historians and film-makers often focus on the most pedantic details and the exchanges can be highly amusing. In general, however, it is those feature films that challenge received wisdoms about the past which come in for the most severe criticism. This is particularly so with films about the kings and queens of England, and is exemplified by the controversies that erupted over two films released 65 years apart. *The Private Life of Henry VIII* (dir. Alexander Korda, 1933) and *Elizabeth* (dir. Shekhar Kapur, 1998) were both highly publicised films, championed for the cultural and economic prestige they brought to the British film industry. In both cases, however, historians objected to the films' representation of their royal protagonists. In *The Private Life of Henry VIII* it was the question of the king's table manners that provoked censure. The Earl of Cottenham regretted that 'a great king should be portrayed to the world as a vulgar buffoon... In this film Henry VIII is held up to the world at large as a strutting mountebank, petulant, shallow, discourteous and of revolting habits.' He felt that the popularity of the film and the laughs that greeted the notorious banqueting scene were 'a sad commentary on our time'. Another correspondent thought it 'a pity that English history should be made cheap and tawdry'. Alexander Korda, for his part, claimed that he had 'tried to give the atmosphere of the epoch' and asserted what has become the standard response of film-makers to charges of historical inaccuracy: 'To judge this effort by the standards of history books, or even historical novels, is certainly an unjustifiable point of view.'[13] This exchange took place in the letters columns of the *Daily Telegraph*, which also led the attack on *Elizabeth* some six and a half decades later. In this case the controversy centred on the film's suggestion that the 'virgin queen' was in fact nothing of the sort. 'To question Elizabeth's virtue 400 years after her death is not just a blackguardly slur upon a good, Christian woman, but an insult to our fathers who fought for her', an enraged editorial declared. 'It should rouse England to chivalrous anger.' The newspaper cited a leading Tudor historian, asserting that '[t]here is no doubt among serious historians that Elizabeth I died *virgo intacta*'. The director replied that 'her virginity is a matter of interpretation'.[14]

That the historical film should provoke such controversy suggests that there is more at stake here than just the issue of historical accuracy. The historical film raises questions such as whose history is being represented, by whom and for whom? The theme of identity is central to the genre: class, gender and specifically national identities are among its principal concerns. The historical film is not merely offering a representation of the past; in most instances it is offering a representation of a specifically national past. National histories are fiercely protected and contested. Nothing better illustrates this than the hysterical reaction in the British press to Hollywood films that distort the historical record of 'our finest hour' such as *Objective Burma!* (dir. Raoul Walsh, 1945) and *U-571* (dir. Jonathan Mostow, 2000). The scenario reports of the British Board of Film Censors provide a revealing anecdote of the extent to which the censors saw themselves as guardians of national history. When Columbia Pictures proposed a film based on Comyns Beaumont's notorious book *The Private Life of the Virgin Queen* in 1947 – a work claiming that Sir Francis Bacon and the Earl of Essex were Elizabeth's sons from a secret marriage – it received short shrift from the examiner who thought it 'a deplorable book in that it poses as historical truth'. 'It is known that some American films have twisted and adapted OUR history to suit THEIR needs,' the report went on, 'but it would be reprehensible if a British producer followed suit by basing a film on this travesty of history.'[15] Yet, as we shall see, British film-makers have proved equally adept at adapting the past to meet their own cultural and ideological concerns.

The subject matter of the historical film involves a special relationship with notions of nationhood and national identity. The

British historical film offers a popular version of the past that promotes dominant myths about the British historical experience for lay audiences who do not comprise large numbers of professional historians. The use of the word 'myths' in this context should not imply that historical films have no basis in fact, but rather that they tend to endorse narratives that accord with popular views of history. Thus British historical films present Britain as leading the resistance to tyranny and oppression (*Fire Over England, This England, Henry V*), dramatise British pluck and courage in adverse conditions (*Scott of the Antarctic, A Night to Remember*) and foreground notable British achievements in fields such as exploration (*Rhodes of Africa, David Livingstone*), aviation (*They Flew Alone, The First of the Few*), invention (*The Magic Box*) and sport (*Chariots of Fire*). The central role of the monarchy in British history is attested to by the preponderance of films dealing with the 'private lives' of rulers such as Henry VIII, Elizabeth I and Queen Victoria. The favourite periods for producers of historical films, moreover, have tended to be those which give rise to narratives of national greatness: the Tudor period, which saw the emergence of England as a great power; the Victorian period, which saw industrial progress and imperial expansion; and the Second World War, which in the popular imagination remains 'our finest hour'. In contrast, there have been relatively few films about periods of internal conflict such as the Dark Ages (*Alfred the Great*) or the English Civil War (*Cromwell, To Kill A King*).

In each of the case studies that comprise the main body of this book I have chosen films in which representations of the national past are both culturally and historically specific. The historical film, in common with all genres, is not a fixed, static entity, but rather one that is subject to a continuous process of change and transformation. It changes in response to a range of determinants: industrial, economic, social, cultural and political. To this end I have chosen a baker's dozen of films produced at different moments that all reward close analysis. As I could easily have chosen an entirely different selection of films, the criteria for selection require explanation. First, the films themselves have to be classified as British according to the industry's own benchmarks (thus allowing the inclusion of MGM's *Beau Brummell*, but ruling out Mel Gibson's *Braveheart*) and their narrative focus must be on an aspect of British history. Second, they must be commercial feature films that had a full UK release. This excludes semi-documentary films such as Kevin Brownlow's *Winstanley* and television films such as Peter Watkins's *Culloden*, though I have referred to these, and other, examples in passing where I felt comparison with theatrical features was warranted. And third, I have opted for only one film per director or production company, though I have, necessarily, included references to other films by the same hands where appropriate.

For the 1930s and 1940s – the decades when cinema-going was, in A.J.P. Taylor's oft-quoted phrase, 'the essential social habit of the age'[16] – I have selected three case studies per decade. For the 1930s I have focused on the three most important producers of historical films: Alexander Korda (*The Private Life of Henry VIII*), Michael Balcon (*The Iron Duke*) and Herbert Wilcox (*Victoria the Great* and *Sixty Glorious Years*). Alexander Korda was the pre-eminent British producer of the decade and no study of the British historical film could omit *The Private Life of Henry VIII* which remains 'the archetypal film of the genre'.[17] This is the film that is seen as making the breakthrough for British films in the American market, thus attesting to its economic significance for the industry. It also encapsulates many of the debates around the question of a national cinema: a film with a uniquely British subject that was written and produced largely by European émigrés. *The Iron Duke* is a rather less well known film that has not been given similar prominence in British cinema historiography as *Henry VIII*. It is a more overtly political film, using the story of Wellington at the Congress of Vienna to draw contemporary parallels with the Treaty of Versailles and the treatment of Germany after the First World War. Its explicitly pro-appeasement narrative largely reflects British public opinion in the mid-1930s. In contrast, Herbert Wilcox's two 'Victoria' biopics – *Victoria the Great* and *Sixty Glorious Years*, which are included together because they are, to all intents and purposes, two halves of one larger film – can be seen as calls for national unity in the changing political climate of the later 1930s. Both films respond to contemporary political circum-stances: *Victoria the Great* extols the virtues of constitutional monarchy in the wake of the Abdication Crisis of 1936, while *Sixty Glorious Years* is an anti-appeasement narrative whose release coincided with the Munich Agreement of 1938.

The 1940s divide into the war and post-war years. For the war I have chosen one now largely forgotten film (*This England*) and one that is established within the canon of classic British cinema (*Henry V*). Both are propaganda films, but they use history in different ways. *This England* is a cheaply made historical pageant that uses an episodic narrative to invoke resistance to domestic tyrants and foreign invaders. It is an essentially defensive narrative that reflects the defiant mood of 1940. Laurence Olivier's film of *Henry V*, by contrast, is an expensively produced, Technicolor epic that interprets Shakespeare's play for 1944 as Britain is shown taking the offensive. Produced with the full support of the Ministry of Information, *Henry V* represents the most explicit example of a film that mobilises the past in response to the present. For the post-war period, Ealing Studios' *Scott of the Antarctic* is a sober tribute to a national hero who represents a particular code of British masculinity. The tragic yet uplifting story of Scott's Antarctic expedition of 1911–12 took on a special resonance in the years of post-war austerity when Britain was perceived as a nation in decline.

The 1950s, often characterised as the 'doldrums era' of British cinema, saw the onset of a long, slow decline in cinema-going. The film industry attempted to lure audiences back into the cinemas with size and spectacle. The two films representing the 1950s, although very different in narrative and visual style, were part of this strategy. *Beau Brummell*, produced in Britain by MGM, is an example of the 'Hollywood British' films of the decade. Its focus on personal ambition and desire and its colourful, expressive visual style are in stark contrast to the Rank Organisation's *A Night to Remember*, a sober, black-and-white reconstruction of the sinking of the *Titanic*, in which personal desire is subordinated to group effort. The two films also reveal significant differences in critical reception: while *A Night to Remember* was praised as a sincere and unsensational film in the best tradition of British film-making, *Beau Brummell* was universally denounced by British critics as an overblown travesty of history from an American company.

The 1960s were a turbulent decade of fundamental and far-reaching social change that also witnessed rapid changes in British film culture, from the social realism of the 'new wave' to the colourful fantasy of James Bond. *Zulu* is a transitional film which looks back to the heyday of the imperial adventure epic whilst also anticipating the anti-war films that were to follow later in the decade. Its representations of empire and race have made it an unfashionable film within the academy, though it remains a popular favourite, not least for its celebration of the courage of Welsh soldiers at the Battle of Rorke's Drift. In contrast, *The Charge of the Light Brigade* is an explicitly anti-militarist film that uses the historic disaster to make a polemical attack on a range of targets, including the British establishment and class system, and American involvement in the Vietnam War. Unlike *Zulu*, however, the film was not a popular success – a failing attributed to its fragmentary narrative.

By the 1970s the British film industry was in a state of almost perpetual crisis: levels of production declined, audiences fragmented and American films dominated the box office more than ever before. Thus I have selected only one film per decade for the 1970s, 1980s and 1990s, reflecting the contraction of the production sector and the declining visibility of British films on British screens. The 1970s are represented by *Henry VIII and His Six Wives*, one of a cycle of historical biopics that exemplified the persistence of traditional film-making practices at a time when cinema audiences were dissipating. A film version of an acclaimed television serial, it was a sign of shifting cultural capital in the film and television industries. The success of *Chariots of Fire* at the 1982 Academy Awards in Hollywood seemed to herald a revival of fortunes for the British film industry. This film of British sporting triumph has been claimed by critics as both a left-wing and a right-wing text that, depending upon one's interpretation, can be seen as either a critique or an endorsement of the social and political values of Thatcherism. Finally, *Elizabeth* was one of a cycle of films that revived the royal biopic in the 1990s, at a time when the British Royal Family was coming under greater public scrutiny and criticism than ever before. Its portrait of a young queen at the centre of political intrigues has drawn comparisons with Diana, Princess of Wales, who died in a car accident as the film went into production. As well as rehearsing familiar motifs of the tension between the public duty and private life of the monarch, *Elizabeth* is notable for its expressive visual style and its baroque *mise-en-scène*.

It is my contention that each of these films – some in more direct and explicit ways than others – invoke parallels between past and present. Sometimes, as Ken Loach's remark suggests, this imparting of contemporary meaning into a historical film is entirely conscious on the film-maker's part. In other cases, as we shall see, there may not necessarily have been any such intent but, nevertheless, contemporary meaning has been read into the film by critics or historians. In such cases, of course, there is always an inherent danger that the meanings thus identified demonstrate the textual ingenuity of the critic in reading the film rather than the intent of those who made it. All textual criticism, of course, is interpretative. This is why any attempt to analyse the meaning of a particular film or group of films should be grounded in contextual as well as textual analysis. Essentially, this is what differentiates the approach of the film historian from other commentators whose interest lies solely in the aesthetic or formal analysis of films. My own position, for what it is worth, is that the interpretative analysis of films becomes justified only when the historical circumstances of production and reception have first been established. Only in this way can we be certain whether the meanings we read into the films were intended by the film-makers themselves or were identified by contemporaries. Otherwise the interpretation of films can become an arid intellectual exercise, designed more to demonstrate one's own familiarity with the latest fashionable trend in cultural theory than to shed any light upon the actual texts that ostensibly are the object of the analysis.

The research method underpinning this study is empiricist. In addition to the films themselves, my primary sources include official documents, studio records, private papers, autobiographies, scripts, press books, trade papers and film journals, and reviews from a wide range of newspapers and periodicals. Each case study begins by placing the film concerned within the institutional and economic contexts of the British film industry at the time it was produced. Feature films are products of an industry whose primary motive is commercial and which is only secondarily influenced by cultural and artistic concerns. Each chapter then proceeds to examine the production history: the process through which the film came to the screen. Here we need to consider in particular the question of creative agency: to what extent were the content and style of the film due to the input of certain individuals (directors, producers, writers, cinematographers, set and costume designers, actors) and how far was the film shaped by external influences (such as political or censorial intervention)? For, as Sue Harper rightly reminds us, filmic representations 'are simply the traces left by the struggles for dominance during the production process – by the contest for creative control'.[18] In this regard it is significant, contrary to the *auteur* theory that traditionally assigns creative agency to the director, that the most influential figures in historical film production in British cinema have tended to be producers:

studio records reveal that *Scott of the Antarctic* was as much Michael Balcon's film as it was Charles Frend's, the prominence accorded to themes of Welshness in *Zulu* suggests the hand of producer-star Stanley Baker rather than director Cy Endfield, and *Chariots of Fire* was regarded within trade discourse as David Puttnam's film rather than Hugh Hudson's. It takes a strong director, such as Tony Richardson (*The Charge of the Light Brigade*) or Shekhar Kapur (*Elizabeth*), to impose their own vision and style on a film. In contrast, directors like Victor Saville (*The Iron Duke*), David Macdonald (*This England*) and Roy Baker (*A Night to Remember*) were contract directors who saw their role as being simply to transfer the script to the screen. Following the histories of production, each chapter proceeds to examine the histories of reception. This is a part of film history where the sources are more fragmentary and are difficult to interpret. Quantitative evidence of reception (in terms of box-office receipts) is not always available. Not until 1969 did distributors declare their receipts from individual films to the trade press; nor do company accounts or Board of Trade records always reveal precise figures. For some films, especially from the earlier periods, we have to rely on the informed estimates of the trade press, though, for the 1930s at least, John Sedgwick's statistical research into popular film preferences does provide more empirically grounded data.[19] Qualitative evidence of reception consists chiefly of reviews, which are not necessarily representative of the responses of cinema-goers, though other sources (such as fan magazines and the work of Mass-Observation) offer insights into the popular reception of certain films. The contexts of production and reception having been established, only then do I offer my own analysis of the films. I am interested principally in what I have called their narrative ideologies: that is the attitudes, assumptions and beliefs that inform the filmic narratives.[20] It is impossible to be entirely objective about cultural artefacts such as films, and, while I hope that my discussion is based on empirical analysis of the films rather than on my own subjective response, readers will nevertheless identify the films of which I am particularly fond. Perhaps this is no bad thing. Good scholarship should be tempered with passion, and I come to this subject with a passionate belief in the social significance and cultural value of British cinema. If this book demonstrates but one thing, it is that the British historical film rewards close investigation, both for its own sake and for the light it sheds on aspects of the British historical experience over the last 70 years.

1

Merrie England:
The Private Life of Henry VIII
(1933)

*T*HE *Private Life of Henry VIII* is a landmark film in the history of
British cinema. It was the first major historical film since the advent
of talking pictures and is credited with reviving a genre that had been
dormant since the silent period; it was the film that established Alexander
Korda as the pre-eminent British producer of the 1930s; and it was the
first British talking picture to become a significant commercial success in
the international market. Its production history has been well
documented by film historians, as have its critical and popular reception
both in Britain and in the United States.[1] Yet most critical discussion of
the film focuses on its significance to the industry rather than on its
content or its qualities as a film. Most commentators agree with Roy
Armes's assessment in his 1978 book *A Critical History of British
Cinema*: 'In retrospect the film is hardly a masterpiece, but in the 1930s it
was a phenomenon – immensely popular in the United States and giving
Korda just that aura of success which he needed to find backing for his
ambitious plans.'[2] My own argument in respect of *The Private Life of
Henry VIII* is that it should be regarded not only as a significant
production achievement for British cinema, but also as a cultural artefact
of considerable importance. Sue Harper has already shown how '*Henry
VIII* instigated a major debate on the historical film in general';[3] but there
is also a strong case to argue that the film was part of a project to establish
a type of 'national film' that would have wide popular appeal.

That said, however, it is impossible to understand the cultural significance of *The Private Life of Henry VIII* without placing it in the context of British cinema in the early 1930s. This was a period when, as Rachael Low put it, 'British film production was either quality or quota'.[4] It was a paradoxical period of apparent stability at the level of industrial infrastructure but of acute instability in terms of production trends and economic viability. It was a time of upheaval followed by consolidation for the film industry with the arrival of talking pictures in the late 1920s and the consequent conversion of studios and cinemas to sound. As in the United States, the costs of sound conversion consolidated economic power within the industry as a number of large, vertically integrated combines emerged through the amalgamation of separate production, distribution and exhibition interests. The formation of the Gaumont-British Picture Corporation (GBPC) in 1927 and British International Pictures (BIP) in 1928 marked the birth of a duopoly that, albeit with subsequent changes in name and control, would dominate the British film industry for decades to come. GBPC, backed by the merchant bankers the Ostrer brothers, was the largest of the two combines, born from an amalgamation of the distributor Gaumont, which already owned its own film studio at Lime Grove, another two distribution companies (Ideal Films and W&F Film Service) and several chains of cinemas. Its leading position was augmented by a production agreement with Gainsborough Pictures in 1928 and by the acquisition of the Provincial Cinematograph Theatres Company, the country's largest cinema circuit, in 1929. By now GBPC controlled a total of 296 cinemas – over twice as many as its rival – and had a production capacity of some 18 to 20 films a year.[5] The second combine was much more the creation of one individual, Scottish businessman John Maxwell, who added a production company (British National Pictures) to his existing distribution and exhibition interests (Wardour Films and Associated British Cinemas) to create British International Pictures. BIP, which changed its name to Associated British Picture Corporation (ABPC) in 1933, owned the largest production facility in Britain in the early 1930s, Elstree Studios, and controlled 118 cinemas.[6] In addition to these two combines, there existed a number of independent producers, ranging from, at the one end, those with ambitions to make 'quality' films, such as Herbert Wilcox's British & Dominions Film Corporation and Basil Dean's Associated Talking Pictures, to, at the other end, smaller outfits specialising in the production of 'quota' films, such as the British Lion Film Corporation, Julius Hagen's Twickenham Film Studios and Norman Loudon's Sound City Films.

The early 1930s was the time when the phenomenon of the notorious 'quota quickies' was at its height. These were an unforeseen consequence of the Cinematograph Films Act of 1927 which, in an attempt to protect the British film industry against American competition, had imposed a minimum quota of British films on distributors and exhibitors. The quota for exhibitors began at 5 per cent, but there were to be phased increases until it reached 20 per cent by 1936, while the quota for distributors was set 2.5 per cent higher. The effects of the Quota Act, as it became known, were mixed. On the one hand, it did result in British films receiving greater screen time and thus gave a much-needed boost to the British production sector. British films' share of their home market rose from a mere 4 per cent in 1926 and 1927, before the introduction of the quota, to 12 per cent in 1928, 19 per cent by 1930 and 24 per cent by 1932 (indicating that in the early 1930s exhibitors were actually showing more British films than they were required to by the Act).[7] At the same time, the number of British-made feature films increased from a low of 37 in 1926 and 45 in 1927 to 72 in 1928, 92 in 1930, 143 in 1932 and 182 in 1934.[8] On the other hand, however, many of these films were quickly and cheaply made, and came to be derided for their minimal production values. An official report into the film industry later blamed the proliferation of low-budget films on 'American renters [who] gradually became "sponsors" of a series of cheap films which had little or no entertainment value even for the meanest taste. By financing these "quota quickies", which gave employment but no prestige to the British industry, the foreign renters fulfilled their quota obligations without impairing the collective advantage of their own product.'[9] While the poor reputation of the quota quickies has since come in for some long-overdue critical rehabilitation – they provided a training ground for future directors including Michael Powell and Carol Reed, and some of them were perfectly competent and entertaining genre films in their own right – the numbers in which they were produced did nothing to dispel the notion that the majority of British films were cheap and shoddy affairs.

It is against this background of 'quality' films on the one hand and 'quota' films on the other that Alexander Korda's entry into British film production should be seen. Korda, the flamboyant Hungarian émigré, had been active as a film-maker both in Europe and in Hollywood before arriving in Britain in 1931. His film-making career began in his native country during the First World War and he quickly established himself as a major figure in the industry. Political turmoil in the aftermath of the war led to Korda's exile and he spent the 1920s working as a peripatetic film-maker in Austria, Germany and America. He returned to Europe at the beginning of the 1930s, first to France, where he directed *Marius* (1931), the first film in a trilogy of adaptations of Marcel Pagnol's successful plays, and then to Britain, where he would remain for the rest of the decade. He directed one quota film for Paramount Pictures (*Service for Ladies*) before establishing London Film Productions in 1932. Korda's production strategy in the short term was geared towards making quota films – he produced, though did not direct, five more films for Paramount – though his ambition was to move into the more prestigious 'quality' end of the market. *The Private Life of Henry VIII*, for which he secured a distribution agreement from the US company United Artists, was to be the film that established Korda in the first division of film production in Britain.[10]

There are several stories about the origins of *The Private Life of Henry VIII*. Perhaps the most well known – and, indeed, the one popularised by Korda himself – was that he was inspired to make the film when, shortly after his arrival in London, he heard a cabbie singing the music hall song 'I'm 'Enery the Eighth I Am' and misunderstood it to be about King Henry VIII rather than the eighth husband of a much-married widow.[11] Another story is that Korda was looking for a starring vehicle for Charles Laughton and noted the actor's likeness to a portrait of Henry VIII.[12] Michael Korda, Alexander's nephew, has pooh-poohed these accounts of the film's origins, only to promote several myths of his own. In particular, Michael Korda suggests that *The Private Life of Henry VIII* was a gamble on his uncle's part, that it was made on a low budget, and that its success took Korda by surprise:

Alex himself never thought of *Henry VIII* as a classic – in fact he went out of his way to prevent it being presented as one. He knew better than anyone that the film was a hasty attempt to put together all the elements that were available to him on a shoestring budget. Once he had succeeded, much to his own surprise, he spent the rest of his life selling the film, borrowing against it, buying it back and re-releasing it throughout the world...Alex well understood the accidental nature of *Henry VIII*. There was no central vision behind it.[13]

It is surprising that Michael Korda, who in his memoir is usually at great pains to assert his uncle's vision and tenacity, should not credit him with greater insight on this occasion. Indeed, far from being a hastily produced, cheaply made film, *The Private Life of Henry VIII* shows every indication of having been a deliberate and calculated example of the kind of 'prestige' film that was a rarity in British cinema at the time. Its success was no accident.

For one thing, it is disingenuous of Michael Korda to claim that the film was made 'on a shoestring budget'. There are various estimates of the film's production cost. Journalist Ernest Betts, in the introduction to a published version of the screenplay, stated that it was made for £59,000. Betts seems to imply this was relatively cheap: 'Some of its scenes cost only £10 or £12. It had no highly paid stars with the exception of Charles Laughton; all the other members of the cast worked for negligible salaries and for the pleasure of the adventure.'[14] Yet, while this figure was roughly comparable to the average production cost of a Hollywood movie in the early 1930s, it was substantially more than most British films of the time. Linda Wood estimates that the average cost of a British film in 1932 was £9,250 (a low figure owing to the preponderance of quota films that could reputedly be made for as little as £1 per foot) and that even by 1936 it was only £18,000.[15] It has also transpired that the sum quoted at the time significantly underestimated the film's actual cost. London Film Productions' own records indicate that the final cost was £93,710. While this figure would be exceeded by several of Korda's productions later in the 1930s, *The Private Life of Henry VIII* was still one of the most expensive British films of its day. It met the industry's own benchmarks of cost and quality and was certainly no 'shoestring' production.[16]

There is much other evidence, besides its cost, to indicate that *The Private Life of Henry VIII* was intended from the outset as a highly prestigious film. Details of its production (at the British & Dominions Imperial Studios at Elstree) were widely reported in the press; the story was serialised in the magazine *Film Weekly* several months before it was released; and the screenplay was published in book form in 1934.[17] Unusually, the film's London trade show (at the Cambridge Theatre on 17 August 1933) took place two months before its West End première (at the Leicester Square Theatre on 24 October 1933). In the interim, the film had also been accorded a 'World Première' at the Lord Byron Cinema in Paris on 1 October and an American première at the Radio City Music Hall in New York on 12 October. The unusual release pattern for the film, indeed, seems uncannily to anticipate the release strategies of modern blockbusters, with publicity circulating months in advance and a series of premières at prestigious locations in different capital cities. This is hardly the sign of a producer unsure about the commercial potential of his film and further suggests that the success of *The Private Life of Henry VIII* was entirely calculated on Korda's part.

As for the claim that there was 'no central vision behind it', this simply does not stand up to scrutiny. Korda was both producer and director of *The Private Life of Henry VIII* and the film shows his imprimatur at every stage of its production. Although the story is credited to Lajos Biro (a fellow Hungarian) and the dialogue to Arthur Wimperis, it seems likely that Korda also had a hand in writing the screenplay. Wimperis admitted as much when he remarked in a *Picturegoer* article in 1934: 'In my own case there are three of us in collaboration – first and foremost Alexander Korda (privately known as Alexander the Cruel, owing to the merciless manner in which he dismisses our pet ideas!), who has forgotten more about story construction than most people ever know.'[18] Furthermore, *The Private Life of Henry VIII* is consistent with Korda's previous work, which included several historical and/or costume films, including *The Prince and the Pauper* (*Seine Majestät, das Bettelkind*, 1920) and *Samson and Delilah* (*Samson und Delilah*, 1922) in Austria, *A Tragedy in the House of Habsburg* (*Tragödie im Hause Habsburg*, 1924) in Germany and *The Private Life of Helen of Troy* (1927) in Hollywood. The latter film, based on a historical novel of the same title by John Erskine and starring Korda's then wife Maria as Helen and Ricardo Cortez as Paris, has been seen by some commentators as the model for *The Private Life of Henry VIII*. Korda's biographer Charles Drazin, for example, considers that it was nothing less than 'a calculated attempt to repeat Alex's previous box-office hit, *The Private Life of Helen of Troy*'.[19]

Korda, for his part, was clear about where his ambitions lay. He saw *The Private Life of Henry VIII* as an example of what he termed the 'international film'. This, he insisted, had been the basis of his production strategy since making *The Prince and the Pauper* in 1920:

> Ever since then I have thought in terms of international films and no other. I might put it epigrammatically and say I believe that international films are what good directors make. And though I have made many bad films in my life I always hope to be a good director. But perhaps the phrase 'international film' is a little ambiguous. I do not mean that a film must try to suit the psychology and manners of every country in which it is going to be shown. On the contrary, to be really international a film must first of all be truly and intensely national. It must be true to the matter in it . . . In my case, if I may say so, it is because *The Private Life of Henry VIII* is English to the backbone I feel it will appeal and succeed abroad.[20]

Korda's definition of the 'international film' was loose, even contradictory; as with many of his pronouncements it was intuitive rather than rational. He believed that *The Private Life of Henry VIII* would succeed in the international market because its story and subject, while arising from British history, would be familiar to overseas audiences. The thing to avoid, Korda believed, was 'to set out to try to suit everybody . . . The result will be a mongrel film which belongs to no country.' It is ironic that some of the films which Korda made following *The Private Life of Henry VIII* – including *The Private Life of Don Juan*, *Catherine the Great* and *Rembrandt* – might be seen as examples of such mongrel films in so far as they were British-made but did not concern specifically British subjects.

While Korda spoke of the 'international film', however, critics were championing *The Private Life of Henry VIII* as a specifically British film. It was greeted with a chorus of patriotic praise by film journalists who were quick to recognise it as a major production achievement. *Picturegoer*, for example, considered it 'the best production that has ever been turned out from a British studio – and there are no exceptions'.[21] *Kinematograph Weekly* declared that it 'is a masterly British achievement, and its box office success is assured'.[22] And the American showbusiness bible *Variety* acclaimed it as 'the finest picture which has come out of England to date'. 'The business this film will do', the reviewer added, 'should convince England's flicker producers that their contention of prejudice on this side of the Atlantic has always been a fallacy.'[23] British producers had long believed that their films were given short shrift by American distributors; *The Private Life of Henry VIII* was to be the film that seemingly disproved the rule.

It was, indeed, the North American release of *The Private Life of Henry VIII* which assured its success. London Films' records indicate that, although by April 1937 the film had recorded a net profit of £116,290, its British box-office receipts amounted to £81,825 – a sum less than its actual production cost.[24] The accepted wisdom in the British film industry was that a film of the expense of *Henry VIII* stood little chance of recovering its costs in the domestic market, as an editorial in *World Film News* towards the end of 1936 made clear: 'The risk in making ambitious films is a very considerable one for England. The home market is small. It is not sufficient to return with any certainty the cost of a film like *Henry VIII*, and it is incapable of returning the cost of *Mutiny on the Bounty*. The foreign market is in American hands.'[25] In the case of *Henry VIII*, at least, the risk paid off. It was reported to have set a record for the Radio City Music Hall with a first-day gross of $18,400.[26] Sarah Street calculates that it grossed $469,646 in the United States (approximately £104,366 based on an exchange rate of $4.50 to £1) and that it was United Artists' seventh top-grossing release of 1933.[27]

There are other indices of a film's popularity besides box-office receipts. The most useful – in the sense that it allows comparisons to be made between films regardless of ticket prices or inflation – is the number of paid admissions to see a particular film. Although no such information is available for this period of British cinema history, some indication of the relative popularity of individual films is provided by John Sedgwick's statistical research into popular film preferences in the 1930s. Sedgwick calculates that *The Private Life of Henry VIII* was the second most popular film released in 1933 and the most popular British film of the year. The most popular film of the year was *Cavalcade*, a 'Hollywood British' film based on Noël Coward's play, with *Henry VIII* coming in ahead of the monster movie *King Kong* and the Cecil B. De Mille historical epic *The Sign of the Cross*, which also, coincidentally, starred Charles Laughton as Emperor Nero. The second most popular British film, in eighth place overall, was Victor Saville's adaptation of J.B. Priestley's *The Good Companions*.[28]

The popular success of *The Private Life of Henry VIII* was such that it immediately became the yardstick against which other British films were judged. It was frequently revived and reissued, even though, in hindsight, critics felt that 'it does not now stand out from other British films as strikingly as it did when it was first shown'.[29] In 1933, however, *The Private Life of Henry VIII* made a tremendous impact, and not only at the box office. It became a central point of reference in the emergence of a critical discourse around the notion of the 'national film' – a discourse that unwittingly anticipated later theoretical debates about the definition of national cinema. The film raises issues that have since preoccupied film studies, particularly the question of whether a national cinema is to be defined through content and representation or how far it also depends on the creative personnel involved.

Eric Rhode later remarked that with *The Private Life of Henry VIII* Korda 'tried to sell the Englishness of the English to a world public'.[30] His comment echoes the views of contemporaries who saw the film as expressing an uncomplicated sense of national identity. Ernest Betts, for instance, described it as 'a film of taste, of wit, of good, boisterous humour, as English as a Sussex field'.[31] Similar metaphors abounded in the reviews. C.A. Lejeune, film critic of the *Observer*, declared that '*Henry VIII* is national to the backbone... It is the British prestige picture that we have been demanding for ten years back, not pedantic, not jingoistic, but as broadly and staunchly English as a baron of beef and a tankard of the best homebrew.' Lejeune nuanced her assessment, however, by suggesting that it was not content alone, but also the manner of treatment, that made it a distinctively national film:

> The fact that the hero is a monarch of England does not necessarily make it a national picture. We once had a film called *The Virgin Queen*, and the less said about that the better. *Henry VIII* is national because it has been seen from the typical English slant, which combines a kind of forthright and blundering honesty with a childish naivety of humour. Henry is an English hero not because he is a king, but in spite of it. His life story belongs to the people of later generations, not because it is in the history books, but because it is crude and generous

and vulgar enough to establish an England about which history books could be made.[32]

As if anticipating one of the qualifications that would be levelled against its status as a purely national film, moreover, Lejeune also remarked: 'The fact that it was directed by a Hungarian does not change its birthright.'

Critics who claimed *The Private Life of Henry VIII* as a national film, therefore, did so on the basis of its content and treatment, emphasising in particular its qualities of humour and its popular approach to history. There was another view, however, which argued that it was not so much the content as the production personnel involved that accounted for a film's national characteristics. Richard Griffith later argued that *The Private Life of Henry VIII* 'had little British about it except its subject, its stars, and that it was made near London. Its story, direction, photography, settings and music were all by Continentals.'[33] In addition to Korda himself, the key creative personnel included two other Hungarians (scenarist Lajos Biro and set designer Vincent Korda), one Frenchman (photographer Georges Périnal), one German (composer Kurt Schroeder) and one American (editor Harold Young).

To what extent does the involvement of overseas talent make a film like *The Private Life of Henry VIII* any less national? To answer this question it is necessary to consider the nature of the British film industry at the time. It is only recently that historians have started to examine the role of émigré film-makers in Britain in the 1930s, but, as Kevin Gough-Yates has forcefully argued, the 'history of British cinema of the period is inextricably linked with that of the exiled European film-makers'.[34] The roll call of European émigrés included, but was not limited to, directors such as Paul Czinner (Hungarian), Karl Grune (Austrian), Lothar Mendes (German) and Berthold Viertel (Austrian), writer Emeric Pressburger (Hungarian), art directors Alfred Junge (German) and Oscar Werndorff (German), cinematographers Curt Courant (German), Mutz Greenbaum (German), Otto Heller (Czech) and Günther Krampf (Austrian), composers Walter Goehr (Austrian) and Hans May (Austrian) and actors Elisabeth Bergner (Polish), Peter Lorre (Hungarian), Lucie Mannheim (German), Lilli Palmer (Austrian), Walter Rilla (German) and Conrad Veidt (German). The majority of these were refugees from Nazism who came to Britain in the early and mid-1930s. The technical artists,

Gough-Yates avers, 'introduced a combination of technical skill and aesthetic confidence to Britain and its backward industry'.[35] To this list of 'continentals', furthermore, can be added several American journeyman directors plying their trade in Britain, such as William K. Howard, T. Hayes Hunter, Bernard Vorhaus and Tim Whelan. There was nothing particularly unusual, therefore, about the 'foreign' involvement in the production of *The Private Life of Henry VIII*.

There were, and are still, different opinions about the prominence of foreign artistes in British cinema. An anonymous article in *World Film News* in 1936 complained that 'the preponderance of aliens in key positions in the industry... tends to produce a product lacking national character'.[36] Korda, whose films were the main target of this narrow-minded nationalism, naturally held a different view on the question of 'foreign' influence:

> An outsider often makes the best job of a national film. He is not cumbered with excessively detailed knowledge and associations. He gets a fresh slant on things... The best Hungarian film I have ever seen was made by the Belgian, Jacques Feyder. I believe that [René] Clair could make a better London picture than any of the English directors – a London film that would be international. I know there are people who think it odd that a Hungarian from Hollywood should direct an English historical film, but I can't see their argument.[37]

It was to be a part of Korda's production strategy that he would employ foreign directors, including René Clair (*The Ghost Goes West*), Paul Czinner (*Catherine the Great*), Jacques Feyder (*Knight Without Armour*) and Josef Von Sternberg (*I, Claudius*). This was part and parcel of his strategy to produce 'international films' that would win both critical prestige and popular acclaim. There is some substance, however, to Korda's belief that an overseas director can make a better job of a 'national film'. It is difficult to imagine any native British directors of the 1930s, with the possible exception of Alfred Hitchcock, treating the story of Henry VIII with the same bawdy humour and irreverence of Korda – and Hitchcock specialised in modern thrillers rather than costume pictures. Dilys Powell, for one, felt that the 'script had a daring which might not have been possible under an English director'.[38]

Whatever their national origin, however, émigré film-makers were working within the institutional and social framework of British cinema which militated against any wholesale adoption of 'foreign' styles or working practices. It is unlikely that *The Private Life of Henry VIII* would have been the success it was if it had seemed too 'foreign' for British – or for that matter American – audiences. Betts approved of the fact that it had been made 'without attempting anything unusual in photography or cutting, or deafening the ear with the obtrusive technique of the Russian school'.[39]

The charge has often been made against British films, not without some justification it must be said, that they seem 'uncinematic' in comparison to American and European films. This view was particularly strong in the early 1930s when both film critics and cinema exhibitors complained that British films lacked the technical polish and professional slickness of Hollywood movies. British films were thought to lack pace, to be too 'stagey' and to contain too much dialogue at the expense of action. American reviews of *The Private Life of Henry VIII* prove illuminating in this respect. *Variety* felt that technically the film was on a par with American productions, adding, in a significant aside: 'Coming from England, it is magnificent.'[40] But the critic Rob Wagner, writing in the magazine that bore his name, was less enthusiastic about certain technical aspects of the film:

> The critics have generally agreed that this production is equal to Hollywood's best. I do not agree with their agreement. The acting – yes; Alexander Korda's direction is almost as good as Lubitsch's; the sets, costumes and props, yes; sometimes better. But in camera and laboratory work, no. Flat lighting, hard and cruel, spoils – for pictorially sensitive me! – many scenes. They haven't yet learned how to cheat stereoscopic. In certain shots the figures are fastened to the background.[41]

There was a perception in certain quarters, therefore, that the film still exhibited the flat staging and lack of visual flair that characterised so many British films of the time.

However, it has been argued by more recent commentators that the apparent staginess of British films, rather than being a sign of technical inferiority, was a conscious aesthetic strategy adopted to differentiate them from the products of classical Hollywood cinema. This argument has been advanced most cogently by Andrew Higson, who asserts that 'to accuse such films of being primitive, or uncinematic, or too literary, or too theatrical, as many critics have done over the years, is to fail to take into account the particular conditions of this differentiation. Uncinematic may simply mean not like classical Hollywood cinema.'[42] For Higson, as for other advocates of a British, or English, 'heritage' cinema, aspects of form such as frontal staging, long takes and a predominantly stationary camera are all intended to enhance a film's pictorial qualities. This is especially important in respect of costume films, where the authenticity of the *mise-en-scène*, especially in terms of sets and costumes (aspects of *The Private Life of Henry VIII* singled out for praise by the critics), is an important factor. One commentator has argued that the editing of *The Private Life of Henry VIII* differs from the 'invisible' continuity editing of classical Hollywood in that 'nearly every cut jolts as the camera moves from one ideal perspective to another. Each shot is conceived separately, as a pictorial whole, rather than as a temporal process, narrative.'[43] There is a preponderance of medium and long shots but fewer close ups than the typical Hollywood film; many scenes are filmed as frontal tableaux and, while the camera is mobile, there is a relative absence of movement within the frame. The formal composition of the film, therefore, privileges the individual shot rather than sequences of shots (montage). The best example of this is Laughton's first appearance. In certain respects this is a classic star entrance: he first appears just over six minutes into the film, after several scenes establishing the circumstances of Anne Boleyn's execution and the king's forthcoming marriage to Jane Seymour. The ladies of the bedchamber are preparing the king's wedding bed when there is a sudden cutaway to the king himself. It is a perfectly symmetrical shot, framed by the door, with Henry/Laughton standing in the centre, resplendent in his royal robes, his legs apart and his hands on his hips. The image is so close to the famous portrait of Henry by Holbein the Younger that it would be too much of a coincidence for it to have been unintentional.

Evidence that visual authenticity was a major preoccupation of the film-makers can be discerned from the production discourse around the film. Reports in the trade press were at pains to emphasise its authenticity, especially concerning sets, set dressings and costumes. Although most of the sets are relatively modest in size, they are given

1. Charles Laughton's appearance in *The Private Life of Henry VIII* was modelled on Holbein's portrait of the King.

a more sumptuous appearance through the dressings, which included reproductions of Holbein tapestries. The largest set constructed for the film was 'a reproduction of the Great Hall at Hampton Court, [which] is the last word in magnificence', while an 'exact replica' of the bridge leading into Hampton Court was built in the studio grounds.[44] Other indicators of the authenticity intended for the film were the use of a falconry expert and the inclusion of songs written by Henry himself, notably 'What Shall I Do for Love?'.

In this respect, however, there was a wide gulf between the production discourse and the reactions of professional historians. The film's claim to authenticity was firmly rejected by Charles Beard, who took it soundly to task in the pages of *Sight and Sound* on the grounds that 'it is feeble history, bad psychology and worse archeology...The production displays a lamentable lack of knowledge of the manners, customs and practices of the Court in the third and fourth decades of the sixteenth century, and a hopeless ignorance of almost all the material details, which differentiate this period from those which preceded and followed it.' Beard was a specialist on arms and heraldry and he went on to describe the many historical infelicities, some of them absurdly pedantic, such as the Earl of Essex not wearing his Lesser George Garter ('as he was bound to do by the Statutes of the Order'), the king's shoe buckles being on the inside of his feet rather than the outside ('Mr Laughton wears his spurs like a cowboy'), the Gentlemen of the Court wearing their swords within the palace precincts, the Yeomen of the Guard wearing the wrong uniforms and carrying the wrong weapons, and the executioner of Anne Boleyn using a German fighting sword of 1580 ('He would, moreover, never have sharpened his instrument upon a grindstone; he would have honed it'). The furniture was 'a hotch-potch of all periods, mostly of the middle and second half of the seventeenth century', while the 'gardens bear no resemblance to those at Hampton Court as they were at the period'.[45] In view of Beard's critique, it should be noted that the 'technical adviser' for *The Private Life of Henry VIII*, Philip Lindsay, was not a professional historian but a historical novelist, a clear indication that dramatic qualities were more important to Korda than points of historical detail.

The critical reception of *The Private Life of Henry VIII* indicates a range of responses to the use of history in the film. The national critics for the most part approved of its popular and irreverent representation of 'Merrie England' and felt that its qualities as entertainment outweighed any historical infelicities. A review in *The Times* suggested that the film 'takes as its model the modern biography' and was apparently not too concerned that it did not adhere too strictly to the historical record: 'It assumes the rights of a Creevey at the court of Henry, revealing the more awkward inventions of the muse of history, and at times taking the business out of her hand to invent them for her.' It added that the 'use of modern parallels is ingenious and there is not too much of it – a talkative barber and a woman who is asked not to block the view of an execution by wearing her hat are the most obvious examples of this dangerous device'.[46] Campbell Dixon in the *Daily Telegraph* felt that it 'may not be the best of history, but is certainly first-class comedy'.[47] The *Manchester Guardian*, while noting that the narrative focused 'more on the personal taste of the king than on political complications', considered that 'from the point of view of entertainment the picture rightly sets out to be gossipy satire'.[48] And on the occasion of its reissue in 1946, the *Tribune*, usually no admirer of Korda's films, attributed its success to its lavish production values and its populism. 'To this film, for the first time in Britain, the Formula was applied', its film critic remarked. 'No time was wasted on "arty" tricks of photography and direction; no new contribution was made to the technique of film-making...Korda gave the film "the works": all-star cast, costumes, lavish sets, unrationed vulgarity, historical travesty.'[49]

The film press on the whole agreed that the film had found the right balance between history and drama. *Kinematograph Weekly* thought that it 'sketches the private and marital life of Henry VIII with careful regard to fact and detail...The Court scenes are intimate and illuminating and are cleverly made to fit the Rabelaisian figure depicted by the star without losing accuracy in detail.'[50] Forsyth Hardy, writing in the progressive film journal *Cinema Quarterly*, regretted that the 'private life' formula meant the omission of the wider historical background, but accepted, nevertheless, that judged on its own terms the film was entirely successful: 'When it is not the aim of the film to give an impression of England during the momentous years of the Reformation we cannot find fault with it for not having done so. This is the private life of Henry VIII...[and] we must recognise the film's unqualified success within the limits of its title.'[51] Hardy's review is unusual in so far as the intellectual film culture that *Cinema Quarterly* represented was not habitually inclined to favour the British entertainment film, generally prefering documentary and the 'artistic' European film to more mainstream commercial fare.

Some critics on the left, however, disliked the 'private life' formula because it excluded wider historical and social questions. F.D. Klingender, writing in 1937, blamed this trend on Korda's film:

> There could be no clearer indication of this tendency than the title of the film which opened the cycle. Henry VIII, more perhaps than any other monarch in English history, broke down the bulwarks of a whole epoch and paved the way for a new form of society. He created a new ruling class and established a national church. Yet, from his film 'life' all his public actions without exception are eliminated and the attention of the audience is directed exclusively to his private love affairs.[52]

Klingender, characteristically of Marxist critics, was an advocate of a more serious, socially committed cinema that would engage directly with the social issues of the present. He argued that the historical film, as exemplified by *The Private Life of Henry VIII*, marked a deliberate strategy by producers to distract attention away from such questions: 'Yet by transporting its audience to the past it avoided the dangerous ground of contemporary controversy...In this formula history no longer serves to fan the flames of contemporary zeal, it has become a new and refined form of escape.'

Klingender's critique, however, ignored the constraints under which British producers were working. It cannot be denied that Korda would have been attracted to the 'private life' formula because it represented a good commercial prospect. At the same time, however, the nature of film censorship at the time was such that it militated against exploration of the sort of contemporary issues that Klingender and others advocated. The role of the British Board of Film Censors (BBFC) in the 1930s has been extensively documented by historians.[53] The BBFC, though nominally a trade organisation, was fully a part of the British establishment. It exercised a strict censorship policy that was designed to keep any potentially controversial subject matter off the screen. The BBFC concerned itself not just with moral concerns but with social and political matters. Its aim was essentially the preservation of the status quo: no criticism was permitted of institutions such as the monarchy, church, government, police or judiciary, and politically sensitive subjects (such as strikes, industrial unrest, Communism or Fascism) were to be avoided. As Lord Tyrrell of Avon, who became President of the BBFC in 1935, infamously declared: 'We may take pride in observing that there is not a single film showing in London today which deals with any of the burning questions of the day.'[54] In view of the general outlook of the BBFC, therefore, the scope for film-makers to respond to 'contemporary controversy' as Klingender wanted was at best extremely limited.

The historical film, set at a safe distance from the present, was the one genre where an element of social or political commentary might creep in. *The Private Life of Henry VIII* did not have an unproblematic passage through the BBFC, though it was sexual rather than political content that bothered deputy chief censor Colonel J.C. Hanna when he read the script: 'The language throughout may be true to the standards of that period, but it is far too outspoken and coarse for the present day...Delete all suggestion that marriage [to Anne of Cleves] is being consummated.'[55] As the finished film does indeed suggest non-consummation of the marriage (Henry and Anne spend their wedding night playing cards) it would seem that Korda followed Hanna's directive. Following the arrival of talking pictures the BBFC had introduced a system of voluntary pre-production censorship by reading scripts and advising producers whether they would be likely to cause problems. In the event, *The Private Life of Henry VIII* was passed by the BBFC with an 'A' certificate.[56]

How far, then, does *The Private Life of Henry VIII* distance itself from 'the burning questions of the day'? Jeffrey Richards, for one, asserts that the film 'avoids concentration on real issues, social, political, economic, religious problems that might cause controversy, invite censorial intervention or affect profitability'.[57] To some extent this is certainly correct. Thus there is no mention of Henry's break with Rome and the establishment of the Church of England. Indeed, the film omits entirely the first two-thirds of Henry's 38-year reign and begins in 1536 with the execution of his second wife Anne Boleyn and his marriage to Jane Seymour. In focusing on the later years of the reign, *The Private Life of Henry VIII* avoids having to deal with the political consequences of the English Reformation and concentrates instead on the period of Henry's marital affairs. Throughout the film the private and the personal intrude upon the public and the political. There are several occasions when the king discusses foreign policy with his ministers, but these are invariably cut short by the intrusion of his current amour. Early in the film, for example, Jane Seymour interrupts Henry's council with Thomas Cromwell. King and minister are discussing the balance of power in Europe ('Softly, sweetheart, we have affairs of state'); Jane wants his opinion on what she should wear for their wedding ('Listen, darling, this is really important – shall it be the chaplet or the coif?'). Even the politically motivated marriage to Anne of Cleves is presented as a bedroom farce. The focus of the narrative is firmly in the domestic sphere.

Moreover, *The Private Life of Henry VIII* endorses the consensual social politics that were supported by the BBFC and which are a strong feature in British cinema of the 1930s.[58] Henry and his subjects are united by a set of common values and a shared outlook. Henry is responsive to the needs and opinions of his subjects: the royal barber has the role of a sort of King's Fool in so far as Henry takes heed of the views of 'my royal guild of barbers'. The lower classes are represented by the servants who share the king's desire for a male heir: the cook and the kitchen skivvies might be seen as sixteenth-century equivalents of the working-class voters who supported the National Government in the 1930s. The film validates the institution of monarchy, a central plank of consensus politics. One of the recurring themes of the film is the question of whether or not the king should marry again to produce another son. The court talks about him as if he were 'a breeding bull'. When he accepts Cromwell's admonishments to marry Anne of Cleves, one of the most famous lines in the film draws a parallel between sex and patriotism as Henry, on the threshold of the marital bedchamber, declares to the assembled courtiers: 'The things I've done for England!'

An alternative reading of the politics of *The Private Life of Henry VIII*, however, has been advanced by Greg Walker. Far from distancing itself from 'the burning questions of the day', Walker argues that *Henry VIII* 'had a clear political agenda...reflecting a distinct line on British foreign policy, and intervening directly in the internal battles raging within the Conservative party in the early 1930s'.[59] Thus, a key scene early in the film where Henry orders the expansion of the fleet to protect England against the threat of continental powers 'places the film squarely in the middle of the most contentious political issue of the day: rearmament' and 'asserts the need to avoid war through a policy of armed neutrality'.[60] There is a neat coincidence in the fact that it was in the same month as the film's release, October 1933, that Germany withdrew from both the Geneva Disarmament Conference and the League of Nations. Walker suggests the film was ahead of its time in being 'a strident call for re-armament in a political climate dominated by appeasement'.[61]

It is a persuasive reading, even though it is based on just the one scene. That scene, as Walker observes, was significantly revised between script and film. In the published version of the script, Henry recognises the need to expand the fleet but is worried about how this can be financed ('A strong fort at Dover, a strong Fleet in the Channel, and we can laugh in their faces. But the money – the money – we *must* have the money!') He rejects Cromwell's suggestion of increasing taxation as the burden would fall on his subjects ('New taxes? My people are bled white already! Yet a way must be found – *must* be found').[62] This has a clear parallel with the policy of the National Government, the coalition formed in 1931 in response to the economic crisis, which sought to curb expenditure in order to restore sound finance. One of the factors determining the foreign policy of appeasement was the reluctance of the National Government, under Ramsay MacDonald, to increase spending on armaments. In the finished film, however, the question of the cost of rearmament is no longer so prominent. Cromwell advocates 'wise diplomacy', but Henry pooh-poohs him:

> *Henry*: Diplomacy my foot! I'm an Englishman and I can't say one thing and mean another. What I can do is build ships, ships, then more ships.
> *Cromwell*: You mean double the fleet?
> *Henry*: Treble it. Fortify Dover. Rule the sea.
> *Cromwell*: To do that will cost us money.
> *Henry*: To leave it undone will cost us England!

There is an irresistible temptation to read this scene as one where Cromwell represents the Treasury (averse to spending on armaments and therefore pro-appeasement), whereas Henry represents the voice of Tory dissidents like Winston Churchill (anti-appeasement, advocating rearmament regardless of the means to pay). It was only after the general election of 1935 had returned a large Conservative majority that the National Government, now led by Stanley Baldwin, changed its defence policy and initiated a programme of rearmament.

It seems unlikely, however, that contemporaries were alert to these possible meanings in the film; at any rate none of the reviewers seem to have detected them. It is more likely, if the letters pages of the popular film magazines are any sort of guide, that cinema-goers responded more to the historical and visual qualities of films than to any political subtexts.[63] *The Private Life of Henry VIII* presents the past as a site of pleasure and bawdy humour. Its irreverent tone is established in an opening caption: 'Henry VIII had six wives. Catherine of Aragon was the first; but her story is of no particular interest – she was a respectable woman. So Henry divorced her. He then married Anne Boleyn. This marriage also was a failure – but not for the same reason.' The film indicates, therefore, that its interest is in the disreputable aspects of the past. The same irreverent tone is maintained throughout the film: there is much banter and innuendo; the ladies of the court chatter about Henry's sexual appetite; his marital career is described as one of 'chop and change'. The royal servants, especially the cook and his wife, offer the sort of vulgar comic relief that was provided by the supporting characters in Shakespeare's plays:

> *Cook*: A man should try for another son or two if he's a king, eh wife?
> *Wife*: Yes, my man, and even if he's not a king.

Indeed, the script displays a saucy sense of humour that looks forward to its parody some 40 years later in *Carry On Henry* (dir. Gerald Thomas, 1971).

The Englishness of *The Private Life of Henry VIII* – 'as broadly and staunchly English as a baron of beef and a tankard of the best homebrew' – represents the rough rather than the respectable face of popular culture. The film exhibits the bawdiness and innuendo of the provincial music hall. The 'coarse' language identified by Colonel Hanna was something that George Orwell associated with the English lower classes, who 'are devoted to bawdy jokes, and use probably the foulest language in the world'.[64] A scene that particularly irked critics of the film such as Lord Cottenham was the banquet where a belching Henry guzzles his food and throws discarded chicken legs on the floor.

Yet they seem to have missed the irony of the scene: the point is that Henry's behaviour contrasts with his words as he laments the decline of good taste ('No delicacy nowadays...refinement's a thing of the past, manners are dead'). Whether this is an accurate representation of the Tudor court is beside the point; Cottenham himself recognised that the film was in tune with the tastes of the cinema-going public. [65]

Henry and his subjects also share another characteristic of Englishness: xenophobia. It is ironic that a film made largely by foreigners, whose prominence in the film industry caused resentment in some quarters, should take such apparent glee in expressing a sense of popular xenophobia. The English distrust all foreigners. When Holbein is sent to paint a portrait of Anne of Cleves, for example, Henry insists that Peynell is sent 'to watch Holbein':

> *Cromwell:* Your Grace has no faith in German painters?
> *Henry:* Yes, but I have no faith in German beauty.

The published script indicates that the French executioner employed to behead Anne Boleyn is regarded 'with resentment and contempt' by his English assistant and the two men 'should be contrasting types – the Frenchman very supple and willowy, the Englishman very square and powerful'.[66] The characterisation of the French executioner in the film is effete, even effeminate, while the English headsman is plebeian and straight-talking. Orwell observed that 'the famous "insularity" and "xenophobia" of the English is far stronger in the working class...the English working class are outstanding in their abhorrence of foreign habits'.[67] Walker sees the same scene as further evidence of the film's engagement with contemporary issues, arguing that in 'this one scene the film manages to allude simultaneously to the politics of ethnic difference, current international tensions, domestic class conflict, and the consequences of industrial depression'.[68] Thus the English headsman is resentful of his French counterpart ('I was good enough to knock off the queen's five lovers, wasn't I? Then why do they want you over – a Frenchman from Calais?') and is bitter about unemployment in the profession ('It's a damned shame, with half the English executioners out of work as it is!'). Walker insists that 'such references were hardly uncontentious' at a time of record unemployment. The worst month was January 1933 when some 2,979,000 workers were registered as unemployed, representing 22 per cent of the insured workforce in Britain.[69]

2.   Henry is bewitched by the coquettish Catherine Howard (Binnie
Barnes) in *The Private Life of Henry VIII*.

While the film's representation of history might be described as
populist, however, its gender politics are nothing if not conservative.
Henry's own attitude towards women displays an underlying
misogyny in that he realises he can only be happy with an unchallenging
consort. He offers marital guidance to Thomas Culpeper: 'My first wife
was clever, my second was ambitious. Thomas, if you want to be happy,
marry a girl like my sweet little Jane. Marry a stupid woman.' None of
Henry's later marriages proves any more successful than his first two.
He is, in turn, widowed (Jane Seymour), politically outmanœuvred
(Anne of Cleves), cuckolded (Catherine Howard) and hen-pecked
(Catherine Parr). Although Henry is presented as a victim of feminine
wiles, this does not translate into empowerment for the female
characters who are either comic (Elsa Lanchester as Anne of Cleves) or
purely decorative (Merle Oberon as Anne Boleyn, Wendy Barrie as
Jane Seymour, Binnie Barnes as Catherine Howard). The promotional
materials shamelessly emphasised the pulchritudinous appeal of the

starlets and *Variety*, demonstrating that political correctness was unheard of in the 1930s, observed that 'Korda has slipped in another surprise by placing before the king not one but many dainty dishes...and this from England, where one attractive femme screen face to a picture has been a novelty and two a full cargo'.[70] The American trade press, it seems, had no faith in English beauty. Henry's most affectionate relationship turns out to be with the plain Anne of Cleves ('You're the nicest girl I ever married'). He is besotted with the young Catherine Howard and seems genuinely heartbroken when her adultery with Culpeper is revealed. Catherine Parr (Everley Gregg), who appears only at the very end of the film, is a shrewish harridan who nags him mercilessly. The gradual process of Henry's emasculation, put in train when he engages in a wrestling bout in a vain attempt to impress Catherine Howard ('Hard work when a man of fifty wants to show his wife he's no more than thirty'), is completed in old age when he is reduced to guzzling chicken legs behind his wife's back. In the last shot of the film he looks at the camera and says: 'Six wives. And the best of 'em the worst!'

The popular success of *The Private Life of Henry VIII* was such that other producers, both in Britain and in Hollywood, immediately took note. The historical film, unfavoured by the film industry since the coming of sound, was suddenly back in vogue. Thus, as Forsyth Hardy observed early in 1934:

After *Henry VIII*, the deluge. The remarkable and unexpected success of Korda's spectacular experiment with history has sent his fellow-producers scurrying to their text-books, there to search for romantic heroes and heroines with traits of character sufficiently and suitably startling to make the story of their lives attractive on the screen. The search is taking the course we expected, and in addition to four versions of the life of Mary Queen of Scots(!), we are to have Charles II, Louis XVI and Napoleon, Queen Elizabeth, Marie Antoinette and Nell Gwyn.[71]

The most significant aspect of this trend, perhaps, was that so many of the historical films, from both sides of the Atlantic, were on British subjects. Thus, from Hollywood, there came Ronald Colman as Robert Clive (*Clive of India*), Katharine Hepburn as Mary Queen of Scots (*Mary of Scotland*) and Clark Gable as Fletcher Christian

(*Mutiny on the Bounty*, which also starred Charles Laughton as Captain Bligh), while British studios presented Anna Neagle as Nell Gwyn (*Nell Gwyn*), George Arliss as Wellington (*The Iron Duke*), Matheson Lang as Sir Francis Drake (*Drake of England*), Walter Huston as Cecil Rhodes (*Rhodes of Africa*), Nova Pilbeam as Lady Jane Grey (*Tudor Rose*) and Flora Robson as Queen Elizabeth I (*Fire Over England*). It is difficult to generalise about this cycle of historical films, though Klingender observed that as 'the cycle advanced the national sentiment imperceptibly but clearly grew more intense'.[72] The British films were, on the whole, regarded as being more historically accurate; the interest of Hollywood studios in British historical subjects is suggestive of both the cultural and the economic significance of the British market for Hollywood.

Korda, meanwhile, was acclaimed as 'the man who made the world conscious of British films'.[73] In hindsight, *The Private Life of Henry VIII* can be seen as an important early step in a calculated bid to establish himself as a major independent producer. He had already secured a deal to make quality films for distribution by United Artists before *Henry VIII* was released. Following the success of *Henry VIII*, Korda was able to secure the financial backing of the Prudential Assurance Company, which he used to support an ambitious and expensive production programme and the building of a brand new studio complex (London Films had hitherto been a 'tenant' at Elstree). Denham Studios, built at a cost of £1 million, opened in May 1936 and became home to 'half the crack technicians of Europe'.[74] Yet Korda was soon in difficulties. As his films became more expensive they also became less profitable, none of them repeating the spectacular success of *Henry VIII* in the American market. Prudential was so concerned about Korda's profligacy that in 1936 it imposed strict managerial controls on London Films. When, in 1937, the film industry was hit by a slump, Korda was blamed by some trade sources for the 'boom and bust' in the mid-1930s – though, to be fair to Korda, his tactic of financing film production from loans rather than working capital was characteristic of the short-term and speculative nature of the British film industry at the time, while the City institutions that advanced loans without adequate security must also be held to account for the problems that affected the industry.[75] In 1938 Korda was forced to relinquish control of Denham to a consortium backed by J. Arthur Rank and, by the end of the decade, he was again a tenant producer in the studio he had built on the back of the profits from *Henry VIII*.

It would be fair to say that the other historical films Korda made in the 1930s were something of a mixed bag. Graham Greene, at the time a practising film critic as well as a novelist, was one of Korda's most vocal critics. 'He's a great publicist, of course, the Victor Gollancz of the screen', Greene wrote of Korda in 1936. 'Only a great publicist could have put over so many undistinguished and positively bad films as if they were a succession of masterpieces.'[76] Korda's next major film following *Henry VIII* was *Catherine the Great* (dir. Paul Czinner, 1934), a starring vehicle for Czinner's wife, Elisabeth Bergner. It was based on a play co-written by Lajos Biro and, in terms of subject matter and treatment, has a more distinctly 'European' feel than *Henry VIII*. C.A. Lejeune complained that it had 'no national feeling'.[77] In contrast to *Henry VIII*, it places a woman at the centre of the narrative, presenting her as repressing her own desires to become 'mother' of the nation. The casting of Flora Robson as the old Empress anticipated the actress's role as Elizabeth I, and the film has some observations on gender and power ('Women can rule and men can't'; 'There's only one way for a poor defenceless woman to treat a man, and that's to rule him') that Harper attributes to the input of female co-writer Marjorie Deans.[78] *Catherine the Great* was more expensive (£127,868) than *Henry VIII* and earned less from the British market (£58,308). Its relative failure was the first sign of the trend of diminishing returns at the box office that was to afflict Korda's productions throughout the decade.

The unpredictability of popular taste – and proof that Korda's flair for judging it was far from infallible – was rudely demonstrated by the next film he directed, *The Private Life of Don Juan* (1934), which cost £109,977 and returned only half that sum in total (£53,700). It marked a sad end to the screen career of Hollywood legend Douglas Fairbanks Sr and, while Korda was able to extract some pathos from the casting of the 51-year-old Fairbanks as the ageing Lothario, the truth is that the star simply looked too old to be playing a romantic lead opposite starlets such as Merle Oberon, Binnie Barnes and Benita Hume. Korda was on firmer ground with *The Scarlet Pimpernel* (dir. Harold Young, 1935), which was not a historical film proper but a costume swash-buckler, based on the popular tale by Hungarian novelist Baroness Orczy. *The Scarlet Pimpernel* indicates the direction that Korda's films were to take in becoming far more explicitly anti-Fascist as the decade progressed. Britain is presented as a safe haven for refugees from continental oppression and there is an implicit parallel between France during the Reign of Terror and Germany following the 'Night of the Long Knives' (29 June 1934). *The Scarlet Pimpernel* was a popular success – it returned £204,300 against a production cost of £143,521 – and was followed by an inferior sequel, *The Return of the Scarlet Pimpernel* (dir. Hans Schwarz, 1937), in which the allegory was even more explicit. Korda evidently liked the story: he later produced *The Elusive Pimpernel* (dir. Michael Powell, 1951), an expensive Technicolor extravaganza that might have been more interesting if the original idea to make it as a musical had not been abandoned during production.

Rembrandt (1936), which reunited Korda as director with Charles Laughton, playing the seventeenth-century Dutch painter, is probably one of his most underrated films. It was not successful, returning £93,168 against a cost of £140,236, but it is testimony to Korda's financial and intellectual daring that he should have gone ahead with a film that was never likely to be much of a commercial prospect in the first place. The film is notable for its bold, experimental visual style – Vincent Korda designed the sets to resemble the perspectives of Rembrandt's paintings – and for another bravura performance by Laughton as the troubled artist at odds with society's expectations. Greene admired Laughton's 'amazing virtuosity', but concluded that the film 'is chiefly remarkable for the lesson it teaches: that no amount of money spent on expensive sets, no careful photography, will atone for the lack of a story "line", the continuity and drive of a well-constructed plot'.[79] Korda then cast Laughton in an ambitious adaptation of Robert Graves's historical novel *I, Claudius*, to be directed by Josef Von Sternberg, an ill-stared production that was never completed. The film had already run into difficulties, caused by script rewrites and the temperamental behaviour of its star, when co-star Merle Oberon was injured in a car crash and Korda called a halt to the production. The half-hour or so of surviving footage suggests another intense Laughton performance as the insecure, stuttering Claudius and hints of the expressionist visual style that characterised Sternberg's Hollywood films such as *Shanghai Express* and *The Scarlet Empress*.

Fire Over England (dir. William K. Howard, 1937) was one of Korda's pet projects that had a long gestation period, having originally been scheduled for production in 1935 when it was known variously as *Queen Elizabeth*, *Elizabeth of England* and *Gloriana*.[80] Korda, who was to have directed it from a screenplay by Austrian playwright Ferdinand Bruckner, eventually assigned the film to German émigré Erich Pommer to produce. The Bruckner treatment was abandoned and the retitled film became an adaptation of a novel by A.E.W. Mason. The film was Korda's most insistent yet in its overt parallels with the present: Spain/Germany, Philip II/Hitler, the Inquisition/the Gestapo. The message was not lost on contemporaries. Gore Vidal, the American novelist who remembered seeing the film in Washington as a boy, recalled that it 'caused our heads to nod solemnly as we realized that our common Anglo past was again in peril'.[81] *Fire Over England* was successful but not outstandingly so: released early in 1937, its strident call for preparedness against a foreign dictator was probably slightly ahead of its time. Three years later Robson would repeat her critically acclaimed role as Elizabeth in the Hollywood swashbuckler *The Sea Hawk* (dir. Michael Curtiz, 1940), this time opposite Errol Flynn as privateer Captain Geoffrey Thorpe. Produced by Warner Bros. at a time when the United States was still officially neutral, this was an even more explicit call to arms than *Fire Over England* and its overt propagandism was apparent to critics on both sides of the Atlantic.[82]

In the later 1930s Korda's interests turned more and more to the British Empire. The 'empire trilogy' films – *Sanders of the River* (dir. Zoltan Korda, 1935), *The Drum* (dir. Zoltan Korda, 1938) and *The Four Feathers* (dir. Zoltan Korda, 1939) – between them represent most of the narrative and geographical variations possible within the British Empire film. Although invariably grouped together, there are in fact significant differences between the films, though all three promote the ideology of imperialism. *Sanders of the River*, based on the stories by Edgar Wallace, is concerned primarily to justify British colonial administration in West Africa. It is relatively sober in style (filmed, unlike the later two, in black and white) and refrains from excessively jingoistic tub-thumping. It promotes consensus between British and Africans through the relationship between the just, benevolent commissioner (Leslie Banks) and the loyal native chief (Paul Robeson). *The Drum*, while also concerned to support the principle of British rule in India, eschews the somewhat pious moralising of *Sanders* in favour of a tale of the 'Great Game' of empire played out on the Northwest Frontier. The use of Technicolor and location shooting opens up the visual possibilities of the imperial adventure film, though it is in *The Four Feathers* – which is, like *The*

Drum and *Fire Over England*, based on a novel by A.E.W. Mason – that visual spectacle, in the form of lavishly mounted battle sequences and stunning desert landscapes, assumes even greater prominence. *The Four Feathers* presents the deserts of the Sudan as a mythical space for the enactment of a drama of personal courage and moral redemption. It is no longer deemed necessary to justify the imperial mission: it is taken for granted that the campaign to avenge the death of Gordon at Khartoum is justified, allowing the film to focus instead on the efforts of Harry Faversham (John Clements) to redeem his honour. *The Drum* and *The Four Feathers* were set against recognisable historical backgrounds, even if their stories were fictional, and therefore merit inclusion alongside Korda's other historical films.[83]

Almost as interesting as the films Korda made, however, were the films he did not make. He was notorious for announcing films that, for a variety of reasons, never made it to the screen. In 1935 he was one of several producers to plan a film to mark the Silver Jubilee of King George V – *The Iron Duke*, as we will see, was one such film – for which he actually commissioned a treatment from none other than Winston Churchill. Korda had already contracted Churchill to write a series of short films 'dealing with subjects of topical interest', which were never made, and agreed to pay him £10,000 as an advance against 25 per cent of the net profits of the film. Churchill set to work with customary energy in the autumn of 1934 and produced a draft within two weeks. Korda felt that the outline was 'really splendid' but, perhaps with potential censorship difficulties in mind, pointed out that 'in this version politics play too big a part not leaving enough for technical, industrial and other developments in these twenty-five years'.[84] Churchill delivered a full scenario early in 1935. The film was to be structured in three parts – 'Faction', 'War' and 'Survival' – and was to combine a spoken narration with newsreel and studio reconstructions of events including the Coronation, the constitutional crisis of 1910–11, the campaign for women's suffrage, the Agadir Crisis of 1911, the Irish Home Rule problem, the Great War, the Russian Revolution and the Armistice. It is a recognisably Churchillian view of history – a history in which he had played various prominent parts – and is replete with characteristic passages of purple prose. It ends with the direction: 'Roll and uplift of drums into Rule Britannia...breaking into God Save the King.'[85] By this time, however, Korda's enthusiasm for the project was waning. It is not clear precisely why he abandoned the film: perhaps, despite his advice to Churchill, its content remained too political, or perhaps it was just too similar to ABPC's *Royal Cavalcade* (dir. Marcel Varnel *et al.*, 1935), a combination of newsreel footage linked by a number of fictional personal stories. Churchill was disappointed by the abandonment of the project, but was mollified to some extent by Korda's offer of £5,000 compensation for his work.

Churchill was also involved in another abortive Korda project, a film version of T.E. Lawrence's *Revolt in the Desert*. Korda had bought the film rights to this book (an abridged version of Lawrence's *Seven Pillars of Wisdom*) in 1934 and, following Lawrence's death in a motorcyle accident the following year, was granted permission by Lawrence's trustees to proceed with the film. A script was written by Hollywood screenwiter John Monk Saunders and Zoltan Korda was to direct, with Walter Hudd playing Lawrence, but civil unrest in Palestine throughout 1936 scotched plans to send a unit there on location. In 1937 the project was revived, now to be entitled *Lawrence of Arabia* and directed by William K. Howard, with Leslie Howard as Lawrence and Churchill as historical adviser. The Foreign Office became involved, however, when the Turkish Embassy in London objected to the film on the grounds that the Turks were represented as the oppressors of the Arabs. Informal pressure was brought to bear on Korda by the Foreign Office and eventually the BBFC scotched the project by advising him that it would be unlikely to certify the film.[86]

The personal contacts Korda had forged during the 1930s with Tory policitians and senior civil servants such as Sir Robert Vansittart were to be invaluable to both parties during the Second World War. Upon the outbreak of war he produced a propaganda film entitled *The Lion Has Wings* (dirs Michael Powell, Adrian Brunel and Brian Desmond Hurst, 1939) which was endorsed by the Ministry of Information (MOI), responsible for government propaganda, to the extent that the MOI paid for dubbed and subtitled prints for overseas territories and facilitated the film's quick release in the United States.[87] *The Lion Has Wings* was a hodge-podge of newsreel compilation and studio scenes, a tribute to the fighting power of the Royal Air Force that also included the Tilbury sequence from *Fire Over England* for good measure. Korda had planned to move his production base to Hollywood since early in 1939 when he had formed a new company, Alexander Korda Film Productions, that would not be so closely tied to Denham. He relocated to California in the summer of 1940, becoming one of those (along with Alfred Hitchcock and Herbert Wilcox) who were accused of having 'Gone With the Wind Up'. It has long been rumoured that the real reason for Korda's move was that he was involved in secret intelligence work for the British government. While this claim is impossible to substantiate, there is evidence to suggest that Korda was working in a semi-official capacity as a sort of goodwill ambassador for Britain. He was certainly involved in the covert propaganda war conducted by the British to generate sympathy for their cause and to prepare the way for eventual American entry into the war.[88]

Korda's most significant contribution to the propaganda war was his production of *Lady Hamilton* (1941), which he also directed. *Lady Hamilton* – released in America as *That Hamilton Woman!* – was a 'Hollywood British' film made in California but with a significant British involvement, including screenwriter R.C. Sherriff and stars Laurence Olivier and Vivien Leigh, in their first film together since their marriage (the two had previously appeared in *Fire Over England*). It is also clear that, behind the scenes, the film was supported by the Foreign Office as precisely the sort of pro-British film it wanted to be seen in America. The allegorical parallels in the film are even more explicitly drawn than they had been in *Fire Over England*: Nelson/Churchill is the inspirational leader, Napoleon/Hitler is the continental dictator intent on conquest, and Trafalgar/the Battle of Britain is the historic event that saves Britain from invasion. The film was one of those attacked by isolationists in the US Senate in the autumn of 1941 as pro-interventionist propaganda (alongside *The Great Dictator*, *Foreign Correspondent* and *Sergeant York*) before the Japanese attack on Pearl Harbour brought America into the war. It was the film's representation of an adulterous affair between Nelson and Emma Hamilton – reflecting the much-publicised affair between its stars when they were both married to other people – that most concerned the American film censor, Joseph Breen, and obliged the film-makers to include a scene of Nelson regretting the affair and of Emma herself suffering from destitution at the end of her life as punishment for her wrong-doing. It grossed $1,147,000 at the North American box office – 'a healthy if not spectacular gross' – and was the fifth most popular film in Britain in 1941.[89]

There is one particular scene in *Lady Hamilton* where the contemporary resonances are so specific that involvement from the highest level has been suspected. Nelson addresses the Board of the Admirality:

> *Nelson*: Gentlemen, you're celebrating a peace with Napoleon Bonaparte…But, gentlemen, you will never make peace with Napoleon. He doesn't mean peace today. He just wants to gain a little time to rearm himself at sea and to make new alliances with Italy and Spain. All to one purpose – to destroy our empire! Napoleon can never be master of the world until he has smashed us up – and believe me, gentlemen, he means to be master of the world. You cannot make peace with dictators. You have to destroy them! Wipe them out!

It is not only in its anti-appeasement rhetoric that this speech has Churchillian overtones: Nelson's words echo directly part of Churchill's famous 'finest hour' speech of 18 June 1940 ('Hitler knows that he will have to break us in this island or lose the war'). It was rumoured that Churchill himself wrote this part of the film dialogue; even if this is untrue the parallels are too close to have been entirely coincidental. *Lady Hamilton* was reputedly Churchill's favourite film and he was frequently moved to tears by it, including while *en route* on HMS *Prince of Wales* to meet President Roosevelt at Placentia Bay in August 1941.[90]

Korda's historical films, both in Britain and in Hollywood, display a remarkable level of consistency in their representation of the past. They combine a romantic, populist view of history with a degree of visual spectacle that is rare for British cinema in this, or any, period. They also demonstrate the flexibility of the historical film as a genre for responding to 'the burning questions of the day'. What is perhaps more significant, however, is that the most successful of Korda's films were those which focused on specifically British subjects. Korda was knighted in 1942, the first film producer to be so honoured, and, while cynics may suggest that this was his reward for having put Churchill on the payroll in the 1930s, there can be no question that this émigré film-maker did more than anyone to establish the cultural and commercial viability of the British historical film.

2

Age of Appeasement:
The Iron Duke (1935)

The Iron Duke, directed by Victor Saville for Gaumont-British, was one of the films that went into production in the wake of *The Private Life of Henry VIII* as other producers sought to exploit the new-found popularity of the historical film. Yet the ideology and cultural politics of *The Iron Duke* are almost as far removed from the populist style of Korda's film as is possible within a genre. If, on the face of it, the two films are both biopics of great men and star vehicles for their main performers, any similarities end there. *The Iron Duke* is as much concerned with the public as the private life of its protagonist; it is far more reverential in its treatment of its subject as a national hero; and it is more obviously propagandistic in its intent. Parallels with the present are much more obvious in *The Iron Duke* and were noted by contemporary critics. While it might have been expected, however, that a film about one of Britain's greatest soldiers would have been a vehicle for promoting an ideology of militarism or belligerent nationalism, *The Iron Duke* turned out to be quite the opposite: an affirmation of the policy of appeasement and an idealistic plea for peace in a continent riven with distrust between dictators and democracies. That it is less well known than *The Private Life of Henry VIII* may be due in some measure to its endorsement of a discredited foreign policy; it is also because, in the judgement of both contemporary critics and subsequent historians, *The Iron Duke* is simply a less good film.[1]

Gaumont-British was the largest producer-distributor-exhibitor in Britain by the mid-1930s. Its holdings included two studios (Lime

Grove and Islington), some 300 cinemas, film printing works and subsidiary companies producing newsreels (Gaumont-British News) and educational films (GB Instructional). In 1933 the company was reorganised, consolidating the control of the Ostrers and rationalising its two separate distribution arms into one. The departure of C.M. Woolf to join J. Arthur Rank in 1935 left Mark Ostrer as chairman and managing director. Director of production from 1931 until 1936, when he left to head MGM's British operation, was Michael Balcon. Gaumont-British benefited from the fact that it had under contract several top British stars (including Jessie Matthews, Jack Hulbert and Cicely Courtneidge) and an 'impressive trio of directors' (Victor Saville, Walter Forde and, from 1934, Alfred Hitchcock).[2] In the wake of Korda's success with *The Private Life of Henry VIII*, Balcon also saw 'internationalism' as the cornerstone of his production strategy:

> The growth of the film industry in this country during the past few years, and the welcome extended to British pictures, not only in our own Dominions but in the vast American market, have proved beyond doubt that in order to progress still further we must pursue a production policy ever less and less parochial and more and more international in appeal. 'Internationalism' sums up G.B. policy.[3]

Balcon was later to find his greatest critical success as Head of Production at Ealing Studios, where his policy was distinctly national rather than international, but in the 1930s he held to the belief that British films could hold their own in the American market. This differentiated Gaumont-British from its rival ABPC which, following the failure of several big-budget films in the late 1920s, followed a policy of retrenchment and concentrated principally on the production of economical films that would cover their costs in the home market.

Victor Saville had been associated with Balcon since 1919 when they had both joined the Victory Motion Picture Company as film salesmen. Saville joined Gaumont-British in the 1920s, working his way up from production manager to writer to director. Unlike Hitchcock (suspense thrillers) and Forde (thrillers and comedies), Saville was not particularly associated with any genre. 'I cannot say yet that I have developed any particular partiality as to the subjects of the films I make', he told *Picturegoer* in 1933. 'Of course, there will always be drama, comedy and historical plays', he added; 'I do not believe that anything entirely new apart from these categories can be invented, but there must always be a certain amount of originality in any plot if a play is to be a success on the screen.'[4] He won critical plaudits for social dramas promoting the ideology of consensus (*Hindle Wakes*, *The Good Companions*, *South Riding*) and popular acclaim for a series of glossy musicals starring the 'dancing divinity' Jessie Matthews (*Evergreen*, *First A Girl*, *It's Love Again*).[5]

It does not seem that *The Iron Duke* was a personal project of Saville's. Indeed, it has been suggested that 'he was obliged to direct a number of films which were not of his own choosing' as part of Gaumont-British's attempt to enter the American market.[6] Saville came to it following his successes with *The Good Companions* (1933), *I Was A Spy* (1933) and *Evergreen* (1934). There is some evidence to suggest that before *The Iron Duke* Saville had been developing a film about Mary, Queen of Scots, to star Madeleine Carroll (whom he had directed in the First World War drama *I Was A Spy*), but 'the project was shelved because he was unable to obtain a satisfactory story treatment of this complex historical drama'.[7] Saville's account of the origins of *The Iron Duke* claims that it was the outcome of Balcon's wish to make a film marking the Silver Jubilee:

> Nineteen thirty-five was George V's silver jubilee, and early in 1934, Balcon asked who had an idea for a film to help mark the event. The year of accession, 1910, saw Bleriot's flight across the Channel, and the twenty-five years of George's reign saw the rapid progress of the airplane with a great leap forward in the war; then Alcock and Brown's first flight across the Atlantic and Lindbergh's solo flight to Paris; and then, in the thirties, air travel had become commonplace on the continents and we were, via the flying boat, rapidly approaching intercontinental flights. I wanted to take the twenty-five years of George V's reign through the development of the airplane – a worthwhile effort as a contribution to the jubilee celebrations...I am afraid that it never got further than an idea. As a patriotic gesture, it was decided to make a film of Wellington at Waterloo.[8]

The way in which Saville mentions the film almost as an aside at the end of his description of a film that was never made suggests that he made no claim to ownership of *The Iron Duke*. Indeed, he played down his own role in its production, remarking that the 'best sequence in the film was not directed by me. It was shot in Scotland by a second unit: the charge of the Scots Greys at Waterloo with a Cameron Highlander clutching the stirrup of a Scots Grey.'[9]

The Iron Duke was a starring vehicle for George Arliss, the British stage and screen actor who had settled in America in the early 1900s and who was renowned for his portrayal of historical figures, including Voltaire, Richelieu and Disraeli. His stage background made him a star of early talking pictures when precise elocution was deemed necessary for serious acting. He starred in a number of historical biopics including *Disraeli* (1929 – for which he won an Academy Award), *Alexander Hamilton* (1931), *Voltaire* (1933), *The House of Rothschild* (1934) and *Cardinal Richelieu* (1935). The story that an American lady tourist on visiting London and seeing a statue of Disraeli was overheard to say 'What a lovely statue of George Arliss!' is probably as apocryphal as Korda's singing cabbie; however, much the same point was made by the commentator who remarked: 'Lives of all great men remind us how like George Arliss they were'.[10] The recruitment of a Hollywood star such as Arliss can be seen as part of the studio's international strategy, though by the time of *The Iron Duke* Arliss was 66 years old and his period of greatest popularity had passed. Most commentators agree with Richards to the effect that Arliss was 'curious casting for the role of the Duke of Wellington. A slight, round-shouldered figure with equine features and flared nostrils, he lacked the physical authority of almost all the other actors to have played the part – and they include Laurence Olivier, C. Aubrey Smith, Christopher Plummer, John Neville and Torin Thatcher.'[11] In his autobiography, however, Arliss maintained that 'the old duke was in reality exactly my height' and quoted a letter he received from Mrs Muriel Goodchild, *née* Wellesley, great grand niece and biographer of Wellington, who approved of his casting 'for I feel you are the only person I would care to trust with so precious a subject'.[12]

Arliss's autobiography provides further anecdotal evidence that *The Iron Duke* came about after other ideas had been discarded, including an adaptation of *The Forsyte Saga* and biopics of Nelson and Samuel Pepys. It took 'from three to four months to concoct and write and polish the scenario of Wellington'.[13] The film was shot at the Lime Grove Studios, Shepherd's Bush, in less than six weeks (from 3 September to 13 October). The Battle of Waterloo was staged on three

3. George Arliss as *The Iron Duke* directs the Battle of Waterloo.

separate locations: a site near Wormwood Scrubs prison stood in for
the hill from which Wellington and his staff officers watch the battle,
the British infantry squares were shot on Salisbury Plain and the
charge of the Scots Greys was staged at Invergordon.[14] The use of
British troops as extras for the battle sequence suggests a level of
official support for the film, an impression confirmed when the Prince
of Wales attended its première at the Tivoli Cinema on 30 November
1934. *The Iron Duke* was shown in London at the end of the year,
prior to its general release early in 1935.

There is much evidence to suggest that the film-makers were
concerned with the needs of historical authenticity. The shooting
script indicates that certain visual compositions, as in *The Private Life
of Henry VIII*, were modelled on pictorial sources: 'Shot of French
road to duplicate the famous painting of the meeting between
Wellington and Blucher after Waterloo.'[15] Several historical advisers
were employed, including Captain H. Oakes-Jones of the Royal
Fusiliers for the military sequences and Herbert Norris (who also

worked on the studio's production of *Jew Süss*) for costumes and set dressings. Harper sees this as evidence 'that the opinions of academic historians were beginning to be heeded by some parts of the film trade'.[16] The British press book, produced for exhibitors to suggest promotional angles, was at pains to emphasise the authentic period detail of the film and suggested that this was the foremost criteria upon which the film would be judged: 'The ultimate success of such a picture as *The Iron Duke*, or any other dealing with a historical period, depends as much upon the accuracy of reconstruction as upon the quality of the presentation of the story.'[17] This is, to say the least, a disputable claim. The historical infelicities of *The Private Life of Henry VIII* had done nothing to harm its popular success, whereas many critics were to find *The Iron Duke* lacking in dramatic qualities.

The critical response to *The Iron Duke* was, in fact, rather mixed. There was little unanimity, even among the trade press, the purpose of whose reviews it was to sell the film to cinema distributors and exhibitors. Thus, while the *Daily Film Renter* proclaimed it as a 'distinguished production with outstanding box-office appeal' which 'presents a cavalcade of stately pageantry that has seldom been equalled on the screen', *Kinematograph Weekly* was rather more circumspect, feeling that the historical events were not successfully integrated into the narrative: 'The major weakness lies in the story; it introduces all historical events of importance, but touches on them so lightly that they do not mould into a dramatic whole.'[18] Lionel Collier of fan magazine *Picturegoer* found it wanting both as drama and as history: 'It is well enough done technically, but it is deficient in vitality and that essential quality which makes you deeply interested in the characters of a story, and even as a documentary historical film it does not bear too close a scrutiny.' He felt, furthermore, that Arliss was 'miscast' and that he 'makes the conqueror of Napoleon an elderly, garrulous and avuncular sort of person very unlike the popular conception of the "Iron Duke"'.[19] The middle-brow film critics were similarly divided on its merits. Forsyth Hardy in *Cinema Quarterly* acknowledged 'that it attempts a bigger subject than the average sevenpenny novelette or penny dreadful of the screen' but concluded that 'on the screen it lacks life and form, and Victor Saville's direction is flat and uninspired'.[20] But the *Monthly Film Bulletin* held entirely the opposite view: 'The producers' laudable insistence on historical accuracy has not prevented this from being a genuinely dramatic piece, through which the interest of the story never flags. Victor Saville's direction is excellent, and provides some really superb groupings.'[21]

American critics were also divided. This is exemplified by *Variety*, which reviewed the film twice and pronounced a different verdict on each occasion. The London critic of the trade paper felt that 'it is a satisfactory commercial proposition throughout the world' and that it is 'in histrionic and production detail that the film makes its finest impression'. The same critic also approved of the film's staging of the Battle of Waterloo in a short montage of scenes: 'Just a flash or two of the epoch-making battle of Waterloo suffices to give the requisite atmosphere and a mere handful of the Scots Greys with the famous line "Up Guards and at 'em" conjures up sufficient action taking place in this historical battle.'[22] When it was released in America, however, another reviewer suggested that '*The Iron Duke* is but intermittently entertaining' and observed that the battle sequence 'looks like a polite diminutive etching. Famous regiments and celebrated deeds become lifeless tableaux.'[23] This was in marked contrast to the American press book, which urged exhibitors to promote the film on its depiction of the 'blood-stirring, heart-shaking Battle of Waterloo...More hell-bent-for-leather action than in any six Westerns you ever saw.'[24] In this regard there was clearly a discrepancy between the promotional discourse of the film and its reception. The fan magazine *Photoplay* remarked that the 'story of Wellington's triumph is told carefully, thoughtfully, cleverly, though not brilliantly. There is little fire. Even the Battle of Waterloo is pictured in a placid, gentlemanly way with more conversation than bloodshed.'[25] The *New York Times* made much the same point: 'The film, surprisingly enough, is not at its best in the dramatization of Waterloo, which has been so simplified that it seems a rather placid affair on the screen.'[26] It would seem that, by American standards, the action sequences were felt to be lacking in spectacle and excitement.

The critical response to *The Iron Duke*, therefore, focused on the competing demands of historical authenticity and entertainment value. Despite the mixed reviews, however, there is evidence to suggest that *The Iron Duke* was successful at the box office, if not achieving quite the same impact as *The Private Life of Henry VIII*. There is no available record of its British box-office performance, though Sedgwick calculates that it was the fourth most popular film of 1935, behind Paramount's Northwest Frontier adventure *Lives of a Bengal*

Lancer, RKO's Fred Astaire–Ginger Rogers musical *Top Hat* and Korda's *The Scarlet Pimpernel* (released, like *The Iron Duke*, at the end of 1934). It was also the most popular Gaumont-British release of the year, ahead of Hithcock's polished romantic thriller *The 39 Steps*.[27] More surprisingly, perhaps, given the lukewarm response of the American critics, it seems to have done well in the American market, though again not to the same extent as *Henry VIII*. Saville claimed that '*The Iron Duke* brought revenue from its American exhibition, more revenue than infinitely superior pictures, such as *I Was a Spy* or *Evergreen*, had produced'.[28] It was released at a time when, according to British trade sources, 'Gaumont-British and Gainsborough pictures are playing to exceptional business in that continent'.[29] Street concurs that *The Iron Duke* 'did comparatively well' in America alongside other Gaumont-British films including *The 39 Steps*, *Rhodes of Africa*, *First A Girl* and *Evergreen*.[30]

Although *Variety*'s London correspondent had declared that this 'picture is of sufficient importance to warrant columns of comment in any newspaper', *The Iron Duke* did not generate the same level of interest as *The Private Life of Henry VIII*. Nor has it figured prominently in critical discourse around the notion of a British national cinema. The British press book described it 'as truly British in sentiment as it is British in its emotional appeal'. Yet this was felt to be something of a handicap in the American market, where *Variety* felt that the subject and treatment would alienate American audiences:

> Its nationalistic tone dominates to the extent that many Americans will fail to appreciate typically British touches... British-Gaumont [sic] may be presumed to know British sentiment where a national hero is concerned. But in America he is mostly a name only. Few Americans will detect the pious fraud in connection with the fictionized [sic] version of Marshal Ney's execution which flies in the face of history...[H]owever satisfying the touched-up portrait may be to Britons, it's not very glamorous as here treated because the picture is slow.[31]

This verdict, however, was contradicted by none other than Hollywood movie mogul Darryl F. Zanuck, who had advised Arliss against making the film because the Duke of Wellington was *too* familiar to American audiences following his portrayal by C. Aubrey

Smith in *The House of Rothschild*. Zanuck averred that 'any Duke of Wellington who didn't look like Aubrey Smith would not be accepted in the movies'.[32]

In this context there is a significant difference between *The Iron Duke* and *Henry VIII* as star vehicles. Laughton looked so much like the popular image of 'Bluff King Hal' that critics and cinema-goers immediately accepted him in the role. This likeness was due in part to the film modelling Henry's appearance on portraits of the king and in part to the fact that Laughton did not have a fixed star persona before the film. He could, therefore, become Henry in a way that Arliss could not become Wellington, for not only was Arliss so different from the Duke in appearance, he also had an existing star persona with which audiences were already familiar. *The Iron Duke* characterises Wellington in such a way as to make him fit the Arliss persona, rather than Arliss attempting a likeness of Wellington. This point was recognised by the *New York Times*:

> There is a grave likelihood that an unsympathetic historian could commit considerable damage upon the screen play which has been arranged for Mr Arliss. To begin with, the Iron Duke seems to have earned his title because of his icy and punctilious manner, and reputable historians have pointed out that he seldom played the beloved papa to his soldiers. In Mr Arliss's highly amiable performance, however, Wellington, who was only in his middle forties in 1815, becomes a gay and witty old gentleman, much given to informal behaviour.[33]

Thus *The Iron Duke* contains scenes such as Wellington crawling around on all fours playing with his hostess's children and joshing with his officers that are completely at odds with the usual characterisation of the Duke as a stern, patrician, authoritarian figure. The importance is less whether a film characterisation is psychologically accurate according to the best historical knowledge (as, for example, Flora Robson's portrayal of Elizabeth I in *Fire Over England* was held to be) and more whether it accords with the popular image of the historical figure. Arliss himself recognised 'the danger, while portraying historical characters, of running counter to the preconceived ideas of the general public', but claimed that the 'reason I fell into the trap was that I knew too much about the man to start with'.[34] In the case of *The*

Iron Duke, Arliss's performance was both contrary to the popular image of Wellington and unlike the actual historical person. As a military leader Wellington was a strict disciplinarian who famously referred to his own troops as 'the scum of the earth' and inspired respect rather than affection from his men. It was only in his old age, following his retirement from politics, that the Duke became a popular national hero. Yet it was an aged and revered Wellington that Arliss played, entirely inappropriately, in *The Iron Duke.*

It is due in large measure to the miscasting of its star that the 'private life' aspect of *The Iron Duke* is far less successful than in *Henry VIII.* This is most apparent in the sub-plot involving Wellington's relationship with Lady Frances Webster. To believe in the elderly and avuncular Arliss as an object of romantic fascination for a young woman is hardly credible. This aspect of the film is further weakened by the characterisation of Lady Frances as a rather silly *ingénue* who faints upon her first meeting with the man she hero-worships. In contrast to *Henry VIII,* where the protagonist's romantic affairs are the focus of the narrative, *The Iron Duke* is least comfortable in dealing with the private sphere. So redundant is this sub-plot to the main action of the film, indeed, that it is tempting to speculate that it was included only so that the film-makers could include Wellington's famous riposte to the *St Jude's Chronicle* when it threatened to expose his (entirely innocent) friendship with Lady Frances: 'Let 'em publish and be damned!' While the BBFC forbade profanities, it was evidently prepared to allow a mild example when it was a matter of historical record.

Much more central to *The Iron Duke* is the public life of its protagonist. Promotional materials emphasised that the film was concerned with Wellington's role as a statesman and a diplomat as well as a soldier. Surprisingly, perhaps, the film does not end with the defeat of Napoleon on the field of Waterloo; the battle itself takes place half-way through the film and is followed by Wellington's efforts to negotiate a peace settlement at the Congress of Vienna. And it is in this aspect of the film that its contemporary resonances become explicit, to a far greater extent than in *Henry VIII* where political matters had been alluded to only in passing. The narrative of *The Iron Duke,* indeed, is so intricately related to domestic and international politics during the interwar years that it is difficult to escape the conclusion that this aspect of the film was intentional on the part of its makers.

Some 15 years before production of *The Iron Duke*, the Great Powers had again sat down at the negotiating table to agree the settlement of Europe following a devastating war that had altered forever the geopolitical balance of power on the continent. The Paris Peace Conference of 1919, resulting in the signature of the Treaty of Versailles and the other treaties that ended the First World War, had certain historical parallels with the Congress of Vienna in 1815. On both occasions Allied statesmen had met to determine a territorial settlement that would contain the nation held responsible for the war – France in 1815, Germany in 1919 – and to settle the amount of the indemnity payable by the defeated country to the Allies. And on both occasions the Allies came to the negotiating table with their own national interests and political agendas. But there were also significant differences between 1815 and 1919. At Vienna, France, although the defeated power, was represented at the negotiations (Talleyrand, the French foreign minister, was able to broker favourable terms by playing off rivalries between the other Great Powers), whereas Germany was excluded from the Paris Peace Conference and was forced to accept the Treaty of Versailles under threat of the renewal of the war. And the terms of Versailles were far more punitive on Germany than the terms extended to France in 1815. Germany was forced to accept moral responsibility for the outbreak of war – the notorious Article 231, or 'war guilt clause' – and was burdened with crippling reparations of £6,600 million (plus interest) that even some economists at the time regarded as quite unrealistic.

The Versailles Treaty created more problems than it resolved. Germany was left hurt and resentful by her harsh treatment: the treaty was regarded as a diktat and revision of its terms became the aim of German statesmen throughout the interwar period. In France, there was a popular feeling that the treaty had not been punitive enough: it left Germany's frontiers substantially intact and even the establishment of a demilitarised zone in the Rhineland did not allay French fears over the threat to national security still posed by Germany. In Britain, there is evidence of a softening of attitudes towards Germany. In the immediate aftermath of war there had been a popular mood of anti-German feeling and the slogan 'Hang the Kaiser' was bandied about during the general election of December 1918. But the Great War had also been, or so it was supposed, 'the war to end all wars' and there was a realisation among British politicians that reconciliation with

Germany would be not only a sign of magnanimity in victory but also a means of restoring the formerly lucrative trading relationship between the two nations. Britain was represented at Versailles by Prime Minister David Lloyd George, certainly no dove, but not motivated by the spirit of '*la revanche*' that influenced the French. An important difference between the British and French positions was their attitude towards reparations. Lloyd George had fought the general election on the platform of exacting reparations from Germany, but by 1920 he was prepared to agree to their reduction and did not advocate punitive action when Germany defaulted on payments in 1922. In contrast, the French were prepared to extract reparations by force and early in 1923 sent troops to occupy the Ruhr – a move that was condemned by Britain and the United States. The argument that reparations had been unfairly punitive was lent intellectual weight by British economist John Maynard Keynes whose book *The Economic Consequences of the Peace* (1919) argued that they would destabilise the German economy and bring about economic collapse. Keynes's view appeared to be vindicated in 1922–23 when Germany was struck by chronic inflation, blamed on the level of reparations, which in turn led to mass unemployment and acute social distress. From the early 1920s British policy towards Germany and British public opinion were sympathetic to the revision of the Versailles Treaty. The view that Germany had been harshly treated and had cause for grievance at the punitive nature of the treaty was one of the factors that influenced the foreign policy of appeasement during the interwar period.[35]

It is a notable feature of *The Iron Duke* that while the film is ostensibly dealing with the Congress of Vienna, the arguments it advances are far more applicable to the treatment of Germany at Versailles. A lengthy and detailed voice-over narration at the beginning of the film explains the historical background and establishes that a prominent theme of *The Iron Duke* will be the question of the fair treatment of France at the end of the Napoleonic Wars:

> The beginning of the year 1815 finds the world at peace. Napoleon, the raging lion who had wrought havoc in Europe and had shaken for so long the peace of the whole world, is now in captivity. The great European powers – Prussia, Russia and Austria – which had combined to defeat Napoleon believed that they could only achieve security by permanently weakening

France. They deposed Napoleon and brought back to the throne of his ancestors the exiled Bourbon king, Louis the Eighteenth, hoping that in return for his restoration he would accept their guidance. Great Britain, however, had also played her part in the downfall of Napoleon through Wellington's victorious campaign in the Spanish Peninsula. But the Duke was a statesman as well as a soldier. He realised that Napoleon alone had been the enemy, and he had been ordered to Vienna to persuade the Allies that only by fair treatment of the French people could they hope to preserve the peace of Europe from being shattered once more by the prisoner of Elba.

The didactic style of this voice-over allows no space for the spectator to reach his or her own interpretation of the ensuing narrative: from the very beginning, therefore, the film imposes a meaning and asserts the view that fair and just treatment of the defeated enemy rather than the imposition of harsh terms is the key to securing future peace.

The discussion of the treatment of France in *The Iron Duke* is so explicitly informed by the debate that had emerged over Versailles that it seems reasonable to assume this aspect of the film was intentional. The British position is one of reconciliation and fair-mindedness, whereas the other powers are shown to be intent upon seizing the spoils of war and imposing harsh terms on France. Wellington is characterised as a peace-maker and a conciliator: he is the 'dove' in contrast to the 'hawks' represented by Metternich of Austria and Field Marshal Blücher of Prussia. Wellington's insistence on fair treatment and his opposition to an indemnity can be seen in terms of the more conciliatory British attitude towards Germany after 1919:

> *Blücher:* We're not here to ask favours, but to demand rights. We are in the country of the beaten enemy.
> *King of Prussia:* I agree with General Blücher. My people have suffered. They must have some reward. Prussia must have proper strategic frontiers.
> *Wellington:* Speaking as a soldier, it is my opinion that there is only one strategic frontier of any value, and that's a hole in the ground.
> *Blücher:* France must be so weakened that this can never happen again.

King of Prussia: The world must be made safe from France.
Metternich: You say no indemnity – why? What justice is there in that? It's cost us all dearly enough.
Wellington: Idemnities will cost you more, and how are you going to get 'em?
Metternich: Stay here till they're paid. You have your army of occupation.
Wellington: I'm not a bailiff's man. My army's for fighting, not for collecting debts.
Blücher: They must pay – pay – pay!
Wellington: Your majesties, my lords, we all desire one thing – peace. If your policy is to weaken France, do it thoroughly. Take her territory, her population, her resources, but don't imagine that's going to bring you peace. If we insist on taking her territory, war is merely deferred until France is once more strong enough to take what she has lost.

The film therefore makes what seem to be direct references to the treatment afforded Germany after the Great War. Wellington's opposition to an indemnity is almost Keynesian; his refusal to extract an indemnity by force of arms might be seen as an implicit criticism of the French occupation of the Ruhr; and his warning that an unjust settlement would merely defer another war recalls the view of the Allied Commander-in-Chief, Marshal Foch, who in 1919 had referred to Versailles as a 'twenty-year armistice', implying that another war with Germany would be the consequence. Foch's prediction was to prove uncannily accurate.

The ideological position of *The Iron Duke* is asserted again in the final sequence of the film. The ending of any film is important as the resolution of the narrative works to fix the meaning of the film in the mind of the spectator. *The Iron Duke* concludes with Wellington's speech to the House of Lords in which he makes a passionate and witty defence of his successful negotiations at Vienna in response to his critics, such as Earl Grey, who had wanted a harsher settlement with France:

Wellington: The noble lords have asked what reward this country has obtained in return for its unflinching efforts. If material rewards are meant, there are none that is in proportion to the sacrifices made. I could have smuggled home some art treasures

– I might even have rescued a marble Venus for the noble earl. I could have insisted on the thousand million reparations. I could have ruthlessly seized territory. You could have had your pound of flesh, my lords, but France would have bled to death, and you would have found that you had plunged your knife into the heart of Europe. Our rewards will be found in the attainment of the purpose for which we fought – the peace of Europe and the salvation of the world from unexampled tyranny.

Wellington's reference to 'the thousand million reparations' must surely be understood in the context of Versailles. The film is clearly aligning itself with the position of Keynes and other critics of the reparations imposed on Germany. The film ends with Wellington being cheered through the streets of London as he drives home with his wife and sons.

Marcia Landy avers that *The Iron Duke* 'seems unusual for the time in making an idealistic plea for the countries of Europe to put aside differences, national enmities, and ambitions in the interests of peace'.[36] Yet the ideological alignment of the film is not at all unusual in the context of British politics and society in the mid-1930s. While it would be overstating the case ever to describe Britain as a pacifist country, there is much evidence to suggest that the interwar period, especially the decade between the mid-1920s and the mid-1930s, marked the height of anti-war sentiment. In the mid- and late 1920s there was a literary fashion for books about the Great War – including memoirs (Robert Graves's *Goodbye To All That*), plays (R.C. Sherriff's *Journey's End*) and novels (Ernest Raymond's *Tell England*) – that all represented war as a futile enterprise in which brave men suffered for the mistakes of politicians and generals. In the first half of the 1930s there were many indicators that public opinion was in favour of peace and against war. In February 1933, the Oxford Union passed its famous motion that 'This House will in no circumstance fight for King and Country' and in October of the same year John Wilmott, an independent socialist candidate, overturned a large government majority in the East Fulham by-election campaigning on a disarmament platform. In 1934, the Peace Pledge Union was founded; in 1935, ten million people signed a 'Peace Ballot' calling for a reduction of armaments; and in 1936, a group of documentary film-makers led by Paul Rotha produced the short film *Peace of Britain*, urging people to write to their MPs to protest at government spending on armaments. Given this context, the assertion in *The Iron Duke* that Britain's aim was 'the peace of Europe and the salvation of the world from unexampled tyranny' was entirely consistent with the mood of the times.

The nature of public opinion in the 1930s, combined with the view of statesmen and intellectuals that Germany had been harshly treated at Versailles, helped to create the climate for the policy of appeasement. Appeasement – the notion that the grievances of Germany and other powers could be addressed through positive negotiation and making concessions where the reason was thought to be just – was the guiding principle of British foreign policy during the interwar period and was followed by successive British governments under Ramsay MacDonald, Stanley Baldwin and Neville Chamberlain. It is crucial to understand that in the 1930s appeasement was not the dirty word that it has since become. It was widely seen as an entirely reasonable policy whose aim was to resolve international tension through peaceful negotiation and to avoid another war that could have potentially devastating consequences. But the reasons behind appeasement were practical as well as moral. Britain was neither militarily nor economically prepared for war in the 1930s; the defence chiefs were as much concerned with protecting the Empire as with the European situation; the Treasury was concerned that spending on rearmament would upset the delicate recovery from the slump; and the Foreign Office was as distrustful of France as it was fearful of Germany. Thus it was that Britain did not oppose Hitler's action in 1936 when, in violation of Versailles, German troops reoccupied the Rhineland, or in 1938 when Germany effectively annexed Austria through the *Anschluss*. The high-water mark of appeasement came in September 1938 when Chamberlain flew to Munich to negotiate a settlement to the Czechoslovakian crisis and returned to proclaim 'peace with honour... peace for our time'. A.J.P. Taylor later described the Munich Agreement as 'a triumph for all that was best and most enlightened in British life; a triumph for those who had preached equal justice between peoples; a triumph for those who had courageously denounced the short-sightedness of Versailles'.[37] A similar belief in equal justice between peoples and a commitment to fair dealing in international affairs is evident in *The Iron Duke*.

How far were the politics of *The Iron Duke* apparent to contemporaries? Forsyth Hardy, for one, detected the contemporary resonances: 'In the course of the spectacular flirting with history, occasionally sentiments are expressed which are capable of modern application – talk among the Allies of demanding indemnity and Wellington's reference in the House of Lords to Britain's implication in European affairs'.[38] Where there is less hard evidence is whether this 'modern application' was intentional on the part of the film-makers, though the film itself is so overt in this regard that it is difficult to believe it was anything other than deliberate. But whose was the intelligence behind it? Unlike Korda's films, where their politics can be attributed to his control, the situation is less clear with Gaumont-British. The internationalism of the film would seem to fit in with Saville's politics; he was described by Sir John Woolf as having 'a very international outlook and was a liberal by nature'.[39] But Saville, as we have seen, had no particular investment of his own in the film. Harper argues that Balcon exercised greater control over the film than Saville and that *The Iron Duke*'s overt propagandism, its middle-class orientation, and its avoidance of the erotic were the result of Balcon's overall studio control'.[40] The moral optimism of *The Iron Duke*, certainly, is characteristic of other films produced during Balcon's regime at Gaumont-British, notably *Jew Süss* (dir. Lothar Mendes, 1934).

There is, however, another possibility: that the film reflected Arliss's views. He had a hand in writing the script – at least according to his autobiography – and by his own admission was attracted by subjects preaching the gospel of internationalism and peaceful co-existence. He believed in 'the idea that we have a right to expect honourable dealings between nations just as we look for it in individuals'.[41] He was referring specifically to the next film he made at Gaumont-British, *East Meets West* (dir. Herbert Mason, 1936), though the sentiment would apply equally well to *The Iron Duke*. *East Meets West* is a political melodrama set in the fictional Sultanate of Rungay where the British and an unnamed Eastern power (but clearly meant to be Japan) are vying for influence and strategic advantage. As the Sultan, Arliss again asserts the need for peace: 'I desire the friendship of all nations ... I have noticed that when the integrity of a small nation is threatened, that sooner or later it becomes a battlefield. War is a foolish argument and must be avoided.' The film alludes to the view, popular on the left during the interwar period, that wars were caused by the manufacturers of armaments. Carter, a British Customs officer, is an advocate of armed intervention:

> *Carter:* A British cruiser and a party of marines could have Rungay in twenty-four hours.
> *Dr Fergusson:* It's hot heads like you that keep the munitions factories busy.

The Sultan of Rungay is a wily diplomat who plays the British and the 'Eastern' ambassadors against each other. Although the Eastern ambassador Dr Shaghu is characterised as a devious oriental, the British ambassador Sir Henry Mallory (Godfrey Tearle) is not entirely sympathetic either, threatening gunboat diplomacy and demanding that Carter, who has been arrested for rum-running in 'dry' Rungay, should be handed back to the British ('White men must be punished by white men'). The Sultan asserts the neutrality of his country and manipulates events so that both Britain and the Eastern power sign a friendship treaty with Rungay in which they pledge economic aid (which the Sultan wants to improve roads and sanitation) in return for a guarantee that the other power will not be allowed to establish a naval base there: 'You want security and you have bought it with money which you would otherwise have wasted in powder and shot. I have saved you thousands of lives and millions of money.'

The argument that Arliss as much as anyone else was responsible for the ideological undercurrent of these films is lent further credence by his next film for Gaumont-British, *His Lordship* (dir. Herbert Mason, 1936), another drama of political intrigue in which Arliss plays both the Foreign Secretary Lord Dunchester and his identical twin brother Richard Fraser. The plot revolves around a political crisis in a fictional Middle Eastern state, Kasra, where the Emir has been assassinated by treacherous ministers who have succeeded in framing an Englishman for the murder. Dunchester is characterised as a belligerent statesman in the Palmerstonian mould who is quick to advocate force to resolve the dispute: 'There are only two ways of dealing with these orientals – try persuasion and, if that fails, we'll send an armed force.' In one ideologically charged scene, Dunchester makes a speech in favour of war and is shouted down by an audience of dockers – an assertion that the working classes are in favour of peace. The National Government, which had been re-elected by a large majority in 1935, was committed to a policy of collective security through the League of Nations and to the principle of 'all sanctions short of war'. In the event it is Fraser, who has lived in Kasra and speaks Arabic, who takes his brother's place in the decisive negotiations, exposes the treachery and averts a war. In contrast to his bellicose brother, Fraser is characterised as an appeaser who believes that British interests can be maintained through peaceful means rather than by resorting to war. His familiarity with Arabic language and customs might also link him to that other great British idealist, T.E. Lawrence, who had died a year earlier.

Arliss's films for Gaumont-British, and *The Iron Duke* in particular, are very much tracts for their times. They now appear dated, as much by their politics as by Arliss's highly mannered style of performance. Arliss retired from the screen following the lively pirate film *Dr Syn* (dir. Roy William Neill, 1937) and died in 1946. Gaumont-British, meanwhile, was beset by a bitter boardroom power struggle between the Ostrers and John Maxwell of ABPC who acquired shares and a seat on the board in 1936 and attempted over the next two years to wrest control of the company away from the Ostrers. It is little wonder that against such a background of institutional instability several of the studio's biggest talents decided to leave: Balcon and Saville both left in 1936, followed the next year by Alfred Hitchcock. The slump that affected the British film industry in 1937 was felt at Gaumont-British, which responded with a policy of retrenchment and economy. It ceased distributing its own films early in 1937 and the Lime Grove studio was closed later the same year. It retreated from making any more ambitious historical/costume films: a Dufaycolour film of *Rob Roy* with Michael Redgrave and Margaret Lockwood – successfully teamed in *The Lady Vanishes*, Hitchcock's last film for Gaumont/Gainsborough – was announced in 1938 but never made.[42] The corporation's most consistently successful films of the late 1930s came from its Gainsborough subsidiary, in the form of comedies featuring music-hall stars such as Will Hay and the Crazy Gang. Thus it was that by the end of the decade Gaumont-British had reverted to a sort of 'domestic' film, successful in the home market but with little potential for export, that represented the antithesis of the ambitious 'international' film exemplified by the likes of *The Iron Duke*. At the outbreak of the Second World War Gaumont-British was a mere shadow of the studio it had been only a few years earlier and would soon be incorporated within the rapidly expanding empire of J. Arthur Rank.

3

Monarchy and Empire:
Victoria the Great (1937) and
Sixty Glorious Years (1938)

T HE flexibility of the historical film as a vehicle for propaganda
during the 1930s is no better exemplified than in the extraordinary
case of *Victoria the Great* and *Sixty Glorious Years*. Herbert Wilcox,
who produced and directed both films, accomplished the remarkable
feat of presenting what was effectively the same story, with much the
same characters and cast, in two films, released in successive years,
which both won critical and popular acclaim. It would be inaccurate to
describe *Sixty Glorious Years* as a sequel to *Victoria the Great* in the
sense of taking up where the first film finished; it is, rather, a remake
which spans the same time period and dramatises many of the same
incidents. To all intents and purposes, they are two separate halves of
one larger film: in 1942, indeed, Wilcox released an edited compilation
of both films under the title *Queen Victoria*. The particular significance
of the 'Victoria' films for this study is that they demonstrate how the
same historical events could be used to fit different political and
ideological ends. Both films assert the need for national unity, but they
do so in response to different circumstances: thus *Victoria the Great* is
concerned principally to validate the institution of monarchy in the
wake of the Abdication Crisis of 1936, whereas *Sixty Glorious Years* is
a strident call for national preparedness that was released shortly after
the Munich Agreement of 1938.[1]

Like Korda, Herbert Wilcox was an independent producer whose
ambitions lay at the quality end of the market. Like Balcon and Saville,

he entered the film industry as a renter in 1919 and moved into production in the early 1920s. He bought the Imperial Studios at Elstree in 1926 and founded the British & Dominions Film Corporation in 1927. Wilcox was one of the first British producers to recognise the significance of talking pictures and even travelled to Hollywood to gain experience in using sound technology. He adopted Hollywood methods of production and imported American stars such as Dorothy Gish and Will Rogers. It was Wilcox who launched the screen careers of Sydney Howard, Jack Buchanan, Tom Walls, Ralph Lynn and Anna Neagle. Neagle, whom Wilcox first directed in the musical *Goodnight Vienna* (1931), was to become one of the major British female stars for the next two decades. Wilcox moulded her star persona through several transformations – from musical comedies to costume dramas to contemporary romantic melodramas – which demonstrated a knack for judging changes in popular taste. It was a romantic as well as a professional partnership: Wilcox and Neagle married in 1943 after a decade as lovers.

As a film-maker, however, Wilcox was the antithesis of Korda. His films are chiefly characterised by their aesthetic and cultural conservatism. As a director he had little visual imagination and tended towards flat and static compositions; many of his films were adaptations of stage plays. Throughout his career he demonstrated a tendency to repeat formulas that had already proved successful. The Victoria films were not the only examples of stories he made twice. He directed two versions of *Nell Gwyn* (with Dorothy Gish in 1926 and Anna Neagle in 1934) and two versions of Reginald Berkeley's play *Dawn* (with Sybil Thorndike in 1928 and Anna Neagle in 1939, made in Hollywood as *Nurse Edith Cavell*). The 1926 *Nell Gwyn* had been a considerable success in the United States, where it was afforded a prestigious New York première and a high-profile 'roadshow' release.[2] The 1934 *Nell Gwyn* was clearly influenced by *The Private Life of Henry VIII*, with its focus on romantic affairs at court. The film is replete with salacious detail, exposed *décolletage* and *risqué* dialogue ('We'll roll in the hay till the sun gets low'; 'A bold and merry slut'). It was shown in the United States only after substantial cuts had been made and a moralising prologue added, at the insistence of the Production Code Administration, which showed Nell destitute towards the end of her life.[3]

Wilcox produced and directed four historical films during the 1930s, all starring Anna Neagle: *Nell Gwyn*, *Peg of Old Drury* (1935),

Victoria the Great and *Sixty Glorious Years*. There is less thematic and
stylistic consistency in his films than is evident in Korda's work,
suggesting either that Wilcox lacked the same clearly defined view of
history, or, conversely, that he was more flexible in responding to
production trends and changes in popular taste. The four films divide
neatly into two pairs. On the one hand, *Nell Gwyn* and *Peg of Old
Drury* represent the past as a site of pleasure, feature disrespectable
lower-class protagonists and afford greater prominence to female
desire. On the other hand, the two Victoria biopics subordinate desire
to duty and represent the past in terms of a strict bourgeois morality.
It is possible that the changing nature of Neagle's roles in these films
– an upwards trajectory from courtesan to queen – reflected Wilcox's
increasing sense of reverence for his star.

In common with other British producers, Wilcox was affected by
the instability of the film market in the 1930s. He was known for over-
production, investing his working capital in several films at the same
time.[4] In 1936, the British & Dominions (B&D) studio was gutted by
fire, and the insurance money allowed Wilcox to make a fresh start. The
strategy he followed over the next few years was geared towards both
the domestic and international markets. In 1936, he set up Herbert
Wilcox Productions with a view to making modestly budgeted films for
the home market. Then, in 1937, he incorporated Imperator Film
Productions which, he planned, 'will make from four to six pictures a
year at a cost of approximately £100,000 each. They will be made with
an eye to the world market.'[5] Wilcox was extended credit by Korda to
film at Denham (it is worth remembering that Korda had made *The
Private Life of Henry VIII* at the old B&D studio) and the first film to
be produced by Imperator was *Victoria the Great*.

Wilcox later described *Victoria the Great* as 'the biggest gamble I
had ever taken'. He claimed to have turned down an offer to make the
film in co-operation with Korda ('Not this time, Alex') and gave as his
reason a long-standing personal interest in the project:

> This was the one film I had always wanted to make. I suppose
> the ambition was there, deep down, before I even dreamed I
> would make pictures; when I was the hungry young boy
> scrounging stale sandwiches from Brighton restaurants, and had
> seen Edward VII dozing on a seat on the Hove sea-front with
> his back to the statue of Queen Victoria. And stuck in my mind

for ever were the words I shouted as a Brighton newsboy the day she died: 'Death of Queen Victoria.'[6]

That the film could be made at all was because of the lifting of an official ban on portrayals of Queen Victoria. King George V had made clear his wish that there should be no stage or screen portrayals of his grandmother during his lifetime. The Lord Chamberlain, responsible for theatre censorship, had willingly acquiesced to the king's wish and the BBFC adopted the same policy in respect of cinema. It had already blocked a film script entitled *The Girlhood of Queen Victoria* in 1934 and had rejected a film adaptation of Laurence Housman's play *Victoria Regina*, which had been performed to acclaim in New York, in 1936. Following the death of George V, however, it became clear that Edward VIII was more amenable to the notion of a biopic of Queen Victoria. Wilcox claimed that the king gave him permission to proceed with the film in 1936, allegedly after his companion, Mrs Simpson, had mentioned the Housman play.[7] It was not until six months after the Abdication, however, that the royal ban was finally lifted by agreement between the Lord Chamberlain and the President of the BBFC in June 1937, the centenary of Queen Victoria's accession.[8] Wilcox must have been confident the ban would be lifted, as *Victoria the Great* had already gone before the cameras. It was filmed at Denham over six weeks during April and May 1937.[9]

Victoria the Great was an expensive production, costing some £150,000 according to Wilcox's autobiography. Wilcox secured distribution through RKO Radio Pictures (he broke with General Film Distributors, which had hitherto handled his films, when C.M. Woolf objected to his casting 'chorus girl' Neagle as Queen Victoria). The screenplay was by Miles Malleson (who had scripted Wilcox's previous historical films) and Charles de Grandcourt. In common with other major historical films at the time, there was an emphasis on research and authenticity. Wilcox claimed that 'six months were spent in intensive research before the script was finally completed'.[10] Neagle, who had researched her role as Nell Gwyn even to the extent of imitating Nell's laugh and adopting a Cockney accent, absorbed herself in biographies of the queen and read diaries and letters of the period. The film itself asserts its own authenticity through a pre-title caption which announces: 'Every incident is founded on historic fact and the political utterances by various statesmen are authentic.'

Evidence regarding the extent of official support for the film is contradictory. In his autobiography Wilcox claimed that no 'royal locations were made available nor details of the royal household off duty'. [11] But in an article for *Film Weekly* at the time he suggested that only 'the wonderful facilities granted by the authorities made it possible for us to secure authentic reconstructions of apartments hitherto kept strictly private'.[12] The film's credits afford generous acknowledgement for the assistance provided by Windsor Castle, St James's Palace, Buckingham Palace and St Paul's Cathedral and claim that the film uses 'the actual coach used by Queen Victoria at the Diamond Jubilee'. The balance of evidence, therefore, would seem to be that there was some level of official support for the production. Certainly, the perception of some overseas commentators was that *Victoria the Great* had an aura of offialdom about it. The *New Yorker*, for example, remarked: 'It is, you can see at once, something almost official, a kind of state document.'[13]

Victoria the Great was premièred – rather unusually – in Ottawa, in the presence of the Governor General of Canada, Lord Tweedsmuir, better known as the novelist and historian John Buchan. In Britain, where it opened at the Leicester Square Theatre, it had probably the best reception of any British film since *The Private Life of Henry VIII*, being hailed both as an outstanding production achievement and as a superb example of the historical genre. Thus *Kine Weekly* called it 'one of the finest prestige pictures to be produced in this country' and a 'brilliant visualisation of one of the greatest periods in English history'.[14] *Film Weekly* declared that it 'is likely to do more for the prestige of the British picture than any since *The Private Life of Henry VIII*'.[15] Even the *Monthly Film Bulletin*, often quite jaundiced in its appreciation of such obviously patriotic fare, concurred that it 'is unquestionably one of the finest pictures yet made in this country, and it is at the same time one of the most interesting'.[16] The rapturous reception afforded the film is significant in two particular respects. First, it provides evidence of the genuine support and affection for the monarchy that existed in Britain at the time, in so far as many of the critics seemed to be responding to the subject matter as much as they were to the film itself. And second, it needs to be seen in the context of the economic crisis that hit the British film industry in 1937. The success of *Victoria the Great* was especially timely, given the failure of several expensive films during the previous year (*Rembrandt, Knight*

Without Armour) and the collapse of several of the smaller independent producers. One contemporary source even suggested that *Victoria* itself was very nearly a casualty: '*Victoria the Great* was made during the time that the British film slump had reached its lowest depth. Half way through the production money ran short and for a few days the fate of the film hung in the balance.'[17]

What did critics make of the film itself? There was almost unanimous praise for the performances of Neagle and Anton Walbrook as the Prince Consort, and admiration for the production values, though several critics felt that the switch to Technicolor in the last reel spoiled the ending of the film. *The Times*, for example, thought that the 'pageantry of the Jubilee is blurred by colour'.[18] As far as its approach to history was concerned, most critics approved of the decision to focus on the relationship between Victoria and Albert at the expense of the wider political and social background. Thus *Picturegoer* felt that Wilcox 'has treated a vast subject in a manner which gives us history with a smile, which, be it said, has a subtle distinction from being given "history without tears" as the text books sometimes have it'.[19] *Film Weekly* concurred: 'It necessarily omits a vast amount of incident of that longest of British reigns; but there can be no just criticism on this score, since the film's chief concern is obviously with the romance between Victoria and Albert and their long partnership.'[20] And the *Monthly Film Bulletin* also approved of the decision to concentrate on domestic drama: 'With so vast a field before him the director had to decide where he would place his emphasis. His choice has fallen on *la vie intime*, and he has given us a vivid picture of the home life and romance of Victoria and Albert, set against a background of great events recorded with considerable regard for historical accuracy.' It added that the 'direction is imaginative and sympathetic, and shows understanding of a great age and great characters. His [Wilcox's] touch is sure, and his restraint admirable.'[21]

Moreover, *Victoria the Great* even won over the Historical Association, which rarely had a good word for the historical feature film. In this regard, at least, Wilcox's research paid dividends. Professor Hearnshaw, who had been so critical of Korda's *Fire Over England* for its mixing of fact and fiction, found *Victoria the Great* much more to his satisfaction:

With regard to the historicity and accuracy of the film

representation of the scenes depicted, I think it safe to say that never before has so much care been taken to eliminate error, or so much skill been shown in reproducing exactly the topographical backgrounds. The buildings, the costumes, the furniture, the modes of lighting – all are reproduced with marvellous correctness. Even the speeches of the leading actors are generally composed of authentic utterances, authoritatively reported.[22]

High praise indeed from Hearnshaw, one of the staunchest critics of the historical film, though he did find space to list a dozen 'minor deviations from fact', including the date of the first meeting between Victoria and Albert and the assumption that she did not speak German. It seems that even Wilcox's research was not foolproof: the film uses the proclamation of accession of Edward VII (concluding with the word 'Dominions') rather than that of Victoria, and anachronistically features Elgar's *Pomp and Circumstance* being played when Victoria is proclaimed Empress of India in 1877, some 30 years before the music was written.

There were, however, some dissenting voices amidst the chorus of praise. Critics on the left attacked the film, as they had done *The Private Life of Henry VIII*, for its narrative focus on the personal rather than the public. The Marxist documentarist Basil Wright, who, like Graham Greene, was somewhat improbably employed as a film critic for the *Spectator*, observed that 'behind these finely presented personalities of Queen and Consort, one looks instinctively for an indication, however roughly sketched, of the amazing vigour, the overwhelming and monstrous forces of intellectual and technical advance, the sprawling *mélange* of squalor and respectability, which were the essence of that amazing era... These are denied; the impact of the outside world is in palace terms only.'[23] The *New Statesman* regretted the omission of any mention of social reform: 'The makers of this film have been pleased to call it the story of a glorious reign. It is hardly that. The glories of the reign – factory acts, the improvements in prisons, the removal of some of the grossest forms of judicial savagery, the reform of nursing and a hundred other humane acts are left to the imagination.'[24] In fact, the film does allude to social reform, albeit only in passing, though the left-wing critics of *Victoria the Great* again ignored the constraints imposed upon film-makers by the BBFC. There was little scope for the film to examine social issues, even if it had been part of Wilcox's agenda to do so.

There is no firm evidence of the film's box-office performance; contemporary reports that it grossed over £1 million would seem somewhat exaggerated. Wilcox claimed 'that the distributor's gross of *Victoria the Great* had been £305,000, a very small proportion of which had come from the US market'.[25] Sedgwick calculates that it was the most popular British film of 1937 and fourth overall, behind *Lost Horizon*, *The Good Earth* and *A Star is Born*.[26] There is, however, some qualitative evidence of its reception. Mass-Observation, the social survey organisation founded in 1937, was particularly interested in people's cinema-going habits and the sort of films they liked. A survey of cinema audiences in Bolton, carried out in March 1938 in three cinemas chosen to represent the upper, middle and lower price ranges, found that *Victoria the Great* was the favourite film amongst respondents and that it was liked equally by men and women. Of the individual comments about the film, the majority were highly positive ('*Victoria the Great* is the best picture I have ever seen. I hope there are more like it – starring Anna Neagle'; 'I went a few weeks ago to see *Victoria the Great* and thought it one of the best pictures I had ever seen'; one respondent described it as 'perfect'), with only one expressing any disappointment ('The film *Victoria the Great* did not reach expectations, and although I am very fond of Historical films, I found it rather boring').[27] Leslie Halliwell, later the doyen of amateur film historians, recalled the sense of occasion felt in Bolton when the recently opened Odeon cinema 'capped its own triumph in the booking of *Victoria the Great* by having its star, Anna Neagle, make a personal appearance on the first night...It was the closest we had come to cinema glamour, and we were duly awed.'[28]

In America, the film was premièred at the Radio City Music Hall, where, according to Wilcox, it played to 'packed houses'.[29] American critics admired the production values of the film, though some of them found it too episodic and slow-moving. It seems to have been successful in the large metropolitan centres of the East Coast, where its British pedigree was seen as a cultural indicator of its prestige. Frank S. Nugent in the *New York Times* called it 'a regal biography and a royal treat'.[30] Welford Beaton, writing in the *Hollywood Spectator*, drew particular attention to the 'matchless English landscapes, imposing interiors and groups of handsomely uniformed men and gorgeously attired women, all photographed with an artistic skill Hollywood cannot match'.[31] In common with other British

4. Regal Neagle: Anna Neagle as *Victoria the Great*.

historical films, therefore, the pictorial qualities of *Victoria the Great* were singled out to differentiate it from Hollywood movies. There were echoes of the British critics, however, in that the use of colour in the last reel was felt by some to be inappropriate. Thus Herb Sterne pronounced: 'Technicolor is used for a final, and foolishly blatant, note. A mistake to try so abruptly to bridge the gap between soft photography and hues.'[32]

It would be fair to describe *Victoria the Great* as a 'theatrical' or 'literary' film: it is shot largely in tableaux and makes extensive use of inter-titles and captions that serve much the same purpose as chapter headings in a book. It is an episodic narrative that has the feeling more of a pageant than a film, especially in later sequences. Its relatively static composition throws greater emphasis on narrative than on aspects of form and visual style. In this regard the film's politics are more overt than in either *The Private Life of Henry VIII* or *The Iron Duke*. *Victoria the Great* is an explicit endorsement of consensus politics and of the role of the monarchy in maintaining stability. Thus the young Victoria becomes queen at a time of political tension and social unrest ('Europe on the verge of war, England on the verge of revolution, and a girl on the throne!' one courtier remarks early in the film) and the early years of her reign are beset with domestic problems. An assassin attempts to shoot the Queen and Prince Consort while they are riding in their carriage on Constitution Hill; Victoria is shocked to read of the plight of the poor in *Oliver Twist* ('Such accounts of poverty and squalor! Surely such degradation and starvation cannot exist?'); and an angry mob protesting against the Corn Laws throws stones through the windows of Buckingham Palace. The repeal of the Corn Laws is presented as a just and necessary measure to relieve the poverty of those who, as Sir Robert Peel puts it, 'earn their daily bread by the sweat of their brow'. In supporting the repeal of the Corn Laws, Victoria is shown acting in the interests of her subjects rather than for the vested interests of the gentlemen farmers and landed aristocracy.

In the second half of the film, the focus of the narrative switches from domestic to foreign affairs. Having supported one prime minister (Peel), the royal couple are now shown opposing another (Palmerston) over the *Trent* incident of 1861, when there was a threat that Britain might enter the American Civil War on the side of the Confederacy. An inter-title goes so far as to refer to Palmerston's 'dictatorial threat of war with the Federal Government of the United States' and it is suggested that he wants to bring about 'the final dissolution of the United States of America'. In contrast, an inter-title assures us, 'Victoria and Albert stood together for peace'. The Prince Consort intervenes by rewriting Palmerston's inflammatory protest, producing a diplomatic and conciliatory note that averts the danger of war and brings the two nations closer together. Albert refers to the Americans as 'people of your own blood' and to this extent the film endorses the notion of shared political and cultural heritage between Great Britain and the United States. Following her husband's death, Victoria withdraws from public view, becoming the 'Widow of Windsor', re-emerging in 1877 with her proclamation as Empress of India – an event which marks the beginning of 'the most glorious period in the history of the British Empire'. The speech of Lord Beaconsfield (Disraeli) – seen earlier in the film opposing the repeal of the Corn Laws – summarises the progress and achievements of Victoria's reign and pays tribute to the Queen's role as a servant of the national interest:

> *Lord Beaconsfield:* Your Majesty, for many years now, with untiring energy, with the widest sympathy, and with an indomitable sense of duty, you have applied yourself to the work of government with greater ardour and greater industry than any of your predecessors. You have watched England grow from an agricultural country to a land of railways, telegraphs, canals, factories and ports – from whence her shipping sails out over seven seas and the four corners of the world. You have seen the worst horrors of poverty disappear – children no longer slave in the mills, nor women in the mines. Under your great kindliness have been born a greater kindliness between rich and poor.

This emphasis on industrial and social progress is reminiscent of the publicity of the National Government in the 1930s. Its tone is remarkably similar, for example, to the Gaumont-British newsreel item 'The World Today' (27 August 1936) which had contrasted international strife (Spain, Abyssinia, Palestine) with the social and political stability of 'fortunate Britain – still with its tradition of sanity, the rock of stability amid the eddying stream of world affairs'. The story went on to assert that Britain's industries 'have risen from the slough of despond which clogged the wheels of progress in the depression of the last decade' and concluded with an unequivocal endorsement of the monarchy as the symbol of a united and prosperous nation: 'And above all we look to the head of this great nation whose example and courage have won the admiration and envious respect of other nations less happy. Every member of the royal family works unselfishly and without stint in the cause of social service.' The similarity in language and tone to *Victoria the Great* is quite apparent: Beaconsfield's speech of 1877 seems to have been written with audiences of 1937 in mind.

There are clear echoes of the present in the film's attitude towards the British Empire. Victoria sees herself 'not so much as a queen, or an empress, but as a mother, or perhaps I should say as a grandmother of a great family'. The notion of the British Empire as a family of nations united by principles of 'democracy, tolerance and freedom' reached its height in the inter-war period. 'This Great Family' was the title of the Empire-wide programme that preceded George V's Christmas broadcast in 1935.[33] And the political and economic ties within the Empire had been strengthened by the Ottawa Conference of 1932, which adopted the doctrine of imperial preference. Victoria refers to 'all my dominions overseas' (mentioning specifically Australia, Canada, New Zealand and South Africa) in 1877, at a time when only Canada had actually been accorded dominion status and over 30 years before the Union of South Africa had even been created. When she says of India that she wishes 'to see my new subjects on an equality with the other British subjects of the Crown – happy, contented and flourishing', it is difficult not to see it as a veiled reference to the 1935 Government of India Act, which allowed a greater level of autonomy for the Indian provinces within a federal structure. The British Empire referred to in *Victoria the Great* is essentially the Empire of the 1930s rather than the Empire of the 1870s.

The treatment of monarchy in *Victoria the Great* is nothing if not reverential. Wilcox said that the film 'was designed as a tribute to the woman, rather than as a testament to the historical greatness of the monarch'.[34] Yet in paying tribute to Victoria, the film also acts as an endorsement of the institution of monarchy. There are, again, contemporary parallels. Victoria's interventions in politics over the Corn Laws and the *Trent* incident might be seen to refer to George V's interventions over the Parliament Act of 1911 (which curbed the powers of the unelected House of Lords) and over the formation of the National Government in 1931: the monarch becomes involved in politics in order to safeguard social justice and national security. The reign of George V saw a growing affection between the sovereign and the public, evident in the popular Silver Jubilee celebrations of May 1935. His death in January 1936 heralded the short and troubled reign of his eldest son, Edward VIII. Edward had been a popular figure as Prince of Wales and had evinced concern for social deprivation, but his reign was overshadowed by his relationship with a twice-divorced American socialite, Wallis Simpson. It is difficult today to appreciate the seismic impact of Edward's decision to relinquish the throne in order to marry 'the woman I love'. The constitutional crisis had been kept out of the press until December 1936, by which time the king's hand been forced by his government. Prime Minister Stanley Baldwin believed that marriage to a divorcée would be incompatible with the king's position as Supreme Governor of the Church of England, and was supported by politicians of all parties and by the prime ministers of the dominions. Edward was presented with a stark choice: to give up Mrs Simpson or to give up his throne. He chose to abdicate, anouncing his decision in a radio broadcast on 10 December. Wilcox's autobiography gives some indication of the shock effect of the Abdication:

> On 10th December 1936 I was in Waring and Gillow's, selecting materials for the decor of *Victoria the Great*, when suddenly the noise gave way to an ominous quiet as the BBC announcement came over clear as a bell: 'I, Edward VIII, King of Great Britain and the Dominions beyond the seas, Emperor of India...' I sat down sharply and listened to the word 'abdicate'. I heard no more, I only knew that the King who, during a short reign in which he was never crowned, had made it possible for me to produce the film of his great-grandmother, was no longer a King and had gone into exile.[35]

Edward was succeeded by his brother Albert, Duke of York, who took the title of George VI, while the former king was made Duke of Windsor and went into voluntary exile in France where he married Mrs Simpson on 3 June 1937, ten days after his brother's coronation.

The official response to the Abdication Crisis can be seen from the way in which it was reported in the newsreels of the time. The links between the newsreel companies and the National Government have been well documented by historians: the newsreels were inclined to support the government, even though their editors clung to the mantra of independence.[36] The newsreels had done much to promote Edward VIII as a dutiful and socially responsible king. On his succession, for example, a British Movietone feature entitled 'Edward VIII: An Appreciation' (27 January 1936) had declared that 'a son worthy of his father has succeeded to the throne'. Gaumont-British's 'The World Today' (27 August 1936) had similarly stated that 'already in the short time since his succession, he has proved a worthy successor to his great father and to his grandfather, Edward the Peacemaker'. But the Abdication damaged Edward's reputation – only a handful of MPs, including Winston Churchill, supported him – and it is clear thereafter that the newsreels were anxious to distance themselves from him. Thus the newsreel coverage of the Abdication focused less on Edward's decision than on building up the image of his successor. A British Movietone story, significantly entitled 'Amen: The end of a tragic chapter in British Imperial History' (10 December 1936), testified to the impact of the crisis with its declaration that 'the whole emotional life of the nation – indeed of the entire British race – has seemed to hang poised in suspense'. A shot of a solitary woman kneeling in prayer 'typifies the Empire's distress'. While the commentary suggests some sympathy for the king's position, it makes it clear that he has brought the crisis upon himself: 'To be placed in the position of having to choose between love and the throne is one of life's most tragic dilemmas – even if the dilemma is of the king's own making.' The rest of the story, however, focuses upon the Duke and Duchess of York, who, it claims, have long been aware 'that they may some day be summoned to the supreme responsibility of the Crown'. The item was immediately followed by another ('Sequel: Promise of a new reign') which made no reference at all to Edward and declared that 'it already seems natural to speak of the Duke and Duchess of York as their majesties the king and queen'. There is emphasis on the Duke of York's interest in industry and his annual camps at Southwold for promoting understanding between boys of different social backgrounds. The Gaumont-British item 'Our New King and Queen' (10 December 1936) declared confidently: 'In the hands of King Albert [sic] we may rest assured that the dignity of the Crown, so well established by his beloved father, is in safe keeping.' The embarrassment of Edward was therefore expunged, while the newsreels were at pains to build up a picture of the new king as a dedicated public servant and to promote, in contrast to his brother, but in common with his father, a happy home life, with the two young princesses, Elizabeth and Margaret Rose, much to the fore.

Richards sees *Victoria the Great* as providing 'reassurance in the essential soundness of the monarchy' in the wake of the Abdication Crisis.[37] Victoria is presented as the model of a modern monarch: she has an unflinching sense of duty which sees her always put matters of state before personal affairs. Even her honeymoon is cut short ('I am the Queen – business cannot stop and want for anything. Even two days is a long time to be away'). It is a sense of duty that Albert comes to share: he sits up all night, despite his failing health, to rewrite Palmerston's provocative note to the Americans, knowing that otherwise there could be war. Like the newsreels, therefore, *Victoria the Great* projects an image of the monarchy centred upon the values of duty, service and sacrifice. Significantly, given the Anglicisation of the royal family's name – the German name of Saxe-Coburg Gotha was changed to Windsor during the Great War – *Victoria the Great* is at some pains to emphasise the Anglo-German connection. However, it is abundantly clear that it is Victoria who rules and Albert who is the consort. He initially chafes at this role as he had expected to play a more prominent part in politics, but is regarded as a 'foreign interloper' by some of the political classes.

There is contradictory evidence as to whether Wilcox set out immediately to capitalise on the success of *Victoria the Great* by making the film over again. His autobiography suggests that he did: 'After *Victoria the Great* it seemed that anything I did could be nothing but an anti-climax. But I found a way to overcome this. The Victoria story had been only lightly touched on. I would make a sequel in colour and call it *Sixty Glorious Years*.'[38] According to the trade press, however, his next planned vehicle for Neagle was to have been a film of *Lady Hamilton* with C. Aubrey Smith as Sir William Hamilton.[39] Smith, then based in Hollywood, came back to Britain in the spring of 1938 to make the film, but shortly before production was due to commence at Denham Wilcox announced that he was not going ahead with it because Gabriel Pascal was planning a film entitled *Nelson* and Wilcox was 'convinced it is a mistake for producers to compete with similar subjects'.[40] (In the event, Pascal's Nelson film did not materialise; Korda went on to make *Lady Hamilton* in Hollywood in 1940.) Wilcox then announced that Smith would play the Duke of Wellington in *Sixty Glorious Years* and that the film would start production within two weeks. Thus it would seem that the decision to proceed with the Victoria 'sequel' was more *ad hoc* than Wilcox later suggested.

As it happened the two-week estimate was premature even for Wilcox, renowned for his ability to work quickly. The studio interiors for *Sixty Glorious Years* were shot at Denham in four weeks during June 1938 – concurrent with the Wilcox-produced *A Royal Divorce* (dir. Jack Raymond) about the affair of Napoleon and Josephine – followed by another six weeks of location work filming exteriors at Buckingham Palace, Windsor, Balmoral and Osborne.[41] Wilcox averred that King George VI co-operated fully with the production and 'granted every request except the wearing of the Balmoral tartan, which was private and only for the use of the royal family'.[42] *Sixty Glorious Years* was one of the first British features made in three-strip Technicolor – the cinematographer, as on *Victoria the Great*, was Freddie Young, working under the nominal supervision of American 'color director' Natalie Kalmus – and must therefore be presumed to have been an even more expensive production than its predecessor, though there is no clear indication of its cost. Wilcox assembled much the same cast: Neagle, Walbrook, Walter Rilla (Prince Ernst), Charles Carson (Sir Robert Peel), Felix Aylmer (Palmerston), Derrick de Marney (Disraeli), Henry Hallatt (Joseph Chamberlain) and Gordon McLeod (John Brown) all reprised their roles, with Malcolm Keen replacing Arthur Young as Gladstone and C. Aubrey Smith reprising the role of Wellington, which he had played to popular acclaim in *The House of Rothschild* for Twentieth Century Films in 1934.

Wilcox later acknowledged that *Sixty Glorious Years* was influenced by the political circumstances of the time. He said that it was made 'at a time critical to our national history. Hitler was making threatening noises and in London appeasement was in the air. I sought out Sir Robert Vansittart at the Foreign Office, who for years had advocated a strong line towards Germany.'[43] The involvement of Vansittart is crucial to understanding the politics of *Sixty Glorious Years*. Vansittart was Permanent Under-Secretary of State at the Foreign Office from 1930 to 1938, when his anti-appeasement views resulted in him being moved to a grand-sounding but essentially honorary post as Chief Diplomatic

Adviser to His Majesty's Government. Vansittart had close contacts with a number of film producers, including Korda and Basil Dean, and believed in the value of film as a medium of propaganda. Michael Powell described Vansittart as a man who was 'afraid of nothing and nobody – a fascinating and complex personality, a charming man, a neglected prophet who, like Winston Churchill, had been ignored and driven into the wilderness by the little men'.[44] Vansittart accepted the offer to co-write the film ('Just the thing we need at the moment') with Malleson and acted as an intermediary between Wilcox and Buckingham Palace.

Sixty Glorious Years premièred at the Odeon, Leicester Square, on 14 October 1938 in the presence of Queen Mary. The reception was as enthusiastic as it had been for *Victoria the Great*, with a number of critics considering it at least the equal if not an improvement upon its predecessor. *The Times* proclaimed it 'a triumphant success' and felt that the episodic structure 'is certainly far more successful in this respect than the previous film or the play, and it does show some of the possibilities for first-class historical films in the future'.[45] Sydney Carroll in the *Sunday Times* declared that it 'merits exhibition as a historical and authentic document...in every school and educational institute in the United Kingdom'.[46] *Film Weekly* felt that it was 'better balanced than its predecessor' and predicted that 'it will have as much, if not more, appeal to British filmgoers'.[47] In America, however, where the film was again shown at the Radio City Music Hall, critics were less impressed. Nugent predicted that it would not repeat the success of its predecessor, as 'to put it bluntly, Victoria isn't news any more...It isn't that the film is dull, or dully presented...But not even the best story-teller should expect applause when he repeats himself.'[48] *Sixty Glorious Years* was again distributed by RKO, though it was not until 1940, when different circumstances prevailed, that it went on general release in the United States.

The dissenting voices were the same as for *Victoria the Great* and for much the same reasons. Basil Wright complained that both 'the director and the star seem to labour under the impression that they are producing something important, and this gives what is really an inoffensive picture a kind of humourless pomp. Incidentally the Indian Mutiny and the Boer War, not to mention other rather inglorious campaigns in Africa and Afghanistan, are omitted: the Crimea and the Sudan alone disturb this love-life of a queen.'[49] The *New Statesman* found it 'difficult to understand the praise which, even in the most respectable press, has been showered upon *Sixty Glorious Years*. Anybody who possesses even a small acquaintance with the history and personalities of the nineteenth century must recognise that the thing is a travesty of the truth.' 'It is significant, in these days,' the review went on, 'that a widespread and grossly inaccurate view of history should be disseminated by showing Gladstone simply as the man who left Gordon to his fate, [and] Disraeli as the man who bought the Suez Canal for England.'[50] *World Film News* was even more blunt in its criticism both of the film and of the critics who had praised it: '*Sixty Glorious Years* is a propaganda film. It has the unanimous support of all our newspapers; even the left wing papers, who ignore the political effect of films, endorse it.'[51]

What is abundantly clear from the reviews – both positive and negative – is that critics were very attuned to the parallels between the historical narrative and the present day. Even the trade press, generally the least likely to identify such readings, remarked upon this aspect of the film. *Today's Cinema*, for example, observed that 'in addition to recreating the past in fascinating detail it has a message for today that cannot be ignored'.[52] C.A. Lejeune was in no doubt that this was the input of Vansittart, 'whose name appears on the credit sheets, by his own request, without its official handle. Close readers of the political columns of the newspapers will remember that Sir Robert is adviser to the Cabinet, and that his name was frequently mentioned last month in reports of inner discussions on the crisis.' [53]

The crisis to which Lejeune referred was, of course, the Sudeten Crisis of September 1938 which had provided a major test of the policy of appeasement towards Germany. Hitler, emboldened by the success of his reoccupation of the Rhineland in March 1936 and by the *Anschluss* with Austria in March 1938 – both against the terms of the Treaty of Versailles – now demanded that the Sudetenland, an area of north-western Czechoslovakia, should be ceded to Germany. The Sudetenland never had been part of Germany – it had belonged to Austria–Hungary until 1919 – but it was home to some three million German-speaking people whom Hitler wanted to incorporate within his Greater German Reich. Neville Chamberlain, a firm believer in appeasement as a means of resolving international disputes and grievances, flew to Germany three times during September 1938 to attempt a negotiated settlement to the crisis that threatened to plunge Europe into war. The Munich Agreement (29 September) – signed by

Hitler, Chamberlain, Mussolini of Italy and the French Prime Minister Daladier – ceded the Sudetenland to Germany while guaranteeing the territorial integrity of the rest of Czechoslovakia. Chamberlain returned to Britain and proclaimed 'peace with honour'. There was widespread popular support for the Munich Agreement at the time and only a few Tory dissidents – Churchill, Anthony Eden, Duff Cooper – spoke out against it.

The newsreels again demonstrate how the National Government sought to influence public opinion over appeasement in the late 1930s. 'The World Today', for example, had included reference both to appeasement and to its critics that hardly could have been lost on contemporaries: 'Statesmen who may have drawn upon themselves criticism from time to time have nevertheless worked tirelessly for peace at home and abroad. As we look back we realise that their efforts have brought this country safely through the innumerable crises that have beset it in the past few years.' (Given the date of the newsreel – August 1936 – the crises that it alludes to would in all certainty have been Mussolini's invasion of Abyssinia in 1935, Hitler's reoccupation of the Rhineland and the outbreak of the Spanish Civil War.) British Movietone's report 'The Rhine' (12 March 1936) reflects the British government's response to the Rhineland crisis in its passive acceptance of Hitler's action as 'an accomplished fact' and expresses the hope that 'out of the difficult situation may be rebuilt a new peace system on a surer foundation' – thus promoting the pro-appeasement argument that the redress of Germany's grievances would secure peace. In the aftermath of Munich, British Movietone's 'The Crisis Passes' (3 October 1938) described Chamberlain unequivocally as 'the saviour of peace' and 'the man who averted another Armageddon'.

At the same time, however, the newsreels indicate that the government was far from blind to the threat of the dictators, as some of its critics, both at the time and since, alleged. The National Government had been re-elected in 1935 on a policy of 'no great armaments' but, in practice, appeasement went hand-in-hand with rearmament, for both Baldwin and then Chamberlain recognised that increasing international tension necessitated a credible defence policy. Newsreels such as British Movietone's 'Is there to be an armaments race?' (7 March 1935) and British Paramount's 'Where stands peace?' (16 November 1936) argue that Britain was being compelled to build up her armed forces because of the rearmament undertaken by other nations. The latter story made it clear where the threat lay, describing Germany, Austria and Italy as 'three powerful nations in arms who openly jeer at the League of Nations and the ideal of collective security'. Gaumont-British's 'Britain's re-armament plan' (18 February 1937) sought to address domestic criticism of the policy by explicitly linking rearmament to employment: 'This means no remission in taxation, but it gives security. Even more than that it will reduce the figure of unemployment – more ships mean more men at work... Security will bring prosperity.' Even in the wake of Munich it is clear that the newsreels were still seeking to mobilise public opinion in support of continued rearmament. Gaumont-British's 'Armistice 1918–1938' (14 November 1938) is a curiously contradictory item: it follows the service of remembrance at the Cenotaph in Whitehall and an accompanying assertion of the desire for peace ('They died to give us peace. They have given us peace for twenty years. It is the duty of all nations to preserve peace forever') with a call for rearmament and national preparedness ('There need never be another Cenotaph if Britain is strong enough to defy the threat of war... We in Britain have a hatred of war, but to fear war is to provoke it'). On this evidence, at least, the view that the British government had been entirely hoodwinked by Hitler at Munich simply does not stand up to scrutiny. It is evident that the necessity for rearmament was recognised long before Munich, and that Munich itself did not halt but, in fact, accelerated the mobilisation of British public opinion behind rearmament.

It would be misleading, therefore, to regard *Sixty Glorious Years* as an isolated case in its assertion of the need to protect Britain's national security. Where it is different from the newsreels, however, is that, in addition to its call for national preparedness, it is critical of the policy of appeasement adopted towards the aggressor nations. It is not strictly accurate to suggest that *Sixty Glorious Years* replicates the 'same arrangement of politics and narrative structures' as *Victoria the Great*.[54] In fact, there is a subtle but highly significant ideological realignment from the earlier film. Thus, while *Sixty Glorious Years* dramatises several of the same incidents as *Victoria the Great*, including the repeal of the Corn Laws and the *Trent* incident, they are afforded less narrative space this time around and greater prominence is given to foreign affairs, especially the Crimean War and the siege of Khartoum. This is where the hand of Vansittart becomes most apparent. For example, the characterisation of Lord Palmerston is subtly different from that of *Victoria the Great*. The Crimean War, passed over in an inter-title in the first film, becomes the occasion for the rehearsal of arguments between 'conciliation' (supported by Victoria and Albert) and belligerence (adopted by Palmerston). Described in the first film as 'dictatorial', Palmerston now offers reasoned argument for his assertive foreign policy:

> *Lord Palmerston:* Now the British lion's got to do a little roaring.
> *Lord John Russell:* That's a dangerous spirit.
> *Palmerston:* There's one thing more dangerous still, and that's not to stand up when you're in danger.
> *Russell:* The Queen always says you exaggerate, Palmerston, and she's right. With a little concession -
> *Palmerston:* Concession! My dear Russell, you're like those two young innocents at Windsor. You think that one can reach safety by feeding cutlets to a tiger, or beans to a bear.
> *Russell:* You're too picturesque. Only facts count. And the fact is the Czar has sent the Queen this letter which bears every mark of a sincere desire to preserve the peace of Europe.
> *Palmerston:* So long as this country is anything or has anything we shall go on receiving letters from 'Yours Truly' or 'Yours Sincerely'. Beware of 'Yours Very Sincerely', Russell.

It is irresistible to see Palmerston here as speaking for Vansittart and against the 'innocents' of the Foreign Office, who clung to the belief that Hitler's promises were sincere and that it was possible to reach a settlement of the outstanding grievances. *Sixty Glorious Years* thus argues the case against appeasement as explicitly as *The Iron Duke*, only four years earlier, had argued in its favour.

The views of Palmerston/Vansittart prevail to the extent that later in the film it is the Queen herself who advocates firm action in a politically charged exchange with Gladstone over his tardiness in sending a relief force to Gordon at Khartoum in 1884:

> *Queen Victoria:* Mr Gladstone, I cannot conceal from you my disquiet at the delay in your measures for the relief of General Gordon.
> *Gladstone:* Your Majesty, everything possible is being done.
> *Queen Victoria:* No, Mr Gladstone, everything the government

thinks possible. General Gordon has been besieged in Khartoum since March. Only in August has it been decided to relieve him, and only now, in November, has the relief force under Sir Garnet Wolsey started out. These tardy races against time are neither to my taste nor to our credit.

Gladstone: Believe me, ma'am, I understand your anxiety.

Queen Victoria: Oh, it is more than anxiety, it is anguish, Mr Gladstone. This great Christian soldier means something to the world as well as to us. If we fail him, posterity will not forget.

Gladstone: Your Majesty may rest assured -

Queen Victoria: I cannot rest, however much I am assured. I am haunted by the dread that we may too late. That is the danger to which this country so often exposes itself. One day it may be our undoing.

It is important to remember that the script was written several months before Munich, though with the film released only weeks after

5. *Sixty Glorious Years*: The Queen is not amused when her Prime Minister Gladstone (Malcolm Keen) hesitates to relieve General Gordon at Khartoum.

Chamberlain's proclamation of 'peace with honour', its politics became even more topical. Khartoum/Munich: it is an irresistible parallel. Public opinion had turned against Gladstone, who was accused of abandoning Gordon to his fate; critics of Munich, both at the time and since, held that Britain had betrayed Czechoslovakia, leaving the country weakened and indirectly encouraging Hitler's territorial ambitions in that it convinced him that Britain would do anything to avoid war. When Germany marched into the rump of Czechoslovakia in March 1939, the folly of Munich was seemingly exposed and the territorial guarantee made to Czechoslovakia looked like an empty promise. Chamberlain now changed his policy and pledged to guarantee Poland's integrity; and, while it seems that personally he hoped for a peaceful settlement to resolve the Polish Crisis in September 1939, Britain began to prepare in earnest for the war that she had tried for so long to avoid.[55]

The contemporary parallels were even more obvious when the film was belatedly released in America in 1940. As Herb Sterne recognised:

> Time and events have conspired to make certain facets of more contemporary interest than they were in 1937 [sic]. We are reminded that though Britain attempted to appease Russia, finally sending her unprepared armies into the field miserably fed, poorly clothed, and lacking in proper fighting equipment, she eventually won the Crimean War. Too, there is an account of the endless red tape and foolishly incompetent handling of the Khartoum incident that ended in the needless death of Gordon. Although the British procrastinated and retribution came late, again the soldiers of Empire conquered. In this particular instance, may history repeat itself![56]

This time, however, the parallels were an accident of timing: not even Vansittart could have predicted the severity of the military setbacks that affected Britain's war effort in 1940.

There is more to *Sixty Glorious Years*, however, than just its 'turgid propagandism'.[57] Visually and aesthetically it is a superior film to *Victoria*, the Technicolor cinematography – more subdued than in the bright primary colour of Korda's *The Drum* and *The Four Feathers* – allowing subtle touches, such as Disraeli's bowl of yellow primroses, as well as spectacular vignettes, such as the Charge of the Light

Brigade and the siege of Khartoum, both glimpsed in short montage sequences that recall the staging of the Battle of Waterloo in *The Iron Duke*. It is also more confident in its use of cultural motifs, including quotations from Tennyson ('The Gallant Six Hundred') and Kipling ('Lest we forget') to link the unwieldy and episodic narrative together, while the death of Gordon is modelled on G.W. Joy's famous painting – a device that Basil Dearden would borrow four decades later in *Khartoum* (1966). This time it is Albert rather than Victoria who reads of the plight of the poor through Dickens (*Sketches by Boz*). Less space is given to domestic unrest and more attention is afforded to the cultural and scientific achievements of Victoria's reign, including the building of Crystal Palace for the Great Exhibition of 1851, which is planned by Albert 'to promote a better understanding between all the peoples'. Victoria is credited not only with the inscription of the medal which bears her name ('For Valour') but also with supporting the efforts of Florence Nightingale to improve care for the wounded following her distressing visit to a military hospital. While the focus of the narrative remains resolutely on the domestic sphere, it broadens the canvas of its predecessor so that it is more successful as a portrait of the age – albeit, as critics realised, one that fitted the cultural and ideological determinants of British cinema of the 1930s.

The popular success of *Sixty Glorious Years* further enhanced Wilcox's prestige and his standing with the American studios. At the end of 1938 he annouced a new production deal with RKO which 'provides for three to four films a year, at an average cost of £150,000, with substantial financial backing from the American company'.[58] It was suggested that both Fred Astaire and Ginger Rogers would star, separately, in Imperator/RKO films. Wilcox had intended the next Neagle vehicle to be a biopic of music-hall legend Marie Lloyd – a choice of subject that again demonstrates his safety-first policy of adhering to a successful formula, since Neagle had already played an actress (Peg Woffington) in *Peg of Old Drury* – though the film fell through when he was unable to persuade Cary Grant to play Lloyd's husband Alec Hurley.[59] Wilcox's first film under the new deal with RKO was *Nurse Edith Cavell*, made in Hollywood and based on the play *Dawn* that Wilcox had already filmed in 1928. The politics of the film are interesting in so far as *Nurse Edith Cavell* is essentially a pacifist story about an English nurse shot by the Germans as a spy during the First World War. 'With war on the horizon we intended this to be an *anti-war* film', Neagle claimed in her autobiography.[60] It is suggestive that the politics of Wilcox's films may not necessarily have been due to Wilcox, but rather arose from the particular sources he used and the writers he employed. Certainly there are significant differences between *Nurse Edith Cavell* and *Sixty Glorious Years* that make it difficult to plot a linear trajectory from one film to the next.

It is instructive to compare Wilcox's later career with Korda's in so far as it was the conservative Wilcox who better managed to negotiate changes in popular taste than the more daring Korda. He elected to remain in Hollywood for the duration of the war, following the instruction of British ambassador Lord Lothian 'to keep the English idiom and way of life before American audiences'.[61] He directed Neagle in three musicals in 1940-41 (*Irene, No No Nanette, Sunny*) and was instrumental in the production of *Forever and A Day* (1943), an episodic pro-British propaganda effort using most of the 'Hollywood British' film colony and with the profits distributed to various war charities. *Forever and A Day* is a pageant, similar in style to the Victoria films, which charts the course of British history between 1804 and 1940 through the story of a house and the two families that live in it. Each episode was made by a different director (René Clair, Edmund Goulding, Cedric Hardwicke, Frank Lloyd, Victor Saville, Robert Stevenson and Wilcox himself), and the writers included C.S. Forester, James Hilton and R.C. Sherriff among many others.[62] Wilcox also made two films in Britain for RKO using the company's 'frozen funds' (during the war the Treasury limited the amount of dollar remittances American companies could withdraw from the distribution of their films in Britain; these monies could, however, be invested in productions in British studios). These two films were a biopic of pioneer aviatrix Amy Johnson (*They Flew Alone*, 1941) and a topical spy drama (*Yellow Canary*, 1943), both, of course, starring Anna Neagle.

Returning to Britain permanently at the end of the war, the now-married Wilcox and Neagle achieved their biggest popular success since the Victoria films with the frothy romantic drama *I Live in Grosvenor Square*, (1945) that was one of the biggest box-office hits of the year. *I Live in Grosvenor Square*, a cross-class and trans-national love story between an English aristocrat (Neagle) and a working-class American serving in the US forces (played by Dean Jagger), was one of several of British films of the mid-1940s addressing the question of

Anglo-American relations – others included *A Canterbury Tale* (dir. Michael Powell, 1944), *The Way to the Stars* (dir. Anthony Asquith, 1945) and *A Matter of Life and Death* (dir. Michael Powell, 1946). It was to be the first in a cycle of 'London films' – so-called because their titles all referred to famous London locations – in which Neagle starred with Michael Wilding: *Piccadilly Incident* (1946), *The Courtneys of Curzon Street* (1947), *Spring in Park Lane* (1948) and *Maytime in Mayfair* (1949).

The 'London' films were not the sort of fare that critics liked, being found wanting in the qualities of documentary-style realism and emotional restraint that had become the twin yardsticks of critically respectable cinema by the mid-1940s, but their blend of romance and melodrama ensured their popular success at a time when British audiences did not wish to be reminded of the climate of austerity. Neagle called them 'pleasant films about pleasant people'.[63] *The Courtneys of Curzon Street* was the leading film at the British box office in 1947, earning £390,000 against a cost of £280,000, and *Spring in Park Lane* was the biggest attraction of 1948, costing £220,000 and returning £405,000.[64] The 'London' cycle can be seen as a middle-class riposte to the Gainsborough melodramas with their sensational stories and transgressive heroines. In contrast, there is nothing very transgressive about the 'London' films which, while ostensibly concerned with mobility across the class structure, ultimately work to endorse middle-class values. The main contrast is that between Neagle and her principal rival as Britain's leading female star of the time, Margaret Lockwood. While the Gainsborough melodramas completely transformed Lockwood's image from the respectable girl-next-door of her 1930s films to a passionate, sexually charged adventuress, Neagle's had gone in entirely the opposite direction, from the coquettish flirt of *Nell Gwyn* to the 'regal Neagle' whose sexuality was held in check by bourgeois respectability. To a large extent her image reflected Wilcox's romantic infatuation with his own wife. In his autobiography he wrote unashamedly and unselfconsciously that 'Anna, with her fair loveliness, blue eyes and beautiful skin, plus her innate integrity as an actress, sublimated, both as a woman and artist, my spiritual and physical needs and ideals'.[65]

There was yet one more transformation in Neagle's screen persona to come: national heroine. Wilcox cast her as Special Operations Executive (SOE) agent Odette Sansom in *Odette* (1950), one of the leading box-office attractions of the year, and a film that is credited with reviving the popularity of the war film in the 1950s after a lean period in the immediate post-war years. Again, Wilcox can be seen as an astute judge of popular taste: the true stories of SOE agents such as Odette and Violette Szabo – later played by Virginia McKenna in *Carve Her Name With Pride* (dir. Lewis Gilbert, 1958) – had been revealed only after the war and he was the first to realise their commercial potential. *Odette* harks back to wartime feature films in its use of documentary-style techniques to impart a sense of authenticity – including an appearance by Odette's real SOE superior – and contains a harrowing sequence of Odette's capture and torture by the Germans. It is one of Neagle's best and most intense performances as she charts Odette's progress from middle-class housewife to secret agent to concentration camp victim/survivor. *Odette* was followed by *The Lady With A Lamp* (1951), a biopic of Florence Nightingale which reunited Neagle with her erstwhile co-star Michael Wilding. It was another popular success, chiefly notable for its reverential treatment of its subject.

Wilcox's business instincts deserted him in the 1950s: he lost money investing in the British Lion Film Corporation and turned down an opportunity to invest in commercial television. He admitted candidly in his autobiography that he paid the price for becoming 'a little too cock-sure of being able to turn out hit after hit'.[66] His later films were largely undistinguished; bankruptcy ended his career in the 1960s. Neagle, for her part, returned to her first persona as a song-and-dance star of the stage and enjoyed great success in *Charlie Girl*, for which she played 2,062 performances between 1965 and 1971.[67] *Sixty Glorious Years*, in the meantime, was successfully reissued in the mid-1970s, when one critic claimed it as 'an outstanding example of film craftsmanship which has hardly dated at all in any major particular'.[68] However, and in conclusion, it would probably be fair to say that the true significance of the Victoria films resides less in their qualities as films than in their status as historical documents – documents not only of the life and times of Queen Victoria but also of the social and political circumstances of the late 1930s.

4

Class and Nation:
This England (1941)

IN the short feature film *The Volunteer* (1943), a recruiting film made for the Admiralty by Michael Powell and Emeric Pressburger, Lieutenant-Commander Ralph Richardson, RNVR, shows the audience around Denham Studios. 'We were making a propaganda film', he says. 'At the outbreak of war, actors dived into historical costumes and declaimed powerful speeches about the wooden walls of England.' It was during the Second World War that the historical film was put to its most obviously propagandistic use. *This England*, an early-war example of the genre, is precisely the sort of film that Richardson (or Pressburger) may have had in mind. It has been largely forgotten in histories of British cinema; when it is mentioned it is usually only to be dismissed as a crude and simplistic propaganda effort.[1] *This England* was not well regarded even at the time. Leslie Halliwell, who was taken to see it in Bolton by his school's history master, thought it 'an abysmal propaganda film' and recalled that 'the history master roared with derisive laughter at the inept and extremely boring goings-on'.[2] *This England* is certainly no forgotten master-piece. However, it is significant in so far as it represents the first attempt during the war to mobilise the past in order to address social divisions and to promote the need for national unity. It was also the first example of what Charles Barr has since described as 'a wartime series, almost a genre in itself, of "heritage" films' – a cycle that culminated in Laurence Olivier's production of *Henry V*.[3]

The Second World War is regarded by many as the 'golden age' of

British cinema. Just as the nation experienced its 'finest hour', so did the film industry. Cinema attendances rose during the war, reaching a peak of 30 million a week in 1945 (in 1939, for comparison, the average weekly attendance had been 19 million).[4] The film industry, although affected by wartime shortages, the rationing of film stock and the recruitment of many of its personnel into the services, responded to the changed circumstances by producing films serving the national need for both entertainment and propaganda. Critics of the time saw evidence of an overall improvement in the quality of British film production even as its quantity declined. 'Everyone recognises now that there has been an extraordinary renaissance in British feature-film production since about 1940', Roger Manvell wrote in 1946. He felt that films reflected 'the new spirit of Britain challenged at last to undertake a war which she had been uncomfortably avoiding for too long'. British films of the war exhibited 'an understanding of emotional values and a faithfulness to the environment in which the story was set', while the realism they exhibited placed Britain 'in the forefront of progressive cinema today'.[5] Among the classic films of the war were *In Which We Serve*, *The Foreman Went to France*, *The First of the Few*, *Thunder Rock*, *The Life and Death of Colonel Blimp*, *San Demetrio, London*, *The Gentle Sex*, *Millions Like Us*, *This Happy Breed*, *The Way Ahead* and *The Way to the Stars*. British film-making, as represented by films such as these, Manvell averred, 'is bound to the national life of Britain, to our people, our cities and our rich and varied countryside'.[6]

Most of the canonical films of the war were made between 1942 and 1945; earlier attempts at projecting the nation at war were regarded as too crude and melodramatic to be effective propaganda. The first propaganda feature of the war, Korda's *The Lion Has Wings* (1939), was dismissed by Graham Greene on the grounds that as 'a statement of war aims, one feels, this leaves the world beyond Roedean still expectant'.[7] The most successful British film of 1940, according to the trade press, was the naval drama *Convoy* (dir. Penrose Tennyson), though the journal *Documentary News Letter* – successor to *Cinema Quarterly* and *World Film News* as an organ for the progressive voices in the film industry – disliked it because it gave 'the impression that the main business of the Navy was resolving triangles involving officers' wives'.[8] *Ships With Wings* (dir. Sergei Nolbandov, 1941) was similarly written off because 'the propaganda line of the film would be more appropriate to a Ruritanian campaign than the

Second World War'.[9] *This England* also belongs to the early period of the war when British films had not yet attained the level of realism that Manvell, and others, so admired. It is perhaps significant that John Clements, the dashing officer hero of both *Convoy* and *Ships With Wings*, was also one of the stars of *This England*.

This England was produced by British National, an independent production company formed in 1934 by J. Arthur Rank, the Methodist flour millionaire, and Lady Yule, widow of the Anglo-Indian jute magnate Sir David Yule, with the intent of making religious films for the Sunday school movement in which Rank was a prominent figure. British National's first feature was *The Turn of the Tide* (dir. Norman Walker, 1935), based on a novel by Leo Walmsley about two families in a North Yorkshire fishing village. Rank sold his interest in the company to Lady Yule in 1937 as he concentrated on building his film empire. British National's production was undistinguished throughout the late 1930s, comprising low-budget thrillers and comedies, but the company's acquisition of its own studio signalled its intent 'to make films of greater importance'.[10] Early in the war it produced three major films that each brought a measure of prestige to the company: *Gaslight* (dir. Thorold Dickinson, 1940), a highly atmospheric costume thriller adapted from a play by Patrick Hamilton; the spy thriller *Contraband* (dir. Michael Powell, 1940); and *Love on the Dole* (dir. John Baxter, 1941), the critically acclaimed adaptation of Walter Greenwood's novel that had been blocked by the BBFC during the 1930s but which now fitted the wartime mood of optimism for a better future. Head of Production at British National was John Corfield, whom Powell described as 'one of those men who are scared to death by every decision they make, but can't resist making them'.[11] Corfield, like other producers during the war, believed in a type of national film that reflected the mood of the British people:

A virile and independent film industry is an essential adjunct of any democracy in time of war. Films serve the dual purpose of providing escape for the people from the stress and boredom of war and carrying a message – to every country in which they are shown. Further, there is inherent in the war-time psychology of any people an intense nationalism, which can only be satisfied, so far as pictures satisfy it, by nationally conceived pictures, made by their own people.[12]

Corfield's idea of a 'nationally conceived' film, therefore, was different from Korda's in so far as he believed it must be one made by home-grown talent. British National, indeed, was less inclined to employ émigrés than other independent producers such as London Films, Two Cities or even Ealing Studios, which in 1940 had lured the Brazilian film-maker Alberto Cavalcanti away from the General Post Office (GPO) Film Unit.

This England was announced as part of the British National production schedule in the summer of 1940. This was a time of acute crisis for the country, which now stood alone against Germany following the fall of France and faced the threat of imminent invasion. The prevailing mood of the time was one of determination and defiance, and this is the mood that pervades *This England*. Corfield suggested that he was prompted to turn to a historical subject in response to the rapidly changing war situation:

> The swift march of events these days is such that the average film producer has difficulty in keeping abreast of current happenings. For instance, in *Contraband* our neutral Danish skipper in the film became right out of date. Similarly, we had preparations ready to start on a big Anglo-French subject. Finally, I suggested to our script writers that as the only thing seeming to survive all storms and stresses was the countryside of England, here was something lasting.[13]

There is evidence to suggest that, originally at least, *This England* was intended as a rather more ambitious film than it ultimately became. It was to have been filmed on real locations rather than in the studio – as, indeed, was *The Turn of the Tide* – and it would be 'probably in Technicolor'. 'It will be filmed largely out of doors and will be the most ambitious subject the company has undertaken so far', the press announcement declared. 'It will be a spectacular cavalcade of the English countryside, from the time of the Roman Invasion right up till 1940, when, once more, invasion looms up as a possibility.' It is only speculation whether or not this was a deliberate reference to *Cavalcade*, though with its episodic narrative focusing on an English family *This England* clearly bore affinities with the 1933 Noël Coward saga. Production economies, however, soon took their toll. British National had neither the budget nor the facilities that had been available to the Fox Film Corporation. There was no more talk of Technicolor, and by the time the film was on the studio floor the Romans had disappeared from the narrative. There is no clear indication of the film's cost, though British National's chairman George Parish said that between July 1939 and January 1941 the company made 12 feature films at a total cost of £225,000.[14]

This England was shot, during the Blitz in the autumn of 1940, at British National Studios, with some exterior locations around Welwyn. It was an original screenplay by A.R. Rawlinson and Bridget Boland, who had both worked on *Gaslight*, with dialogue by Emlyn Williams, the Welsh actor and playwright who also appeared in the film in 'his capacity as a licensed representative of the lower classes'.[15] Its director, David Macdonald, was a former Malaya rubber planter who had entered the film industry in Hollywood as an assistant to Cecil B. DeMille before returning to Britain where he directed a number of low-budget programmers for British National. Earlier in 1940 he had been recruited by the GPO Film Unit to direct the narrative-documentary *Men of the Lightship* and following *This England* he would join the Army Film Unit, where he commanded the No. 1 Film and Photographic Section and worked with Roy Boulting on the production of the actuality documentaries *Desert Victory* (1943) and *Burma Victory* (1945). After the war Macdonald would direct several historical biopics, including *Christopher Columbus* and *The Bad Lord Byron* (both 1949), and the costume swashbuckler *The Moonraker* (1957).

This England is an episodic narrative that focuses on five moments in English history. Each is a moment of crisis and adversity; on each occasion crisis is averted and adversity is overcome through a show of national unity and a reaffirmation of traditional social values. A voice-over narration explains that the story of one rural community is intended to represent the entire nation: 'This England, among whose hills and valleys since the beginning of time have stood old farms and villages. The story of Rookeby's farm and the village of Clevely is the story of them all.' The film begins in 1940 as an American journalist, Ann (Constance Cummings), visiting Clevely, is impressed by the fortitude of the villagers during an air raid: 'I felt this morning that to you people, all this is nothing new at all. You've been doing it for centuries.' She is befriended by farmer John Rookeby (John Clements), also an officer in the Home Guard, and air-raid warden

6. 'This earth, this realm, this England': labourer Appleyard
(Emlyn Williams, *left*), American visitor Ann (Constance
Cummings) and farmer Rookeby (John Clements) find common
cause in the modern segment of *This England*.

Appleyard (Emlyn Williams), a labourer on Rookeby's farm. They
proceed to tell her the story of the village through the ages. The
presence of Cummings, an American actress based in Britain since the
mid-1930s following her marriage to theatre producer Benn W. Levy
– she also appeared in Ealing's *The Foreman Went to France* (1942) –
places *This England* within a lineage of wartime films, intended to
explain Britain and the British people to American audiences, which
also includes Powell and Pressburger's *49th Parallel* (1941) and *A
Canterbury Tale* (1944). A series of flashbacks follows, with
continuity maintained through the device of using the same actors in
each episode. While there is continuity in cast and narrative, however,
each episode is to some extent stylistically different. These differences
can be related to other filmic representations of the past drawn from
both British and Hollywood cinema.

   In the first episode, set in 1086, 20 years after the Norman
Conquest, the village is under the heel of an oppressive Norman baron

who detests the 'British scum'. The baron's young son Hugo, however, is befriended by Rookeby and other villagers. When Hugo asks 'Do you hate my father?', Martin the blacksmith replies: 'I reckon if he leaves us fairly alone we shall do our work and bear him no grudge.' But the baron refuses to leave the serfs alone, failing to heed his churchman's warning that 'the English must not be roused'. He denies the serfs the right to farm their own land and orders instead that they should work as forced labourers to build a new approach road to the castle. The theme of the cruel Normans as oppressors of the peaceable Saxons has been popularised in myth; its most enduring filmic representation had been in Hollywood's *The Adventures of Robin Hood* (dir. Michael Curtiz, 1938). Interestingly, however, *This England* never once refers to the Saxons, preferring to call them 'English' or (anachronistically) 'British' (perhaps 'Saxon' sounded too Germanic in 1940). When Norman soldiers confiscate their tools, Rookeby leads a revolt of the serfs, frees the imprisoned Appleyard and kills the baron. The churchman commends Hugo to the villagers as their new master – 'a child who already has the spirit of tolerance… a Norman birthed in your ways and understanding'.

The second episode, set in 1588 during the approach of the Spanish Armada, seems to anticipate the popular Gainsborough melodramas that were to be the box-office sensation of the mid-1940s. It is both the most sensational episode in terms of narrative and also visually the most expressive. Rookeby is now a tenant farmer, Appleyard one of his labourers. A gypsy girl is shipwrecked and is offered shelter by Rookeby, who finds himself attracted to her, though Appleyard dislikes her, calling her a 'Spanish witch' and distrusting her because she reads books. Rookeby responds to the Queen's call for timber for ships by felling several oaks, but is reprimanded for doing so by Lord Clevely's steward, who cites 'such wearisome encumberances as bylaws and bylaws'. Rookeby's response is to the point: 'To hell with the bylaws! We're in the middle of a war!' The steward informs Rookeby that Lord Clevely, an absentee landlord, has decided to enclose the common ground around the village, leaving Rookeby with the unfarmable Hangman's Hill. At this point Rookeby decides to leave for a life on the 'open road' with the gypsy girl. Cummings's role in this episode can be seen as a prototype of the sort of parts played by Margaret Lockwood in *The Man in Grey* (1943) and *The Wicked Lady* (1945), the seductive temptress who comes between the man and his duty, though the gypsy girl (who is never named) is less calculating than the characteristic Lockwood heroine and her downfall occurs not through the excesses of her own behaviour but rather because of the prejudices of others. It is Appleyard who on this occasion takes matters into his own hands, first killing the steward to retrieve the enclosure order, then rousing the villagers to hate the girl by suggesting she has lit a bonfire to signal the Spanish Armada. Pursued by an angry mob, the girl jumps to her death from a clifftop; news arrives that the Armada has been defeated. 'We have our land again', says a relieved Appleyard.

The third episode, set in 1804 during the Napoleonic Wars, has fewer obvious generic reference points, though its theme of agrarian depression and consequent unrest would later be explored in *Captain Boycott* (dir. Frank Launder, 1947). It begins with Rookeby as an idle gentleman of leisure, while Appleyard is an itinerant beggar. Rookeby blames the decline of farming on mechanisation: 'No labour to be had and no money bags to pay wages with ... the machines turn out as much in a week as I can pay my lads in a month.' The present Lord Clevely, now a close friend of Rookeby's, reveals that he faces bankruptcy because of his gambling debts, and is forced to sell his estate to 'an ironmonger fellow – one of these new rich upstarts made me an offer'. Rookeby wins the right to keep his farm in a game of cards, but Clevely hangs himself before the agreement is confirmed. Rookeby meets new landlord Josiah Much and his daughter, whom he marries. The farm is abandoned as Rookeby moves into the big house with his family. At the christening party for his son, however, Rookeby's conscience is touched when he hears of the death from malnutrition of Ben the ploughman's child and he is roused to action by an impassioned speech from Appleyard. Rookeby resolves to return to farming, joined by his wife and by Appleyard.

The final episode occurs on Armistice night in 1918. It is filmed in an austere, bleak style on just two sets – the interior and exterior of the village pub – and resembles *Love on the Dole* with its small, claustrophobic settings. Rookeby (officer) and Appleyard (private) have both served in the Great War; Rookeby has won the Victoria Cross but has lost his eyesight. In the village pub, they leave the revelry, along with a young mother – Rookeby's distant cousin – whose child has been taken from her following the death of the child's father at Vimy Ridge. Rookeby says that he 'can smell the fields'.

'They was always worth fighting for', Appleyard remarks. 'Yes, every
time', agrees Rookeby. 'And will be again.' The three figures walk off
together into the foggy night as Rookeby begins to recite 'that fine bit
of Shakespeare'. A dissolve allows the Rookeby of 1940 to complete
the verse.[16]

This England was promoted as a 'national saga that will be the
worthy successor of those previous epics of the screen which have
shown England in all its glory'.[17] Released in May 1941, however, it
failed to set the box office alight and left critics largely unimpressed.
C.A. Lejeune felt that it 'is badly handicapped by its format'; while
accepting that the 'idea is sound enough and timely, too – the long,
strong pull on its sons of a plot of English soil', she disliked it because
it 'has been turned into one of those dreary reincarnation affairs'.[18] The
Monthly Film Bulletin complained that 'it has been conceived
theatrically and without a proper understanding of the limitations and
possibilities of the film medium. Not even its production qualities are
all that could be desired.'[19] The obvious propaganda element put off
the *New Statesman*: '*This England* isn't impressive; in fact, it is the
sort of patriotic film we do worst.'[20]

American critics were no more impressed than their British
counterparts. The *Motion Picture Herald* felt that it fell short of its
intentions: 'It is one of those instances...where the canvas is more
ambitious than the palette; probably producers and director can be
pardoned for failing adequately to compress the story or the spirit of
the British nation into 8,000 feet of celluloid.' 'There is little subtle or
imaginative about the treatment and the development seems to lack
melodramatic climaxes', the trade paper remarked, though added a
caveat that 'the spirit of the stuff is ardent and here and there a flash of
patriotic hyperbole will stir the natives'.[21] It was not released in
America until November 1941, when it was shown at the World
Theatre in New York, a cinema previously specialising in French films
that had now adopted a 'British only' policy. 'As a film to emphasize
a new policy, as well as a new point of view *This England* is peculiarly
effective – as effective as waving the Union Jack', wrote Bosley
Crowther. 'But as a sample of motion picture competence it leaves a
great deal to be desired, for the story is manufactured fable with no
dramatic coherence or suspense, the performances are forced and
uneven and the production is generally poor'. Crowther, clearly, was
alienated by the propaganda content of the film, concluding that 'the

simple and obvious fact is that *This England* was struck off in an emotional whirl; the fervor of patriotism blazes brightly throughout. And although the purpose is noble and the idea is provocative, the whole thing smacks too blatantly of bombast and pageantry.'[22]

This England failed to impress, therefore, either as propaganda or as entertainment. It is easy to deride the film for its poor production values and for its occasionally risible dialogue, accents and wigs. Emlyn Williams told his wife that in their serf costumes the cast ended up 'looking like a series of Lesbian hockey mistresses who've lost their sticks'.[23] Yet, while accepting its many flaws, *This England* is not without interest. It was the first fully fledged attempt to use a historical narrative for film propaganda during the war and is therefore worthy of attention in its own right, as well as for comparisons with later examples of the genre. It is also interesting for the precise use to which history is put, for, whatever its shortcomings as an exercise in film-making, *This England* employs the past in a very different way than the inspirational stories of leaders and national heroes exemplified by films that followed, such as *The Prime Minister*, *The Young Mr Pitt* and *Henry V*. Moreover, the film has given rise to vastly different readings among the few film historians to have considered it. Thus, on the one hand, Harper laments 'the extreme cultural conservatism of the film', whereas, on the other hand, Richards detects in it 'a distinctly radical element which mirrors the shift to the left in the national mood and the desire for a juster, fairer and more humane post-war society'.[24] Which, if either, of these interpretations is most correct?

The social politics of *This England*, certainly, are nothing if not conservative. There is none of the egalitarianism or suggestion of social levelling that characterises other wartime films such as *Fires Were Started* or *Millions Like Us*. Instead, *This England* depicts English society as hierarchical and paternalistic. It is posited on a commonality of interest between landowners and labourers: the former have a social responsibility towards the latter, while the labourers offer their loyalty to their employers. There are two occasions in the film (the Armada and Napoleonic episodes) when Rookeby fails to discharge his social responsibilities towards the labourers; he is reminded of his duty by Appleyard, who, nevertheless, remains properly deferential towards his employer and knows his place in the social hierarchy. When external forces threaten to upset the balance they are either removed entirely (the gypsy girl) or assimilated into the social order (Josiah Much and his daughter, whom Rookeby marries). The film's view of society is static: there is no suggestion of social change, while industrialisation is deplored because it saps the countryside of vitality. In a number of respects, indeed, *This England* is reminiscent of the 'one nation' Toryism of the nineteenth century. Its suggestion of a bond between landowners and labourers recalls the 'Young England' movement of the 1840s that had advocated a form of benevolent feudalism to preserve the social structure and counter the rise of the middle and professional classes. This was the mood expressed in the novels of the young Benjamin Disraeli, particularly *Coningsby* and *Sybil*. The Rookeby of 1804 follows the example of Harry Coningsby, who had married Edith Millbank, a daughter of the 'millocracy'.

This England also belongs to a conservative tradition of defining the essence of national identity in terms of the rural and the pastoral. The 'rural myth' can be seen as a cultural response to the rapid industrialisation and urbanisation of the nineteenth century; its proponents saw traditional social values disappearing under the onslaught of the Industrial Revolution and looked back nostalgically to a pre-industrial Arcadian golden age. The rural myth was probably at its height between the 1880s and the 1940s, with the two world wars, especially, throwing into sharp relief the essence of 'what we are fighting for'. The celebration of the countryside as the source of national strength found its most famous expression in the poetry of Rupert Brooke ('There'll always be an England while there's a country lane/As long as there's a cottage small beside a field of grain'), though the image of England as a rural paradise was also widely disseminated through novels, music, painting and film. Its persistence during the Second World War is evident at different levels of cultural production, both official and unofficial: the British Council sponsored films on subjects such as Kew Gardens, English inns and rural waterways; propaganda posters by artists such as Frank Newbould were steeped in imagery of rolling fields and green hills; and *Picture Post* ran photo features on subjects such as 'Sunday Afternoon in England' (a sleepy village street full of sheep) and published Cecil Day Lewis's tribute to 'The English Village'.[25] This was the image that, time and again, was offered up as what the war was being fought to preserve. To take just one example, rural essayist Anthony Armstrong, author of books such as *Cottage into House* and *We Like the Country*, concluded his 1941 book *Village at War* thus: 'There are many worse ways of dying, than in defence of the village street, the village church, the village pub, the cottages, houses, gardens, farms and fields that go to make up England. As we used to think, and one of us once said on a summer evening of our first patrols on the Downs, looking over the Weald below, "Worth fighting for, isn't it?"'[26]

The social historian Angus Calder later expressed surprise that 'during the war, many writers who should have known better implied that the soldiers and airmen were dying to preserve an essentially rural Britain'.[27] The rural myth had long ceased to have any bearing on reality by the Second World War, when four-fifths of British people lived in towns and only six per cent of the population were employed in agriculture. Yet this point had already been rejected by George Orwell who, in a review of *This England*, observed that 'as in nearly all patriotic films and literature, the implication all along is that England is an agricultural country and that its inhabitants, millions of whom would not know the difference between a turnip and a broccoli if they saw them growing in a field, derive their patriotism from a passionate love of the English soil. Are such films good for morale in wartime? They may be.'[28] It is not difficult to understand the appeal of the rural myth at a time when British towns and cities were being bombed by the *Luftwaffe*. Buildings could be destroyed but the countryside could not; thus it became a fitting motif to symbolise the indestructability of the nation. It is precisely this idea of the countryside as the indestructable backbone of England that is expressed in *This England*. The film is prefaced with a poem before the titles:

> The earth of England is an old, old earth,
> Her autumn mists, her brambleberry flame,
> Her tangled rain soaked grass, were still the same –
> Time out of mind before the Romans came –
> Though from the skies men hurl their slaughter down,
> Still there will be the bracken turning brown.

These lines express the idea that the earth remains the same regardless of the tide of events, that as long as the earth survives there will indeed always be an England. It is an idea that is repeatedly driven home throughout the film, most especially by Appleyard. In the Armada episode, for example, when the gypsy girl is tempting Rookeby to leave, Appleyard tries to impress upon her his and Rookeby's historic ties to the land:

> *Appleyard:* Under that oak tree John Rookeby's father met King Henry VIII while he was out hunting and His Majesty passed the time of day. At a gate beside that hedgerow my grandfather William Appleyard died of a stroke. The field beyond that hedgerow was first turned under the plough of my great great grandfather. Look, listen. Can you see them? Their arms waving? Can you hear what these ghosts are saying? Is not this worth fighting for?

Here again the film posits a static view of the past, emphasising continuity in land ownership and social relationships. The film suggests, forcefully, that it is Rookeby's and Appleyard's destiny to remain tied to the land through the generations.

In its representation of a hierarchical society and its employment of pastoral imagery, therefore, *This England* can legitimately be described as ideologically conservative. Yet there are other aspects to the film which, if not actually radical, are tinged with a sort of radicalism that sits, at times uncomfortably, alongside its essential conservatism. For one thing, there is a sense in which the land – and the social responsibilities that come with it – are a burden. This is most explicit in the Napoleonic episode where the bankrupt Lord Clevely is prompted to declare: 'It's this past of ours that's a curse – this sticky, clinging, damnable creeper of an English past.' He has frittered away his fortune on gambling and is forced to sell his estate to meet his debts. As Rookeby's farm is part of the estate, Rookeby and Clevely play cards to determine its fate. Rookeby is somewhat less than overjoyed to win: 'Those damnable acres have won again!' Both aristocrat and yeoman farmer, therefore, are prepared to relinquish the land. It is significant in this respect that it is Appleyard, the labourer, who reminds Rookeby that he is a farmer first and foremost: 'But you don't belong, Master Rookeby, you don't belong. You can make your hands as fine as you like with gentleman's rings and wash them with the best soap that money can buy, but there's one thing you'll never get out of your nails and that's earth – village earth.'

Another radical element of *This England* is its representation of social injustice. This is no rose-tinted view of the past: English history is shown to have had its share of tyrants and oppressors; relations between the classes are tinged with bitterness and hostility; and there is a frank acknowledgement of the economic distress endured by the lower classes. *This England* may be unique as the only example of a wartime film to include domestic, as opposed to foreign, tyranny. The Norman episode suggests that traditional English liberties have been eroded following the Conquest. The blame is laid at the door of the baron, who is characterised as an interloper, unable to understand the rights of his subjects:

> *Baron:* What do you mean – liberty?
> *Churchman:* I mean, sir, that just as you claim rights for the king, these serfs claim rights from you. They are human creatures, born of woman as you are, and their rights cannot be denied.

The Norman baron might be considered an aberration as he is not English-born. Within a generation, it is suggested, the Normans have adapted to English traditions and liberties. 'It is a poor conqueror who lays his eggs in England and sees them hatched out Englishmen', remarks Appleyard. The baron's descendant in the Armada episode is that stock villain of country folklore: the absentee landlord who wishes to enclose the land. In 1086 the serfs had resorted to rebellion to depose a tyrant; in 1588 one murder is sufficient to safeguard the common law and traditional liberties. Nevertheless, it is an extreme solution to the problem.

It is in the Napoleonic episode that social divisions are most explicitly laid bare. To this extent the film shows some awareness of history: the later eighteenth century had seen a widening of the gulf between rich and poor as a combination of industrialisation, population growth and a cycle of agrarian depression made life more difficult for those at the bottom of the social scale. There is a background of social unrest:

> *Rookeby's wife:* Is it bad in the village?
> *Rookeby:* Brewing worse every day. My farm rotting before their eyes. Rumours of war. Bread riots.

Rookeby's wife, initially characterised as a spoiled heiress, believes the problem should be left to others ('That's to keep the politicians awake at night, not you'). Rookeby's conscience is gradually reawakened, however, when the village doctor informs him that the ploughman's son, born two days after Rookeby's, is dying because he has 'not enough to eat'. Appleyard implies that the child's death is a consequence of Rookeby turning his back on the farm: 'That babe died because good rich land has gone to waste.' The uninvited entry of Appleyard and other villagers into the Rookeby household during the christening party for Rookeby's son is perhaps the most powerful moment in the film, deriving its dramatic force from the contrast between rich and poor: 'Fine place you've got here, or your wife's father I should say. Gold and silver, silks and satins, a grand lady, a good smell from the kitchen.' There is a distinct edginess to the confrontation between the classes which is rather too easily resolved by Rookeby's decision to return to farming and Appleyard's eagerness to join him.

The social problems of 1086, 1588 and 1804 were all at sufficient remove from the present to be containable and safe. The Armistice of 1918, however, was a much more recent event. Interestingly, this is perhaps the bleakest episode in the film, a bleakness due not only to its visual texture but also to its prevailing tone of pessimism. The three protagonists have all been damaged, either physically or emotionally, by the Great War: Rookeby is blind, the girl has lost her husband or boyfriend, and, while nothing is said specifically about Appleyard, he noticeably does not participate in the public celebrations that mark the end of the war. All three stand apart from the crowd and do not join in the communal singing. Rookeby's fate might be seen as an allusion to the unfulfilled promise of 'homes fit for heroes' made by British politicians at the end of the war, while the girl's plight – her child has been taken from her by its grandparents who believe she is an unfit mother – is also suggestive of social inequality. The script reserves its most severe criticism, however, for those who believed the Great War would be the last war. One of the villagers believes that disarmament and reconciliation with the former foe will bring peace: 'Eternal peace in this dear, dear land of ours, as Shakespeare put it, our homes and happiness secure, but no rancour. The British lion, as it were, in the great-hearted meakness of its victory, is going to lie with the German lion.' When the villagers see Rookeby standing at the back of the pub, they demand a speech from 'the local VC'. He is reluctant to come forward, but is prompted by Appleyard and the girl. His speech is interesting in so far as it reveals not only his awareness of the futility of the Great War but also his uncertainty and fears about the future:

> *Rookeby:* Ladies and gentlemen, I'm no speaker but a farmer,
> though I've been a soldier for so long now that I've almost
> forgotten what it's like to be a farmer. I'm going to be one from
> now on, thank God. Bit of a crock but I'll do my best. Be a bit
> of a change for me, I'll tell you, to see the soil – to *hear* the soil
> – being put to better use than what I saw over in Flanders. That
> was a good speech just now and that's a fine bit of Shakespeare
> we should all know. And if all that comes true it will be a great
> thing for us. But it's a tall order. I don't want to cast any cold
> water tonight, but if anything goes wrong with that programme
> there'll be the devil to pay. And it won't be us that have to pay
> – we've paid enough, some of us – it'll be our children. We
> know they won't fail us, coming of good old fighting stock, but
> we don't want to see that. Solutions, not words.

This speech, obviously, represents the attitude of 1940 rather than that of
1918, when there was a widespread belief that the Great War would be the
'war to end all wars'. His warning is dismissed by the other villagers who
attribute his pessimism to his wartime experiences ('Cynical, poor fellow,
but after all he's been through small wonder'). In hindsight, of course,
Rookeby's pessimism would prove well founded: Germany was left
aggrieved following her defeat and the hoped-for reconciliation was not
achieved. Implicitly, therefore, the film is critical of those who had
preached disarmament and appeasement following the Great War.

It might not, on the face of it, seem especially radical of *This
England* to look back critically at the failure to achieve a lasting peace
in 1918. Similar statements warning against the danger of complacency
and the mistaken faith in reconciliation are to be found in several other
wartime films, including *The Life and Death of Colonel Blimp* (1943)
and *This Happy Breed* (1944). What is significant about *This England*,
however, is that it was one of the first feature films of the war to
express this view. Written in the summer of 1940, in the aftermath of
the evacuation from Dunkirk, *This England* emerged from the same
political and social climate as the political pamphlet *Guilty Men* by
'Cato' (actually three left-wing journalists, Michael Foot, Peter
Howard and Frank Owen), which had launched a savage attack on the
politicians of the 1930s who had appeased Germany and led Britain

into a war for which she was unprepared. Rookeby's speech warning against complacency is a watered-down version of the trenchant criticism of *Guilty Men*, not so much in terms of what he says as in the fact that he is responding to an advocate of pacifism and disarmament. *Guilty Men* can itself be seen as part of the radical shift in popular opinion that took place in the aftermath of Dunkirk, a shift that was also reflected in J.B. Priestley's radio broadcasts in the 'Postscripts' series on the BBC and in the Boulting Brothers' film *The Dawn Guard* (1941) for the MOI's series of five-minute films. There was a mood, albeit at first quite vaguely expressed, that the war was being fought not just to defeat Nazism but also to build a better future for the people of Britain. This was the mood that would culminate, five years later, in the election of a Labour government under Clement Attlee. The crucial moment of change, however, as far as such things can ever be pinned down, occurred in the summer of 1940.[29]

It would be stretching the point to suggest that *This England* expresses the mood of wartime populism that originated in 1940. Indeed, with its suggestion that the war was being fought to preserve the past rather than to build the future, *This England* would appear to have very little in common with later wartime feature films such as the Boultings' *Thunder Rock* (1942) and Ealing's *They Came to a City* (1944). In one important respect, however, *This England* does embody the mood of 1940: the emphasis on social unity in response to an external threat. The recurring theme of the film is how, at moments of crisis, the English overcome their own differences and unite to face the common enemy. The Elizabethan and Napoleonic episodes are both set against the threat of invasion by foreign despots. The comic drilling of the local militia in 1588, a sort of Elizabethan *Dad's Army*, implies a parallel with the formation of the Home Guard in 1940. It is worth stressing that *This England* was made when invasion remained a very real threat, prompting Robert Murphy to observe that 'the film has an urgency and a harshness that later films celebrating "this England" lacked'.[30]

That the summer of 1940 did indeed witness a feeling of national unity transcending class and social barriers can hardly be disputed even by the most jaundiced of commentators. If historians have subsequently debated whether the war effected any fundamental or lasting social change, there is ample evidence to suggest that the British people did metaphorically close ranks in the aftermath of Dunkirk. It is only to be expected, of course, that propaganda films such as the GPO

Film Unit's *Britain at Bay* – written and narrated by J.B. Priestley and providing a visual equivalent of his radio 'Postscripts' – would stress national unity and social cohesion. More revealing, perhaps, is the evidence provided by independent sources. George Orwell could never be described as a member of the establishment; his disdain for the English class system was well known and *The Road to Wigan Pier* (1936), one of the milestones of English political journalism, ranks alongside *Love on the Dole* as a polemic against social inequality. It was in *The Lion and the Unicorn* – written between August and October 1940, and published by Secker & Warburg in February 1941 – that Orwell brilliantly evoked the contradictions of the English character. In one famous passage he describes the emotional ties that bind the nation together despite the inequalities of the class system:

> England is the most class-ridden country under the sun. It is a land of snobbery and privilege, ruled largely by the old and silly. But in any calculation about it one has got to take into account its emotional unity, the tendency of nearly all its inhabitants to come together in moments of supreme crisis...England is not the jewelled isle of Shakespeare's much-quoted message, nor is it the inferno depicted by Dr Goebbels. More than either it resembles a family, a rather stuffy Victorian family, with not many black sheep in it but with all its cupboards bursting with skeletons. It has rich relations who have to be kow-towed to and poor relations who are horribly sat upon, and there is a deep conspiracy of silence about the source of the family income. It is a family in which the young are generally thwarted and most of the power is in the hands of irresponsible uncles and bedridden aunts. Still, it is a family. It has its private language and its common memories, and at the approach of an enemy it closes its ranks.[31]

It is precisely this closing of ranks and the tendency of its people to come together in times of crisis that is the spirit invoked by *This England*.

Orwell argued, furthermore, that the sense of national unity overcame differences between the different regions of what should properly be called the United Kingdom:

> It is quite true that the so-called races of Britain feel themselves to be very different from one another. A Scotsman, for instance,

does not thank you if you call him an Englishman. You can see the hesitation we feel on this point by the fact that we call our islands by no less than six different names, England, Britain, Great Britain, the British Isles, the United Kingdom and, in very exalted moments, Albion. Even the differences between north and south England loom large in our own eyes. But somehow these differences fade away the moment that any two Britons are confronted by a European. It is very rare to meet a foreigner, other than an American, who can distinguish between English and Scots or even English and Irish...Looked at from the outside, even the cockney and Yorkshireman have a strong family resemblance.[32]

An indiscriminate use of 'Britain', 'England' and the other names was a characteristic of wartime cinema. It is particularly evident in *This England*, which uses 'British' anachronistically in the Norman sequence but reverts thereafter to using 'English', even on occasions where 'British' would be more appropriate. For all the cultural resonances of the title, however, one reason for *This England*'s failure to make any impression at the box office may have been its apparent privileging of just one part of the United Kingdom. Indeed, prints of the film shown in Scottish cinemas were tactfully re-entitled *Our Heritage*.

Ultimately, perhaps, the combination of conservatism and radicalism in *This England* is neither contradictory nor unusual. The co-existence of both elements is entirely consistent with events in Britain in 1940. Thus, on the one hand, there was the popular reaction against the 'Guilty Men' and the 'Men of Munich' – Neville Chamberlain, Lord Halifax, Sir Samuel Hoare – who had, or so it was now believed, failed to recognise the threat posed by Hitler and who were held responsible for the mess in which the country found itself. And, at the same time, there was the emergence of a public discourse over war aims that, in the view of progressive left/liberal opinion, had as much to do with social justice as with military victory. This was the mood summed up by Priestley in his 'Postscript' of 21 July when he spoke about the opportunity to 'really plan and build up a nobler world in which ordinary, decent folk can not only find justice and security but also beauty and delight'.[33] On the other hand, however, this was the Britain led by one of its most totemic, right-wing figures – Churchill – who had no truck with talk of social reconstruction and whose policy was simply 'victory at all costs'. And Churchill, whose world-view could hardly be described as progressive, would remain a hugely popular figure even while the groundswell of popular opinion that would eventually remove him from office in 1945 grew. As the historian Paul Addison remarked: 'The year 1940 has gone down in our annals as the time when all sections of the nation put aside their peacetime differences, and closed ranks under the leadership of Churchill – "their finest hour". It should also go down as the year when the foundations of political power shifted decisively leftward for a decade.'[34]

This England was a film very much of and for its moment. A few years later and it would have appeared ridiculously dated. It is a sign of its failure as propaganda that there were no attempts to repeat its epic (in ambition if not in execution) chronicle of history through the ages. Perhaps the nearest equivalent – and deriving its title from the same source – was *This Happy Breed*, directed by David Lean from the play by Noël Coward and representing a sort of civilian equivalent of the same team's naval epic *In Which We Serve*. *This Happy Breed* focuses on the fictional Gibbons family of 17 Sycamore Road, Clapham, against the background of real events between the wars (the General Strike, the Abdication, Munich). However, any similarities with *This England* end there. *This Happy Breed* was a far more successful projection of the English character, being acclaimed for its realism and for the restrained performances of its cast (Robert Newton, Celia Johnson, John Mills, Kay Walsh). It also benefited from higher production values, including Technicolor, than had been possible for *This England*, produced as it was by Cineguild under the aegis of the Rank Organisation. There were also important ideological differences. Whereas *This England* had defined the essence of Englishness as residing in the countryside, *This Happy Breed* focused on the suburban lower middle classes (represented in the person of Newton's staunchly Conservative Frank Gibbons) as the backbone of national stability and solidarity. It was both a critical and a popular success, the biggest British box-office attraction of 1944 and an early example of the sort of 'quality' film that middlebrow critics admired.[35]

British National, for its part, enjoyed its biggest successes of the war with two films it backed from independent film-makers. Leslie Howard's *Pimpernel Smith* (1941) was perhaps the actor-director's finest hour, a wartime reworking of the Scarlet Pimpernel, whom Howard had played for Korda in 1934, but recasting the Pimpernel as

an apparently absent-minded professor of archeology who risks his
life to rescue scientists, artists and men of letters from inside Nazi
Germany. The film dramatises the ideological differences between
democracy (represented by Howard's Professor Horatio Smith) and
Fascism (personified by the thuggish, though cunning, Gestapo chief
General von Graum, played with subtle menace by Francis L.
Sullivan). It is the foremost wartime tribute to the qualities of the
gentleman hero: patriotic, chivalrous, romantic, humorous, gentle,
courageous, self-effacing. Howard deploys familiar motifs of
Englishness, including the poetry of Rupert Brooke ('Let me pack and
take a train/ And get me to England again'), and suggests that the
secret weapon of the English is their sense of humour. *Pimpernel
Smith* describes itself as a 'fantasy' and its whimsical treatment was not
to the liking of those critics who preferred a more straightforward
realism, though its popular success suggests that, as far as cinema-
goers were concerned, realism was not necessarily the foremost
criterion of good entertainment.[36] Powell and Pressburger's *One of
Our Aircraft is Missing* (1942), backed by British National when
Rank's General Film Distributors turned it down, fits more
comfortably within the canon of British wartime cinema. Its narrative
of a bomber crew shot down over the Netherlands and escaping to
freedom with the assistance of the Dutch resistance uses a familiar
device of wartime films, namely the heterogeneous social group whose
bonding becomes a metaphor for national unity – a motif also
employed in *Nine Men*, *San Demetrio, London* and *The Way Ahead*.
It was made in the realistic, understated style of narrative
documentaries such as *Target for Tonight* and can be seen as an early
example of the 'wartime wedding' that critics identified between the
commercial feature film and the documentary style.

   Powell and Pressburger were also responsible for British cinema's
most ambitious attempt to examine the rural myth. The aim of *A
Canterbury Tale*, said Powell, 'was to examine the values for which we
were fighting and to do it through the eyes of a young American who
was training in England'.[37] The film begins with travellers on the
Pilgrims' Way in medieval times and then switches to the present
through a brilliant ellipsis: a falcon thrown into the air becomes a
Spitfire in a single cut. The narrator explains that while the
countryside remains the same six hundred years on, 'another kind of
pilgrim walks the way'. The film follows three modern-day pilgrims

travelling to Canterbury who meet in a Kentish village: an American soldier (played by Sergeant John Sweet of the US Army), a British sergeant (Dennis Price) and an English girl in the Land Army (Sheila Sim). They find the village of Chillingbourne being terrorised by a mysterious 'glueman', a nocturnal phantom who under cover of the blackout pours glue into girls' hair. It transpires that the 'glueman' is none other than local magistrate Thomas Colpeper (Eric Portman), who has resorted to the attacks in order to vent his frustration that servicemen prefer the company of the local girls to attending his lectures on natural history. Colpeper is an eccentric rather than a dangerous villain: he emerges ultimately as a sympathetic figure and warms to the three 'pilgrims' when he realises that they too are interested in the traditions and values of the countryside. Finally, the protagonists make their way to Canterbury, where they all experience an emotional catharsis: the girl learns that her fiancé, missing in action, is safe and well, the American receives news from home after a long silence, and the British soldier fulfils his childhood dream of playing the organ in the cathedral.[38]

A Canterbury Tale is a fable of spiritual renewal as the three modern pilgrims who find their way to Canterbury come to understand the eternal values of the countryside. It is a far more polished film than *This England*, benefiting from location filming in the Kentish countryside and in Canterbury itself, but its cultural values are much the same: it represents a conservative notion of national identity which defines 'Englishness' through the traditions and customs of the rural past. It was not a box-office success. The critical response was one of bafflement, and, though its reputation has been enhanced since its restoration, along with other Powell and Pressburger films, by the National Film Archive in the 1970s, it remains something of a curate's egg. The failure of both *This England* and *A Canterbury Tale* to find either a wide public or a sympathetic response during the war illustrates the difficulty of dramatising complex motifs of history and heritage. Neither film is able to find a narrative framework that is able to give clear expression to the ideas and values they are validating. When it came to mobilising the past for wartime propaganda, British cinema was to enjoy far better results with inspirational narratives of national heroes. And the most successful of these was released in the same year as both *This Happy Breed* and *A Canterbury Tale*.

5

Cry God for Larry, England and St George: *Henry V* (1944)

IN 1947 Laurence Olivier was presented with a special Academy Award in recognition of his 'outstanding production achievement as actor, producer and director in bringing *Henry V* to the screen'. His majestic 1944 Technicolor film of *Henry V* is widely regarded as one of the masterpieces of British cinema and a landmark in the filmic interpretation of Shakespeare. It is both a historical film (a narrative of the English king's victorious campaign against the French in 1415 culminating in the Battle of Agincourt) and a costume film (an adaptation of the play *King Henry the Fifth* by William Shakespeare).[1] Released in the wake of D-Day and the campaign in Normandy, *Henry V* is an unashamedly patriotic, triumphalist epic in which an English army crosses the Channel to vanquish a mighty continental foe. Indeed, the film asserts its own status as propaganda by means of a caption preceeding the opening titles: 'To the Commandos and Airborne Troops of Great Britain – the spirit of whose ancestors it has humbly been attempted to recapture in some ensuing scenes – this picture is dedicated.'[2] *Henry V* was the most expensive British film of the war – it eventually cost some £475,000 – but, like *The Private Life of Henry VIII* a decade earlier, it brought both economic and cultural prestige to the British film industry. It was the first Shakespearean film to reach a mass audience and was critically and commercially successful in the United States.

The background to the film involves a complex matrix of wartime commerce, culture and propaganda. *Henry V* brings together two separate, and largely unrelated, histories: the emergence of J. Arthur Rank as the dominant figure in the British film industry and the role of the Ministry of Information (MOI) in promoting an officially endorsed wartime film culture. The story of Rank's rise from miller to movie mogul is well documented.[3] Rank first became interested in films through his membership of the Religious Film Society, of which he was treasurer; it was his dissatisfaction with the quality of religious films that prompted his first venture into film finance in 1934 with a film called *The Mastership of Christ*. Later that year he joined with Lady Yule to create British National. It was the lacklustre handling of British National's *The Turn of the Tide* by its distributor, Gaumont-British, that prompted Rank in 1935 to set up General Film Distributors (GFD) in association with paper magnate Lord Portal and former Gaumont-British executive C.M. Woolf. GFD was followed in 1936 by the General Cinema Finance Corporation (GCFC), backed by the National Provincial Bank. GCFC, which became the parent company of GFD, also bought shares in Universal Pictures, thus securing a steady supply of films from one of the Hollywood majors. Having established himself as a distributor and financier, the next step for Rank was to move into production. He invested in a consortium to build Pinewood Studios in Buckinghamshire, which opened in September 1936 as a rental studio that hired floor space and facilities to independent producers including Herbert Wilcox and Gabriel Pascal. In 1938 Rank acquired Denham Studios from the debt-ridden Korda and in 1939 he bought the newly built Amalgamated Studios at Elstree (which he immediately leased to the government for storage, as the decline in production in the late 1930s meant that Rank was unable to keep all his studios full). Then, in 1941, Rank bought the Odeon cinema chain, following the death of its founder Oscar Deutsch. Within the space of only a few years, therefore, Rank had acquired interests in the production, distribution and exhibition sectors of the industry. He had, in effect, created a third vertically integrated group. The three quickly became two, however, when Rank bought the Ostrers' shares in Gaumont-British in October 1941 and so brought the ailing giant within the orbit of his own empire. Rank now owned or controlled over half of the total studio space in Britain, the largest distributor and two (Gaumont-British and Odeon) of the three principal cinema chains, amounting to over 600 cinemas.

The most remarkable thing about the growth of the Rank empire was that, rather like the British Empire, it came about more or less by

accident. As Rachael Low attests: 'Rank's progress in the industry...
was not so much a deliberate attempt to take it by storm as a step by
step response to changing events, drawing him further and further
along the road to power.'[4] Its growth was so rapid, moreover, that the
rest of the film industry was caught off guard. It was only late in 1941
that the 'shock effect', as Geoffrey Macnab puts it, began to register.[5]
Concern was expressed by smaller producers, led by Michael Balcon
of Ealing Studios, about Rank's dominant position in the film industry
and the monopolistic tendencies it represented. Rank countered this
view by arguing that it was necessary to consolidate power in order to
protect the British film industry against American competition. To be
fair to Rank, he never had a monopoly in the strictest sense: the British
film industry is best described as a duopoly (the Rank Organisation
and ABPC); GFD was only one of eight major distributors (six of the
eight were American); and Rank's 619 cinemas represented less than
one-seventh of the 4,618 cinemas licensed in 1941.[6] However, the
industry's concerns were sufficient for the President of the Board of
Trade, Hugh Dalton, to set up a committee, chaired by City banker
Albert Palache, to investigate 'Tendencies to Monopoly in the
Cinematograph Film Industry'. The Palache Report of 1944 was a
compromise: it expressed concern that two companies (Rank and
ABPC) owned a quarter of all cinemas and drew attention to their
links with American studios (Rank with Universal, ABPC with
Warner Bros.) but drew short of advocating the dismantling of the
duopoly. Instead, it recommended that restrictions should be imposed
on the further acquisition of cinemas and that there should be no
discrimination against independent producers in the renting of films.
Rank and ABPC both agreed not to buy any more cinemas without
seeking permission from the Board of Trade.[7]

The irony of the Palache Report is that many of the independent
producers it sought to protect were, in fact, operating under the aegis of
the Rank Organisation. In 1942 Rank had established Independent
Producers Ltd in order to provide production finance and facilities for
independents such as The Archers (Michael Powell and Emeric
Pressburger), Individual Pictures (Frank Launder and Sidney Gilliat),
Cineguild (David Lean, Anthony Havelock-Allan and Ronald Neame),
Wessex Films (Ian Dalrymple) and Gabriel Pascal. For a period of four
or five years in the mid-1940s, these film-makers experienced a level of
both artistic and budgetary freedom that was unprecedented in British

cinema. Rank was prepared to invest in 'prestige' films and to sponsor creativity and innovation. The artistic flowering of British cinema in the mid-1940s that produced films such as Powell and Pressburger's *The Life and Death of Colonel Blimp* (1943), *A Matter of Life and Death* (1946), *Black Narcissus* (1947) and *The Red Shoes* (1948), David Lean's *Brief Encounter* (1945), *Great Expectations* (1946) and *Oliver Twist* (1948), and Gabriel Pascal's *Caesar and Cleopatra* (1945) could not have occurred without Rank's patronage. These films were the antithesis of economic or aesthetic conservatism. David Lean testified to the commercial and artistic conditions which the members of Independent Producers enjoyed under Rank:

> J. Arthur Rank is often spoken of as an all-embracing monopolist who must be watched lest he crush the creative talents of the British film industry. Let the facts speak for themselves, and I doubt if any group of film-makers in the world can claim as much freedom. We of Independent Producers can make any subject we wish, with as much money as we think that subject should have spent on it. We can cast whatever actors we choose, and we have no interference at all in the way the film is made. No one sees the films until they are finished, and no cuts are made without the consent of the Director or Producer, and, what's more, not one of us is bound by any form of contract.[8]

These conditions would not last, but, for a few short years in the mid-1940s, independent producers enjoyed the benevolent patronage of the Rank Organisation. It is in this context of both economic and creative freedom that the production of *Henry V* needs to be understood.

The second context in which *Henry V* should be placed is the film propaganda policy of the MOI. It is evident that the official agencies responsible for promoting the British war effort both at home and abroad – the MOI, the Foreign Office and the British Council – attached great importance to history.[9] In 1939 the International Propaganda and Broadcasting Enquiry, sponsored by the Royal Institute of International Affairs to lay down what it considered were the basic principles of propaganda for the embryonic MOI, had included among its list of observations: 'Trappings and pageantry inherited from the past form valuable propaganda for stability' and 'A particularly effective means of propaganda is the idealisation of national heroes'.[10] The MOI's own Programme for Film Propaganda, drafted by Sir Kenneth Clark, the second Director of the Films Division, early in 1940 echoed this view in its suggestion that 'we may also consider films of heroic actions, histories of national heroes (Captain Scott) etc., although these may easily become too obvious'.[11] Although the MOI turned its back on subsidising feature film production following Powell and Pressburger's *49th Parallel* (1941) – the Treasury advanced just under £60,000 towards the film with a similar amount being put up by Rank – it was active throughout the war in suggesting appropriate topics to producers. In March 1942, for example, Clark's successor, Jack Beddington, invited to attend meetings of the British Film Producers Association, 'mentioned the story of Mary Kingsley and her life on the Gold Coast, which portrayed past events connected with the foundation of the British Empire'.[12] While in the event the Mary Kingsley film was not made, there are various other examples of historical feature films that accord so closely with official policy that it seems reasonable to assume some level of MOI involvement.

The Prime Minister (dir. Thorold Dickinson, 1941), produced in Britain by Warner Bros. with its 'frozen funds', is a biopic starring John Gielgud as Disraeli. The film asserts its patriotic credentials by presenting Disraeli as a national hero ('I think you can do great things for England', Lord Melbourne tells the young statesman) and a tireless servant of his country. There are parallels with Wilcox's *Sixty Glorious Years* in the narrative strategy of replaying the appeasement debates of the 1930s through the events of the nineteenth century, in this case the Congress of Berlin in 1878, where Disraeli stands firm by defending a small, weak nation (Turkey) against the territorial ambitions of larger powers (Russia and Germany) and returns having brokered 'peace with honour'. There are also similarities with Korda's *Lady Hamilton* as Disraeli's speech to his Cabinet recalls Nelson's address to the Admiralty: 'Europe at the moment is at the mercy of the most ruthless band of autocrats the world has yet seen. They recognise one argument and one argument alone – force – and that is the argument I beg you to use now for the sake of peace and for the sake of England.' *The Prime Minister* was made at a time when Britain had no allies and when the Nazi–Soviet Pact was still in force, thus both Germany and

Russia are presented as hostile powers. It has not stood the test of time: the propaganda is didactic, the film itself undistinguished, and its reception from press and public alike was largely indifferent.[13]

The Young Mr Pitt (dir. Carol Reed, 1942), a more expensive (£250,000) and polished film than *The Prime Minister*, was also produced in Britain with backing from a Hollywood studio (Twentieth Century-Fox). Robert Donat starred as William Pitt, presented as a social reformer at home and as a patriot in foreign affairs. He opposes domestic corruption in the person of his political rival Fox (Robert Morley) and foreign tyranny in the form of Napoleon (Herbert Lom). Once again there are clear contemporary parallels: Pitt is cast in Churchillian mould as an inspirational and visionary leader who is distrusted by the political establishment but enjoys popular support in the country; Britain is shown as the defender of small countries against aggressor nations; appeasement of foreign tyrants (the Treaty of Amiens) is shown as a misguided and futile foreign policy; Britain suffers initial reverses in the war and the army has to be evacuated (from Dunkirk no less) but is saved by a famous victory (Trafalgar). The contemporary parallels were readily apparent to contemporaries. *Picture Post* remarked:

> In 1940, when Hitler threatened England with invasion, it was natural to recall the time, nearly a century and a half before, when Napoleon made the same threat – particularly so since Napoleon's failure encouraged the hope that his twentieth-century imitator would be no more successful. And, since we are now led by a Prime Minister who typifies the spirit of resistance to a tyrant's ambitions, it is equally natural to recall the career of William Pitt the Younger.[14]

The film was a popular success when it was released in the summer of 1942, with *Today's Cinema* declaring: 'Never has any film more perfectly expressed the feeling and temper of the British people in times of stress and trouble such as we are passing through today.'[15]

Richards describes *The Young Mr Pitt* as 'almost a textbook demonstration of the MoI's interpretation of history'.[16] The MOI promoted a particular narrative of British history in which Britain was presented as a pioneer of social reform, the champion of the underdog and the defender of freedom – all notions that inform *The Young Mr*

Pitt. There is evidence of discreet official input into the film in so far as Viscount Castlerosse, *Sunday Express* gossip columnist and one of the MOI's favoured journalists, is credited on the film for 'dramatic narrative and additional dialogue' – the screenplay was by Frank Launder and Sidney Gilliat – and it was one of the British films approved for sending to the Soviet Union.

The production history of *Henry V* similarly shows evidence of official involvement, for, while the MOI did not finance the film, it clearly provided much assistance from behind the scenes. For one thing, it facilitated the release of Laurence Olivier from the Fleet Air Arm to star in the film. This was a sure sign of official approval: in 1942 the ministry had refused to arrange the same actor's release when Michael Powell wanted him for *The Life and Death of Colonel Blimp*.[17] Olivier later claimed that the idea to make *Henry V* came directly from the MOI Films Division. In his autobiography the actor wrote:

> I was summoned to the Ministry of Information to see Jack Beddington, who was side-kick for the Minister on any question which concerned show-business propaganda. He asked me to undertake two pictures intended to enhance the British cause. One was *The Demi-Paradise*, whose object was to win the British public over to the idea of liking the Russians ... After *Demi-Paradise*, I would be required to make a picture of Shakespeare's *Henry V*. The pull of this play as popular propaganda, I could see, might be far more potent than the first project, and the pull on my artistic ambitions was intoxicating.[18]

Both *The Demi-Paradise* (dir. Anthony Asquith, 1943) and *Henry V* were produced by Two Cities Films, furthermore, which of all the production companies was probably the most closely involved with the official film propaganda machinery. Two Cities had just produced Noël Coward and David Lean's naval epic *In Which We Serve*, which Rank's GFD had declined to back on grounds of cost. It was to Two Cities that the MOI turned when it wanted a feature film made about British colonial administration in Africa (*Men of Two Worlds*) and it was Two Cities that the Army Kinematograph Service approached when it wanted a film to do for the Army what *In Which We Serve* had done for the Royal Navy (*The Way Ahead*). So intimately was Two Cities integrated into the official propaganda effort that its managing director, Italian émigré Filippo Del Giudice, told Beddington that 'it is the policy of this Company not to make any films, whether on subjects connected directly with the war or not, without the approval of the Ministry of Information'.[19] Del Giudice was confident of securing official support for *Henry V*: 'As you will see from the first outline of this great undertaking, every care has been taken to stress the propaganda angle of this subject and we need your help to secure facilities which will enable us to bring about a production which will certainly be a pride to the Industry.'[20]

Henry V was a natural choice for a propaganda film. The theatre critic Alan Dent, who worked with Olivier on the adaptation of the play for the screen, described it as 'by far the most patriotic, most pro-England play that Shakespeare ever penned'.[21] The subject lent itself easily to patriotic display and was a favourite at moments of national crisis: the Old Vic produced it every year during the First World War. Olivier's association with the play dated back to 1937 when he had starred in a spectacular production to mark the coronation of George VI.[22] In May 1942 Olivier recited passages from the play, including Henry's stirring orations at Harfleur ('Once more unto the breach, dear friends, once more') and on Crispin's Day ('We few, we happy few, we band of brothers'), for a short radio programme called *Into Battle* and later that year appeared in a full radio broadcast of the play. *Into Battle* had been produced by Dallas Bower, a pre-war television producer who in 1940-41 had worked for the MOI Films Division as Supervisor of Production. Olivier acknowledged that it was Bower 'who had originally conceived the idea' of *Henry V*.[23] He first planned it for television in the late 1930s, but this idea had to be aborted when television was suspended on the outbreak of war. Bower then worked on a film treatment. On 28 October 1942 he wrote to Olivier: 'I am very pleased indeed by the turn of events concerning "Henry V". Del Giudice has bought my treatment. He proposes that you shall produce and play the King and that I shall act as your Associate Producer.' There was, however, the problem of finding a suitable director:

> The question of a director has yet to be solved. Naturally I am bitterly disappointed that nobody appears to have sufficient faith in such abilities as I may have in this capacity, but I understand the sort of difficulties Del is faced with, and I think that if it were a matter which rested on his decision alone, he

would chance his money on me...We must, however, have a director who is not only an imaginative technician, but he must also believe in the possibilities of a Shakespearean cinema as a whole. So few directors do, I find. The ones that do are shocking bad technicians with no hard training behind them.[24]

Several directors were mentioned in connection with the film, including William Wyler, who had directed Olivier in *Wuthering Heights* for Samuel Goldwyn in 1939 but who turned down *Henry V* (Wyler was currently in Britain making films for the US Army Air Force), and Carol Reed, who was, however, engaged in making *The Way Ahead* for Two Cities at the time. Terence Young, a screenwriter who had directed the action scenes for the RKO British war melodrama *Dangerous Moonlight* (dir. Brian Desmond Hurst, 1941), was approached to direct in collaboration with Olivier (rather as David Lean had done with Noël Coward for *In Which We Serve*), but could not secure release from the services (Young was in the Guards Armoured Division) for the necessary length of time. In the event it was decided that Olivier would direct the film himself, his contract with Two Cities giving him full creative control over all aspects of the production. Olivier was paid £20,000 to produce, direct and act in the film, with a promise of 20 per cent of the profits, and a further £15,000 not to appear in another film for 18 months following the release of *Henry V*.[25]

It is unclear how much of Bower's treatment remains in the finished film of *Henry V*: from the evidence of the Laurence Olivier Archive it would seem that the dramatic structure and adaptation were largely the work of Alan Dent and Olivier himself. In his introduction to a published version of the screenplay, Olivier disingenuously remarked that 'we made only a few minute alterations in the text, and the cuts are even less than those invariably made in a stage production'.[26] Even the most cursory comparison of the play text and the film reveals this to be entirely untrue. In fact, the play was severely edited, over a third of the text being expunged. To some extent this was to make space for the Battle of Agincourt, the spectacular set piece that would be the highlight of the film. To an even greater extent, however, the cuts were made in order to remove anything that contradicted official propaganda directives. Dent's notes recognised that the adaptation needed to be 'tactfully handled and its parts carefully distributed' and referred to 'awkward obstacles' that would have to be overcome. The subplot of three disaffected subjects (the Earl of Cambridge, Sir Thomas Grey and Lord Scroop of Masham) who are executed for treason after plotting to kill Henry was cut entirely. Dent made no apology for the omission: 'The entire episode of the Cambridge–Grey–Scroop conspiracy, for example, goes by the board and this film's makers will have no more artistic qualms about this excision than they will have about removing all difficult and obscure lines and passages, and all textual redundancies.'[27] Other parts that were cut included references to the divine right of kings (incompatible with modern British democracy), the threat posed to England from the Scots (contradicting the idea of national unity) and Henry's order to his soldiers to execute their prisoners (the sanctioning of a war atrocity).[28]

The propaganda imperative of *Henry V* was to present Henry's victory at Agincourt as an allegory of the present war. Here there is evidence that the meaning eventually overlaid onto the film was not that which the film-makers had originally intended. It is impossible to read the dedication to 'the Commandos and Airborne Troops of Great Britain' as a reference to anything other than the offensives of 1944, specifically D-Day and Arnhem.[29] However, Dent's notes suggest another parallel was intended by emphasising how the English army at Agincourt faced vastly overwhelming odds:

> Surely this is comparable with Britain's hour in the autumn and winter of 1940, when a 'pitiful few' during the Battle of Britain went up into the skies, hour after hour, week after week, and kept a powerful invader at bay. These modern warriors of the skies were worn too: tired, nerve-wracked, but they had that same courage and won the day as King Henry and his soldiers won theirs centuries ago. This parallel is very significant and of immense exploitation value from the viewpoint of the ordinary public.[30]

As the film was nearing completion by the time of the Normandy Landings, with just the opticals to be finished, the dedication was an opportunity to assert the topicality of the film for war-weary audiences who were starting to tire of combat films. *The Way Ahead*, coincidentally released in London on 6 June 1944, was not a box-office success, though critics admired its authenticity and realism.[31]

It was in Dent's treatment notes, furthermore, that the idea of 'opening up' the play took shape. There are broadly speaking two ways of adapting Elizabethan drama for cinema: the 'theatrical' mode which treats it as a piece of filmed theatre (often criticised as 'shooting from the front row of the stalls') or the 'cinematic' mode which treats it naturalistically, using realistic sets and locations (but against which dialogue in blank verse can seem incongruous). *Henry V*, however, would combine both modes. It was to begin in the theatrical mode, with a reconstruction of a performance at the Globe Playhouse by the Lord Chamberlain's Men on 1 May 1600, including scenes of the theatre audience and the actors in the wings, and would then gradually open out into the cinematic mode for the Battle of Agincourt, to be shot in all its Technicolor glory as a set piece of action and spectacle. Dent modestly credited this idea to Shakespeare himself as the play 'clamours almost categorically for film treatment. The Chorus repeatedly confesses that the theatre is too limited a medium for the stirring events here depicted or described.'[32] The prologue spoken by the Chorus implores the audience to use their imagination in visualising the spectacle ('can this cockpit hold/The vasty fields of France? or may we cram/Within this wooden O the very casques/That did affright the air at Agincourt?'). The transition from the stage of the Globe to the field of Agincourt is managed through a series of painted backgrounds and studio sets that move from extreme stylisation (the embarking ships at Southampton) to naturalism (the English camp scenes at Agincourt). The scenic backdrops were modelled on a fifteenth-century illuminated manuscript, *Les Très Riches Heures du Duc de Berri*, which art director Paul Sheriff and costume designer Roger Furse consulted 'to learn how people dressed and behaved and what the architecture and landscape, which formed the background of their lives, looked like'.[33] This assumed a great deal of cultural competence on the part of the film's spectators in decoding the imagery.

Henry V had a much longer production period than most films, owing to the complexity of the production and the logistical difficulties involved in shooting the Agincourt sequence on location in Eire. This was necessary, according to the trade press, because of 'the impossibility in this country of utilising suitable backgrounds or to obtain the large numbers of men and horses necessary for the battle sequences'.[34] The irony of shooting a patriotic epic about an English king in republican, neutral Eire was not lost on commentators. One

Irish newspaper remarked caustically that 'Irishmen are to be asked to join the British and French Armies again…Stranger than fiction – one would think it the last place they'd bring Henry.'[35] The extras cast for the battle were drawn largely from the ranks of the Irish Local Defence Force. Such an unlikely source of recruits was a subject of amusement for 'Sagitarrius', the satirical poet of the *New Statesman*, who penned a pastiche of Henry's Harfleur speech ('Once more rehearse the scene, good Celts, once more') in response:

> Advance, you stout Sinn Feiners, brawny supers
> Whose limbs were made in Eire, show us here
> That you are worth your wages; which I doubt not,
> Are ten times more than those of Harry's bowmen!
> And he that doth enact this scene with me,
> Let him never be so Republican
> He is this day King Harry's follower!
> On to the charge! though there is none of you
> But hath a neutral lustre in his eye,
> And say, this day I act an Englishman!
> Now set the teeth, hold hard the breath, and strike!
> Follow your leader, and upon your cue
> Charge for St Patrick and the Emerald Isle![36]

One vistor to the set was none other than Irish Prime Minister Éamonn de Valéra, who told Olivier that he 'had a really pleasant afternoon', despite having to watch the English win.[37]

The first shots of *Henry V* were taken on 7 June 1943, on the estate of Lord Powerscourt in Enniskerry, and the studio scenes at Denham were completed in the second week of January 1944.[38] Poor weather conditions in Eire and the subsequent extension of both the location and studio shooting schedules meant that the film exceeded its original budget of £325,700 and that the final production cost came in at £474,888.[39] A consequence of the escalating cost was that Del Giudice was forced to turn to the Rank Organisation for support. Two Cities already had a distribution deal with Rank through which GFD advanced funds for production (to be repaid from the rental receipts as was normal practice). In 1943, however, Del Giudice obtained a special loan from GFD in order that Two Cities could carry on with production of *Henry V*, *Tawny Pipit* and *English Without Tears* (a follow-up to Two Cities' first success, *French Without Tears*, both based on Terence Rattigan plays). The price exacted by Rank was high. Del Giudice signed over to GFD 75 per cent of the profits of *Henry V* in all markets.[40] A further condition was that Rank join the Two Cities board. In effect, Del Giudice was now reliant on Rank and Two Cities had come within the orbit of the Rank empire. Del Giudice became increasingly frustrated at the loss of his independence, as he saw it, and soon came into conflict with the Rank management. 'I shall go on fighting, my dear Larry; as you must know, from time to time I fight like hell for matters of principle', he wrote to Olivier in October 1946. 'It is rather tiring but some good occasionally results from it. It is a pity that Arthur is surrounded by so many small people.'[41] A few months later, however, Del Giudice gave up the fight and sold his shares in Two Cities, leaving the company he had co-founded in 1937.

The falling-out between Del Giudice and Rank was to some extent a consequence of the problems that had beset the distribution of *Henry V*. Rank was a businessman who had little personal interest in films, regarding them as commodities rather than art. Thus, while he seems to have been impressed by *Henry V* which 'has, I think, brought special credit and added prestige to the British Film Industry both in this country and abroad', he was at the same time doubtful of its commercial potential, adding that 'it may be extremely difficult to arrange for an adequate showing of the film in the USA, owing to recent events over which none of us has any control'.[42] He asked Olivier to cut the 140-minute film by 40 minutes, but Olivier was able to persuade Rank that the cuts he asked for would be damaging to the film and maintained his 'director's cut'.[43] *Henry V* was one of the first films to be handled by Eagle-Lion, a new distribution arm set up by Rank in 1944 for the purpose of selling his 'prestige' pictures in the international market. Eagle-Lion's managing director, E.T. Carr, complimented Olivier that he had been 'able to produce a classic and keep it as such, and at the same time present entertainment in its very highest form, which the masses will relish'.[44] There is evidence, however, that Eagle-Lion were unsure how to handle *Henry V*, its length and its Shakespearean parentage being seen as drawbacks. It was initially given a limited distribution, showing at a select handful of West End cinemas, before a wider general release in the summer of 1945. Even so there is evidence to suggest that Eagle-Lion were less than wholeheartedly behind the film. Clayton Hutton, an Eagle-Lion executive and friend of Olivier's, who had written a book on the making of the film, wrote despairingly: 'I really have put up a fight *internally*, on this particular picture, inside our own Corporation. Half of them, in spite of the enormous success it has had, are half hearted on it even now, yet what little success they admit of it, those few seem to think they have created it.'[45]

For all that it is now widely recognised as one of the greatest of all British films of the 1940s, the reception of *Henry V* was in fact rather uneven. Reviews of the film reveal a range of responses to its status as entertainment, art and adaptation. *The Times* thought it a triumph on all counts: 'A great play has been made into a great film and Shakespeare has survived the transition.'[46] The *Manchester Guardian* found it 'a film with boldness, colour, and sweep, with fine acting, a sense of poetry and motion, and, over all, a play of imagination'.[47] Several critics echoed the views of Carr that *Henry V* made Shakeaspeare accessible to a mass audience. Oliver Bell, Director of the British Film Institute, thought it 'a noticeable achievement of purely British cinema, not least because it will introduce Shakespeare to millions who would not dream of seeing the play performed on stage'.[48] Here there seems to have been consonance between the views of the BFI (at this time concerned as much with the aim of film education as with the idea of film art) and some cinema-goers. Several of the respondents to a survey of film preferences conducted by sociologist J.P. Mayer, published in 1948 as *British Cinemas and their Audiences*, were clearly of a similar mind. One 17-year- old female wrote:

> It is only just lately that we have seen Shakespeare successfully served up as a palatable and exceedingly colourful if not dainty dish for cinema audiences to masticate. I refer to Laurence Olivier's production of *Henry V* – a vitally interesting experiment which opens up new hopes for those longing to see Shakespeare appreciated by the masses.[49]

Another respondent, a 24-year-old woman, saw *Henry V* as 'the beginning, I hope, of a series of Shakespeare plays brought to the screen, what a pleasure to hear our English language spoken correctly and in such beautiful tones'.[50]

The educational value of *Henry V* was stressed in its promotional materials, which, rather disingenuously, claimed that it 'is not somebody's idea of Shakespeare's masterpiece. It is a faithful, sincere and entirely successful adaptation to the screen.'[51] Cinema exhibitors were encouraged to arrange special morning and matinée performances for schoolchildren; some local education authorities, including Olivier's home town of Brighton, even paid for children to see it – a policy that must have delighted exhibitors. A schoolmaster reviewing the film for *Sight and Sound* considered that it 'opens a new prospect, rich in promise for the new schools and colleges as they begin to provide new audiences for the cinema'. He went on to declare that the epithet of 'masterpiece' was 'overwhelmingly deserved... as a film, as a production of a Shakespeare play and as a description of a historical epoch'. His only criticism, which ran against the grain of the film critics, was of the Agincourt sequence on the grounds that 'much happens that is historically inaccurate. That long charge, for instance, would have been quite impossible to men and horses loaded with armour as they were.'[52]

For a number of the middle-brow film critics, committed as they were to the aesthetic potential of the medium and eager to assert its independence from other art forms, *Henry V* seemed to provide evidence in support of their view. 'I cannot believe that the majestic pageantry of Agincourt in this film is inferior, in art or truth, to the customary stage spectacle of knots of gentlemen bashing around in tin shins', Dilys Powell remarked.[53] C.A. Lejeune concurred: 'The charge of the cavalry at Agincourt, with its accelerating rhythm of music and movement, is one of the most exciting sequences I can remember on the screen, applying to the practicality of drama the poetry of pure mathematics.'[54] While most critics preferred the cinematic to the theatrical aspects of the film, Roger Manvell admired both, describing it as 'a beautiful rendering of the play from the theatrical point of view, [which] achieves a certain cinematic quality in the prose scenes where Shakespeare's speech is at its most intimate, idiomatic and realistic'. He also felt that 'Agincourt itself is excellent cinema following the classic example of medieval battle in Eisenstein's *Alexander Nevsky*'.[55]

For other critics, however, the mixture of styles was too uneven to be deemed entirely successful. Richard Winnington called it a 'patchwork' of a film that 'stumbles in confusion' for most of the time, though he felt that 'Britain has found here, in those moments which are of the cinema, and are unclouded to staginess, the real approach not only to Shakespeare but to the treasure chest of her history'.[56]

William Whitebait found the 'metamorphosis' from one style to another 'rather uneasy', but felt that it 'comes beautifully to life' on the field of Agincourt.[57] The sense of exasperation that some critics felt was expressed by Ernest Betts, who pronounced it 'the most difficult, annoying, beautiful, boring, exciting, wordy, baffling picture yet made. It is good and it is bad. It has a sort of damnable excellence.'[58]

The popular reception of the film was similarly divided. It seems to have done well in certain up-market cinemas. It opened in London on 27 November 1944 at the Carlton, Haymarket, where it ran for 16 weeks and grossed £50,536.[59] However, this success was not repeated across the country and outside the West End of London it fared rather less well. One of Del Giudice's associates reported that the manager of the Odeon in Birmingham 'was nervous of the picture as a whole lot of other Managers I have met were'; one commentator saw it with a 'bored and restive audience' at Muswell Hill; and Halliwell recalled it showing at the Odeon in Bolton 'before the most scattered and paltry house I remembered seeing'.[60] By August 1947 it had grossed a total £248,996 in Britain (a figure that illustrates just how remarkable its showing at the Carlton had been), of which the distributor claimed £165,929.[61] While *Henry V* was not unsuccessful, its appeal was limited, in the main, to more discerning cinema-goers. One of Mayer's respondents, for example, a 54-year-old bank clerk, named *Henry V* as one of the films, along with *The Great Mr Handel* and *Wilson*, 'which were not popular successes, but which appealed to me greatly'.[62] It did not have the populist appeal of, say, the Gainsborough melodramas that were the leading box-office attractions of the mid-1940s. This was much to the chagrin of Olivier:

> I have explained to Rank before that this film is for the good of his name, not his pocket, and if members of his organisation cannot see that these sort of films are better for his name than 'Wicked Lady' or 'Madonna of the Seven Moons', however many millions they may take in the Box office, then he and his organisation will have done no more for British films than Bungalows have done for architecture.[63]

To be fair to Rank, there is no evidence that he preferred *The Wicked Lady* to *Henry V*, but he was astute enough as a businessman to realise that most cinema-goers did.

Olivier's own view of *Henry V* was that it 'should be used as a kind of national gesture', to which end he advocated special screenings for schools and the armed services.[64] He also maintained that 'the primary motive behind the production was not the making of a financially successful film but the making of an artistically successful film…Our primary object must be to give the minority pleasure, and the majority the possibility of grasping that pleasure.'[65] If this sounds an extremely elitist view of cultural provision (as indeed it is), it is nevertheless consistent with the prevailing critical discourse of the time, which regarded British cinema as having come of age during the war. *Henry V* was an early example of what John Ellis has termed 'the quality film adventure': it was one of a series of films in 1944–48 (others include *This Happy Breed*, *Brief Encounter*, *Waterloo Road*, *Great Expectations*, *Odd Man Out*, *The Red Shoes* and *Oliver Twist*) that were seen to mark the emergence of a British school of film-making that was the equal of both the technical artistry of Hollywood and the formal innovation of European cinemas.[66] Within the industry, certainly, there was much acclaim for *Henry V*, one American documentarist describing it as 'perhaps the greatest contribution to the use of the film medium since the coming of sound'.[67]

All hyperbole aside, there is no denying that *Henry V* is a film of great technical and artistic achievement – all the more remarkable considering that it was Olivier's first time in the director's chair. It has a near-perfect structural and aesthetic symmetry. The sequential structure of the film follows the pattern A–B–C–D–E–F–E–D–C–B–A. The opening titles are presented as Elizabethan script on a handbill ('*The Chronicle History of King Henry the Fift with his battell fought at Agincourt in France by Will Shakespeare*') against the sound of a trumpet fanfare (A), followed by an overhead crane shot of a model of Elizabethan London that finally settles on the Globe Theatre (B). The narrative proper begins with the staging of a performance of the play at the Globe, including an abridged version of Act I at Henry's court, in which he decides to press his claim to the French throne, based upon the case presented to him by the Archbishop of Canterbury, and Act II Scene 1, which introduces the comic relief characters Bardolph, Nym and Ancient Pistol at the Boar's Head Tavern in Eastcheap (C). The end of the overtly theatrical part of the film is signalled by the Chorus drawing a curtain across the stage, after which a succession of scenes are set against painted backdrops and stylised sets (D). These include Henry's

7. 'Cry God for Harry, England and St George': Laurence Olivier
directed and starred in the patriotic spectacular *Henry V*.

embarcation at Southampton (a heavily abridged Act II Scene 2), the death back in London of Sir John Falstaff (incorporated from *Henry IV Part 2*), the introduction of the French court (Act II Scene 4) and most of Act III, including the siege of Harfleur and the introduction of Princess Katharine. The sets become less stylised up to the scenes in the English and French camps the night before Agincourt (Act IV Scenes 1–2). The morning of Agincourt, including the challenge of the French herald, Mountjoy, for Henry to surrender (Act IV Scene 3), are studio scenes using back projection rather than paintings (E). A matte painting showing the disposition of the opposing armies opens the battle itself, which consists mostly of exteriors and culminates in Henry's defeat of the Constable of France in single combat – a dramatic addition that is not in the play (F). The battle marks the two-thirds point of the narrative; the last third of the film reverses the formal pattern. Thus the aftermath of the battle is represented through a combination of exteriors (F) and back projections (E); scenes in the English camp (Act V Scene 1) and at the French court where Henry courts Princess Katharine (Act V Scene 2) are enacted against painted backdrops (D); the Chorus delivers the epilogue back on the stage of the Globe (C); and the film concludes with another model shot of London (B) and the closing credits written on a handbill (A).

Within this formal structure, *Henry V* contrives to represent a virtual compendium of the aesthetic history of film up to that point. The different techniques employed in the film all have their analogues in various stylistic trends and movements. Thus, the theatrical scenes and painted backcloths recall the method of filming Shakespearean drama in the early years of cinema, involving little more than scenes from the plays shot in tableaux from the front of the stage. The stylised sets and paintings are highly reminiscent of the cinema of German Expressionism with its forced perspectives and disorienting angles, particularly the scenes at Southampton and at the gates of Harfleur. And the Agincourt sequence employs the montage techniques of Soviet cinema, with its rapid editing and violent juxtapositions between shots. Many critics, both at the time and since, have compared Olivier's Agincourt to the Battle on the Ice in Sergei Eisenstein's *Alexander Nevsky* (1938). There are some striking similarities: the depth of the *mise-en-scène*, the formal organisation around planes of movement and stasis, the matching of images to the music. Yet even Eisenstein at his best never created a moment to equal the celebrated long tracking shot of the French knights as they build from a walk to a canter to a gallop in their charge against the English lines. Olivier, for his part, never confirmed that he had based Agincourt on Eisenstein. However, in a letter to George Macy he offered a different explanation for the orchestration of the battle: 'The importance to me of this probably unimportant point lies in an English left to right movement rule, and a French right to left movement rule which I had adopted in the film in order really to promote a theory that I have always had (though probably not the first to have it) regarding the rules of the English stage.'[68]

Agincourt provides the visual and narrative climax of the film: the resounding defeat of the enemy, in all its flamboyant might, by the heavily outnumbered English. This was the *raison d'être* of the film and its meaning was explicit: for France read Germany and for 1415 read 1944 (or 1940). That it concerns a specifically English victory was in itself significant, moreover, in the context of 1944–45. Unlike *This England*, which belongs to the period of the war when Britain was without allies, *Henry V* belongs to a later period when Britain was one-third of what Churchill called the Grand Alliance with the Soviet Union and the United States. Ever since 'Operation Barbarossa', the German attack that had started the war on the Russian Front in June 1941, Soviet leader Stalin had been complaining that the Soviet Union was bearing the brunt of the fighting and was pressuring Churchill to launch a Second Front against Germany in the West. The British campaign against the German and Italian armies in North Africa was regarded as a sideshow by Stalin, whose attitude can be read between the lines of his reply to Churchill after the British Prime Minister had sent him a print of *Desert Victory*, the documentary film of the Battle of El Alamein: 'The film depicts magnificently how Britain is fighting, and stigmatises those scoundrels (there are such people also in our country) who are asserting that Britain is not fighting at all, but is merely an onlooker.'[69] El Alamein had been politically as well as militarily important as it marked a significant British victory before the deployment of American forces in the European theatre. Between the end of 1942 and the middle of 1944 the British still had more men in the field in Europe than the United States, but the massive build-up of US troops in preparation for 'Operation Overlord' meant this would no longer be the case for the Normandy campaign. It was an indication of the shifting balance of power within the Anglo-American alliance that the appointment of a Supreme Commander Allied Expeditionary Force went to an American (Eisenhower). In this context, *Henry V* was a timely reminder of Britain's military contribution to the war at a time when the Americans had more men in the field in Western Europe.

Henry V is a testament to the fighting spirit of the British (though the film itself refers to the English, consistent with both the fifteenth century when the events took place and the end of the sixteenth century when the play was written). It presents the war against France as a righteous crusade ('we are coming on/To venge us as we may, and put forth/Our rightful hand in a well-hallowed cause') which has the support of the people ('Now all the youth in England are on fire'). Henry's oration to inspire his demoralised troops at Harfleur is replete with warlike imagery ('But when the blast of war blows in our ears/Then imitate the action of the tiger/Stiffen the sinews, conjure up the blood/Disguise fair nature with hard-favoured rage'), while his speech before Agincourt asserts the special honour bestowed upon the army that sets them apart from those at home ('And gentlemen in

8. 'We few, we happy few, we band of brothers': Henry inspires his troops before the battle in *Henry V*.

England now a-bed/Shall think themselves accurs'd they were not here/And hold their manhoods cheap while any speaks/That fought with us upon Saint Crispin's Day'). To this extent *Henry V* explores similar themes to other wartime films such as *The Life and Death of Colonel Blimp* (the necessity of fighting a total war) and *The Way Ahead* (how civilians are turned into soldiers).

The patiotic impulse of *Henry V* is greatly enhanced by its music. The recruitment of William Walton to compose the film's score exemplified a trend in British wartime cinema that saw established classical composers turn their talents to film, others including Sir Arnold Bax (*Malta, GC*), Constant Lambert (*Merchant Seamen*) and Ralph Vaughan Williams (*49th Parallel, Coastal Command*). This in turn can be seen as part of a larger cultural trend during the war which saw the boundaries between elite and popular culture crossed, if not actually broken – a trend of which *Henry V* was part. The composer Hubert Clifford believed that Walton's score for *Henry V* revealed 'an authentic English voice' equal to Elgar and Vaughan Williams.[70] The score is as much a pastiche of styles as the film itself, ranging from mock-Elizabethan court music for the Globe scenes to a rousing march reminiscent of Walton's own majestic *Crown Imperial* (composed for the coronation of George VI) for the embarcation of English ships at Southampton. The scoring of the main battle sequence is as ritualistic as the visual presentation: drum rolls, fanfares of horns announcing the French, a woodwind response for the English archers, and a *crescendo* of strings to signify the beat of the horses' hooves as they break into a charge.

Henry V also exemplifies the key ideological imperative of wartime cinema: asserting national unity and social cohesion in support of the war effort. It was for this reason that all references to internal dissent were excised from the film. The film has no room for the play's suggestion of revolt by 'the weasel Scots' or for the treachery of the 'three corrupted men'. Instead, the film emphasises unity, consciously interpreting the 'four captains' as an allegory of the home nations and casting them accordingly: English (Michael Shepley as Gower), Irish (Niall MacGinnis as Macmorris), Scottish (John Laurie as Jamy) and Welsh (Esmond Knight as Fluellen). The political entity of a United Kingdom had not existed in Shakespeare's day, of course, and to this extent these scenes, depicting an essential unity of purpose behind the good-natured joshing and rivalry, have greater resonance in the film.

The film also embodies the spirit of the 'people's war' in alluding to a shared kinship regardless of social status ('For he today that sheds his blood with me/Shall be my brother, be he ne'er so base'). A theme of the film is how, in adversity, the English/British find common purpose and a common bond.

As king, of course, Henry himself can never be entirely of the people, despite his own attempt to strip away the illusion of royalty in his discussion, while in mufti, with common soldier Michael Williams ('For I think the king is but a man as I am. The violet smells to him as it doth to me. His ceremonies laid by, in his nakedness he appears but a man'). Henry is reassured by the loyalty of his men, who make clear their willingness to fight if he requires it of them. *Henry V* is nothing if not a paen to leadership. Olivier's Henry is represented as an inspirational leader who rallies his men both in his words and in his actions (his duel with the Constable of France which decides the battle). His special status is asserted by camera shots during the battle that isolate Henry in the frame and thus present him as being apart from his men (Leni Reifenstahl had used much the same technique in *Triumph of the Will*). He is also associated with visual signifiers of England, sharing the shot with the Cross of St George (the standard that follows Henry throughout the battle). The imagery, both visual and verbal, works to represent Henry in chivalric mould as a knightly defender of his nation.

The representation of leadership also carries contemporary overtones. It was a shared characteristic of both British and German films during the war that they used biopics of past national leaders to allude to the present. Thus Hitler was represented on screen as Bismarck (*Bismarck*) and Frederick the Great (*The Great King*), while Churchill had already appeared in the guises of Disraeli (*The Prime Minister*) and William Pitt (*The Young Mr Pitt*). *Henry V* is the ultimate Churchillian film, not least because Henry's stirring orations are so similar in tone to Churchill's inspirational speeches. Churchill often resorted to quasi-Shakespearean rhetorical flourishes, in which, for example, 'men of arms' performed 'feats of valour'. There is evidence that Churchill, an avid film fan, saw and liked *Henry V*: Del Giudice reported that 'the Prime Minister...seems to have been enormously enthusiastic and wants to see the film again'.[71]

While *Henry V* extols the virtues of the English, however, it is less than charitable in its characterisation of the French. The French leaders, particularly the Dauphin, are arrogant and aloof, in contrast to Henry, who, even in his moment of victory, is humble. An exception is the Constable, who is prepared to die with honour ('Let life be short, else shame be long'). The inclusion of the scene where a group of French knights raid the English camp and kill all the boys attending the luggage (''Tis expressly against the law of arms') is clearly meant to imply parallels with German atrocities such as the massacres of Lidice and Oradour. Yet the represention of the French as the enemy was problematic when the film was shown in France two years after the war. An official of the Quai d'Orsay (the Ministry of Foreign Affairs) felt that the content of the film was 'extremely painful and almost intolerable' on account of its representation of 'the moral faults and weaknesses of the French'.[72] Olivier, who opposed all attempts to cut the film for overseas distribution, conceded over this particular case.[73] It was, perhaps, unfortunate that the French happened to be represented as the enemy, not least given the highly fractious relationship between Churchill and Free French leader Charles De Gaulle, though some of the play's most insulting lines about the French were cut and the resolution of the narrative is the sealing of a marriage alliance ''twixt England and fair France'.

For a film that is so notable for its martial and triumphalist tone, the fact that *Henry V* ends with a promise of the reconciliation of national enmities is significant. The vanquished enemy has become a friend; the alliance, symbolised in the marriage of Henry and Katharine, offers the promise of peace. This had always been in the film-makers' minds. Dent's working notes state: 'It may also be noted that although in the play our enemy, France, is necessarily somewhat traduced, the ultimate message which issues from it dictates the strongest grounds and sews the most promising seeds for the lasting friendship of the two nations.'[74] It is not entirely clear whether Dent was thinking of Anglo-French relations (the two countries signed a new alliance in 1947, the year that *Henry V* was released in France) or the possibility of a new Anglo-German accord after the war. However, there is no question that the resolution of the film – the total defeat of the enemy, followed by the forging of an alliance that linked the nations together – anticipated the geopolitical realignment of Europe after the end of the war. Germany was divided and, while the East came under Soviet political control, in the West a new democratic state was created with the establishment in 1949 of the Federal Republic of

Germany, which, within a few years, had joined NATO (North Atlantic Treaty Organisation) and would be a founding member of the European Common Market. While *Henry V* does not address the 'German question' as directly as films such as Humphrey Jennings's *A Defeated People* (1945), it does, nevertheless, allude to the issue of post-war policy and suggests that a more peaceful and stable future may result from the war.

The propagandist intent of *Henry V*, so crucial during its production in 1943–44, was, however, less significant when the film came to be released in America, almost a year after the end of the war in Europe. The war was won and there was no longer any need to persuade the Americans, or anyone else for that matter, of the moral fibre and fighting spirit of Great Britain. Instead, *Henry V* was to serve a different purpose: to fly the flag for the British film industry as part of Rank's attempt to open up the American market for British films. There is evidence, indeed, that the film was seen as a potential flagship of Rank's American strategy almost two years before it finally reached the United States. As early as July 1944, months before the film was even released in Britain, E.T. Carr was writing to Arthur Kelly of United Artists to tell him that '*Henry V* is one of the greatest productions that has ever been made from an entertainment and technical point of view, and coming out of a British Studio, working under the difficulties we are all experiencing at the moment, it is an achievement nothing short of miraculous'. It is evident that Carr was trying to sell the film as a harbinger of things to come: 'I am sure you can readily visualise, if this is the sort of product our Group are turning out now, what Mr Rank will do when the war is over.'[75] Just as Henry's army had conquered France, so, now, it was believed, would *Henry V* conquer the American market.

The critical reception of *Henry V* in the United States was generally positive, with the film being much admired by middlebrow critics who responded to its status as 'art'. For Bosley Crowther it was 'a stunningly brilliant and intriguing screen spectacle, rich in theatrical invention, in heroic imagery and also gracefully regardful of the conventions of the Elizabethan stage'.[76] Charles Faber in the *Hollywood Review* called it 'a masterpiece of unexampled integrity'.[77] One of the film's greatest admirers was James Agee, whose review for *Time* magazine declared: 'The movies have produced one of their great works of art.'[78] Agee was so overwhelmed by the film that in another review, this time for the *Nation*, he wrote: 'I am not a Tory, a monarchist, a catholic, a medievalist, an Englishman, or, despite all the good that it engenders, a lover of war; but the beauty and power of this traditional exercise was such that, watching it, I wished I was, thought I was, and was proud of it.'[79] Amid the hyperbole, however, a cautionary note was sounded by *Variety*, which, while admiring the production values and artistic ambitions of the film, added that 'it will go right over the average audience'.[80]

The popular reception of *Henry V* followed a similar pattern to that in Britain. It was most successful in large metropolitan centres, where it was shown at up-market cinemas, playing to packed houses at the Esquire Theatre in Boston, and running for 46 consecutive weeks at the New York City Centre on Broadway – a record for a British film. United Artists, which handled the American distribution, adopted a release strategy 'that depended less on general release and more on selective roadshow programming aimed primarily at schools and the educated audience'.[81] However, Olivier again had to defend the film from what he regarded as the cultural philistinism of the distributors, who wanted to shorten it by cutting all the scenes featuring the character of Pistol: 'Those critics and friends of the classics and students in every single university in the United States, whom we now stand a chance to gain as friends of British pictures, will be irreparably lost if we do anything so inartistic as to try and present a Shakespearean play without one of the chief characters in an obvious effort to gain commercial prestige.'[82]

The circumstances of its release in America turned *Henry V* into a site of contestation between, on one level, culture and commerce, and, on another level, the British film industry and Hollywood. *Henry V* won the first round in the contest when it was voted best picture of 1946 (and Olivier the best actor) by the National Board of Review of Motion Pictures (ahead of *Rome, Open City*, *The Best Years of Our Lives* and *Brief Encounter*). This gave Rank hope that *Henry V* would repeat its success at the annual Academy Awards in March 1947. Jerry Dale of Rank's New York office averred that 'we are doing a great deal of propagandising of the Academy of Arts and Sciences [*sic*] and will do all we can to keep them fully aware of "Henry"'. However, he added: 'It seems to be some sort of a conclusion that Goldwyn's picture "Best Years" will get the Academy Award, although we still hope right will prevail and "Henry" will get it. Undoubtedly Olivier will get the best acting honor.'[83] In the event *The Best Years of Our Lives* won seven Academy Awards including Best Film, Best Director (William Wyler), Best Screenplay (Robert E. Sherwood) and Best Actor (Fredric March). Dale suggested there had been a conspiracy to prevent *Henry V* from winning and that the special award for Olivier arose from a guilty conscience within the Academy: 'Naturally, we are simply livid with rage at the whole thing. It was certainly a "stop Britain at any price" year in Hollywood... I am sure the good men of the Academy must have been embarrassed over the lack of votes by the Hollywood contingent for "Henry" and decided to do the next best thing.'[84] The Academy of Motion Picture Arts and Sciences, it seems, was a more implacable foe for *Henry V* than the French had been.

That said, however, there is no question that *Henry V* was a significant success in the American market. It was one of several British films of the late 1940s (all backed by Rank) that grossed over $1 million in the United States, others include *Caesar and Cleopatra*, *The Red Shoes* and *Hamlet*.[85] The success of *Henry V* was all the more remarkable given the sometimes difficult relations that existed between Britain and Hollywood at the time: the imposition of an *ad valorem* duty on film imports by the Chancellor of the Exchequer, Hugh Dalton, in August 1947 had brought about a retaliatory boycott of the British market by the Motion Picture Export Association, the overseas arm of the US Motion Picture Producers and Distributors Association, until the duty was removed nine months later. However, it is ironic that those who reaped the success of *Henry V* were not those who had made it, including Del Giudice who had left Two Cities, but the distributors (both British and American) who had wanted to cut it. Thus, of the film's $965,686 gross receipts in America by September 1947, United Artists claimed $246,551 and, following expenses and deductions, some $632,082 (£157,145) was remitted to Britain.[86] Despite the reports of its record-breaking grosses, it was not until 1949 that *Henry V* showed a profit on GFD's books; even then the percentage of profits owed to Olivier was a cause of much dispute with the Rank Organisation.[87]

The Academy Awards that had been denied *Henry V* were forthcoming for *Hamlet* (1948), which won for Best Picture (the first such honour for a British film) and Best Actor. *Hamlet* reunited most of the production team of *Henry V*, including Olivier as actor-director, Alan Dent, William Walton, Roger Furse and Carmen Dillon.

Hamlet might be regarded as better Shakespeare than *Henry V* but is certainly less effective cinema: attempting to create atmosphere, the camera spends excessive time wandering around the corridors and ramparts of the castle of Elsinore. Nevertheless, its grosses in the United States ($3,250,000) proved that *Henry V* had been no fluke and that a market could be found for Shakeapearean cinema if properly handled.[88] The third film in Olivier's Shakespearean trilogy was *Richard III* (1955), made this time for London Films, again in association with Dent, Walton, Furse and Dillon. *Richard III* to some extent repeats the formal and aesthetic strategy of *Henry V*, with stylised sets followed by a realistic staging of the Battle of Bosworth, though it is chiefly notable for Olivier's marvellously grotesque performance as the hunch-backed king.

It was in the year of Olivier's death, 1989, that his cinematic masterpiece was remade by the actor probably most deserving of the 'new Olivier' tag. Like Olivier, Kenneth Branagh chose *Henry V* for his first film project and also directed as well as playing Henry. And, like Olivier, Branagh had previously played the role on stage, in a 1984 production for the Royal Shakespeare Company (most of the cast reprise their roles for the film). There, however, the comparisons end. Branagh's *Henry V*, produced by his own company, Renaissance Films, in association with the BBC and the Samuel Goldwyn Company, is very different in conception and style from Olivier's. In particular, Branagh distanced himself from the overt propaganda of the earlier film: 'The more I thought about it, the more convinced I became that here was a play to be reclaimed from jingoism and its World War Two associations.'[89] Branagh's film has often been compared unfavourably with Olivier's. As a film, indeed, it is technically less adventurous, though to be fair to Branagh he did have not anything like the budget available to Olivier. The fact is that both films are adaptations of the play, informed by and responding to the times in which they were made; neither should be regarded as the definitive version. In its own way Branagh's *Henry V* is just as much a product of its own time (post-Falklands, Thatcherite Britain) as Olivier's had been. A comparison between the two films reveals how the same source material may be intepreted in radically different ways, depending upon the contexts of production.[90]

In many respects Branagh's film is the complete opposite of Olivier's: anti-heroic rather than heroic, sombre rather than triumphalist, intimate rather than spectacular, realistic rather than stylised. It is darker in tone, not only visually but also in terms of performance. Branagh restores many of the textual cuts made by Olivier, reinserting the Cambridge–Grey–Scroop conspiracy and featuring the hanging of Bardolph for looting. There is a fuller engagement with the rationale for going to war and an implicit parallel is made between the reasons of the bishops for supporting Henry's campaign against France (to divert attention from the idea of confiscating Church lands) and the idea (seriously mooted by some on the left) that the Thatcher government had engineered the Falklands War in order to divert attention from unemployment and social problems at home. Branagh makes the occasional homage to Olivier, for example in filming the Crispin's Day speech with Henry standing on a cart, but his understated, naturalistic performance style is very different from Olivier's highly theatrical bombast. In contrast to Olivier's declamation of the set-piece orations, there is a sense in which the more quietly spoken Branagh is pleading with his men to fight rather than inspiring them to do so. And Patrick Doyle's music, conducted by Simon Rattle, is elegaic and lyrical in contrast to the triumphalism of Walton.

The major difference between the two films, however, is in their staging of the Battle of Agincourt. If Olivier's Agincourt had been modelled on Eisenstein's *Alexander Nevsky*, then Branagh's is closer to Akira Kurosawa's *Seven Samurai*: a bloody and brutal affair, fought in the mud and rain and using slow-motion sequences. Here there are no neat lines of knights, their spotless armour gleaming in the sunshine. Instead, the battle lines collapse into a *mêlée* of confusion in which it is difficult to distinguish one side from the other. It is almost certainly closer to the historical reality of a medieval battle than Olivier's: there are scenes of throats being cut and of the looting of the dead. Henry himself does not stand apart from his men as in the Olivier film but fights among them, his face and tunic splattered with mud, throwing himself in rage upon the French herald when he discovers the killing of the luggage boys. Agincourt may be a victory, but it is hardly a triumph: the English troops are too exhausted to celebrate their victory and the playing of *Non nobis* as they march away is more of a lament than a celebration.

The extent to which *Henry V* can be interpreted as a tract for the times in which it is performed was demonstrated again in the spring of

2003. Nicholas Hytner's modern-dress production for the National Theatre, with Adrian Lester as Henry, was a conscious allegory of the Anglo-American war to 'liberate' Iraq from the dictatorship of Saddam Hussein. Act I of the play, in which Henry and his courtiers debate the legal case for the invasion of France, was performed so as to highlight the contemporary parallels as Britain and the United States failed to secure the approval of the United Nations Security Council for their invasion of Iraq. The production emphasised that Henry's invasion of France, far from being defensive, is an act of territorial aggression against a sovereign nation. Lester played Henry as a ruthless and brutal warlord who, in the last act, virtually forces himself on a terrified Princess Katharine. A more different interpretation from Olivier's Henry could hardly be imagined, yet both were based on the same source material. To this extent, the criticisms of Shakespearean purists that Olivier's film is a very selective interpretation of *Henry V* in cutting large swathes of the text rather misses the point: Hytner's production was equally selective in emphasising particular aspects of the play. Much of the enduring fascination of Shakespeare is that his work remains relevant to successive generations. It was with good reason that Jan Kott entitled the English version of his book *Shakespeare – Our Contemporary* (1965). And the themes of patriotism, war and leadership that inform *Henry V* were never more relevant than in the embattled and war-torn Britain of 1944.

6

The Dunkirk Spirit:
Scott of the Antarctic (1948)

S COTT of the Antarctic, directed by Charles Frend for Ealing Studios, can be seen, like *Henry V*, as an example of the British 'prestige' film of the 1940s. It was an expensive production, made in Technicolor and featuring extensive overseas locations; a score was commissioned from Ralph Vaughan Williams, which the composer subsequently used as the basis of his Seventh Symphony (*Sinfonia Antarctica*); the film was chosen as the third Royal Command Film Performance and was the subject of a commemorative book about its making. It is a well-known film, but has not received a great deal of critical attention.[1] Its relative neglect, rather like the British war films of the 1950s with which it bears a number of affinities, can probably be explained by its ideological and aesthetic conservatism. *Scott of the Antarctic* is the example *par excellence* of what the intellectual French journal *Cahiers du Cinéma* called 'la convention anglaise': a sober, unsensational narrative of emotional restraint and a visual style that strictly enforces realism and authenticity.[2] This is a style of cinema that has fallen from favour in the wake of the critical reclamation of more sensational fare such as the Gainsborough costume melodramas and the Hammer horror films, and the attention given to flamboyant individual film-makers such as Michael Powell and Ken Russell. It was Russell, indeed, who derided *Scott of the Antarctic* as a film in which 'half a dozen thick Brits pull a sled halfway across Antarctica, in order to plant a Union Jack at the South Pole'.[3]

Ealing Studios, along with Gainsborough, and later Hammer, was one of several medium-sized independent (or semi-independent) British film companies that owned their own production facilities but relied on the larger circuits for the distribution and exhibition of their films. A film studio had been built in the West London suburb of Ealing by Will Barker, the early British pioneer, before the First World War, though the facility which subsequently became known as Ealing Studios was built at the beginning of the 1930s by theatre producer Basil Dean and his accountant partner R.P. Baker, to act as a permanent production base for their company, Associated Talking Pictures (ATP). Dean had ambitions to make quality film adaptations of plays and novels – *Lorna Doone* (dir. Basil Dean, 1934) and *Midshipman Easy* (dir. Carol Reed, 1935) were probably the most successful examples of this policy – but ATP achieved its biggest popular acclaim with two cycles of low-budget, lowbrow star vehicles for music-hall artistes Gracie Fields and George Formby. By the late 1930s, however, ATP's fortunes were in decline and Dean returned to his first career in the theatre. He was replaced by Michael Balcon, who, after his brief and unhappy stint at MGM-British, moved to Ealing, first as a tenant producer – his first film at the studio was an Edgar Wallace adaptation, *The Gaunt Stranger* (dir. Walter Forde, 1938) – and then as Head of Production. 'By this time, I was convinced that my future lay with Ealing', Balcon confided in his autobiography. 'The studio was ideal, I got on well with everybody there, and, of course, above everything else was the pleasure of renewing my relationship with [Reg] Baker in a partnership which continued, through good times and bad, until the end of 1958.'[4] Associated Talking Pictures was renamed Ealing Studios early in 1940 and one of the most celebrated chapters in British cinema history was about to begin.

Balcon's production policy initially maintained some continuity with Dean's – star vehicles for comedians George Formby and Will Hay proliferated between 1939 and 1942 – though there were also early examples of the sort of realistic films for which Ealing would become known during the war, notably *There Ain't No Justice* and *The Proud Valley*. After producing the critically derided but very popular patriotic flag-wavers *Convoy* and *Ships With Wings*, Ealing switched direction with a series of more realistic war films notable for their qualities of emotional restraint and sober heroics: *The Foreman Went to France*, *Went the Day Well?*, *Nine Men*, *The Bells Go Down* and *San Demetrio, London*. Films such as these exemplified the 'wartime wedding' between commercial feature film production and the realistic style of the documentary school, not least because Balcon recruited two leading documentarists, Alberto Cavalcanti and Harry Watt, to work at Ealing. Ealing came to be known as 'the studio with the team spirit' and the majority of its films during and after the war were made by a small nucleus of directors (Harry Watt, Charles Frend, Charles Crichton, Basil Dearden, Robert Hamer and Alexander Mackendrick) and writers (Roger Macdougall, Angus Macphail, John Dighton, Diana Morgan, Monja Danischewsky and T.E.B. Clarke).[5] There were also common themes running through Ealing's films which extolled the values of community, tolerance, decency, duty and public service. It is a consistent and identifiable studio ethos which crosses generic boundaries, from war films to comedies, and which represents a distinct production ideology.

Balcon claimed in his autobiography that 'my ruling passion has always been the building up of a native industry with its roots firmly planted in the soil of this country'.[6] It is a claim that requires some qualification: his production policy at Gaumont-British, after all, had been based around the notion of 'internationalism', in common with other major British producers of the 1930s. At Ealing, however, Balcon came to focus increasingly on films that were essentially national both in subject matter and in treatment. Writing in *Sight and Sound* in 1941, he expressed an entirely different point of view from that which he had held only five years earlier: 'The British producer can make no greater mistake than to have the American market in mind when planning and costing a picture. Not in that way will the British film ever become representative of British culture.'[7] Through-out the war he was a passionate advocate of a British national cinema that was different from Hollywood and an outspoken critic of the Rank Organisation that he felt had become too powerful for the good of the industry – though, ironically, from 1944 Ealing was dependent upon Rank for distribution and part-financing of its films. Balcon, in common with the middlebrow film critics of the time, undoubtedly believed that 'it is the influence of realism on the British film in wartime which has given it its new and individual character and which has weaned it away from being an amateur and clumsy pastiche of its Hollywood counterpart'.[8]

The most celebrated of Ealing's post-war films, without any

question, are the classic comedies made between the late 1940s and the mid-1950s, including *Passport to Pimlico*, *Whisky Galore!*, *Kind Hearts and Coronets*, *The Lavender Hill Mob*, *The Man in the White Suit*, *The Titfield Thunderbolt*, *The Maggie* and *The Ladykillers*. Although there are significant differences between individual films in the canon, this group of films have so often been grouped together that the term 'Ealing comedy' – like 'Gainsborough melodrama' and 'Hammer horror' – has become a shorthand for a particular style of film, in this case one characterised by its whimsical humour and nostalgic picture of an idealised, imaginary nation of stubborn eccentrics and harmless anarchists.[9] The reason why the Ealing comedies have received so much attention within British film historiography is that they were, and are, central to a particular critical project to construct a national cinema based around their typically 'English' qualities. It must be remembered, however, that the famous comedies were numerically in a minority among Ealing's entire output during these years and that they constituted only part of a balanced production programme that also included war films (*Against the Wind*, *The Cruel Sea*), costume dramas (*Pink String and Sealing Wax*, *Saraband for Dead Lovers*), literary adaptations (*Nicholas Nickleby*, *The Loves of Joanna Godden*), contemporary crime films (*The Blue Lamp*, *Pool of London*), social problem films (*I Believe in You*, *Mandy*), portmanteau films (*Dead of Night*, *Train of Events*), Australian 'outback westerns' (*The Overlanders*, *Eureka Stockade*) and colonial adventure films (*Where No Vultures Fly*, *West of Zanzibar*). Ealing's post-war production policy, indeed, fulfils what Balcon had stated in 1945 as his aim that 'the world...must be presented with a complete picture of Britain'. This 'complete picture' included 'Britain as a leader in Social Reform in the defeat of social injustices and a champion of civil liberties; Britain as a patron and parent of great writing, painting and music; Britain as a questing explorer, adventurer and trader; Britain as the home of great industry and craftsmanship; Britain as a mighty military power standing alone and undaunted against terrifying aggression'.[10]

Balcon's declaration of his production policy was made in response to a plan by the MOI 'to flood liberated Europe with films' that would be 'official screen documents of what we have achieved and to what we aspire'. The Labour government elected in 1945, while dismantling the MOI, nevertheless held similar views about the role of film in the projection of Britain. There was, however, a shift of emphasis from the overt propaganda of films like *Henry V*. Sir Stafford Cripps was one of several Labour ministers who took a keen interest in the film industry, telling a Rank Organisation meeting in 1947: 'It is not propaganda that we want in our films, but a national interpretation of what is good and interesting, amusing and hopeful in our cultural and historical heritage.'[11] As President of the Board of Trade, Cripps drafted a far-ranging government plan to assist the film industry, including the provision of finance for independent producers and the promotion of documentary and educational films, but the scheme foundered in the face of opposition from the Treasury, which remained hostile to the idea of subsidising commercial film production.[12]

Scott of the Antarctic, clearly, represents Ealing's projection of 'Britain as a questing explorer'. The story of Captain Robert Falcon Scott and his ill-fated expedition to reach the South Pole in 1912 had made a deep and lasting impression on the public imagination. It was a story that had the hallmarks of both tragedy and triumph: a tragedy in so far as Scott and his companions were beaten in their attempt to be the first men to the Pole by a rival Norwegian expedition led by Roald Amundsen and then perished from cold and starvation on their return journey, yet curiously also a triumph of the human spirit and personal courage in the face of overwhelming adversity. The discovery of Scott's journals and their publication in 1913 contributed to the mythologising of the doomed expedition: the discovery that they had been beaten to the Pole ('It is a terrible disappointment, and I am very sorry for my loyal companions'); the arduous trek back towards their base camp ('We've had a horrid day and not covered good mileage'); the death from frostbite of Petty Officer Evans ('It is a terrible thing to lose a companion in this way, but calm reflection shows that there could not have been a better ending to the terrible anxieties of the past week'); the heroic self-sacrifice of Captain Oates ('He said, "I am just going outside and may be some time." He went out into the blizzard and we have not seen him since') and Scott's realisation that his own death and those of his remaining companions were not far away ('I do not think we can hope for any better things now. We shall stick it out to the end, but we are getting weaker, and the end cannot be far'). In particular, Scott's journals and the letters he wrote for family and friends reveal a sense of patriotism that is entirely in accord with the age in which he lived. To his wife, Kathleen, Scott wrote that 'we have given our lives for our

country – we have actually made the longest journey on record, and we
have been the first Englishmen at the South Pole'. To his friend J.M.
Barrie, he wrote: 'We are showing that Englishmen can still die with a
bold spirit, fighting it out to the end...I think this makes an example
for Englishmen of the future, and that the country ought to help those
who are left behind to mourn us.' The last entry in Scott's journal was:
'For God's sake look after our people.'[13]

Scott's expedition had been accompanied by a photographer and
cinematographer, Herbert G. Ponting, who took a Newman-Sinclair
camera specially adapted to function in the Antarctic. Ponting exposed
some 25,000 feet of film as well as taking hundreds of still photographs
in making a pictorial record of the expedition that was shown to the
public at home in several different versions. *With Captain Scott to the
South Pole*, released by Gaumont, opened in London on 16 November
1911 while Scott was still making for the Pole – Ponting had gone as far
as the Great Ice Barrier – and was shown in America in 1912. Following
Scott's death Ponting bought the rights to the Gaumont film and used
it in lectures. He released a feature-length version under the title *The
Great White Silence* in 1924 and a re-edited sound version, with his own
commentary, as *90° South* in 1933. The latter film was introduced by
Vice-Admiral E.R.G.R. Evans, who, as Lieutenant Evans, had been
Scott's deputy and had later served with distinction in the First World
War. It is essentially a travelogue and nature documentary, showing the
outward journey of Scott's expedition on the *Terra Nova* and including
much footage of seals and penguins in their natural habitat. It is
characterised by some breathtaking shots of the Antarctic landscape;
one particular image – a shot of the *Terra Nova* taken from inside a
cavern of ice – is so striking that it was reconstructed in colour, through
a matte painting, for the Ealing film. For the final attempt to reach the
Pole, the film uses maps and extracts from Scott's journals – these
techniques would be employed again in the Ealing film – and the
commentary stresses the patriotism of Scott and his companions.
Ponting avers that they met their end 'happy in the knowledge that they
died for the honour of their country'. Ponting intended that *90° South*
should be 'an historical national possession' and a copy was accepted by
the Duke of York on behalf of the British Film Institute. Ponting died
in 1935, however, without ever having made any profit from his various
Antarctic presentations.[14]

The initiative to make *Scott of the Antarctic*, according to Balcon,

came from director Charles Frend. Frend had started as an editor at
Gaumont-British in the 1930s, working with Hitchcock on several
films, before joining Ealing as a director in 1941, where his films
before *Scott* were *The Foreman Went to France*, *San Demetrio,
London*, *Johnny Frenchman* and *The Loves of Joanna Godden*. Balcon
wrote that Frend 'had been looking for a long time for a subject of
genuinely epic dimensions and in Scott's last expedition he found it'.[15]
Although a film about Captain Scott had been suggested by Sir
Kenneth Clark in 1940, it is easy to see why, as a story ending in
failure, such a film was not made during the war. It was only after the
war, moreover, that overseas shooting on the sort of locations required
for *Scott* could be undertaken. A small camera unit was sent to
Antarctica late in 1946, before a script had been prepared, to shoot
'atmospheric scenes that we shall need in any case'.[16] The draft script
was prepared jointly by Walter Meade and Ivor Montagu. Meade was
a former Indian army cavalry officer and African tobacco farmer who
joined Ealing as a writer in the 1930s on the strength of having been
stage manager for some of Basil Dean's productions at the Drury Lane
Theatre. Montagu, the socialist son of Lord and Lady Swaythling, was
a leading figure in the progressive film movement of the interwar
years, co-founding the Film Society in London in 1925 and translating
Eisenstein's writings into English; he worked at Gainsborough in the
1920s and at Gaumont-British during the 1930s, where he
collaborated with Hitchcock as associate producer of *The 39 Steps*,
Secret Agent and *Sabotage*. Montagu's notes suggest that he mapped
out the dramatic structure of the film while Mead concentrated on the
research.[17] Montagu originally envisaged including more of Scott's
domestic life, including his first meeting with Kathleen and his
proposal on the Solent, and had more details of the outward voyage
where the *Terra Nova* runs into a storm. Associate producer Sidney
Cole – an Ealing veteran who, like Montagu, was a left-wing activist,
having worked with Thorold Dickinson on his documentaries about
the Spanish Civil War, and who was a leading figure in the Association
of Cine Technicians – felt that the script need pruning. 'I am still
concerned about the length of the script and anything you can do to
get it down without losing the facts that we agreed on, will be
gratefully received and certainly by Mick', he told Montagu in
October 1947, when location filming was already underway in
Norway.[18] The finished script was revised by Cole and Frend and an

'additional dialogue' credit was accorded to playwright Mary Haley Bell, wife of star John Mills who had been cast as Scott.

The exteriors for *Scott of the Antarctic* were shot in Switzerland (where the Aletsch glacier stood in for the Beardmore glacier in the Antarctic) and Norway (where the high, flat plateau of Hardanger Jøkel was used to replicate the landscape around the South Pole itself). The Norwegian locations, especially, were extremely difficult, though this was to work to the film's advantage in so far as the actors look as if they are enduring the same sort of physical hardships as Scott and his men. The studio interiors were shot between New Year and Easter 1948.[19] At a cost of £371,588, *Scott of the Antarctic* was Ealing's most expensive production to date (the costume melodrama *Saraband for Dead Lovers*, made concurrently with *Scott*, and also in Technicolor, was only slightly less costly) and almost twice the average amount of an Ealing feature in the late 1940s.[20] It was a considerable strain on the studio's resources, as Balcon admitted in a letter to Mills:

> It is true that we are really a single-picture outfit here and there is always a little difficulty in raising two absolutely first-class units at the same time, but we thought we had done everything possible in the case of 'Scott'. The trouble was that we were always bound by seasonal demands and were not able to wait until it was the most convenient time for us to tackle the picture...I want you to know that 'Scott' is recognised as the most important picture we have ever tackled. It is the one nearest to all our hearts and nothing will be left undone which can make things go smoothly.[21]

The necessity of undertaking location shooting first, so that studio interiors could be matched to the exteriors, had meant that the Norwegian unit had to film in autumn, when the climatic conditions were deteriorating, rather than in spring, when they would have been improving.

Scott's expedition, in the words of David James – a member of the British Antarctic Survey who was employed as technical adviser for the film, was 'a story particularly British and particularly well suited to film presentation'.[22] The producers went to greater lengths than ever to ensure authenticity. Relatives and survivors of the expedition were consulted, including Lord Mountevans (as Lieutenant Evans now was), zoologist Apsley Cherry-Garrard and geologist Professor Frank

Debenham (now Director of the Scott Polar Institute at Cambridge). Ealing's art department even consulted Norwegian astronomer Professor Karl Störmer, a leading authority on the Aurora Borealis, about the likely appearance of the night sky over Antarctica in 1912.[23] Actors were chosen for their physical resemblance to the characters, including John Mills as Scott and, as his four companions in the final dash for the Pole, Harold Warrender as Dr Wilson, Reginald Beckwith as 'Birdie' Bowers, Derek Bond as 'Soldier' Oates and James Roberston Justice as 'Taff' Evans. The group shot of the party at the Pole is modelled directly on the actual photograph taken there by Bowers. This extreme commitment to authenticity was integral to the film, though there were some, including Mills, who felt that it was dramatically limiting. After seeing a rough cut, Mills complained to Cole that 'it has Documentary stamped all over it. We must, of course, be honest and true to the original story, which is magnificent, but we must also see to it that it is entertainment with a capital E...I am sure that the Public must be moved by the Film and not merely interested and at times fascinated by something curiously remote and apart from them.'[24] In expressing his reservations Mills anticipated the reactions of some critics to the film.

Mills later said that he found Scott 'a fascinatingly complex character' but felt that he was unable 'to delve more deeply' into his personality 'because of the possibility of upsetting characters still living'.[25] There is every indication that the film met with the approval of the relatives and survivors. Balcon averred that Scott's widow, Lady Kennet as she now was, gave her 'passionate support for the project'.[26] 'In so far as I can be said to represent the Scott group,' Frank Debenham told Balcon, 'may I thank you on [their] behalf for both undertaking the film and selecting such good people to make it what it is, a true and restrained picture of what happened, paying visual tribute to the memory of that five.'[27] This verdict must have been music to Balcon's ears as terms like 'true' and 'restrained' were very much in tune with the realist critical discourse that dominated British film culture in the 1940s. He replied that 'I have never been happier than when working on *Scott of the Antarctic*, and what is more, I have a conviction that it will be appreciated, not only through the length and breadth of this land, but throughout the world wherever English speaking films are played'.[28]

There is much evidence, also, to suggest that *Scott of the Antarctic* met with official approval. It had been applauded by the BBFC, whose script examiner had proclaimed it 'a magnificent film' and 'a monumental story'.[29] When it was chosen as the Royal Command Film Performance for 1948, the chairman of the selection committee revealed that 'not only was our decision unanimous but it was reached practically instantaneously'. Sir Henry French evidently approved of its celebration of courage and the national character: 'I felt as your film reached the inevitable end that there was more cause for pride that our nation had produced those five men than for grief that they had met their end in such a heroic effort.'[30] J. Arthur Rank, who had backed the production financially and would handle its distribution, wrote a warm note to Balcon to say that 'I enjoyed "Scott" very much indeed – there were some really great moments & I am sure it will entertain & uplift'. 'In my view,' he added, 'we will be able to road show it in America & I believe it will do very well.'[31] Rank's view of the uplifting qualities of *Scott of the Antarctic* were shared by the Christian Cinema and Religious Film Society, which promoted films that endorsed Christian values:

> It is part of the duty of the Christian Cinema and Religious Film Society to bring to your notice films upholding Christian Ideals, and we consider that *Scott of the Antarctic* is a subject worthy of your recommendation. Much has been said by Christian people throughout the country in criticism of the films which are being shown on the screens of our Cinemas, but little is, in fact, being done about it. We believe that if films of the standard of *Scott of the Antarctic* are given the support of those who hold to such standards, they will have considerable effect in convincing the film producers that there is a public for something better than the films which sometimes bring discredit upon the film industry.[32]

There was a range of critical responses to the film. The most positive reviews, on the whole responding to the story rather than to the technical or aesthetic qualities of the film, came from the popular press. There were some reviewers for whom *Scott of the Antarctic* represented nothing less than a tribute to all that they perceived was best about the British character. Ewart Hodgson in the *News of the World* was one of its champions, declaring 'that the very nature of the characters in the story and the way they behave and talk is so British as to be beyond the comprehension of anyone not born in this country and brought up in accordance with our way of life...*Scott of the Antarctic* is a towering motion picture that could only have been made by Britons.'[33] Elspeth Grant in the *Daily Graphic* 'felt very proud' having watched it and declared: 'If you can look at this honest, undemonstrative, unboastful account of a great though lost endeavour, chivalrously undertaken and carried out with loyalty, courage and almost unbelievable hardihood and fortitude by men of your nation, without feeling an upsurge of pride – then I wonder at you.'[34] The *Sunday Dispatch* saw the film as a riposte to those who believed that Britain was a nation in decline: 'Such a film as *Scott* is welcome at a time when other races speak disparagingly of our "crumbling Empire" and our "lack of spirit". It should make those who have listened too closely to such talk believe afresh that ours is the finest breed of men on this earth.'[35] The reference to a 'crumbling Empire' is almost certainly a reference to the loss of India – long regarded as the 'jewel in the crown' of the British Empire – which had become independent in August 1947.

The middlebrow critics, as would be expected, approved of its semi-documentary style and its quality of emotional restraint. Dilys Powell, comparing it favourably with the Crown Film Unit's wartime Technicolor documentary *Western Approaches* (dir. Pat Jackson, 1944), felt that 'for once we have a film of an episode in history without resort to heroics. The success of this plain reconstruction is the justification of the documentary style in the commercial cinema.'[36] *The Times* reviewed the film twice and on both occasions lauded its authenticity: 'Perhaps we shall praise the film most in saying that it nowhere, neither in fact nor in sentiment, seems to run counter to Scott's journals'; the second review 'confirms the first impression of its fidelity to Scott's journals, and also of the restraint with which the film had avoided the obvious temptation of intruding false sentiment into its account of the final stages of the journey'.[37] This view was shared, perhaps surprisingly, by the *Daily Worker*, mouthpiece of the Communist Party of Great Britain and hardly renowned for its support for British imperial heroes. Yet its film critic of the time, Honor Arundel, declared that 'it is the documentary quality of *Scott of the Antarctic* which makes it one of the best British films I have seen for a long time. The technique of letting facts speak for themselves, of having a group of actors who really subordinate their personalities to their parts, of having dialogue and setting both inobtrusive in their very authenticity – all this is in the traditions of inspired documentary.'[38] For these critics, therefore, *Scott of the Antarctic* was seen as the legacy of the 'wartime wedding' between the documentary and the commercial feature film and exhibited the characteristics that had been so admired in wartime cinema.

There were various other critics, however, who, echoing John Mills, felt that 'inspired documentary' on its own was insufficient and found the film wanting on a dramatic level. C.A. Lejeune, surprisingly, thought that moments such as the discovery that Scott's party had been beaten to the South Pole and the death of Captain Oates were 'less effective because both these points are deliberately underplayed. No doubt this reticence is true to fact, but it weakens the piece by robbing it of legitimate dramatic climax, and, in weakening the piece, diminishes the heroes' own stature.'[39] Matthew Norgate in the *Tribune* also felt that the deaths of the protagonists 'could have been made a series of climaxes if they had been portrayed more dramatically than was aesthetically permissible...British understatement, in fact, becomes a greater handicap than ice and blizzard.'[40] The *Daily Telegraph* concurred: 'The commendable intention to avoid melodrama at all costs has, perhaps, been paid for too dearly: the genuinely dramatic has been avoided also. A continuously stiff upper lip, so useful at minus 40 deg F., becomes on the screen less of an asset.'[41]

Some reviews complained that the film did not provide any insight into its characters. The *Sunday Graphic* felt that 'the screen-writers have made the mistake of concentrating too much on Scott's epic march to the South Pole and too little on the men who made it'.[42] The *Evening Standard* agreed that 'both camera and script have concentrated so intensely on the Antarctic journey itself that the men have lost their individuality in the process'. It went on: 'Had I known why Oates had come all the way from India, something about the background of Bowers and Evans, and what the scientist Wilson was doing in the Antarctic I could have shared and appreciated their aims and desires.'[43] In fact, scenes of Oates in India and of Bowers in the Persian Gulf hearing of the expedition and deciding to volunteer were included in the final script and in all probability were shot, but were cut from the finished film.

The specialist journals were more favourably inclined towards the film. The *Monthly Film Bulletin* thought it 'an outstanding film and a fine tribute to the men who participated'. It felt that the exterior cinematography 'will rank as some of the finest ever seen'.[44] Arthur Vesselo, in his quarterly survey of recent films for *Sight and Sound*, averred 'that I would claim the "Scott" film to be one of the best of its kind ever made'. 'At a moment when British film-making is in the throes of crisis,' he added, 'I think it just to signal here my own appeciation (for what little it may be worth) of a major British film.'[45] And Roger Manvell admired both the aesthetic qualities and the emotional pull of the film:

> The effect is austere, noble and impressive. The icy wastes freeze you with their terrible beauty, while the music expresses distance and grandeur. When the last moments are reached, the canvas of the little tent whips in the wind, and the four men lie looking up into the slender, shaking cone of the narrow shelter that holds out the blizzard. The great emptiness outside is narrowed to four, and then to three men huddled together, each writing his last message to his wife or his mother and then lying down to sleep or die. This is the most perfectly handled dramatic moment in the film, and it does not depend this once on landscape, colour or music; it is a simple studio sequence.[46]

'I prophesy a long life and world festival honours for *Scott of the Antarctic*', Manvell added. 'It shows more clearly than most films the co-operative nature of film-making and the lengths to which a studio team is prepared to go when they undertake a subject which inspires their respect.'

In the event, *Scott of the Antarctic* did not win any major honours – the British Film Academy Award for Best British Film that year went to Carol Reed's *The Fallen Idol* – and its record at the box office was solid rather than spectacular. It was listed among the notable attractions of 1949 by the trade press, but even so returned only £214,223 (under three-fifths of its production cost).[47] Despite Rank's prediction of success, it failed to make any impact in America, a failure which Balcon attributed to its subject matter: 'The American public has no interest in failure, even if it is a heroic failure, and certainly they do not easily accept other people's legends.'[48] The American critics had been lukewarm. Even Bosley Crowther, who admired it, conceded that 'this is not the sort of picture one should choose for a jolly good time'.[49] There is evidence to suggest, however, that it was appreciated in the Soviet Union, where it was shown to workers' film clubs as well as at a diplomatic function in Moscow to which leading Russian film-makers were invited. 'Unfortunately Pudovkin was down with a cold and unable to come,' Montagu reported, 'but Dovchenko and others were there, and the former obviously liked it very much, praising it as a British tribute to a national historical example of our own of the fortitude of man, and particularly praising Charles Frend's big close-ups from the return journey onward, pointing out that these give the film its reality and human content, bringing to life the significance of the landscapes.'[50]

Scott of the Antarctic was indeed conceived as 'a national historical example ... of the fortitude of man'. It is an epic in the literal sense of the Latin epos: a narrative that celebrates heroic endeavour and achievement. Ivor Montagu's working notes indicate that the theme of the film was the contest between man and the environment: 'Introducing the Antarctic – its mystery and power. Introducing Scott, destined from youth to combat it, the strange mixture of dream and practicality, efficient naval officer and hankering romantic adventurer.'[51] This sense of destiny is evident from the beginning of the film in the magnificently evocative title music of Vaughan Williams, which establishes the spirit of quest and endeavour through an ascending scale that climbs slowly upwards, slips back and then resumes the climb. The main theme recurs throughout the film – for example, in the journey up the Beardmore glacier and in the final, doomed trek back from the Pole. The main titles are followed by extracts from Scott's journal, as he returns from the Antarctic on the Discovery in 1904, in which he describes the Antarctic as 'vast, mysterious, inhospitable'. Shots of the Antarctic landscape – mountains, vast snowscapes, ice floes – are accompanied by an eerie lento, using xylophone, glockenspiel, harp and bells, before the rise of a wordless female chorus which evokes both the beauty and the danger of the continent. Like the mythical sirens of Antheomoessa, whose songs lured mariners to their doom, the pull of the Antarctic will be too strong for Scott who, the film thus establishes from the outset, is destined to return there and die.[52]

Charles Barr describes Scott of the Antarctic as 'a strange, dreamy,

9. *Scott of the Antarctic*: Captain Scott (John Mills, *right*) persuades
Dr Wilson (Harold Warrender) to join him on another Antarctic
expedition, but Oriana Wilson (Anne Firth) is not happy.

elegiac film, [and] often a moving one'.[53] For all that it is informed by
a rigorous authenticity of treatment, the tone of the film is epic and
portentous. The exterior cinematography – the Antarctic and Swiss
locations were shot by Osmond Borradaile and the Norwegian
locations by Geoffrey Unsworth, with Jack Cardiff supervising the
studio shooting – is nothing short of magnificent. The Antarctic is
represented as more than a mere physical location; it is also a spiritual
space in which occurs an epic tale of great courage and endeavour.
Characters repeatedly express their sense of awe at the natural
environment: Scott's reaction upon arriving at the Pole is 'Great God!
This is an awful place'. The exteriors emphasise the vast, white empti-
ness of the Antarctic with long shots in which the men themselves
appear as tiny dots against a sheet of snow. Frend's direction at times
resembles the great westerns of John Ford, not only in the use of
landscape but also in the studio sequences that use close-ups to express

in images what remains unsaid in words. The early scene of Scott's arrival at the Wilsons' home is a classic example: Oriana Wilson's expression upon seeing Scott and the silent exchange of glances between them indicate clearly that Oriana resents Scott's presence and fears that he is going to take her husband from her – which, indeed, is the ultimate outcome.

The narrative ideologies of *Scott of the Antarctic* revolve around codes of patriotism and masculinity. These codes are expressed through the attitudes and behaviour of Scott and his colleagues. Scott's public rationale for the expedition is to further scientific knowledge, but it is made clear that his ambition to reach the Pole is motivated by patriotism ('I think an Englishman should get there first'). Oates and Bowers join the expedition for the adventure. Wilson, the scientist, is less obsessed with reaching the Pole than Scott ('I don't believe I want to get somewhere first just for the sake of doing it'), but still cannot resist the opportunity to go when Scott promises him 'the best-equipped expedition ever'. Scott maintains that the aim of the expedition is scientific, but when news arrives that Amundsen's rival Norwegian party is making for the South Pole, instead of the North Pole as assumed, it becomes a matter of pride for Scott that the English expedition should reach it first. Thus he declares that 'the whole resources of the entire expedition will be devoted to getting four men into a position from which they can make their final bid for the Pole'. Scott's 'bitter disappointment' upon reaching the Pole after Amundsen arises from his wounded national pride. Significantly, none of the party can bring himself to smile when they take a group photograph of themselves at the Pole. In this respect, the emphasis of the film is different from *90° South*, which stresses the scientific nature of the expedition and includes the bid for the Pole itself as a coda rather than as the primary objective.

Andrew Spicer rightly observes that *Scott of the Antarctic* 'gives enormous emphasis to unspoken masculine accord, to a spareness of words and dialogue'.[54] Scott and his party all exhibit characteristics that are regarded as peculiarly British: emotional restraint, quiet courage, stoical acceptance of the hardships they face and a self-deprecating sense of humour. They have a shared, understood code of behaviour in which self-control and restraint are paramount. A revealing anecdote of how the display of emotion was strictly regulated comes from the autobiography of Kenneth More, who played 'Teddy' Evans. More averred that his 'big scene' in which Evans broke down and wept upon being told by Scott that he was not to be in the final group to head for the Pole was cut from the film.[55] However, the scene as described in the shooting script is exactly as it played in the film, suggesting that it was never the intention that Evans should display emotion in this way: 'Even with this news, which must come as an extra sledgehammer blow adding to his disappointment, Teddy Evans has his feelings under tight control.'[56] The masculine ethos of the film is that emotion is a private thing and that any public display would be both unmanly and, moreover, un-British. This attitude is perfectly summed up in one of the extracts taken from Scott's journal written during the return journey: 'Among ourselves we are unendingly cheerful, but what each man feels in his heart I can only guess.'

Scott of the Antarctic is a very male-oriented film. This is characteristic of Ealing, a studio generally more comfortable in the world of men than the world of women (as seen, for example, in the prisoner-of-war camp in *The Captive Heart*, the police station in *The Blue Lamp* and the warship in *The Cruel Sea*). In *Scott* women are peripheral to the narrative and are represented principally by the loyal and dutiful wives of Scott and Wilson who say goodbye to their husbands in New Zealand and thereafter feature only in flashbacks. The goodbyes themselves seem passionless – Scott and Wilson both kiss their wives on the cheek – prompting Walter Mead to complain that the scene is 'almost too undemonstrative and is rather reminiscent of two ladies – not necessarily friends – embracing with due regard to lipstick'.[57] The film displays an unease about romantic relationships and the female presence that borders on anxiety. Despite the Christmas toast to 'wives and sweethearts', Scott and his companions are clearly more comfortable in the company of other men, while Oates prefers his ponies. Women become, quite literally, invisible: Scott and Wilson both talk of not being able to see their wives' faces when they write letters. A scene in which Ponting delivers a music-hall rhyming monologue about the difficulties of getting into a sleeping-bag ('On the outside grows the furside, on the inside grows the skinside') is interpreted by Harper as 'a covert metaphor for female genitalia – a site of danger and distaste if the manner of the verse's delivery and the explorers' sniggering response is read aright'.[58] If this is so, however, it was missed entirely by contemporaries, including both the critics and Balcon, whose attitude towards female sexuality was conservative in the extreme.

One of the charges levelled against *Scott of the Antarctic* – unfairly, given that Ealing had to take account of the sensitivities of relatives and survivors – is that it is uncritical of Scott himself, who is presented with 'due reverence as a British hero'.[59] Scott is shown as making mistakes, but these are not commented upon. Against the advice of the Norwegian explorer Nansen to take only dogs to haul the sledges ('A dog is an animal. When a dog is finished, he is still some use to other dogs and to man if necessary'), Scott relies on a combination of motor tractors (which soon break down in the cold), Siberian ponies (which delay his start as they cannot withstand the coldest temperatures) and dogs (which he sends back on reaching the Beardmore glacier, declaring that thereafter 'we'll ask no more of machines and animals'). The folly of this decision is revealed when Scott's party reach the Pole and see dog prints left by Amundsen's team. Scott also decides to take five men on the final push for the Pole, though they have rations only for four. It is an arbitrary decision that he does not explain. This decision is recognised now to have contributed to the eventual fate of the five, but the film does not examine it critically.

Ultimately, the film contributes to the mythologisation of the Scott expedition rather than attempting to debunk it. It would be almost 40 years before a revisionist account of the story would be told in Central Television's production *The Last Place on Earth* (1985). It is, in large measure, because of its reliance on Scott's journals as an authenticating device that *Scott of the Antarctic* endorses the Scott myth – a myth of which Scott himself was the author (I should point out that I am using the word 'myth' not to imply that this record of events is incorrect but rather to suggest that it represents the widely accepted popular account of what happened). There is an emphasis on the British code of chivalry: thus Bowers is described as 'an undefeated little sportsman' and Oates as 'a brave man and a gallant gentleman'. On the return journey, the men refuse to give in to despair and maintain their outward optimism despite the setbacks and deteriorating weather ('Letting up a little, I think'; 'We'll make it in no time'). Gradually, their physical condition deteriorates, but even so they refuse to despair. Petty Officer Evans, suffering from frostbite and gangrene after cutting a finger, repeatedly insists that nothing is wrong ('Only a cut, sir'; 'Nothing sir, quite alright. Only a bit awkward, that's all'; 'It's alright, sir, quite well') right up to the moment of his death. The death of Captain Oates is presented with great dignity and restraint. Oates, suffering the agony of frostbitten feet, simply stands up, says 'I'm just going outside. I may be away some time', and walks out of the tent. Scott, realising what Oates is doing, prevents Bowers from going after him. The last shot of Oates is of him walking into a blizzard, a bent, staggering figure resembling the contemporary painting by J.C. Dollman. Oates's self-sacrifice, laying down his own life in the hope that his companions may survive, exemplifies an ethos of secular Christianity that is also apparent in the last letters written by Wilson and Bowers, in which they both speak of being reunited with their families in the afterlife. The remaining three men die in their tent and are discovered the following spring. Scott's diary is retrieved, and with it the record of their final days on which the myth largely rests. The last shot of the film is of a cross marking the place where their bodies were found, with a close up of the inscription: 'To strive, to seek, to find and not to yield.'

Scott of the Antarctic is a study of failure, but also of finding strength and dignity in that failure. In this respect it exemplifies a peculiarly British trait of celebrating failure rather than triumph. Many of the most enduring episodes of popular British history are heroic defeats (Boudicca, the Battle of Hastings, the Charge of the Light Brigade, Gordon's death at Khartoum) and even many of Britain's most celebrated battles are far from being outright victories (Rorke's Drift, the Somme, Passchendaele). Probably the most mythologised event of the Second World War from the British perspective was not El Alamein or D-Day or even the Battle of Britain, but Dunkirk – the hastily conceived and daringly executed operation to evacuate the British Expeditionary Force from France after it had been cut off following the German breakthrough in May 1940. Although Churchill was quick to assert that 'wars are not won by evacuations', Dunkirk was immediately hailed as a 'miracle' or a 'deliverance'. British Movietone's newsreel 'Epic of Dunkirk' (6 June 1940), for example, featured a triumphalist commentary describing 'the great withdrawal' and testifying to 'the success of this amazing military exploit'. J.B. Priestley, in his 'Postscript' broadcast of 5 June, saw Dunkirk as symbolic of the national character:

Nothing, I feel, could be more English than this Battle of Dunkirk, both in its beginning and its end, its folly and its grandeur...What began as a miserable blunder, a catalogue of misfortunes and miscalculations, ended as an epic of gallantry. We have a queer habit – and you can see it running through our history – of conjuring up such transformations. Out of a black gulf of humiliation and despair, rises a sun of blazing glory.[60]

This could almost have been a description of *Scott of the Antarctic*, exposing both the folly and the grandeur of the expedition. Scott's party are beset by 'a catalogue of misfortunes and miscalculations'; they face 'the black gulf of humiliation and despair' when they find they have been beaten to the Pole; their return journey is 'an epic of gallantry'. The film even ends with 'The Return of the Sun' (described as such by an on-screen title), which brings to light the courage and fortitude of the expedition through the discovery of Scott's journal.

This not to suggest that *Scott of the Antarctic* was consciously intended by its makers as an allegory of Dunkirk. It is more that the film expresses the same spirit of backs-against-the-wall determination that had been much in evidence during the war years and had come to be known as 'the Dunkirk spirit'. The final entry in Scott's journal testifies that they met their ends with dignity and stoicism rather than defeatism or despair: 'I do not regret this journey. We tooks risks; we knew we took them; things have come out against us, therefore we have no cause for complaint.' 'Mustn't grumble' was an oft-heard phrase of the war years: it also sums up the outlook of Petty Officer Evans even as he dies. In a sense, *Scott of the Antarctic* is a disguised war film. It is perhaps significant that it shares the naval theme of Charles Frend's two most critically acclaimed films, *San Demetrio, London* (1943) and *The Cruel Sea* (1953): the director seems to have felt most comfortable with subjects dealing with masculinity and heroism.

Ten years later, Ealing and John Mills were reunited for one of the studio's last films, *Dunkirk* (dir. Leslie Norman, 1958), which explores quite similar ground to *Scott*. Ealing had ceased to operate its own production facility in 1955 – the studio itself was sold to the BBC – and Balcon, breaking with the Rank Organisation, had entered into a production deal with MGM. *Dunkirk* was produced with the blessing and support of the War Office and is defined by the same rigorous attention to authenticity that had characterised *Scott*. Like *Scott*, it was chosen for the Royal Film Performance – an indicator of its semi-official status in contemporary film culture.

10. 'I do not regret this journey': Scott makes his last diary entry, remaining stoical to the end in *Scott of the Antarctic*.

Unlike *Scott*, however, it was profitable at the box office, with a total gross of $2,060,000 against a production cost of $1,025,000. [61]

    Dunkirk is a representative example of the British war film of the 1950s, providing a sober, detached, retrospective look at the events of the war. Film historians have dismissed it in much the same terms as *Scott of the Antarctic*. Harper, for example, notes its 'emotionally frozen quality'.[62] Barr describes it as 'very dull indeed, and this dullness is rather admirable...it is honest. The film shows a dispirited, sluggish country blundering its way to war – a picture consistent with the films Ealing was making in those years.'[63] Certainly, *Dunkirk* is an ideologically backward-looking film and an aesthetically conservative one, though that is not to say that it is entirely lacking in interest. Perhaps to a greater degree than any war film since Noël Coward and David Lean's *In Which We Serve* (1942), the narrative structure of *Dunkirk* links the services and the home front through its parallel stories of an army platoon left behind during the British retreat and the civilians who man the flotilla of small boats sent to help in the evacuation – stories which eventually are linked on the beaches of Dunkirk itself. It is also, to an even greater extent than *Scott*, conjuring up an inspiring story from the past as a response to the perception of Britain's decline as an imperial power. For Dunkirk, read Suez: the British army is plucked from the beaches following a disastrous intervention on foreign shores. This point was not lost on William Whitebait of the *New Statesman*, who saw a direct link between the war films of the 1950s and Britain's status in the world:

> So while we 'adventure' at Suez, in the cinemas we are still thrashing Rommel – and discovering that he was a gentleman! – sweeping the Atlantic of submarines, sending the few to scatter Goering's many. The more we lose face in the world's counsels, the grander, in our excessively modest way, we swell in this illusionary mirror held up by the screen. It is less a spur to morale than a salve to wounded pride; and as art or entertainment, dreadfully dull.[64]

The war film, Whitebait felt, 'creates an imaginary present in which we can go on enjoying our finest hours'. Like the historical film, it is a genre that responds to contemporary society through reworking stories of the past. This is particularly so with *post-bellum* war films like *Dunkirk* that are themselves set in the recent past but which, unlike the films made during the war itself, are detached from the propaganda imperatives of wartime cinema. The war film is also informed strongly by narrative ideologies of nationhood, class and masculinity similar to those apparent in the historical film.

When Ealing Studios itself was sold in 1955, a plaque was put up with the inscription: 'Here during a quarter of a century many films were made projecting Britain and the British character.'[65] Perhaps to a greater extent than any other production company, the projection of Britain had been central to the ethos of Ealing under Balcon's leadership. That it was a selective and partial projection of Britain cannot be denied: Ealing's Britain was essentially middle class and conservative in its representation of social change and, especially, gender. It is usually argued, not without justification, that Ealing stagnated during the 1950s and could not keep pace with the changes that were becoming apparent in British society towards the end of the decade. Certainly, a film like *Scott of the Antarctic*, with its emphasis on the ideals of patriotism, duty and sacrifice, would have seemed out of place in the film culture that gave rise to the 'Angry Young Men' and British new wave cinema. Yet, in so many ways, it seems the perfect British film for the late 1940s: retrospective and backward-looking, perhaps, but also giving expression to the spirit of determination and stoical endurance that had seen Britain through six years of total war. Criticisms that *Scott* is a cold film – visually, aesthetically, emotionally – are misplaced. It exhibits an epic grandeur that is rare in British cinema and certainly one that is absent from other historical films of the late 1940s such as *Bonnie Prince Charlie* (dir. Anthony Kimmins, 1948) and *Christopher Columbus* (dir. David Macdonald, 1949). It is a film that has been unfairly marginalised in British cinema history. It deserves to be recognised not only as one of the major production achievements of Ealing Studios but also as an exemplar of the type of national film that Balcon espoused.

7

Hollywood's England:
Beau Brummell (1954)

*B*EAU *Brummell*, directed by Curtis Bernhardt for MGM British, is to some extent the odd one out in this study in so far as it was made by a Hollywood studio and needs to be seen within the context not only of British cinema but also of studio policy in Culver City, California. It is legitimate to include the film here as it was filmed in Britain with a largely British cast, was concerned with a British historical subject, and, for legal purposes, was registered as British under Board of Trade regulations. The fact that it was chosen for the Royal Film Performance of 1954 is suggestive of the degree of cultural prestige attached to the film, but British critics were united in their condemnation of what they regarded as a travesty of history by an American company. As a combination of American money and British cultural capital, however, *Beau Brummell* is a fascinating hybrid that offers a significantly different representation of the past than other historical films of the time. If it is less concerned with the holy grail of historical authenticity than most British historical films – a failing attributed by critics to its American parentage – it is also more visually sumptuous and elegant, demonstrating not only the level of production values associated with Hollywood but also the idea of the past as a site of pleasure. With its narrative focus on personal ambition and desire – the very obverse of *Scott of the Antarctic* – *Beau Brummell* incorporates certain aspects of the classical Hollywood melodrama into the historical narrative.[1]

By the early 1950s the British film industry had begun its long, inexorable decline. All the statistical evidence points towards the waning popularity of cinema-going as a social practice: the total number of annual cinema admissions dropped from 1,365 million in 1951 to 500 million by 1960, with the concomitant effect that the number of cinemas in Britain also fell – from 4,581 to 3,034 – over the same period. With ticket prices rising only steadily in line with inflation, total box-office grosses fell from over £108 million in 1951 to less than £64 million by 1960.[2] Anecdotal evidence supports the picture of an industry in decline. Leslie Halliwell recalled a dispiriting return to his home town of Bolton in 1949: 'The cinemas on my home ground were already showing signs of wear and tear, spiritual as well as physical. Attendances had fallen off, and the old sense of occasion was sadly lacking. Most of the halls now saw little future for themselves. Their heyday was certainly gone.'[3] The conventional explanation for the decline of cinema-going is the emergence of television as a genuine mass medium – the number of television licences increased from just over three-quarters of a million in 1951 to almost ten and a half million by 1960 – though other factors, including competing leisure activities and a gradually increasing level of consumer affluence, also need to be taken into account.[4]

The decline in cinema-going inevitably impacted upon the structure of the industry, which underwent major changes in the 1950s. The number of smaller production companies fell as they either shut down entirely (Gainsborough) or came increasingly within the orbit of the Rank Organisation (Ealing). Korda attempted to re-establish London Film Productions as a force to be reckoned with following his wartime sojourn in the United States but, despite the success of *The Third Man* (dir. Carol Reed, 1949) – a co-production with David O. Selznick – found that he was unable to repeat the successes of the 1930s. His production of *Bonnie Prince Charlie* was an expensive flop, and, while he backed Powell and Pressburger following their departure from Rank with *Gone to Earth* (1950), *The Elusive Pimpernel* (1951) and *The Tales of Hoffmann* (1951), the results were generally disappointing, both artistically and commercially. British production increasingly came to be dominated by the 'big three' of Rank, ABPC and British Lion. The level of production remained stable throughout the 1950s, usually between 80 and 90 films a year, though an increasing number of these were made with financial backing from Hollywood. During the 1950s, there were around 170

'Hollywood British' films – made in Britain with American money – which were divided roughly equally between first and second features.[5]

The American presence in the British production and distribution sectors in the 1950s was different from the situation that had pertained in the 1930s. In the 1930s US distributors had needed to fill their quota obligations and so had either bought films from British 'poverty row' producers or had established their own production facilities in Britain by buying small studios: Warner Bros. bought Teddington Studios in 1931, Twentieth Century-Fox bought Wembley Studios in 1936. The revised Cinematograph Films Act of 1938, however, in a largely successful attempt to remedy the curse of the 'quota quickies', had introduced criteria of cost and quality that meant distributors could count films as double or even triple quota depending on their production cost. MGM, which set up its own British production arm in the late 1930s, focused exclusively on the production of top-notch product that would appeal to both British and American audiences. Its first production, *A Yank at Oxford* (dir. Jack Conway, 1937), was the first film to be registered for triple quota and was followed by prestigious productions of *The Citadel* (dir. King Vidor, 1938) and *Goodbye, Mr Chips* (dir. Sam Wood, 1939), though the outbreak of the Second World War curtailed the studio's plans for more British-made films.[6] After the war, however, MGM decided to re-establish its British production base on a more permanent footing. In 1948 it bought the Amalgamated Studios at Borehamwood (Elstree), a modern complex built by Paul Soskin in the late 1930s but never completed and which had been used for storage during the war before passing to the Prudential. At the same time there was a revision of the quota legislation, which set exhibitors' quota at 45 per cent (reduced to 30 per cent in 1950) but abolished the quota for renters entirely. Why, then, now that distributors were no longer required to handle any British-made films at all, was Hollywood, led by MGM, keen to re-establish itself in the British production sector?

There are, in fact, several reasons that help to explain the British production strategy of Hollywood studios in the 1950s. Ever since the arrival of talking pictures, Britain had been Hollywood's most lucrative overseas market, and, given that most Hollywood A-pictures were dependent upon overseas revenues for the bulk of their profits, the importance of the British market should not be underestimated.

Thus it was in Hollywood's interest to make films that would appeal to British audiences, which would naturally include films with British subjects and locations. The British Treasury's limitations on dollar remittances, introduced during the war and reaffirmed by the Anglo-American Film Agreement of 1948, meant that American companies held 'frozen funds' from the distribution of their films in Britain that they had to re-invest in Britain. Moreover, the devaluation of sterling in 1949 and the lower labour costs in Britain meant that it was cheaper to produce films in Britain than in Hollywood. Another incentive was provided, albeit unwittingly, by the establishment of the British Film Production Fund for three years (later extended) from 1951. This was funded by a levy on ticket sales – known as the Eady Levy after the Treasury official who devised it – which exhibitors agreed to in return for the abolition of entertainments tax. Every British film would receive a sum of money in proportion to the distributor's receipts. To qualify for the Eady Levy a film needed to be made in Britain or the Commonwealth, with 75 per cent of the labour costs paid to British workers. In effect, the levy amounted to a subsidy for commercial success: the major beneficiaries were the most successful producers. In the 1953–54 financial year, for example, the three major British distributors (GFD, British Lion and Associated British Pathé) claimed £1,386,328, over half the total of £2,498,187 payable through the Production Fund. During the same period, the eight leading American distributors (Columbia, MGM, Paramount, Republic, RKO, Twentieth Century-Fox, United Artists and Warner Bros.) drew £187,467 from the Production Fund for their eligible films.[7] These were the circumstances, then, in which American companies found it advantageous to establish a production base in Britain.

As Sue Harper has shown, a considerable amount of 'Hollywood British' production in the 1950s was in the historical/costume genre.[8] The costume swashbuckler was especially in vogue: Warner Bros. produced *Captain Horatio Hornblower RN* (dir. Raoul Walsh, 1950), starring Gregory Peck as C.S. Forester's British naval hero of the Napoleonic Wars, and followed it with an adaptation of Robert Louis Stevenson's *The Master of Ballantrae* (dir. William Keighley, 1953) starring Errol Flynn; Walt Disney produced *The Story of Robin Hood and His Merrie Men* (dir. Ken Annakin, 1952) and *Rob Roy, the Highland Rogue* (dir. Harold French, 1953), both starring Richard Todd, and its own Stevenson adaptation, *Kidnapped* (dir. Robert

Stevenson, 1959), with Peter Finch; and MGM British achieved its biggest popular success with a cycle of chivalric epics starring Robert Taylor, the erstwhile Yank at Oxford: *Ivanhoe* (dir. Richard Thorpe, 1952), *Knights of the Round Table* (dir. Richard Thorpe, 1953) and *The Adventures of Quentin Durward* (dir. Richard Thorpe, 1955). Along with the Hollywood-made swashbucklers of the same time – MGM remade both *The Prisoner of Zenda* (dir. Richard Thorpe, 1952) and *Scaramouche* (dir. George Sidney, 1952) as starring vehicles for Stewart Granger – these films represent what Richards has described as the 'last great age of cinematic chivalry'.[9] It is significant that they used British stories and were often adapted from British writers: this indicates that in the 1950s Hollywood still saw Britain as an important market.

Beau Brummell needs to be seen within the context of this vogue for British historical subjects in the 1950s. It followed on from MGM's *Young Bess* (dir. George Sidney, 1953), a historical fiction of the love affair between the future Elizabeth I (Jean Simmons) and Thomas Seymour (Stewart Granger), with Charles Laughton reprising his famous role as Henry VIII. The timing of this film, released to coincide with the Coronation of another Queen Elizabeth in June 1953, was not lost on contemporaries, though there were significant differences between British and American critical responses: while one British critic felt that 'the total lack of resemblances in appearance and character between the two Elizabeths would make such parallels worthless', an American reviewer suggested that even though she 'does not look nearly so much like the historic Queen Elizabeth… one can understand why Producer Sidney Franklin concentrated on purely photogenic elements and selected such an actress as Miss Simmons'.[10] When MGM decided to make a second film adaptation of Clyde Fitch's play about the famed Regency dandy Beau Brummell, previously filmed as a silent with John Barrymore in 1924, the natural choice for the title role was the male star of *Young Bess*, for Granger was now typecast in costume parts following his films for Gainsborough in the 1940s and for MGM in the 1950s. As in *Young Bess*, his female co-star was a British-born Hollywood leading lady (Elizabeth Taylor), while the supporting cast consisted principally of British character actors (Peter Ustinov as the Prince of Wales, Robert Morley as George III, James Hayter as the valet Mortimer). The production made use of British technical personnel so that it would qualify for the Eady Levy, though, as it had for the British swashbucklers, MGM flew in an experienced Hollywood studio director, the German-born Curtis Bernhardt, who had something of a reputation as a director of 'women's pictures' such as *A Stolen Life* (1946) and *Miss Sadie Thompson* (1953). At a reported cost of $3 million (£1.2 million), *Beau Brummell* was in the higher-budget end of Hollywood productions of the mid-1950s and ten times more than the £120,000 average of a British feature film.[11]

Beau Brummell opened in the United States in October 1954, a month before it was shown in Britain as the year's Royal Film Performance. In America, the film's British subject matter was seen as an indication of cultural value and prestige. 'Producer Sam Zimbalist has endowed the new era of wide screen with a costume class filmed in England, that is destined for top-chock repertory in its autumnal years', declared the *Motion Picture Herald*.[12] Bosley Crowther in the *New York Times* expressed a similar view about its 'class': 'It was produced in England, so that such things as hussars on parade, the furnishings of palaces and mansions and a sequence of a fox-hunt in full cry have an uncommon richness, a genuine cachet.' In a prescient aside, however, Crowther added that there 'may be some fidgeting when they see it at the Royal Command Performance in London next month'.[13]

There must have been much fidgeting indeed on the part of the British critics, as *Beau Brummell* met with a resounding chorus of disapproval when it was shown in the presence of the Queen, the Duke of Edinburgh and Princess Margaret at the Empire, Leicester Square, on 15 November.[14] There were two principal complaints: that it contained blatant historical inaccuracies and that it was boring into the bargain. C.A. Lejeune thought it 'horrid history, which might be forgiven if it were also greatly entertaining. Unhappily, this isn't so.'[15] William Whitebait found it 'a fiction so feeble and dreary that even the film-makers must have had doubts about putting it on celluloid'.[16] Derek Granger of the *Financial Times* considered it to be 'almost everything the man wasn't: genteel, tedious, unstylish, inelegant, dull' and claimed that he would have preferred it to be an 'outrageous American travesty...rather than the niminy-piminy stuff served here which seems neither good plain history nor roaring Hollywood licence'.[17] Fred Majdalany in the *Daily Mail* labelled it 'an interminable and pointless tale of the Regency'.[18] Thomas Spencer in the *Daily Worker* decried it as 'Americanised English history, with most of the point missing' and complained that it 'fails completely...in conveying any real sense of period'.[19] And Paul Dehn of the *News Chronicle* called it 'one of the dullest falsifications of history that can ever have been uttered before a British Queen'.[20]

The critical response to the film, therefore, was consistent across both the quality and popular press and the political spectrum. The film was found wanting both as history and as entertainment. It is unusual to find such a unanimity of response to a film across such a wide range of reviewers. It is evident that for many of the national critics the point of contention was the selection of *Beau Brummell* for the Royal Film Performance. *Time and Tide* felt that the film had been accorded a significance it did not deserve, calling it 'a routine piece of commercial flummery that would have been dismissed in a few lines if it had not been singled out for what is after all the most distinguished film function of the year'.[21] Much the same view was voiced by the *Manchester Guardian*: 'It is no bad specimen of its thoroughly unabashed kind, but why, it may be asked, should such a film be considered particularly suitable for a royal performance?'[22] Conservative MP Sir Beverley Baxter, commissioned to review the film for the *Evening Standard*, concluded that 'it is a queer dish to set before the Queen'.[23] Another critic felt that it was an act of 'stupendous bad taste' to present this particular film before the Queen on the grounds that 'royalty is turned into a farce and the monarchy played for cheap laughs'. Leonard Mosley in the *Daily Express*, however, seems to have been the only critic to detect 'an oblique reference to the Duke and Duchess of Windsor' in so far as the Prince of Wales is prevented from marrying Mrs Fitzherbert.[24] It is reasonable to assume that, for British audiences at least, the Prince's dilemma ('Would you give up a woman you love simply to sit on the throne?') would have brought to mind the Abdication Crisis of 1936.

The rubbishing of *Beau Brummell* brought to a head a sense of dissatisfaction with the Royal Film Performance that had clearly been brewing amongst the national critics for some time. The previous choices for this prestigious occasion had been *A Matter of Life and Death* (dir. Michael Powell, 1946), *The Bishop's Wife* (dir. Henry Koster, 1947), *Scott of the Antarctic* (1948), *The Forsyte Saga* (dir. Compton Bennett, 1949), *The Mudlark* (dir. Jean Negulesco, 1950), *Where No Vultures Fly* (dir. Harry Watt, 1951), *Because You're Mine* (dir. Alexander Hall, 1952) and *Rob Roy, the Highland Rogue* (1953). Dilys Powell averred that the choice of film was made on 'an understanding that if an English film was chosen one year, an American film would be chosen the next'. In fact, two British films were shown in successive years, 1950 and 1951, though Powell suggested this was not such an anomaly because in the case of *The Mudlark* 'the film was written and directed by Americans and was not really English at all'. (*The Mudlark* had been written by Nunnally Johnson and directed by Jean Negulesco and had starred Irene Dunne as Queen Victoria.) *Beau Brummell* seemed a natural choice as it was, in effect, an Anglo-American film, though Powell declared that 'I can find no more excuses for this poor, dull piece'.[25] Majdalany concurred that the choices for the Royal Film 'conform to a pattern of safety that becomes clearer every year. The chosen offerings must carefully avoid being original, serious, controversial, or even faintly adult. Not surprisingly, films which oblige by avoiding these pitfalls generally contrive also to avoid being entertaining.'[26]

The trade press, for its part, recognised that 'the selection of the Royal Film is one of those items over which Fleet Street is always ready to snoop a few reporters' and declared, quite reasonably, 'that the sheer appropriateness of the subject must quite naturally and properly weigh in the choice of the final film'. *Kine Weekly* reported that *Beau Brummell* had been chosen from a shortlist of three films: the other two were 'a Hollywood drama of very considerable achievement... [but] essentially a heavy picture, and scarcely the right subject for a festival night' and 'a British film [that] was said to be a very diverting and perhaps rather cheeky comedy'.[27] The problem, of course, was who was to decide what sort of film was appropriate and what was not. The selection panel for the Royal Film Performance consisted of representatives from trade bodies such as the British Film Producers Association and the Cinema Exhibitors Association. In the wake of the controversy over *Beau Brummell*, Korda suggested that the panel should be reconstituted to comprise the Lord Chamberlain, the chairman of the Critics' Circle and 'someone within the industry unconnected with any production or distribution organisation'.[28] But despite some limited changes, film industry representatives in one capacity or another continued to make the selection. The Royal Film Performances in the years following *Beau Brummell* were equally safe choices of subject: the lightweight romantic thriller *To Catch A Thief* (dir. Alfred Hitchcock, 1955), the patriotic war film *The Battle of the River Plate* (dir. Michael Powell, 1956) and the rather lacklustre

MGM–Gene Kelly musical *Les Girls* (dir. George Cukor, 1957).[29]

It is evident, therefore, that *Beau Brummell* became a site of cultural contestation for British critics arising as much from contextual factors as from the content of the film itself. Yet in focusing on its appropriateness for a Royal Film Performance, the critics missed many of the film's points of interest. *Beau Brummell* is indeed an 'Americanised' version of British history, recasting characters and events into a narrative imbued with American ideologies of personal ambition and social mobility. These are elements that would later be manifested in *Chariots of Fire*, another Royal Film that achieved considerable success in America. Furthermore, much of the cultural power of *Beau Brummell* is invested not in its narrative but in its visual style, which exhibits much of the same expressive quality in set design and costume that characterised the classic Hollywood melodramas of the 1950s.

'In fairness to *Beau Brummell*,' C.A. Lejeune averred, 'it should be said that the film makes no claims to historical veracity. It is not a record but a romance, borrowing from history only such facts and figures as suit its purpose.'[30] Indeed, to a far greater extent than most historical narratives, *Beau Brummell* is detached from real historical events. Historical characters (William Pitt, Charles Fox, Lord Byron) appear briefly, the Napoleonic Wars are alluded to only in passing, and there is no suggestion of the unrest that affected Britain during the Regency period (the Luddite riots, the 'Peterloo' massacre, Catholic Emancipation). The film is replete with chronological and factual errors: Pitt and Fox (who both died in 1806) are still Prime Minister and Leader of the Opposition at the start of the Regency (1811), while the end of the film has George IV visiting Brummell on his deathbed (George IV died in 1830, ten years before Brummell). The historical infelicities of *Beau Brummell* are so blatant, however, that they throw into sharp relief the ideological intent of the film.

The absence of any sense of historical context in *Beau Brummell* means that it is freer than many historical narratives to utilise the past to its own ends. The Regency is presented as a period of social change and Brummell's rise in society is seen as a consequence of this: 'The bold currents that produce a Beau Brummell are flowing through the vitals of this country', remarks Lord Byron. 'A whole new era is dawning – an era of power looms and iron works, a smoke-stained, industrious, robust era.' Britain in the first half of the 1950s was seen by many as entering into a new era of national self-confidence. The Festival of Britain in 1951 had been conceived as a showcase for British science and industry, while the coronation of Queen Elizabeth II in 1953 – dramatically preceded by the successful ascent of Mount Everest by a British-led expedition – had been hailed by some commentators as the dawn of a new 'Elizabethan' age of national achievement and progress. Brummell's social confidence is displayed through the set dressings and costumes which reveal his elegant and cultured tastes: he collects *objets d'art* and becomes a leader of fashion.

The social politics of *Beau Brummell* are progressive, egalitarian and democratic, reflecting its American parentage. Much is made of Brummell's lowly origins and social background ('My grandfather was a valet, my father was secretary to a nobleman, I'm an obscure army captain') and his friendship with the Prince of Wales is the cause of hostility within political and social circles. The film endorses social

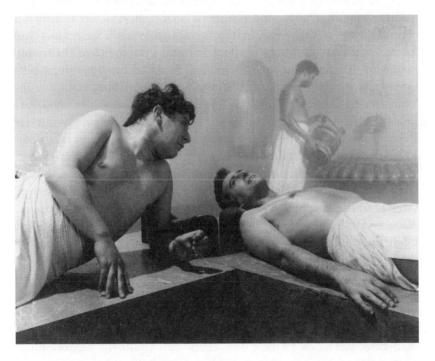

11. *Beau Brummell* explores the nature of intimate male friendship between Brummell (Stewart Granger, *right*) and the Prince of Wales (Peter Ustinov).

mobility and is unequivocal in its assertion that background is no barrier to social advancement ('I do not propose to allow an accident of birth to keep me out. I do not propose to accept inferiority', Brummell tells his valet Mortimer). Brummell dislikes aristocratic privilege and refuses an offer of political patronage from Pitt on the grounds that he would be expected to represent a political faction rather than the interests of those who elected him. But he is also a patriot: his initial criticisms of the Prince are motivated not by personal animosity but rather because a lack of leadership means that 'every day our prestige gets lower and lower – Frenchmen insult us, our colonies desert us, and our future king does nothing'.

Beau Brummell is unusual for a historical film in that it focuses on the nature of male friendship. In contrast to the forced camaraderie of *Scott of the Antarctic*, *Beau Brummell* portrays the relationship between Brummell and the Prince of Wales as one of genuine friendship. Initially, the two men quarrel – Brummell loses his army commission after criticising the regimental uniform designed by the Prince himself ('We are required to wear ridiculously large epaulets just because they have a slimming effect on him') – but they become friends when the Prince realises that Brummell is an honest and sympathetic confidant in contrast to the duplicitous and sycophantic politicians and courtiers he is used to ('All my life I've been surrounded by selfish people. You've proved your honesty'). Unlike the male protagonists of *Scott of the Antarctic*, Brummell and the Prince are able to talk about their feelings towards the women they love but are prevented from marrying: Brummell loves Lady Patricia, who is engaged to Lord Edwin Mercer, the Prince is prevented from marrying his mistress, Maria Fitzherbert, by the conniving Pitt. Moreover, the two men share their confidences in a Turkish bath where they are stripped both physically and emotionally. The women they love, however, have at best only a marginal presence in the narrative; this is very much a film about men.

The codes of masculinity in *Beau Brummell* contrast the commoner Brummell, who is characterised as strong, stoical and loyal, with the Prince of Wales, who is weak, emotional and fickle. The Prince follows Brummell's lead in fashion and relies upon him for advice. He is reduced to tears when his beloved Maria leaves him to live abroad and is even moved to apologise to Brummell for this 'unmanly' behaviour. Brummell, in contrast, conceals his romantic disappointment and does

not outwardly display his emotions, thus maintaining his 'manly'
bearing and demeanour. In one ideologically charged scene, Brummell
sits on the royal throne while George dances, with the Prince telling
him 'that seat becomes you'. When the two men fall out – Brummell
advises the Prince to have his father George III declared insane so that
he may rule as Regent and marry whom he chooses, but Pitt connives
to limit the Regent's powers so that he cannot marry Maria after all – the
Prince reveals his fickleness by banishing Brummell from the court.
Following the quarrel, Brummell is still shown as a stoical and dignified
figure as he dies from tuberculosis. He remains loyal to the Prince,
trying to punch a Frenchman who jeers at the 'fat English pig' when the
latter visits Calais. The message is clear: the commoner Brummell is a
better man than the Prince. Thus *Beau Brummell* shares thematic
affinities with other stories about the relationships between royals and
commoners, including *The Prisoner of Zenda*, *The Prince and the
Pauper* and *The Man in the Iron Mask*.

The prominence accorded to male emotionality in *Beau Brummell*
is rare for British cinema, but there are comparisons to be made with
the male-centred melodramas produced in Hollywood during the
1950s. Films such as *East of Eden* (dir. Elia Kazan, 1955), *Rebel
Without A Cause* (dir. Nicholas Ray, 1955), *Bigger Than Life* (dir.
Nicholas Ray, 1956), *Giant* (dir. George Stevens, 1956), *Tea and
Sympathy* (dir. Vincente Minnelli, 1956), *Written on the Wind* (dir.
Douglas Sirk, 1956) and *Home from the Hill* (dir. Vincente Minnelli,
1960) have sometimes been described as 'male weepies' for the extent
to which they foreground male emotionality and conflict. Although
its director is better known for 'women's pictures', *Beau Brummell* is
in so many respects an archetype of the 'male weepie'. The
relationship between Brummell and the Prince follows the usual
contours of melodrama: antagonism that turns to friendship,
alienation followed by reconciliation. The film ends, significantly, not
with the traditional union of the heterosexual couple but with the
deathbed reconciliation between two men. It could even be argued
that the historical infelicities of *Beau Brummell* (including the
deathbed scene that never actually occurred) represent a deliberate
strategy to create narrative space to enable it to explore the subject of
an intimate male relationship – a subject perhaps more easily
addressed through the conventions of melodrama than through a
discourse of historical authenticity. It is significant in this respect that

most of the Hollywood melodramas of the 1950s were contemporary rather than period narratives.

Another characteristic that *Beau Brummell* shares with the Hollywood melodrama is its privileging of visual style. The sets and costumes of the film are sumptuous and lavish. *Time* remarked that 'Art Director Alfred Junge and Costume Designer Elizabeth Haffenden are in fact the real hero and heroine of this picture'.[31] Junge, who before the war had worked on *The Citadel* and *Goodbye, Mr Chips*, had been brought in to head the art department at MGM British, working on all three Robert Taylor swashbucklers among other films, while Haffenden had been costume designer on most of the key Gainsborough melodramas of the 1940s, including *The Man in Grey*, *Fanny by Gaslight*, *The Wicked Lady* and *Caravan*. Harper suggests that Junge's sets, replete with mirrored doors, columns and drapes, 'interpret the Regency as a period of symmetry and cultural confidence'.[32] Their sheer size – they are evidently built on a grander scale than the films of, say, Ealing or Gainsborough, as one would expect for a major Hollywood studio – also serve to highlight the isolation felt by the protagonists, as in a number of scenes the large sets are sparsely populated. It may be, however, that the visual opulence of the film influenced the British critics in their disapproval of its 'false' sense of history: the dominant critical discourse of the time equated authenticity with a sober, restrained visual style.

It is the costumes, however, which make the most vivid contribution to the 'look' of the film. Brummell is associated with clothes and interior design: he orders his dressing gown to match his bedsheets, and his sartorial tastes determine the fashions of the day. Unlike most colour films of the 1950s, however, including the Hollywood melodramas of Sirk, Ray and Minnelli, where bright and garish primary colours are the order of the day (red representing passion, greens and blues representing loneliness), the costumes of *Beau Brummell* use quite delicate shades that 'encourage the eye to make subtle aesthetic distinctions'.[33] The film's promotional discourse made much of the fashions, but unusually these were centred around the male protagonist rather than the female characters. Granger's 29 costumes were reported to be the most for any male star since Clark Gable's 32 outfits in *Gone With the Wind*. Many of the reviewers compared Granger to a clothes-horse; his is a particularly narcissistic style of performance and it is clear that his tight-fitting stove-pipe breeches and frock coats are cut so as to show off his physique. The presentation of the male body as a source of sartorial elegance and visual pleasure would suggest that the primary audience was assumed to be female – in common with the Gainsborough melodramas in which Granger had starred a decade earlier – though there is a tension here with the promotional discourse that was explicitly aimed at men. The British press book declared: 'It happens to be the first picture that has been "adopted" by an entire industry – the men's apparel business.'[34] MGM arranged tie-ups with organisations such as the National Federation of Merchant Tailors and the Bespoke Tailors Guild. However, there is no evidence to indicate whether the idea of a 'Beau Brummell Fashion Show for Men' was ever taken up by exhibitors.

Beau Brummell was not a box-office success: its total gross of $2.7 million (of which just over $1 million came from the North American market) was less than it cost to make.[35] A major Hollywood studio like MGM could absorb losses on individual films, of course, but by the mid-1950s MGM was an ailing giant that had lost its place at the top of the studio hierarchy. In 1954 it had no film in the annual top ten. Of the films produced by its British studio, only the costume swashbucklers made money, most spectacularly *Ivanhoe* with a total gross of nearly $11 million against a production cost of $3.8 million. This would seem to suggest that cinema-goers in the 1950s preferred their big-budget spectacles to be unabashed works of fiction rather than the uneasy compromise between history and melodrama exemplified by *Beau Brummell*. Following a remake of *The Barretts of Wimpole Street* (dir. Sidney Franklin, 1956), which returned only half its $2.2 million cost, the production strategy of MGM British veered away from expensively mounted costume films and turned towards more modest fare. Its biggest success in the early 1960s, for example, was a series of four, low-cost Miss Marple mysteries starring Margaret Rutherford.[36] The relative failure of *Beau Brummell* is probably best explained by its hybrid status and its original, if unsuccessful, attempt to merge the conventions of the historical film with the Hollywood melodrama. It is too 'Americanised' to work as a genuinely British historical feature film, while its aspirations to 'quality' mean that it lacks the populist appeal of the Gainsborough melodramas. Neither quite one thing nor the other – British or American, serious historical narrative or thoroughly unashamed fiction – *Beau Brummell* did not, ultimately, point the historical film in any new direction.

8

Nearer, My God, To Thee:
A Night to Remember (1958)

A *Night to Remember*, directed by Roy Baker and produced by William MacQuitty for Rank, is in ethos and in style a companion piece to *Scott of the Antarctic* made a decade earlier. For one thing, it was based on a historical event (the tragic sinking of the liner RMS *Titanic*) that not only happened in the same year as the death of Captain Scott and his party but that also came to embody the same values of human courage, stoicism and dignity in the most extreme of circumstances. Furthermore, it was an expensive and prestigious production on which was lavished the full creative and technical resources of the British film industry. With its sober black-and-white aesthetic and its evident concern for historical authenticity, *A Night to Remember* is much more representative of the mainstream of British film-making during the 1950s than the Anglo-American historical film exemplified by *Beau Brummell*. As the 1950s have often, if unfairly, been described as the 'doldrums era' of British cinema, this helps to explain the neglect of *A Night to Remember* by most film historians.[1] Raymond Durgnat – ironically the commentator who coined the 'doldrums' label in the first place – nevertheless recognised the ideological import of the film, which he compared to *Dunkirk*, also released in 1958: 'Not only the *Titanic* in 1912 but Britain's titanic complacency is holed below the waterline. Both these films possess real moral tragedy and beauty, precisely because they admit some cynicism is justified.'[2]

The Rank Organisation remained the biggest producer-distributor-exhibitor in Britain during the 1950s. Rank owned two of the largest studios (Pinewood and Denham), the largest distributor (GFD) and two of the three major cinema circuits (the Odeon and Gaumont chains were, belatedly, merged into a single circuit in 1958). A paradoxical effect of the decline of cinema audiences and the closure of cinemas was that it actually strengthened the position of the two major combines, Rank and APBC, in the exhibition sector, for it was the independent exhibitors who bore the brunt of the closures rather than the major circuits. Thus, while the combines did close some of their less profitable cinemas, their share of the exhibition market increased from 20 per cent in 1950 to 24 per cent by 1960.³ At the level of production, however, the situation was rather less secure. The failure of Rank's ambitious production programme in the late 1940s had incurred losses that necessitated a period of retrenchment and economy. Thus it was that during the 1950s Rank imposed an upper limit of £150,000 on each film produced under the aegis of the organisation. With Rank personally taking a less active role in the film industry (he had to look after the family flour business following the death of his elder brother James), the day-to-day running of the Rank Organisation came increasingly under the control of his associate John Davis. Davis, former managing director of Odeon Theatres Ltd, was an accountant who imposed strict fiscal discipline and whose control over the production process extended to approval of scripts and casting. Davis earned the reputation of the most hated man in the British film industry for his ruthless behaviour towards film-makers and his willingness to wield the hatchet.⁴

The Rank Organisation should be seen not so much as a studio itself, in the manner of the Hollywood majors, but rather as a group of companies that brought various different production interests under the same umbrella. There were three principal Rank production organisations in the 1950s. The first was British Film Makers (BFM, 1951–52), a consortium backed by Rank and the National Film Finance Corporation (NFFC) whereby Rank provided a guarantee of distribution which allowed producers to secure the necessary financial backing. Among the film-makers associated with this group were Anthony Asquith, Betty Box, Ralph Thomas and Anthony Havelock-Allan. However, none of the 14 films produced by BFM was a major box-office success and it was wound up after 18 months. BFM was succeeded by Group Film Producers (1953–55), through which Rank and Davis had tighter control over budgets, scripts and casting in return for providing production finance. Producers would also be obliged to use Rank contract artistes (and to pay their fees) and to film at Pinewood. A third production organisation from 1955, called simply 'Rank', put even greater control in the hands of Davis and Pinewood studio manager Earl St John. Vincent Porter avers that both Davis and St John 'were unimaginative and conservative in their attitude to film and appear to have had little feel for public taste'.[5] The majority of Rank's films of the 1950s were safe, anodyne entertainment films in conventional genres such as comedy (*Genevieve, Doctor in the House* and its sequels) and war films (*Above Us the Waves, The Battle of the River Plate, Reach for the Sky, Ill Met By Moonlight*).[6]

A Night to Remember was the brainchild of William MacQuitty, whose background had been in the Co-operative film movement during the Second World War and who had moved into commercial production in the 1950s. In his autobiography, MacQuitty explained that he had been fascinated by the story of the *Titanic* since his boyhood when he had seen it under construction in Belfast and had witnessed its launch and its departure on its ill-fated maiden voyage.[7] In 1956 MacQuitty bought an option on the film rights to Walter Lord's book *A Night to Remember*, a meticulously researched account of the tragedy that had been on the best-seller lists for six months and had already been adapted for television in America by the NBC network. The trade press predicted a success: '"A Night to Remember" is a great book which should make a great picture.'[8] There had been three previous films of the *Titanic* but none that had any claim to be a definitive historical account. *Atlantic* (dir. E.A. Dupont, 1929) was an early talking picture produced at Elstree by British International Pictures (BIP) in simultaneous British and German language versions – a French language version, making use of scenes from the Dupont versions, was directed by Jean Kemm. It was based on a play by Ernest Raymond called *The Berg* and did not mention the *Titanic* by name (*Atlantic* was the name of the ship in the film), though it was clear that it was based on the *Titanic*. BIP was a pioneer of the multiple-language film and *Atlantic* should be understood within the studio's short-lived international production strategy in the late 1920s, before economic constraints necessitated a shift to more modestly budgeted films.[9] *Titanic* (dir. Herbert Selpin, 1943) was a German propaganda film produced during the Second World War which blamed the disaster on a Jewish–British aristocratic plutocracy who order the captain to sail at full speed in order to win the Blue Ribband for the fastest Atlantic crossing and thus restore the falling share price of the shipping line. This was as fictional as the invention of the German First Officer of the *Titanic* and the ship's orchestra playing German marches as the ship sinks. The 1943 *Titanic* had a curious post-production history: it was never exhibited in Germany during the war – apparently Goebbels thought that scenes of passengers panicking as the ship sank were too reminiscent of Allied bombing – though it was shown in occupied countries. During the shooting of the film, Herbert Selpin was arrested for making alleged derogatory remarks about the armed forces and died in prison under mysterious circumstances. It was released in Germany in 1949 after being passed suitable for exhibition by the German censors, but was withdrawn following a campaign in the British press against what was dubbed 'Goebbels's hate-the-British masterpiece'. *Titanic* is therefore unique as the only film to have been banned both by the Germans and by the British.[10] Another film entitled *Titanic* (dir. Jean Negulesco, 1953) was a full-blown Hollywood studio melodrama, produced by Twentieth Century-Fox. It won an Academy Award for Best Screenplay (by Charles Brackett, Walter Reisch and Richard Breen), though its narrative is essentially a '*Grand Hotel* at sea' rather than a historical reconstruction. It takes fewer liberties with the recorded historical facts than the German film, but focuses exclusively on the American passengers.[11]

Having secured the rights to *A Night to Remember*, MacQuitty had to persuade an initially sceptical John Davis to back the film. Charles Drazin describes MacQuitty as 'one of the very few people able to elicit a warm response from Davis'.[12] It probably also helped that MacQuitty had produced *Above Us the Waves*, one of the leading British box-office films of 1955.[13] *A Night to Remember* was budgeted at just under £500,000 and was therefore in the higher-end cost bracket for British films at the time. It was also a more expensive production than usual for Rank in the 1950s, though this can be explained by a change in the corporation's strategy. In 1956 Rank announced that henceforth he would produce only films 'which had international entertainment appeal' and which could be 'vigorously sold in foreign markets'.[14] There was a certain commercial logic to this in so far as the Rank Organisation earned approximately half its revenues from overseas distribution. What Rank and Davis seemingly failed to realise, however, was that the majority of those revenues came from outside the United States. Rank's announcement of 1956 heralded another attempt to crack the American market, marked by the establishment the following year of Rank Film Distributors of America (RFDA) which was intended to bypass the problems encountered in the past with US distributors over British films. From the late 1950s the Rank Organisation, following a trend set by the Hollywood majors, focused its efforts on the production of fewer but bigger films. *A Night to Remember* should be placed, therefore, in the context of a cycle of international films produced by Rank in the late 1950s that also included *Campbell's Kingdom* (dir. Ralph Thomas, 1957), *A Tale of Two Cities* (dir. Ralph Thomas, 1958), *Ferry to Hong Kong* (dir. Lewis Gilbert, 1959) and *North West Frontier* (dir. J. Lee Thompson, 1959). In the event, this international production strategy was no more successful than it had been before. Rank was unable to repeat its US box-office successes of the 1940s and RFDA was wound up in 1958 after only 18 months. *A Night to Remember*, while mentioned by the British trade press as being 'in the money', was not among the leading box-office attractions of the year and it is not even clear whether the film ever went into profit.[15]

The role of director for *A Night to Remember* was entrusted to Roy Baker, one of a generation of largely unsung British directors (others include Ken Annakin, Terry Bishop, Muriel Box, Lewis Gilbert, Pat Jackson, Jack Lee and Harry Watt) whose careers began in either the pre-war or wartime documentary movement before moving into the commercial film industry in the post-war years. Baker had served in the Army Kinematograph Service (AKS) and had cut his teeth making training films and documentaries. His documentary background is evident in the feature films he made during the late 1940s and the 1950s which are notable for their realism and authenticity. He attracted the attention of Hollywood following *Morning Departure* (1950), a suspenseful and claustrophobic film set aboard a doomed submarine, and worked for Twentieth Century-Fox in the early 1950s before returning to Rank as director of *Jacqueline* (1955), *Tiger in the Smoke* (1956) and *The One That Got Away* (1957). MacQuitty had already approached Baker to direct *Above Us the Waves*, but Baker had turned the offer down 'for the stupid reason that I had already made a submarine story. I was devoted to the idea that I should try something different with every film I made.'[16]

Baker's wish always to 'try something different' helps to explain why 'many critics feel that his work lacks a personal style'.[17] A critical survey of British film-makers by *Sight and Sound* shortly after the release of *A Night to Remember*, for example, suggested that 'Baker has built a reputation for efficiency on a series of pictures not in themselves of the highest distinction'.[18] The claim that Baker was nothing more than an efficient journeyman director is challenged by Richards, who asserts that Baker is 'one of the unsung *auteurs* of British cinema'.[19] This is perhaps an exaggerated claim if an *auteur* is to be understood as a director whose films display a thematic unity and individual stylistic signature: Baker's films vary enormously in subject matter (he was to direct several of the later Hammer horror films as well as doing extensive television work), while the style of his films is less 'showy' than some of his contemporaries (John Guillermin and J. Lee Thompson spring to mind). Baker is probably better described as what the French critics call a *metteur-en-scène*, whose role is primarily to translate the written word into a visual image. In common with many film-makers of his generation, Baker felt that the director's job was 'putting the script on the screen'.[20]

A comparison of the shooting script of *A Night to Remember* and the finished film is instructive in this regard. With the exception of a few deleted scenes and some changes in the dialogue, the script is remarkably close to the film. The most memorable scenes in the film are described in the script. Thus, for example, the scene where passenger Robert Lucas (John Merivale) puts his wife and children in a lifeboat and tenderly kisses his sleeping child on the forehead and then passes him over with the words 'Goodbye, my dear son' is identified by Richards as 'one of the most moving scenes in the film' for the way in which 'the emotion is held in check'.[21] The way this scene is played by the actors and shot by Baker in a medium close-shot followed by a silent exchange of glances between Lucas and Second Officer Lightoller (Kenneth More) is exactly as it is described in the shooting script.[22]

The script for *A Night to Remember* was by Eric Ambler, who had worked with Baker previously on *The October Man* (1947) and *Highly Dangerous* (1950). Ambler, like Baker, had served in the AKS, where his credits included an induction film for new recruits called *The New Lot* (1943), directed by Carol Reed and co-written by Peter Ustinov, which subsequently was expanded into the feature film *The Way Ahead* (1944) – again written by Ambler and Ustinov and directed by Reed. His other screenwriting credits were mostly war films: *The Cruel Sea* (dir. Charles Frend, 1953), *The Purple Plain* (dir. Robert Parrish, 1954) and *Yangtse Incident* (dir. Michael Anderson, 1957). *The Cruel Sea* and *Yangtse Incident* had both been highly praised by British critics for their sober narratives and emotional restraint – qualities that would be paramount throughout *A Night to Remember* – while *Yangtse Incident* also has certain affinities with *A Night to Remember* in so far as it was adapted from a factual account of the escape of the frigate HMS *Amethyst* from Chinese Communists in 1949.

It is clear from the testimony of all those involved in the production of *A Night to Remember* that authenticity was the overriding concern. This was the word used by both the director and the producer: Baker said that it 'presented another challenge of authenticity' (he had recently completed *The One That Got Away*, based on the true story of the only German to escape successfully from a British prisoner-of-war camp and which had included difficult location work) and MacQuitty testified that 'the authenticity we were aiming for would be all-important'.[23] To this end they relied not only on Walter Lord's book, itself based on the fruits of extensive research, but consulted as many survivors of the tragedy as they could find. Joseph Boxhall, Fourth Officer of the *Titanic*, was the technical adviser. Alexander Vetchinsky's set designs were modelled on the actual interior of the *Titanic*, including a reproduction of the painting 'The Approach to the New World' that hung in the first-class smoking room (though in fact it was later established that this was the wrong painting). The decision to shoot the film both in black-and-white and in standard aspect ratio, at a time when colour and widescreen were real possibilities, locates the film within the documentary–realist aesthetic of British cinema which privileged a sober, restrained, economical visual style. As far as deciding which incidents to include in the film, Baker explained the problem thus: 'There was a considerable amount of historical evidence, mostly undisputed but some of it questionable, all of it to be sifted.'[24] To take just one example, there was – and still is – some dispute about the final tune played by the ship's orchestra. It quickly became part of *Titanic* folklore that the hymn 'Nearer, My God, To Thee' was played as the ship went down. From his interviews with survivors, however, Walter Lord concluded that the hymn 'Autumn' ('God of Mercy and Compassion') had been played. Ambler initially opted for 'Autumn' as per Lord's book; the shooting script declares: 'Then the sound of a single violin playing the Episcopal hymn "Autumn" is heard.' In the event, however, the film uses 'Nearer, My God, To Thee', as the British survivors to whom MacQuitty spoke were adamant that this hymn was what they had heard.[25]

A Night to Remember was shot at Pinewood between 15 October 1957 and 4 March 1958, using both a 300-foot section of one side of the *Titanic* and a one-tenth scale model of the entire ship. The scenes of passengers in lifeboats and in the water were shot at Ruislip Lido.[26] The film had an exceptionally large cast: 50 credited actors and 92 speaking parts in total. The film includes many historical characters: Captain Smith and other members of the crew, the *Titanic*'s designer Thomas Andrews, the chairman of the White Star Line J. Bruce Ismay (though he is not referred to by name in the film) and first-class passengers such as Molly Brown, Isidor and Ida Strauss and Benjamin Guggenheim. There are also several composite characters, particularly among the second-class and steerage passengers. The most significant role in terms of narrative agency is Second Officer Herbert Lightoller, played by Kenneth More. Baker described Lightoller as 'the central character but ... not a star part: *primus inter pares* at best'.[27] After Dirk Bogarde, More was the leading British male star of the late 1950s, having recently received both critical and popular acclaim for his performance as war hero Douglas Bader in the biopic *Reach for the Sky* (dir. Lewis Gilbert, 1956). More had also been offered the role of Franz von Werra – the part played by Hardy Kruger – in *The One That Got Away* and turned it down for much the same reason that Baker turned down *Above Us the Waves*: 'I did not feel I could possibly accept the part, because I had just played Bader.' More accepted *A Night to Remember*, however, as he felt it 'was something of which we could be proud: this time I was sure I had made the right choice'.[28]

A Night to Remember was premièred at the Odeon, Leicester Square, on 3 July 1958. Its reception from the trade and popular press was extremely enthusiastic. It was recognised as a major production achievement that brought much-needed prestige to the film industry at a time when it was struggling in the face of declining audiences. Several reviewers resorted to the obvious by labelling it 'a film to remember'. Frank Jackson in *Reynolds News* called it 'one of the finest films to come out of British studios for a long time'.[29] And Peter Burnup in the *News of the World* thought it 'a film that adds new lustre to the British

12. Abandon ship: Second Officer Herbert Lightoller (Kenneth More) directs the evacuation in *A Night to Remember*.

film industry'.[30] It is no surprise that the qualities of the film most admired by the reviewers were its 'realism' and 'restraint', and there was general approval for its matter-of-fact presentation and lack of melodramatic histrionics. *The Times* felt that 'it has clearly been the purpose of the director, Mr Roy Baker, to examine the disaster factually'.[31] Campbell Dixon compared it favourably to previous film versions of the event: '*A Night to Remember* shows that the subject has lost none of its enthralling interest, that the truth is less familiar than one had supposed and that the previous films were even more gratuitously bogus than they seemed to be at the time.'[32] The *Manchester Guardian* declared: 'It may in fact have been much like this. The film, though very big, is intentionally plain...It does not melodramatise or unduly sentimentalise but allows the drama to develop, as it were, of its own true and considerable impetus.'[33] And C.A. Lejeune concluded her review: 'As a clean-cut, unbiased, dramatic presentation of a momentous fact in history, the British film seldom did a better job than this.'[34]

Several reviewers suggested that the film provided an accurate picture of the social conditions and conditioning that prevailed in 1912. Dilys Powell felt that 'the social climate is here. In the confusion of catastrophe the steerage passengers were almost forgotten. Those who managed to reach the boat deck got there, most of them, by luck or pugnacity; it was their place to be saved last (if at all).'[35] David Robinson suggested that the film 'subtly caught the feeling of the period'.[36] Critics on the left were less sure of this, however. Thus William Whitebait complained that 'it evaded the whole social theme'.[37] And Derek Hill wrote sarcastically of the film's indication of class differences between the passengers: 'Underneath this daring social comment, a mere half-century late, is the implication that the days when wealth brought privilege at the expense of others ended the night the *Titanic* went down. But that's a night we can't remember – it hasn't yet come!'[38]

The film journals were less enamoured of the film than the national press. Ken Gay, reviewing it for the new middlebrow film magazine *Films and Filming*, felt that it 'succeeds admirably' in telling the story but that it fell some way short of believable characterisation as it 'was overloaded with a whole army of stage types – Irish peasants, wealthy ladies, footmen, stewards, below deck men, funny foreigners – in none of which we could believe'. 'The class divisions were brought out,' he added, 'but in the way it was done was almost a parody.'[39] The *Monthly Film Bulletin* suggested that the film-makers had missed an opportunity to make a bolder and better film:

> The story of the *Titanic* must have looked ideal cinematic material. It has human drama multiplied some 2,000 times, social significance, the glamour of the sea, the symbolic power of a sinking era, and a strong sense of divine intervention with all its inscrutable beauty. The failure of the Rank Organisation to produce a completely satisfying film out of these elements must be attributed to timidity. The makers seem to have been afraid to adopt a point of view which could give the film meaning either as a story of the gods striking down an arrogant age, or as an indictment of human smallness and negligence, or as a tribute to the human spirit. The result is a worthy, long-drawn-out documentary, with noticeably more honesty about human nature than most films, but little shape or style.[40]

Clearly, the journal was out of sympathy with the aims of the film-makers to recreate the event as authentically as possible and with the anonymous style of Baker's direction. It exemplifies the tendency, even at the time, to disparage the products of the British commercial cinema of the 1950s as well-intentioned but dull.

In America, where the film was released towards the end of 1958, the reception was more mixed than in Britain. The trade press predicted – inaccurately as it turned out – that it was 'a film to win wide audience appeal'.[41] Vincent Canby thought it 'a tremendous film' and predicted that 'Rank Film Distributors have here what can be a real blockbuster for the US market'.[42] But Hollis Alpert was probably closer to the response of American audiences in his comments for the *Saturday Review*:

> Not the *Titanic* again! The English, who have been busy of late recreating their national disasters in film form, have presumably tired of American efforts to reconstruct the sinking of the unsinkable ship, and in *A Night to Remember* have shown how it actually happened...It is rather odd that the English should like to do this kind of picture so much...No one, after seeing the picture, should any longer have the slightest doubt about how and why the *Titanic* floundered. But, do audiences care enough to justify this much work?[43]

Alpert's reference to the tendency of 'the English' to recreate national disasters probably refers to *Dunkirk*, released in America a few months before *A Night to Remember*, which similarly failed to set the box office alight. On the release of that film, Alpert's colleague Arthur Knight had remarked: 'For the past few years, the British film-makers have also been making stabs at a kind of national epic. They have been going back to the incidents in their recent past...as if intent on discovering, in this day of uncertainty and confusion, those values that once spelt survival.'[44]

Why did *A Night to Remember* fail to appeal to American audiences? It cannot have been the subject matter, for there was considerable American interest in the *Titanic* story and the 1953 Fox film had netted domestic rentals of $2,250,000, making it the company's sixth biggest hit of the year.[45] One explanation that has been put forward is that there was a national newspaper strike coinciding with the film's release, so few people would have seen the positive reviews. This is a less than convincing explanation, however, given that positive reviews in influential organs such as the *New York Times* had never automatically translated into large audiences for British films. A more likely explanation, perhaps, involves the nature of American popular cinema in the late 1950s. The biggest box-office hits of those years were spectacular, big-budget, widescreen, colour epics: *The Ten Commandments* (dir. Cecil B. De Mille, 1956), *Around the World in 80 Days* (dir. Michael Anderson, 1956), *The Bridge on the River Kwai* (dir. David Lean, 1957), *South Pacific* (dir. Joshua Logan, 1958) and *Ben-Hur* (dir. William Wyler, 1959). In comparison to films such as these, the modestly budgeted (by Hollywood standards) *A Night to Remember*, made in black-and-white and standard aspect ratio, and with no big-name stars recognisable to American audiences, lacked the sort entertainment value and visual spectacle that audiences seemingly preferred.

It might also be that *A Night to Remember* failed in the American market because it is such a very British film in content, ethos and style. It was the first – and to date the only – film of the *Titanic* to tell the story from the British perspective (*Atlantic*, while made in Britain, had been a 'polyglot' film made in different versions for different markets). The *Titanic* was, of course, an international tragedy: the victims included Irish, Dutch, Danes, Norwegians, Swedes, Germans, Poles, Russians and Chinese. This is a point poignantly captured towards the end of *A Night to Remember* where the film cuts from person to person reciting the Lord's Prayer in their own language as the ship sinks. However, the fact that the *Titanic* was a British-built and British-owned vessel with a British crew does lend a particularly British dimension to the tragedy. Here there is a significant difference between *A Night to Remember* and the 1953 *Titanic*, which had focused exclusively on the American passengers. Indeed, Richards sees *A Night to Remember* as 'a British riposte to Fox's 1953 *Titanic*'.[46] At the level of narrative, certainly, *A Night to Remember* sets out to reclaim the story of the *Titanic* from a British perspective. The film focuses on the crew (all British) and on a cross-section of the passengers (including Americans and Irish, though most of the individually delineated characters, real and composite, are British). There is evidence to suggest this was intentional in so far as the shooting script contains several scenes based around the character of the American Molly Brown which are omitted from the film itself. In the script, she is introduced near the beginning in a scene that has her leaving the Connaught Hotel and bantering with reporters about a rumoured marriage to a French nobleman ('Give me the rugged men of the West. European men? Pooh! Pooh! Pooh! and a bottle of the rum'). In the finished film, she is introduced later in the narrative when the ship has already set sail.

If, then, *A Night to Remember* tells the story of the *Titanic* from a British perspective, what image of the British does it convey? Most obviously it is a testament to the perceived British trait of coolness under pressure: upper lips were never stiffer than on the *Titanic*. Captain Smith twice tells his crew: 'There must be no panic.' (It is reported that Smith told his officers to 'Be British'; oddly, perhaps, he does not say this in the film.) Thus, the ship's officers and stewards are shown calmly organising the filling of lifeboats, the stokers man the pumps in an attempt to keep the ship afloat as long as possible, the wireless operators stay at their post transmitting SOS until the power is gone and the musicians play to calm the passengers' nerves. Officers and men go about their work with stoical acceptance of their fate. 'If any of you feel like praying, you'd better go ahead. The rest can join me in a cup of tea', the Chief Engineer tells his men. The same stoical behaviour is also observed by most of the passengers. Lucas, one of the fictional composite characters, assures Andrews that 'I'm not the panicking kind' when he asks the designer how bad the damage is; Andrews tells him the ship has only an hour left and advises him to get his wife and children into a lifeboat. Lucas replies with grim humour: 'I take it you and I may be in the same boat later.'

However, it would be entirely unfair to suggest that *A Night to Remember* represents such stoical and courageous behaviour as a uniquely British characteristic. It is also apparent in the behaviour of American passengers, who display the same codes of behaviour. The film contains several vignettes that refer specifically to actual persons on board. The elderly Mrs Strauss refuses to leave her husband ('We've always lived together, so why should I leave him now?') and towards the end of the film the millionaire Benjamin Guggenheim appears in full evening dress, accompanied by his valet, to declare: 'We've dressed now in our best and are prepared to go down like gentlemen...If anything were to happen to me, I would want my wife to know that I behaved decently.' This sort of behaviour – recounted by survivors –

embodies the gentlemanly code of honour and chivalry that has historically been part of the common culture and heritage shared by Great Britain and the United States and that was seen by contemporaries as a redeeming feature of the tragedy of the *Titanic*.[47]

A Night to Remember is also concerned with that very British obsession: the subject of class. It was the first film to represent the whole social spectrum of passengers on board the *Titanic*. Both *Atlantic* and the 1953 *Titanic* had focused on the first-class passengers; the 1943 *Titanic* had made an ideological point about the differences between the first-class passengers (British aristocrats and Jewish millionaires) and third-class passengers (many of whom are German) travelling in steerage. *A Night to Remember* includes not only first-class and steerage but also second-class passengers. Indeed, the ship itself is easily seen as a microcosm of British society in 1912 with its distinct social groups. The beginning of the film establishes the social backgrounds of the different types of passengers as we see

13. 'Goodbye, my dear son': Lucas (John Merivale) exhibits emotional restraint in *A Night to Remember*.

representatives of the aristocracy (Sir Richard and his wife), the middle classes (the Clarkes, a young couple on honeymoon) and the lower classes (a group of Irish emigrants) all leaving to board the ship. The same social hierarchy is observed on board the ship with first-class, second-class and steerage accommodation. There are clearly defined lines of demarcation that prevent social mixing: the Clarkes instinctively turn back when they accidentally stray onto the first-class deck, while a steward turns back a group of drunken steerage passengers from a second-class corridor. The barriers are both physical (the locked gates which contain the steerage passengers below decks) and cultural (such as the first-class male passenger who is dissuaded from joining in an impromptu game of deck football with a lump of ice from the berg by his female companion who says frostily: 'But they're steerage passengers!').

That *A Night to Remember* is preoccupied with class is not in question, but how far, if at all, can it be considered a critique of the class system? It is certainly less ideological in its representation of class than the 1943 *Titanic* or, for that matter, the later super-blockbuster Hollywood *Titanic* (dir. James Cameron, 1997). It would probably be fair to say that the film maintains an ironic distance from the social values that prevailed in 1912. This can be seen in the early scene where local children line up to cheer Sir Richard as he leaves the big house and their governess instructs them: 'Now, children... show Sir Richard and Her Ladyship how much we respect them.' 'The workhouse kids – making sure of their Christmas turkey from the home farm', one of the servants remarks sarcastically. This mild critique of social attitudes, however, does not translate into an outright assault on the class system. If the upper classes are mocked for their condescension towards the lower classes and the lower classes for their deference towards their social betters, the film nevertheless shows members of all classes behaving with great courage and decency. Men of all classes accept the principle of 'women and children first' and there is no social preference in the women put into the lifeboats. A few men try hiding among the women and are hauled out of the boats by Lightoller: these seem to include both first-class and steerage passengers.

It has been suggested that *A Night to Remember* is a metaphor for the breaking down of the class system: the sinking of the ship represents the end of the highly structured social order as all passengers, regardless of their social background, are literally in the same boat. To this extent it has sometimes been compared to Noël Coward's *In Which We Serve* (1942), which had similarly presented a ship, in that case the fictional Royal Navy destroyer HMS *Torrin*, as a microcosm of British society. In that film social class had been mapped onto the hierarchy of rank, represented by the three principal characters: the upper/upper-middle-class Captain Kinross (Noël Coward), the lower-middle-class Chief Petty Officer Hardy (Bernard Miles) and the working-class Able Seaman Blake (John Mills). The barriers of rank and class are broken down when the ship is sunk by bombers and the survivors cling to a life raft. Yet there is a crucial ideological difference between *A Night to Remember* and *In Which We Serve*. In Coward's film, natural leadership rests with the upper classes through the character of Kinross (modelled on Coward's aristocratic friend Louis Mountbatten) and it is clear that even in the water he maintains the authority conferred upon him both by his rank and by his class. In *A Night to Remember*, however, leadership is exercised by the middle classes, represented by the ship's officers and pre-eminently by Lightoller. The professionalism of the officers – professionalism being one of the cardinal middle-class virtues – is a recurring theme of the film. It extends not only to the crew of the *Titanic* but also to Captain Rostron of the *Carpathia* who is shown calmly and efficiently preparing his ship to pick up survivors.

That is not to say that *A Night to Remember* is entirely uncritical of British behaviour and attitudes. While the film endorses profes-sionalism and duty, it is critical of complacency. Several characters, including the captain, declare that the *Titanic* is 'unsinkable'; some passengers refuse to believe that the ship is actually sinking. Even Lightoller, reflecting on the disaster, admits to a certain sense of complacency: 'But we were so sure. Even though it's happened, it's still unbelievable. I don't feel I'll ever feel sure again – about anything.' It is tempting to interpret this as a veiled reference to the Suez Crisis, though in the absence of any contextual evidence this must remain a highly speculative reading. In July 1956 President Nasser of Egypt announced the nationalisation of the Suez Canal, owned by a French company in which the British government had a majority share-holding. When diplomatic efforts to reverse Nasser's move failed, Britain and France responded by sending an airborne force that landed at Port Said and seized the Canal. The joint Anglo-French action aroused indignation within the international community and was condemned by the United

Nations. A combination of diplomatic and economic pressure – the value of sterling depreciated during the crisis – brought about a humiliating withdrawal by the British and French forces in November. The Suez Crisis demonstrated that Britain was no longer capable of acting independently to enforce its strategic and economic interests in the Middle East – the United States, significantly, had opposed the action – and, in the view of most historians, accelerated the retreat from empire that gathered pace over the next decade.

While there is no evidence to suggest that *A Night to Remember* was either intended by its makers or seen by contemporary critics as an allegory of the Suez Crisis, there are some more general parallels between the world of 1912 and the world of the late 1950s that are worth elaborating. The sinking of the *Titanic* coincided with a period of political unrest and disturbance in Britain that historians have labelled the 'Edwardian Crisis': there was a wave of strikes between 1910 and 1914, often spilling over into violence, the campaign for women's suffrage was becoming increasingly militant and Ireland was on the verge of civil war over the question of Home Rule. The *Titanic* tragedy, with its accounts of gentlemanly behaviour and human decency, came to be seen as an affirmation of the society and values that were under threat from political and industrial militancy. *A Night to Remember* was made at a time when Britain's post-war mood of complacency had been punctured by Suez and when some voices on both the right and the left were expressing their concern about the decline of Britain – not just in world status but also in moral standards at home. The late 1950s saw increasing social discontent: the Notting Hill race riots of 1958 represented perhaps the first serious social disturbances since the hunger marches of the early 1930s. In the arts, meanwhile, the staging of John Osborne's *Look Back in Anger* at the Royal Court Theatre in May 1956 is generally seen as marking the emergence of the 'Angry Young Men' of stage and literature who took a distinctly jaundiced view of what they perceived as the stagnant, snobbish, class-bound and elitist nature of British society. Osborne was one of the contributors to the polemical arts manifesto *Declaration* in 1957. Another essayist was the film critic and documentarist Lindsay Anderson, who famously described British cinema as 'snobbish, anti-intelligent, emotionally inhibited, wilfully blind to the conditions and problems of the present, [and] dedicated to an out-of-date, exhausted national ideal'.[48]

A Night to Remember, although released the year after Anderson's stinging critique of British cinema, would nevertheless seem to be the sort of film he had in mind. It represents the middlebrow, middle-class mainstream of British cinema during the 1950s, reaffirming the solidity of the existing social order. It was made at probably the last moment in British cinema history when a film of this sort was possible. There is a sense, indeed, in which *A Night to Remember* marks the symbolic end of a particular period of British film-making. The first tremors of a seismic change in British film culture were already being felt in the popular success of the Hammer horror films (*The Curse of Frankenstein* in 1957, *Dracula* in 1958) and the start of the long-running 'Carry On' series (*Carry On Sergeant* in 1958) which brought, respectively, visceral gore and vulgar humour into the mainstream of British popular cinema. Then, at the turn of the decade, *Room at the Top* (dir. Jack Clayton, 1959) and *Saturday Night and Sunday Morning* (dir. Karel Reisz, 1960) marked the emergence of a British 'new wave' cinema that dramatised the discontent and alienation of the two social groups that previously had only marginal representation in film: young adults and the working classes. New wave films were characterised by their warts-and-all representation of abrasive working-class protagonists who swore and drank and exhibited none of the deference towards social authority that had traditionally been the trait of working-class characters in film. And the new wave film-makers themselves represented a generational and cultural shift within the British film industry. They eschewed the restrained, anonymous style of the directors of Baker's generation and instead took every opportunity to draw attention to aspects of form and style. Baker's film career went into decline following *A Night to Remember*. He made two more features in Britain: *The Singer Not the Song* (1960), a conflict-resolution melodrama featuring a bizarrely cast Dirk Bogarde and John Mills as a Mexican bandit and a Catholic priest whose relationship carries overtones of homosexuality, which was a critical and commercial disaster; and the race-relations film *Flame in the Streets* (1961). In common with other directors of his generation, Baker turned to television when feature film work dried up and he spent much of the 1960s directing episodes of detective and adventure series such as *The Saint*, *The Human Jungle*, *Gideon's Way*, *The Avengers* and *The Baron*. He returned to feature films with Hammer Film Productions, beginning with *Quatermass and the Pit* (1967), whereupon he changed his screen credit to Roy Ward Baker in order to avoid confusion with a sound editor at the studio also called Roy Baker.

In his autobiography, Baker wrote that *A Night to Remember* 'gave the Rank Organisation considerable credit for making it. This was something new for the Org, which rightly gained considerable prestige. For years there had been nothing but criticism and downright barracking for all Rank's efforts.'[49] Rank himself was ennobled in 1958 for his services to the British film industry. Ironically, by that time the Rank Organisation had already started to diversify out of the film business. By the late 1950s the corporation was again in financial difficulty, due in large measure to the failure of its international production strategy. In 1958 Rank incurred losses of £1.3 million on film production and distribution; the following year it lost another £900,000.[50] It seems entirely appropriate that *A Night to Remember* should have been one of Rank's last major 'in house' productions as not only does it embody the cultural values that Rank stood for, but it also serves as a metaphor for Rank's inability by the end of the 1950s to navigate the turbulent seas of popular taste. John Davis had by now come to the conclusion that film production on its own was not an economical proposition. In the 1960s he wound down Rank's production activities and invested in only a handful of co-productions where the risk could be shared with another investor, such as Benjamin Fisz's *The Heroes of Telemark* (dir. Anthony Mann, 1965) and Harry Saltzman's *The Ipcress File* (dir. Sidney J. Furie, 1965). He concentrated on distribution and exhibition, and on renting space at Pinewood to independent producers. Davis may have had little cultural taste, but he had the foresight to realise that Rank's long-term survival was dependent upon diversification out of the film industry. Thus it was that the Rank Organisation bought shares in independent television and moved into other areas of the leisure industry such as dance halls, bowling alleys and motorway service stations. By far its most profitable venture, however, was in acquiring the overseas licensing rights to the Xerox photocopying process in 1956. In 1963 Rank Xerox became a full subsidiary of the Rank Organisation and was responsible for half the corporation's profits. *A Night to Remember*, for its part, represents the symbolic end of the period of Rank's dominance of the British film industry and of the sort of respectable film culture that the Rank Organisation embodied.

9

Men of Harlech:
Zulu (1964)

ZULU, directed by American Cy Endfield and produced by Endfield in partnership with Welsh actor Stanley Baker, remains one of the most popular and enduring of the action-oriented historical adventure films that flourished during the first half of the 1960s – a cycle that also includes *The Alamo* (dir. John Wayne, 1960), *Spartacus* (dir. Stanley Kubrick, 1960), *El Cid* (dir. Anthony Mann, 1961), *55 Days at Peking* (dir. Nicholas Ray, 1963) and *Khartoum* (dir. Basil Dearden, 1966). Like all these films, *Zulu* was backed by American capital, though it is undoubtedly British in terms of subject matter, cast, production and representation of history. An account of the Battle of Rorke's Drift during the Zulu War of 1879, *Zulu* is that rarity for British cinema: a genuine epic (in both the popular and the literal meaning of the word) that matches the production values, narrative excitement and visual spectacle of Hollywood at its best. A popular success both in Britain and overseas, *Zulu* was not, however, regarded as a particularly significant film and has only belatedly attracted much critical commentary. Yet in hindsight it clearly represents something of a watershed: *Zulu* can be seen, simultaneously, both as the last, glorious flowering of the old-fashioned imperial adventure epic and as a precursor of the more cynical anti-imperialist films that followed later in the decade. It is largely owing to its ability to support both pro-imperialist and anti-imperialist readings that *Zulu* has recently become the focus of an ideologically charged debate amongst film scholars.[1]

Zulu was made during a period of relative health, both commercially and artistically, for British cinema. Richards summarises the orthodox view when he observes that the '1960s witnessed a revitalization of British cinema and the emergence of a flourishing and diverse film culture after what was widely perceived to be the "doldrums era" of the 1950s'.[2] It was a decade of transition in which the older generation of British film-makers, who had learned their craft during the 1930s and came to prominence during the Second World War (such as Carol Reed, Charles Frend, Harry Watt, David Macdonald, Frank Launder and Sidney Gilliat), were supplanted by a younger generation who had come to maturity in the post-war years and who made their first feature films in the late 1950s or early 1960s (Tony Richardson, Karel Reisz, John Schlesinger, Richard Lester, Lindsay Anderson). Although cinema attendances were still in decline and cinema closures continued throughout the 1960s, production remained stable at around 70 films a year. With the Rank Organisation withdrawing from production and focusing its efforts on distribution and exhibition, and with ABPC seeming to turn out little more than undistinguished comedies, the majority of British films came from independent producers. Two consortia groups established in 1959 represented the first significant challenge to the hold of the Rank/ABPC duopoly for over a decade: Bryanston (Michael Balcon, Tony Richardson, Ronald Neame, John Bryan, Julian Wintle) and Allied Film Makers (Richard Attenborough, Bryan Forbes, Jack Hawkins, Guy Green, Basil Dearden and Michael Relph) were organised as collectives to find financial backing and distribution guarantees. Both groups enjoyed some successes in the early 1960s, but were still dependent on the big distributors (Bryanston on British Lion, Allied on Rank) and had ceased to be significant forces by the mid-1960s.[3]

It was around this time, moreover, that the British film industry belatedly came to terms with the fact that cinema-going was no longer the 'essential social habit' that it had been during the 1930s and 1940s. The supporting feature had all but disappeared by the early 1960s. In 1963 Bill Altria, replacing the veteran Josh Billings as the chief *Kine Weekly* correspondent, identified a new trend: 'The really big pictures – big at the box-office that is – are attracting larger audiences than ever, but the run-of-the-mill films, the type that only a year or so ago were the bread and butter of the business, are barely yielding a crust.'[4] Thus it was that the British film industry followed the example of

Hollywood in shifting towards the production of fewer but bigger films intended to reap success at the box office. This strategy was best exemplified by the James Bond series, beginning in 1962 with *Dr No*, which quickly established itself as the popular film phenomenon of the decade. The Bond movies also highlighted another trend that became increasingly important throughout the decade in so far as they were backed by US dollars (United Artists).

The production history of *Zulu* needs to be understood in this context. Not only was it an example of a 'really big' picture – reportedly the third most successful film at the British box office in 1964 (behind the Bond film *Goldfinger* and the Beatles musical *A Hard Day's Night*)[5] – but it also exemplifies the trend towards what film historians have described as the 'package' rather than the 'studio' mode of production. Rather than being one part of an overall studio production programme, the tendency from the early 1960s was to produce films on an individual basis, sold on a 'package' of director, star and script. This was the case with *Zulu*, a project initiated by Baker and Endfield (who set up Diamond Films specifically to make the film) with Baker as star and Endfield as director. The script, written jointly by Endfield and historian John Prebble, came from a magazine article by Prebble on the Battle of Rorke's Drift that Endfield had read and brought to the attention of Baker.[6] Financial support for the package was provided by American financer-distributor Joseph E. Levine, a flamboyant showman in the Cecil B. De Mille mould, who had started as an exhibitor before becoming an independent distributor in the 1950s, making his fortune by buying cheap foreign films that would not otherwise have been shown in America – most famously the Italian 'peplum' *Hercules* – and marketing them aggressively as 'exploitation' items that would appeal especially to the younger patrons of the new drive-in cinemas. In the 1960s Levine began to invest in more artistic European films, including Godard's *Le Mépris* and Fellini's *8½*. *Zulu* was his first British film, Levine announcing his involvement in November 1962.[7] Levine was evidently attracted to the film as it was the sort he could market successfully: '*Zulu* is our kind of picture. It is big, it has guts and it has all kinds of exploitation values that we can really sink our teeth into.'[8] *Zulu* was made for a reported $3.5 million, though there is evidence to suggest that this figure was inflated for publicity purposes and that the real cost was closer to $1.75 million. In any event, Levine testified that *Zulu* was brought in 'ahead of schedule and under budget'.[9] To put this in context, *Dr No* had cost $950,000 and *Tom Jones* $350,000, meaning that *Zulu* represented a significant investment for a British film, though it was still only a fraction of the $13 million that Columbia invested in Sam Spiegel and David Lean's *Lawrence of Arabia* (1962).[10] Levine's Embassy Pictures released *Zulu* in America, while Paramount Pictures (with whom Levine had a distribution arrangement) handled it throughout the rest of the world.

While the opening credits of the film therefore declare 'Joseph E. Levine presents', *Zulu* was very much the pet project of Stanley Baker who, according to the publicity material circulating around it, persuaded Levine to back the film, which was originally to have been entitled *The Battle of Rorke's Drift*. Allegedly, Levine had agreed on the condition that the title was changed to *Zulu*, as he thought he could sell a film of that title regardless of its content. *Zulu* was the first venture into film production for Baker, a miner's son from South Wales who had established himself as the pre-eminent 'tough guy' actor of British cinema during the 1950s, alternating between 'heavy' villains and abrasive working-class heroes.[11] Baker was attracted to the story of how a garrison of only 105 able-bodied men of the South Wales Borderers, led by an officer of the Royal Engineers with no previous combat experience, held an isolated mission station against an army of some 4,000 Zulu warriors on the day and night of 22-23 January 1879. Evidence that the film was intended, in part at least, as a tribute to the role of Welsh soldiers in the defence of Rorke's Drift is provided by promotional materials which emphasise this very point: 'The story that *Zulu* tells is part of British – particularly Welsh – history of which the country can ever feel proud. Every effort was made to present the subject as authentically as possible.'[12] It is rather ironic, therefore, that the part which Baker himself played in what one critic later dubbed 'the Great Welsh Epic' was in fact the English commanding officer at Rorke's Drift, Lieutenant John Chard.[13]

As producer and star, Baker was the driving force behind *Zulu*, and it seems far more appropriate to locate the film within the context of his *œuvre* than of its director. Cy (Cyril) Endfield was one of the victims of the Hollywood blacklist of suspected communists and fellow travellers following the highly acrimonious investigations into the US film industry by the notorious House Committee on UnAmerican Activities which, in the climate of the early Cold War, more often than not smelt 'reds under the bed'. Endfield was one of those – others included Edward Dmytryk, Carl Foreman and Joseph Losey – who found employment in Britain, where he worked either uncredited or under pseudonyms (for example, he was the 'C. Raker Endfield' who directed *Hell Drivers*, starring Baker, in 1957). While it is always tempting to look for allegorical subtexts in the films of blacklisted writers and directors – *Hell Drivers* with its narrative of a lone driver standing up against corruption in the haulage industry might at a stretch support such a reading – there is no real evidence of this in *Zulu*. Whatever ideological import the film possesses – and it possesses a great deal – would not seem to have come through Endfield.[14]

Zulu was filmed on location in the Royal Natal National Park, South Africa, with the interiors shot at Twickenham Studios in London, during the spring and summer of 1963.[15] For various reasons it proved impossible to shoot on the site of the actual battle, so a replica of the mission and hospital at Rorke's Drift was built on a suitable location 100 miles away. The production was assisted by the South African government, which provided a company of national servicemen to play the defenders of Rorke's Drift – the troops reportedly required special instruction in bayonet-fighting – and by Chief Mangosuthu Buthelezi, nephew of the Paramount Chief of the Zulu Nation (and later Chief Minister of Kwazulu), who advised Baker and Endfield on Zulu battle tactics and played his own great-grandfather, Cetewayo. In addition to Baker, the principal cast comprised Jack Hawkins as Swedish missionary Otto Witt (a composite character based on two chaplains present at Rorke's Drift), Ulla Jacobsson as his daughter (Jacobsson was a Swedish actress who had a brief international career in the 1960s) and Michael Caine, in his first starring role, as Lieutenant Gonville Bromhead of the South Wales Borderers. *Zulu* was premièred at London's Plaza Cinema on 22 January 1964 (the eighty-fifth anniversary of the battle) before going on general release and setting a record number of admissions for the ABC circuit.[16]

The promotional discourse for *Zulu* emphasised its size and spectacle ('Dwarfing the Mightiest! Towering over the Greatest!'). In this sense, the film locates itself within the cycle of large-scale 'epic' films made during the late 1950s and early 1960s, including, further to those already mentioned, westerns such as *The Big Country* (dir. William Wyler, 1958), *The Magnificent Seven* (dir. John Sturges, 1960),

Cimarron (dir. Anthony Mann, 1960) and *How the West Was Won* (dir. Henry Hathaway et al., 1962) and war films such as *The Longest Day* (dir. Andrew Marton et al., 1962), *The Guns of Navarone* (dir. J. Lee Thompson, 1961), *The Great Escape* (dir. John Sturges, 1963) and *Battle of the Bulge* (dir. Ken Annakin, 1965). The proliferation of the action epic at this time was due in large measure to the continuing erosion of the cinema audience and to the perception within the film industry that 'big' films, with high production values, stellar casts and the combination of colour and widescreen, were the most likely means of enticing patrons into the cinemas.[17]

Sheldon Hall has suggested that *Zulu* has an 'equivocal character as an "epic"' on the grounds that the 'battle it describes was relatively minor in national or global impact' and asserts that '*Zulu*'s epic qualities are largely of the folkloric kind, in that it recounts great heroic deeds of the past for the admiration and moral inspiration of present generations'.[18] Whether or not *Zulu* is an epic depends, ultimately, on how this somewhat imprecise generic term is defined. Steve Neale argues that the term 'epic', in the 1950s and 1960s, 'was used to identify, and to sell, two overlapping contemporary trends: films with historical, especially ancient-world settings; and large-scale films of all kinds which used new technologies, high production values and special modes of distribution and exhibition to differentiate themselves both from routine productions and from alternative forms of contemporary entertainment, especially television'.[19] *Zulu* certainly met the film industry's own criteria of an epic. It was a big action-spectacular filmed in Technicolor and Super Technirama 70, one of several widescreen processes in the early 1960s that was used for only a handful of films, in an attempt to differentiate it from the 35-millimetre Panavision, the industry's standard widescreen format by that time. It used two of the common devices of the epic: a portentous score using full orchestra (by John Barry) and a voice-over narration by a major star (Richard Burton) at the beginning and end of the film. And it was accorded a high-profile release, showing at selected showcase cinemas equipped for 70-millimetre projection and stereophonic sound.[20]

Yet *Zulu* is a rare example among sixties epics of a film where spectacle does not overshadow narrative. Even with a running time of 138 minutes (short by the standards of some epics), *Zulu* stands out as a remarkably structured and economical narrative where there is little, if any, surplus: no scene is wasted, story-telling is paramount, and there is no superfluous romantic interest or pious moralising (elements that detract from the two films to which *Zulu* is most obviously comparable, *55 Days at Peking*, featuring Ava Gardner as the some-what improbable romantic interest for Charlton Heston, and *The Alamo*, which features John Wayne pontificating at length about the meaning of the word 'republic'). Structurally, it falls into two roughly equal parts: the build-up to the battle as the garrison at Rorke's Drift prepares to defend the station against the approaching Zulus and the battle itself as the troops repulse wave after wave of Zulu attacks. It seems to me that Hall is correct in his suggestion that *Zulu* 'constitutes material for an epic primarily because of the fantastically disproportionate military odds involved, and the extremes of courage and fortitude required of both the defenders and the attackers'.[21] It is an epic in the literal meaning of the Latin *epos*: a narrative poem celebrating heroic actions. Whatever one's opinion of the cultural and racial politics of *Zulu*, it is impossible to deny that it represents actions that are the stuff of heroism. As the film critic Philip Oakes remarked: 'What *Zulu* celebrates is courage – a virtue which history tends to cut down to size, but which still looks great on the wide screen.'[22]

The critical reception of *Zulu* was mixed, revealing a range of responses to the film's representations of history, patriotism, empire and race. To a large extent, indeed, the critical response anticipates the debate that has since arisen over *Zulu* and for that reason it is worth summarising the main points of contention. The trade press, characteristically, was enthralled by the film's qualities of spectacle and narrative excitement. 'If history could be put over like this in school, teachers would have no problem', declared *Kinematograph Weekly*, suggesting – albeit erroneously – that Endfield 'has kept closely to official records of the action and has wisely realised that the occasion needed very little conventional dramatisation'.[23] *Variety*'s London correspondent saw it very much as Levine's film, averring that it was 'a picture with potent b.o. [box office] potential, and one that also allows ample scope for his flamboyant approach to showmanship'. As far as its representation of heroic deeds was concerned, *Variety* added, it 'keeps the traditional British stiff upper-lip attitudes down to the barest minimum'.[24]

There were some reviewers, particularly from the popular press, who claimed *Zulu* as a patriotic epic, responding to it precisely as Hall suggests as a story 'for the admiration and moral inspiration of present generations'. It is instructive to note, however, that within this discourse reviewers tended to conflate the filmic narrative with the actual battle itself, sometimes to the extent that it is not always clear which they are describing. Every review, it seems, mentioned the fact that 11 VCs – the British Army's highest award for bravery – were won by the defenders of Rorke's Drift. 'I would like to award this film a Victoria Cross of its own', declared Felix Barker in the *Evening News*. 'If ever the phrases "the Thin Red Line" or "last man, last round" had real significance, they get it in the film made by Stanley Baker and Cy Endfield.'[25] (Neither phrase, incidentally, is used in the film.) In an eloquent example of reducing historical events to filmic metaphor, Cecil Wilson of the *Daily Mail* described the defence of Rorke's Drift as 'a classic piece of real-life Errol Flynnery'.[26]

Indeed, it is a characteristic of many critical responses to *Zulu* that they merge filmic and historical discourses. Thus, while placing it within the genre of the British Empire film – a genre that enjoyed its heyday in the 1930s with Hollywood films such as *The Lives of a Bengal Lancer* (dir. Henry Hathaway, 1935), *The Charge of the Light Brigade* (dir. Michael Curtiz, 1936), *Wee Willie Winkie* (dir. John Ford, 1937) and *Gunga Din* (dir. George Stevens, 1939) – critics also recognised, as David Robinson put it, that 'the genre has been modified' to the extent that it 'significantly reflects changing attitudes in the post-war cinema'.[27] There is a greater emphasis in *Zulu* on the carnage of battle and little sense of the jingoism that characterises the films of the 1930s. Yet the two most prominent film review journals of the time differed in their assessment of the film's relationship to its generic predecessors. Thus, on the one hand, *Films and Filming* described it as 'an anti-heroic view of the kind of situation which used to be treated to flag-waving fervour'.[28] On the other hand, however, the *Monthly Film Bulletin* regarded it as 'a typically fashionable war film, paying dutiful lip service to the futility of the slaughter while milking it for thrills', and complained that 'whenever there is a pause in the action the script plunges relentlessly into bathos, with feuding officers, comic other ranks, and all the other trappings of the British War Film Mark I, which one had hoped were safely obsolete'. In contrast to those critics who wanted to award *Zulu* its own VC, the *Monthly Film Bulletin* concluded: 'It seems a very poor tribute to the men who actually fought at Rorke's Drift to portray them on such a comic strip level.'[29]

Most of the middlebrow critics detected evidence in the film of attitudes and values that belonged to the present rather than to the nineteenth century. Interestingly, however, they did not generally approve of this aspect. Thus, Isobel Quigly in the *Spectator* noted 'a modern effort to look carnage in the eye and hate it', but felt, consequently, 'that periods are confused and confusing and spiritual anachronisms abound'.[30] Penelope Gilliat in the *Observer* similarly felt that the 'liberal lines seem a bit out of period. Every soldier there must have called the enemy the fuzzy-wuzzies at the time, and it's like trying to graft a left-wing leaflet on to the Duke of Wellington to make us accept anything else.'[31] Patrick Gibbs concurred in the *Daily Telegraph*: 'This putting of "retrospective views" into people's mouths is unhappy. The dying man who asks "why" or the officer who is "disgusted" hardly give this Empire-building episode a convincing sense of period.'[32] And even Nina Hibbin in the *Daily Worker* – one critic whose reviews usually reflected the ideological orientation of the organ she wrote for – disliked the intrusion of anachronistic sentiments into the film: 'It makes even less sense historically, since the British Army didn't fight its colonial wars of the 1870s with the anti-war mood of the 1960s audience in mind.'[33]

While the British critics detected evidence of 'liberal' ideological posturing in *Zulu*, however, their American counterparts were more bothered by the racial aspects of the film. The *Hollywood Reporter*, while favourably inclined towards the film overall and feeling that 'the story is not weighted in sympathy for white or black', nevertheless anticipated the later academic critiques in suggesting that it was an essentially one-sided picture of events: '*Zulu* is seen from the British point of view. It should be remembered that in today's world this is not the attitude of vast potential audiences.'[34] Bosley Crowther was more outspoken, describing the choice of subject as 'strangely archaic and indiscreet' at a time of 'so much racial tension and anticolonial discord in the world'. He concluded his review for the *New York Times* by asking: '[Is] the ideal of the white man's burden, which this picture tacitly presents (for all its terminal disgust with the slaughter), in the contemporary spirit?'[35] Certainly, the 'moment' of *Zulu* coincided with an increasing international awareness of racial problems. Its production in South Africa came at the height of the apartheid regime and took place only three years after the Sharpeville massacre (21 March 1960) in which some 67 anti-apartheid demonstrators were shot dead and a further 200 wounded by South African police. The film's release in the United States, furthermore, coincided with the passing of the Civil Rights Act (July 1964), and with an increase in black militancy (exemplified by the Harlem riots of the same month) that was a cause of great concern both to moderate Civil Rights leaders and to the liberals in the Johnson administration who had sponsored the Act. Perhaps it is little wonder that, in this climate, *Zulu* underperformed at the US box office.[36]

While *Zulu* can hardly be blamed for the existence of apartheid in South Africa or for racial problems in America, attitudes towards the film – at least within the academy – seem to have been coloured (the verb is used deliberately) by its representation of racial difference. In contrast to its popular reputation – it was successfully reissued in 1967, 1972 and 1976 – *Zulu* was, to say the least, an unfashionable film within an intellectual climate that privileged texts deemed progressive or radical. Raymond Durgnat, the most idiosyncratic of critics and by no means a slave to intellectual fads and fashions, nevertheless found little to admire in *Zulu* (except for its action sequences) and rejected the reading of it as a liberalising narrative:

> The film may seem 'progressive', given its up-from-the-ranks Baker's edging of upper-crust Michael Caine out of command, and the unflattering picture of a drunken and cowardly missionary (Jack Hawkins) and his fine-looking but null daughter (Ulla Jacobsson). Second thoughts are less reassuring. The missionary has made a point of attending native ceremonies in a friendly spirit, in contrast to the whites and Zulus who gallantly go their separate ways. Real understanding is attained through – apartheid, might one say? – whereas those meddling clergymen – like Father Huddleston, perhaps...[37]

It is a contestable reading – the film does not suggest that Chard has risen through the ranks, and, while the character of the Reverend Witt is represented as an appeaser and a drunkard, he is surely no coward – though it set the tone for the academic reputation of *Zulu*.

In the 1980s, as the intellectual climate turned decisively against the imperial project and when it became anathema to suggest that there might ever have been more to the British Empire than conquest and slaughter, *Zulu* came to be seen as an unreconstructed hymn to the 'white man's burden' that was politically disingenuous and ideologically irredeemable. This view was explicit in a programme note written to accompany a screening of *Zulu* at London's National Film Theatre in 1986 as part of a season devoted to 'Images of Empire':

> In the context of 'Images of Empire', this colonial war adventure can only be regarded as exploitative pulp – although in general most reviewers have shown ambivalence towards the film's sheer force and impact (and it was for several years running a Christmas treat on British television during the mid-seventies). What seems to be at play here is some notion of historical authenticity, which not only heightens the film's unquestioned glorification of British heroism, but also disguises its more unsavoury aspects, of which there are many. The tendency in colonial narratives to collapse African characters into a (typically menacing) mass is grandly acknowledged here. And despite the film's apparently 'liberal' gesture, in acknowledging the magnificence of the Zulu warriors – in a romanticised way – the main thrust is clearly towards emphasising the militaristic and, more importantly, spiritual superiority of the hugely outnumbered British.[38]

This is, again, a reading that can be contested – the film's representation of heroism can hardly be described as 'unquestioned glorification' – even though the tone of the opening sentence seems to want to deny the possibility of any alternative readings.

The most sustained ideological critique of the film to date has come in an article by Christopher Sharrett, who, while acknowledging *Zulu* as a 'tautly-directed film that is an instruction to all action filmmakers', proceeds to take it to task on the grounds that 'its liberal ideological veneer cloaks a reliance on a surprising number of generic conventions as well as some key historical distortions and omissions in order to perpetuate its own colonialist political agenda'.[39] He deplores *Zulu* for its 'casual racism' and 'antidemocratic sentiments', absurdly detects an element of 'homophobia' in the characterisation of Bromhead, complains that it ignores the Zulu point-of-view and argues that it deliberately and systematically sets out to assert the superiority of the white British colonisers over the black African colonised subjects. He attacks it for its departures from the historical record, which, he asserts, are nothing less than 'a strategy for bolstering its conservative outlook and its embrace of England's nineteenth-century war policies in South Africa'.[40] Sharrett's critique therefore brings together two particular issues – the accusation of ideological impropriety on the one hand, the charge of historical inauthenticity on the other – that, as we have repeatedly seen, are both characteristic of critical discourses around the historical film.

It is my contention that, in order to analyse the cultural politics of *Zulu* properly, it is absolutely essential to place the film in context. There is little to be gained from judging a film made in the early 1960s in the terms of an intellectual climate prevailing four decades later, any more than there is from judging the events of the nineteenth century by the moral standards of the twenty-first. The first point that must be made is that, whatever its omissions of fact or detail, it was never the intention of the film's creators to present events from the perspective of the Zulus. The charge that it does not do so may be correct, but it is hardly relevant. Partly it is a simple dramatic question – in siege narratives such as *Zulu*, *The Alamo* and *55 Days at Peking* it is dramatically necessary to identify with those who are themselves besieged – but it also involves wider questions of political economy. *Zulu* was made by British and American personnel who could never authentically have 'spoken for' the Zulus even had it been their intention to do so. The production discourse attests to the film-makers' desire to represent the Zulus fairly but, as a British film whose primary markets would be in Britain and in other English-speaking countries, it was both inevitable and desirable that the film would depict events from the British perspective. To accuse *Zulu* of omitting the Zulu point-of-view is as irrelevant as accusing *The Alamo* of neglecting the Mexican perspective or complaining that *Gunga Din* has nothing to say on the subject of Indian nationalism.

Accepting, then, that *Zulu* depicts Rorke's Drift from the British point-of-view, what of the charge that the film distorts the historical record of the actual battle? In this respect, the Zulus may have had less reason to complain than the British. The African tradition of oral history means that Zulu people are familiar with the story of events that occupy an important place in their own history; Chief Buthelezi was happy to co-operate with the film-makers even though he knew that the way the battle was represented on screen involved a considerable degree of dramatic licence. According to most accounts,

Rorke's Drift was a scrappy sort of fight in which the defenders prevailed through sheer stamina rather than superior tactics, but the film represents it as a more disciplined affair, in which the tactics used by both sides – the 'buffalo' formation of the Zulus and the volley-by-ranks rifle-firing of the British – imposes a structure onto the battle and thus assists the viewer's comprehension of the events.[41] There are further deviations from the historical record in the characterisation of the defenders of Rorke's Drift – the families of both Lieutenant Gonville Bromhead and Private Henry Hook complained about the way their ancestors were portrayed – while the role played by others in the battle is omitted entirely.[42] Moreover, two of the most memorable moments in the film – the Welsh soldiers singing a rousing chorus of 'Men of Harlech' as the Zulus make their final assault and the sudden reappearance of the Zulus to salute their 'fellow braves' before withdrawing from the field of battle – are entirely inventions of the scriptwriters.

Zulu is perhaps best understood as a popular mythologisation of history rather than as an authentic historical reconstruction, despite the claim of the promotional discourse. In this respect the film can usefully be compared to the western, which similarly uses a combination of historical material and generic conventions and archetypes in order to represent a popular, if not necessarily historically accurate, narrative of the American past. Sharrett argues (here convincingly) that *Zulu* borrows much of its imagery and conventions from the western: the appearance of the Zulus on the hilltop overlooking Rorke's Drift recalls the appearance of Indians in films such as John Ford's *Stagecoach* and *Fort Apache*; the representation of the Zulus as an undifferentiated mass is similar to the representation of Indians in the western; characters such as the Boer scout Adendorff ('Men Who Know Zulus') perform the same role as frontier scouts in the western; even the cattle stampede in which a number of Zulus are trampled to death could have been taken directly from a western.[43] It is interesting to note, however, that in the extensive scholarly literature devoted to the western genre very little of it is concerned with the issue of historical authenticity.

The representation of history in *Zulu* is intimately connected with a set of overlapping narrative ideologies relating to the themes of nationhood, empire, class, masculinity, race and militarism. The first of these is probably the least contentious. Indeed, the film's critics seem to have little or nothing to say about one of its most interesting facets: its representation of British – and specifically Welsh – national identity. *Zulu* is indeed 'the Great Welsh Epic': the film is replete with verbal and musical references to Welshness that reach a climax in the rendition of 'Men of Harlech' which Private Owen (played by Ivor Emmanuel, a well-known Welsh baritone of the time) leads in response to the war chant of the Zulus:

> *Chard:* Do you think the Welsh can't do better than that, Owen?
> *Owen:* Well, they've got a good bass section, mind, but no top tenors, that's for sure.

This sequence is an invention of the film's own making, though it is not entirely inconsistent with history, given many recorded examples of soldiers turning to popular songs and hymns in order to maintain their morale. Critics were divided on the dramatic value of the scene, but it is an effective example of the cinema's ability to mythologise history in so far as there probably are people who believe that the defenders of Rorke's Drift actually did sing 'Men of Harlech' as the Zulus attacked. Like Eisenstein's Odessa steps, an event that never happened has acquired mythic status through film. The fact that an orchestral version of 'Men of Harlech' is to be heard over the closing credits – before merging into Barry's 'Zulu' theme – is a further indication of the extent to which *Zulu* was intended as a testament to Wales.[44]

It is ironic, however, that a film that has so much to say about Welshness is set at such a distance from Wales itself. The soldiers' feeling of separation from their homeland is a prominent theme – overlapping with the film's equivocal attitude towards empire – that is expressed particularly through the character of Private Thomas. Thomas's touching affection for a sick calf establishes his affinity with the land; his dialogue establishes that he left Wales for a life of excitement but that he now longs to return to the farm: 'I thought I was tired of farming, no adventure in it, like. But when you look at it, this country's not a bit as good as Bala or the Lake there – not really green, like.' The film therefore imagines a rural Wales of green hills and valleys, though, interestingly, the shooting script does contain a reference to the industrialised Wales that did not make it into the finished film:

Thomas: You South Walians, what do you know about the land, seeing as you spend all your time underneath it, like? Digging out coal so's the English can burn it up in their dirty big grates.
Owen: We're not all the time underground, boyo. Anyway, I didn't want to cough out my life at the coal-face like my Da. That's why I enlisted.[45]

Historically, the British Army provided the means through which men from Wales, Scotland, Ireland and the English provinces could serve the Empire. It is impossible when reading this, however, not to be reminded that Baker's own 'Da' had been a miner, though whether this dialogue was a veiled reference to Baker's decision to become an actor is pure speculation.

Yet, if *Zulu* is a testament to the role of Welsh soldiers in building the British Empire, its attitude towards colonialism is equivocal. It is true, certainly, that *Zulu* accepts the fact of the British colonial presence in Southern Africa, though there is nothing in the film to indicate that it actively supports the policy of imperial expansion. In fact, there is a sense of ambivalence towards colonialism running throughout the film. There are several scenes that question the British presence in Africa, though without providing any answers. The enlisted men serving at Rorke's Drift are unable to comprehend what they are doing in Africa and do not understand why they have to fight the Zulus. Thus Private Hook, ordered to knock firing loopholes in the wall of the hospital, retorts: 'Did I ever see a Zulu walk down the City Road? No. So what am I doing here?' As the garrison waits for the Zulus to attack there is a short but significant exchange between the nervous Private Cole, unsettled by the drunken rantings of the Reverend Witt, and the stoical Colour-Sergeant Bourne:

Cole: Why is it us, eh? Why us?
Bourne: Because we're 'ere, lad. Nobody else. Just us.

In a British Empire film of the 1930s, Cole's question would probably have been answered with an earnest homily on the civilising influence of the colonial mission, delivered by an actor such as Sir Guy Standing or C. Aubrey Smith. In *Zulu* there is no answer other than the fact of being 'here'. Later, as Cole dies from his wounds, he keeps on saying 'Why?'; the surgeon can only answer: 'I'm damned if I could tell you why.' Thus the film does not offer a view either for or against the colonial presence in Africa. (Of course, more trenchant critics might regard the failure to adopt an explicitly anti-colonialist position as an implicit endorsement of colonialism, though this strikes me as a theoretically unsound argument.)

Another criticism levelled against *Zulu* is that it offers no historical context either for the Battle of Rorke's Drift itself or for the wider issue of British imperial policy in Southern Africa.[46] The film begins with the aftermath of the Battle of Isandhlwana as Richard Burton reads a dispatch from Lord Chelmsford, commander of the British forces in Natal, to the Secretary of State for War in London: 'I regret to report a very disastrous engagement which took place on the morning of the 22nd January between the Armies of the Zulu King Cetewayo and our own Number 3 Column, comprising Five Companies of the 1st Battalion, 24th Regiment of Foot, and One Company of the 2nd Battalion, a total of nearly 1,500 men, officers and other ranks.'[47] The narration fades and the image dissolves to the battlefield of Isandhlwana strewn with the corpses of red-coated British soldiers. That the film originally had included some context for the Zulu War – and, moreover, from the Zulu perspective – is indicated by a scene in the shooting script that was in all probability shot but which did not, in the event, make it into the final cut. This has a longer version of the scene early in the film at Cetewayo's kraal in which Otto Witt is asked by the Zulu king – through an interpreter, a young boy called Jacob whom Witt has taught English – whether he supports the British:

> *Jacob:* The great Nkosi Cetewayo is angry. He says the red-coated soldiers are already upon his land and wish to take all the hills between the Blood River and the Buffalo.
> *Witt:* I know, Jacob. Tell the King I do not approve of what the British are doing.
> *Jacob:* The great Nkosi Cetewayo says that white-skinned farmers have made a ring about his land like jackals, waiting for the red soldiers to do their killing among the Zulus.
> *Witt:* I know that too.

This scene is interesting both for its explicit references to the British as colonisers – from the Zulus' perspective the 'red soldiers' are the racial 'other' – and for its implicit suggestion of deliberate racial genocide engineered by the Boers. It is unclear why the scene was cut: the fact that it was cut would, on the face of it, lend credence to the criticism that the film sets out deliberately to exclude the Zulu point-of-view, whereas the fact that it was in the script to begin with suggests this was not necessarily always the intent.

This ambivalence towards colonialism is perhaps only to be expected, given the time when *Zulu* was made. The early 1960s witnessed the acceleration of the 'retreat from empire' that had started after the Second World War with the granting of independence to India and Pakistan (1947) and to Palestine (1948), and that had gained momentum in the wake of the Suez Crisis. The bulk of Britain's tropical African empire was wound up between the late 1950s and the mid-1960s: the Gold Coast (1957), Nigeria (1960), Sierra Leone (1961), Tanganyika (1961), Uganda (1962), Kenya (1963), Gambia (1963) and Zambia (1964) all attained their independence at this time. As the geographical extent of the British Empire contracted – and as the notion of 'Empire' itself gave way to that of 'Commonwealth' – it was only to be expected that the nature of the British Empire film would change along with it. Thus, whereas the narrative ideologies of the imperial films of the 1930s (including both British-made and Hollywood films) had been oriented principally towards the expansion of the Empire and asserting the moral imperative of the imperial mission, by the 1950s and 1960s the main theme had become one of defending the Empire. This was evident, for example, in the colonial police films of the 1950s – *Where No Vultures Fly* (dir. Harry Watt, 1951), *West of Zanzibar* (dir. Harry Watt, 1953) – and in the cycle of colonial adventure films adopting a sympathetic (or at least partly sympathetic) attitude towards rebels, such as *Zarak* (dir. Terence Young, 1956), *The Bandit of Zhobe* (dir. John Gilling, 1959) and *The Long Duel* (dir. Ken Annakin, 1967). The most successful of the 'end of empire' films before *Zulu* had been Rank's *North West Frontier*: a fictitious story set during an uprising in 1905, this was essentially a *Boy's Own*-style adventure film but one which allowed a limited critique of colonialism into its narrative and which implied that the days of British rule in India were numbered (an easy enough position to adopt, given that it was made a decade after independence). [48]

It is in its representations of class and masculinity that *Zulu*'s narrative departures from the historical record assume their greatest ideological significance. The characterisation of Private Hook is instructive in this respect. According to the historical record, Hook was a model soldier, one of the Victoria Cross winners for his defence of the hospital, but in the film, as played by James Booth, he becomes (in Bromhead's words) 'a thief, a coward and an insubordinate barrack room lawyer'. Sharrett deplores this 'tomfoolery with one of the legends of the battle' which, he suggests, is meant to imply 'that the worst dregs of British society are more than a match for "a bunch of savages"'.[49] A more likely explanation, however, is simply that the film's Henry Hook is an archetypal sixties rebel of the sort played in British films by actors such as Albert Finney and Tom Courtenay: he is a non-conformist who rails against authority and who puts his own self-interest ahead of others. Even his robust defence of the hospital might be seen as much an act of self-preservation as one of selfless heroism; he is a malingerer who is suffering from nothing worse than a boil and who, during the final roll-call, tries to get back onto the sick list. It was almost *de rigeur* for action-adventure films in the 1960s to feature such a character: it must have seemed to Endfield and Prebble that, in scripting *Zulu*, this sort of role fell most readily onto the part of Private Hook. A similar sort of licence is taken with the characterisation of Colour-Sergeant Bourne, memorably played by Nigel Green. At the time of Rorke's Drift, the real Frank Bourne was 25 years old and was known within the regiment as 'the kid'. In the film he has become a gruff, paternalistic figure – probably for no reason other than that is how non-commissioned officers have usually been characterised in film. It is significant in this respect that not only did most reviewers commend Green's performance, but that several also remarked that it seemed right both in period and in spirit: a case where the stereotype seems more authentic than the real historical person.[50]

That the film embodies contemporary attitudes towards class and masculinity becomes apparent in the characterisation of Chard and Bromhead. Sharrett is correct in his observation that 'the film poses the characters as contrasting masculine styles', but his explanation that this represents 'a typical assault on authority and class structure from the right' is, to say the least, unconvincing.[51] Certainly, the two men are characterised as opposites: Chard, an officer of the Royal Engineers, is rational, practical and level-headed, though with something of a chip on his shoulder about privilege within the army (evidenced in his remark that the order to defend Rorke's Drift rather

14. Contrasting masculinities in *Zulu*: the pragmatic Lieutenant John Chard (Stanley Baker, *left*) and the apparently effete Lieutenant Gonville Bromhead (Michael Caine).

than evacuate it came from 'a military genius – someone's son and heir who got a commission before he learned to shave'), whereas Bromhead, whose family has a long history of distinguished service, at first seems effete, elitist and snobbish. The initial antagonism between them arises from the fact that Chard has commandeered some of Bromhead's men to build a bridge while Bromhead was out hunting and is further exacerbated when Chard takes command of the post by dint of having been commissioned before Bromhead. While dialogue in the film suggests that Bromhead is from an aristocratic family, there is no indication of Chard's social background. Given the time at which *Zulu* was made there is an intriguing, if entirely unwitting, contemporary parallel. The differences in class between Bromhead and Chard are uncannily similar to the differences in personality between the leaders of the two main political parties in 1963–64. Is it perhaps too fanciful to see

Bromhead as the equivalent of the aristocratic, patrician Tory Prime Minister Sir Alec Douglas-Home (the fourteenth Earl of Home, who relinquished his peerage on succeeding the ailing Harold Macmillan in 1963 in order to be able to lead the government in the House of Commons) and Chard as the Labour Leader of the Opposition, Harold Wilson, a grammar-school boy from Huddersfield whose experience as both an Oxford economics don and a wartime civil servant serve as indicators of intellect and professionalism? If Labour's victory in the general election of October 1964 has been seen as a triumph of meritocracy over privilege, it must be borne in mind that Wilson won by the narrowest of margins, a mere five seats – just as the date of Chard's commission predates Bromhead's by only a few months.

Yet the class differences between Chard and Bromhead should not be exaggerated. Ultimately, *Zulu* reinforces the ideology of consensus as Chard and Bromhead learn to work together and come to respect each other's courage and professionalism. When Chard is wounded during the battle, Bromhead tells him: 'We need you! Damn you, we need you!' (thus echoing Chard's earlier despairing plea to the Boer cavalrymen who ride away from the station to return to their farms). Significantly, a line in the shooting script near the end of the film, where Chard's remark towards Bromhead again raises the question of class difference ('You think it's finished now and we can all be jolly comrades-in-arms?'), has been replaced in the film itself by Chard thanking Bromhead for 'what you said earlier': thus the film ends on a note of consensus rather than discord. This is in stark contrast to Tony Richardson's *The Charge of the Light Brigade*, made only four years later, where bitter class differences and petty social antagonisms would be laid bare.

As far as the charge that *Zulu* promotes an ideology of racial superiority is concerned, this is flatly contradicted by the textual evidence of the film. Sharrett detects 'casual racism' in remarks such as Bromhead's comment about the native levies killed alongside British troops at Isandhlwana ('Damn the levies man! More cowardly blacks') and Private Jones's reference to the Zulus as 'a bunch of savages' – attitudes which he claims are 'not really fully refuted'. Leaving aside the fact that these sentiments were probably consistent with the views of most Victorian soldiers – and Sharrett also criticises the film for not being true to its period – it is simply wrong to assert, as he does, that these comments are not refuted. Indeed, the film takes every opportunity to offer a corrective to the instances of 'casual racism' that have quite deliberately been included in the dialogue. And, significantly, it is the South African characters – the 'Men Who Know Zulus' – who provide this corrective view. Thus Bromhead's remark about the levies is immediately rebuffed by Adendorff: 'They died on your side. And who the hell do you think is coming to wipe you out – the Grenadier Guards!?' Similarly, Private Jones is taken to task by Corporal Schiess of the Natal Mounted Police:

> *Schiess:* How far can you red necks march in a day?
> *Jones:* Oh, fifteen, twenty miles, is it?
> *Schiess:* Well, a Zulu regiment can run – *run!* – fifteen miles, and fight a battle at the end of it.

And even if the British soldiers have a poor opinion of the Zulus before the battle, they come to respect the courage of their enemies: 'I think they've got more guts than we have, boyo', remarks Private Owen as the Zulus mount yet another assault.

It is in its attitude towards militarism and warfare that the 'retrospective views' and 'spiritual anachronisms' detected in *Zulu* by critics become most apparent. Despite the views of some commentators to the contrary, *Zulu* is no *Boy's Own* adventure yarn glorifying the 'little wars of empire' of the late nineteenth century. There are no false heroics; the hand-to-hand fighting is shown as bloody and brutal; and there is probably no other film that provides such a vivid impression of the sheer physical exhaustion of battle. It is significant, moreover, that the characters who most consistently express their horror at the consequences of war are the officers, whose role is to provide leadership, rather than the 'damned rankers' who fight with courage and stoical good humour. Thus Surgeon-Major Reynolds, using the church as a makeshift hospital, at one point shouts angrily at Chard: 'Damn you, Chard! Damn all you butchers!' The same metaphor is used by Chard himself after the battle as he and Bromhead survey the burnt-down hospital and reflect on their first experience of combat:

> *Chard:* Well, you've fought your first action.
> *Bromhead:* Does everyone feel like this – afterwards?

15. After the battle: Chard and Bromhead, sickened by the carnage, survey the burnt hospital in *Zulu*.

Chard: How do you feel?
Bromhead: Sick.
Chard: Well, you have to be alive to feel sick.
Bromhead: You asked me, I told you. There's something else. I feel ashamed. Was that how it was for you – the first time?
Chard: First time? Think I could stand this butcher's yard more than once?
Bromhead: I didn't know.
Chard: I told you. I came up here to build a bridge.

These are unlikely to have been the sentiments of professional soldiers of the 1870s (or of any period for that matter), but they are characteristic of the 1960s when the prevailing mood was turning against militarism. The colonial bush wars of the 1950s in Kenya and Malaya had been messy affairs (British tactics against Communist rebels in Malaya anticipated those adopted later by the Americans in Vietnam) that raised questions about the army's role as an instrument of imperial power. *Zulu* was made shortly after the end of National Service in Britain (1959) and thus belongs to a period when the vast majority of young people (who increasingly made up the cinema-going audience) would have had no military experience. It would be inaccurate to describe *Zulu* as a pacifist film (its only pacifist character is the drunken and discredited Witt), but it can reasonably be described as anti-militaristic.[52]

If there is any doubt that *Zulu* was consciously anti-militaristic, it is dispelled by a scene which, again, was cut from the finished film. The shooting script reveals that after the battle Witt (now sober) and Margareta return to Rorke's Drift. This is the occasion for a discussion about the nature of warfare and includes even more explicitly anti-war dialogue:

Margareta: What was it...? I mean...

Chard: What was it like? I suppose we behaved as you said we would. Like animals, wasn't it?

Margareta: And you'll think all this has been glorious?

Chard: (with disgust) Glory's a cheap thank-you from those who profit from a soldier's death!

Margareta: Then the soldier's a fool!

Chard: Yes, he's a fool or he wouldn't have enlisted. *(Harshly)* I'll tell you something... *(then softening)* Perhaps Man is an animal, Miss Witt. But black or white, what distinguished him from the rest of the jungle here today was his courage, his willingness to give his life. Can you understand that? That he was sacrificing himself for something he cherished?

Margareta: For what?

Chard: (a short, bitter laugh) For what? *(and then only half-cynically)* Rorke's Drift will probably become a page in the regimental history, Miss Witt. Something to stiffen a recruit's courage in the next war to which some damn fool commits us.

Margareta: (almost crying in bewilderment) Is that all there is to it?

Chard: (breaks momentarily) Good God, isn't it enough! *(then gentler, wanting to understand it himself)* Now and then all men wonder how much courage they have. And now and then a soldier shows them. Perhaps that's his only purpose.

Margareta: (protesting) No! A man's life should be worth more than that.

Chard: (shaking his head) Not a soldier's life. His country told him the value of that when he enlisted. It's a shilling. One shilling a day.

This bitter and cynical exchange did not make it into the film, perhaps because it strikes the wrong note immediately before Burton lists the winners of the Victoria Cross, though it is tempting to speculate that it would have remained if *Zulu* had been made a few years later.

It is instructive to compare the treatment of militarism in *Zulu* with another film made in the year of *Zulu*'s release and which also involved John Prebble to a significant degree. In 1961 Prebble had published a book on the Battle of Culloden – the last battle to be fought on British soil, in which the Highland supporters of Bonnie Prince Charlie were routed by the Duke of Cumberland's army – that in 1964 was adapted as a television film for the BBC by the director Peter Watkins. Watkins was an amateur film-maker whose early efforts had so impressed Huw Wheldon, then the Head of Documentaries at the BBC, that he invited Watkins to join the corporation. Watkins's first film was *Culloden*, based on Prebble's book, written by Watkins with Prebble acting as historical adviser. As Nicholas J. Cull has demonstrated in his case study of the making of *Culloden*: 'Watkins' script for *Culloden* followed Prebble's account to a remarkable degree. Prebble's book provided both the structure (it focuses on the battle and its aftermath) and most of the detail of Watkins' version.'[53] *Culloden* is an example of what today would be called a 'docu-drama': it uses the techniques of documentary to reconstruct historical events in a realistic manner. In common with his usual working practices, Watkins shot the film on location using non-professional actors and a hand-held 16-millimetre Arriflex camera. However, what distinguishes *Culloden* from other examples of this practice – such as the narrative-documentaries made during the Second World War by the Crown Film Unit – is Watkins's bold and highly innovative use of technique. Thus he filmed *Culloden* in the style of 'window on the world' television current affairs programmes such as *World in Action* and *Panorama*, using interviews to camera by participants and a voice-over narration in the manner of a news reporter. *Culloden* was broadcast on 15 December 1964 and made such an impact on both critics and viewers that it was repeated six weeks later on 31 January 1965.

On the face of it, *Culloden* and *Zulu* seem very different indeed:

low-budget BBC film in grainy black-and-white versus Hollywood-backed epic in Technicolor and widescreen. Yet there are several interesting similarities between them, and not only through the involvement of Prebble. Both are based on battles that have been mythologised in British history; both feature a battle between professional soldiers on one side and an army of less well-equipped 'native' rebels on the other; and both examine the effects of battle on the rank-and-file. There are some direct parallels: a scene in *Culloden* where the English casualty list is read out after the battle recalls the similar scene in *Zulu* where Colour-Sergeant Bourne reads the company roll and crosses out the names of the dead. Where *Culloden* differs from its theatrical cousin, however, is in its depiction of the aftermath of the battle, including the brutal pacification of the Highlands by the redcoats. The BBC's Audience Research Department found that some viewers drew parallels between *Culloden* and contemporary colonial anti-insurgency campaigns: one remarked that 'such utter cruelty reminded me of recent events in the Congo'.[54] And, whereas *Zulu* provides a mythologised version of history, one of Watkins's main aims was to debunk many of the sacred cows of romantic Tartanry. Thus Bonnie Prince Charlie is portrayed as a drunkard who flees the field of battle and abandons his supporters to their fate. The battle sequences are staged differently, too, in so far as Watkins's use of technique – hand-held camera, jump cuts, jarring edits – effectively captures the confusion of battle in contrast to the disciplined tactics of *Zulu*.

Culloden can be seen as an early prototype of what the American postmodernist critic Robert A. Rosenstone later called 'the New History film'. This is a film that 'finds the space to *contest* history, to interrogate either the metanarratives that structure historical knowledge, or smaller historical truths, received notions, conventional images'.[55] In contrast to the more traditional type of historical film exemplified by *Zulu*, with its linear narrative, continuity editing and use of familiar archetypes and conventions, the New History film is characterised by its use of unconventional, experimental devices that draw attention not only to its form but also, by extension, to the nature of historical knowledge itself. Watkins's anachronistic use of interviews to camera (as if television cameras actually were present in 1745) and his adoption of techniques from the Soviet avant-garde (principally montage and typage) provide such devices in *Culloden*.

Indeed, *Culloden* fits perfectly Rosenstone's theoretical model of the New History film in that it 'provides a series of challenges to written history – it tests the boundaries of what we can say about the past and how we can say it, points to the limitations of conventional historical form, suggests new ways to envision the past, and alters our sense of what it is'.[56] The New History film – other examples include *Hiroshima, mon amour* (dir. Alain Resnais, 1959), *Memories of Underdevelopment* (dir. Tomás Gutiérrez Alea, 1968), *Hitler: A Film from Germany* (dir. Hans-Jürgen Syderberg, 1977) and *Walker* (dir. Alex Cox, 1987) – typically exists outside the mainstream or on the margins of commercial film-making and tends to be the work of directors with a self-conscious, highly formalist style.

A belated 'prequel' to *Zulu* appeared 15 years later in the form of *Zulu Dawn* (dir. Douglas Hickox, 1979), an international co-production written by Endfield in collaboration with Anthony Storey and filmed entirely on location in Southern Africa with a stellar cast, including Burt Lancaster, Peter O'Toole, Simon Ward and John Mills. *Zulu Dawn* dramatised the events leading up to the Battle of Isandhlwana and the annihilation of Lord Chelmsford's base camp by the Zulus. If *Zulu* had been equivocal in its attitude towards imperialism, there is no question that *Zulu Dawn* is explicitly anti-imperialist. It provides the sense of historical context that some critics found lacking in *Zulu* and adheres to the historical orthodoxy that the Zulu War was precipitated by Sir Bartle Frere (Mills), the British High Commissioner in Natal, who, against the wishes of the British government in London, is determined to destroy the Zulu nation. Evidence of the film's anti-colonialist ideology is to be found in the parallel drawn between Anglo-Boer policy towards the Zulus and twentieth-century acts of genocide, as Frere declares: 'Let us hope that this will be the final solution to the Zulu problem' (made even more explicit by the phonetic similarity between 'Zulu' and 'Jew'). In common with the unreconstructed imperialists of the earlier film, Frere regards the Zulus as 'violent and murdering barbarians' and considers that Cetewayo's maintenance of his *impis* (armies) constitutes a 'violation of British sovereignty'. He therefore issues an ultimatum that the Zulus must disband their *impis* – a demand that will obviously be unacceptable to Cetewayo – and uses Cetewayo's refusal as an excuse to mount an invasion of Zululand. Moreover, *Zulu Dawn* provides the Zulu perspective that had been absent from *Zulu* and encourages sympathy with Cetewayo's position: 'Do I go to the country of the white man and tell him to change his laws and his customs?...My armies will defend this land from those who would impose their will on us.' There is no doubting that the British are represented as the aggressors and the Zulus as the victims of a deliberately expansionist colonial policy.

To an extent, *Zulu Dawn* employs some of the same archetypes as *Zulu*: the character of irregular Boer soldier Colonel Anthony Durnford (Lancaster) who joins Chelmsford's force is this film's 'Man Who Knows Zulus', and there is another gruff, bewhiskered NCO in Bob Hoskins's Colour-Sergeant Williams who winks reassuringly at one of his lads moments before their line is overrun by Zulus and they are killed. And there are narrative references to the earlier film – for example, as Chelmsford's column marches out to the theme of 'Men of Harlech' played by the regimental band. One of the criticisms levelled against *Zulu* – that it represents the Zulus themselves as an undifferentiated mass – could also be made of this film. On the other hand, *Zulu Dawn* is at some pains to present the British soldiers as individuals, and certainly does not condemn them all as colonialist oppressors. Thus, while there is a clear echo of Bromhead's 'damn the levies' in the remark of Quartermaster Bloomfield (Peter Vaughan) when several native levies drown while crossing a river ('Natives is not on my invoices, Mr Harford, ammunition is and has to be accounted for'), this is contrasted with the more humane and sympathetic view of Lieutenant Harford (Ronald Pickup) who believes the levies should be buried properly and with dignity.

The defeat at Isandhlwana is laid squarely at the door of Chelmsford (O'Toole), who is characterised as an arrogant, careerist officer who seriously underestimates the fighting ability of the Zulus. He regards the Zulus as naughty children who need to be taught a lesson: 'For a savage, as for a child, chastisement is sometimes a kindness.' He commits an elementary tactical blunder by dividing his forces in enemy territory, leaving his base camp exposed at Isandhlwana and leading another column to engage a Zulu *impi* that in the event he cannot locate. He disregards intelligence reports of another *impi* marching on Isandhlwana because he does not believe the Zulus could cross mountainous terrain and is slow to respond to reports that the base camp is under attack. Chelmsford's arrogance is contrasted with the cunning of Cetewayo, who orders three of his warriors to allow themselves to be captured by the British and to provide them with false information under torture. The film ends with Chelmsford returning to Isandhlwana and staring silently at the dead bodies of his troops.

There is much to admire in *Zulu Dawn* – a scene of the Zulus emerging from crevices and swarming *en masse* across the landscape, for example, matches the visual force of their first appearance in *Zulu*, while the lengthy battle sequence is once again impressively staged – though ultimately it is less satisfying than its predecessor as either narrative or spectacle. It did not match the popular success of *Zulu*, perhaps because it could not be claimed as a patriotic epic in the same way. The critics, who it might have been assumed would have been sympathetic towards its anti-colonialist theme, were unenthusiastic. Interestingly, the *Monthly Film Bulletin*, which had felt *Zulu* to be rather old-fashioned, now warmed to it in comparison to *Zulu Dawn*, as Richard Coombs offered a complete *volte face* on the earlier review: 'Not only has Endfield (and his collaborators on this occasion) not added anything to his first film, but he has obscured its trace – which is a pity, because *Zulu*, though not remembered as such, and without the hollow pretensions displayed here, was an intelligent adventure, dovetailing stiff-upper-lip heroism with a certain bafflement about Africa.'[57] In America, where *Zulu Dawn* was not released until mid-1982, its reception was similarly lukewarm. Janet Maslin in the *New York Times* simply felt that it lacked excitement: 'Douglas Hickox…makes *Zulu Dawn* picturesque and proper, if a little dull. For all the mayhem in the movie, there isn't much emotion, even when the fighters are dropping like flies.'[58] In short, while *Zulu Dawn* may be better history than *Zulu* – Maslin also noted that it 'does its best to present both sides of the story' – it is less engaging as a narrative.

The lukewarm reception of *Zulu Dawn* serves to reinforce what a unique and special film *Zulu* itself was and is. For all the debate over its alleged racism and historical inaccuracy that rages within the academy, the frequency with which it is screened on television attests to the special place it holds in British film culture. As one commentator has put it, *Zulu* is 'our epic, a celebration of national courage (but not nationalism) with its eyes wide open'.[59] More specifically, as Peter Stead has argued, the significance of *Zulu* is that it was 'enough to capture the imagination of a Welsh film-going audience who had been denied the historical mythology that should have been truly theirs'.[60] To paraphrase 'Men of Harlech', *Zulu* is the film that will forever be their story. And it remains a fitting testimonial

to the career of its Welsh producer and star, who died from cancer in
1976 at the age of 48, just six weeks after he had been knighted for his
services to the British film industry.

10

Decline and Fall:
The Charge of the Light Brigade
(1968)

*T*HE *Charge of the Light Brigade*, directed by Tony Richardson for Woodfall Films, remains one of the most controversial and misunderstood of British films. It represented a radical new departure both for the historical genre with its iconoclastic and non-heroic representation of a famous disaster (the very obverse of *Scott of the Antarctic* and *A Night to Remember*) and for its director, who had made his name in the British new wave theatre and cinema in the late 1950s. Controversy dogged *The Charge of the Light Brigade* throughout its long and troubled production history, while the release of the film, particularly Richardson's refusal to allow a press screening, provoked a bitter feud between the director and the national critics. In fact, the reception of *The Charge of the Light Brigade* was mixed: some critics found it confusing, while others felt that it was a bold and challenging film that fell just short of greatness. It was a commercial disappointment upon its release, contributing to the demise of Woodfall Films, hitherto one of the most successful independent production companies of the 1960s. Indeed, *The Charge of the Light Brigade* was one of several expensive flops in the late 1960s – others included *Far From the Madding Crowd* (dir. John Schlesinger, 1967), *Alfred the Great* (dir. Clive Donner, 1969) and *Goodbye Mr Chips* (dir. Herbert Ross, 1969) – that were blamed for the withdrawal of American capital from the British film industry. Richardson's career never fully recovered and none of his later films matched the sheer audacity of *The Charge*.[1]

Tony Richardson (born Cecil Antonio Richardson in 1928) was a Yorkshire grammar school boy who won a scholarship to study English at Oxford University and who came to public notice through his direction of John Osborne's *Look Back in Anger* at the Royal Court Theatre in 1956. He was also involved, along with Karel Reisz and Lindsay Anderson, in the Free Cinema movement of the mid-1950s. Free Cinema, a programme of documentary shorts sponsored by the British Film Institute and shown at the National Film Theatre, was a British equivalent of *Cinéma Vérité* in France and Direct Cinema in the United States. It called for a more personal approach to documentary film-making in contrast to the Griersonian tradition that had held sway over the British documentary movement since the early 1930s and that was now perceived as middlebrow and middle class. Free Cinema directors thus made films about subjects which interested them personally: films such as Richardson's *Momma Don't Allow* (1956) and Reisz's *We Are the Lambeth Boys* (1958) exhibit an interest in teenagers, urbanisation and popular culture, whereas Anderson's *Every Day Except Christmas* (1957) is an example of social observation documenting the working day in Covent Garden Market. If Free Cinema was a short-lived movement, it nevertheless had a significant influence in so far as it helped to push the British feature film by the end of the 1950s towards a more direct and down-to-earth engagement with working-class subjects and settings.

Richardson was a key figure in the British new wave cinema that flourished around the turn of the decade. In 1958 he joined with Osborne and Canadian-born producer Harry Saltzman to form Woodfall Films with a view to producing film versions of Osborne's plays. From the outset he cultivated the image of an *auteur*, a film-maker with something to say and a passionate determination to say it. 'It is absolutely vital to get into British films the same sort of impact and sense of life that, what you can call loosely the Angry Young Man cult, has had in the theatre and literary worlds', he told *Films and Filming* in 1959. 'It is a desperate need.'[2] Richardson directed films of Osborne's *Look Back in Anger* (1958) and *The Entertainer* (1960), produced Karel Reisz's film of Alan Sillitoe's *Saturday Night and Sunday Morning* (1960) – the first of Woodfall's films to be a commercial success – and then directed films of Shelagh Delaney's *A*

Taste of Honey (1961) and Sillitoe's *The Loneliness of the Long Distance Runner* (1962). Robert Murphy argues that 'Richardson's films rarely achieve a harmonious artistic unity, but his constant willingness to experiment deserves more credit than it generally receives'.[3] *Look Back in Anger* is an intense, studio-bound drama that reveals its stage origins, but *The Entertainer* is a more cinematic film, notable for its location shooting (in the seaside resort of Morecambe) and fluid camera movements. By the time of *The Loneliness of the Long Distance Runner*, Richardson had absorbed some of the stylistic flourishes of the French *Nouvelle Vague* and deployed devices such as a hand-held camera, jump cuts and speeded-up motion sequences that drew attention to style and form as much as to the content of the film. Penelope Houston, however, felt that the imitation of the *Nouvelle Vague* style was not entirely effective: 'But the echoes of *Les Quatre Cents Coups* also point the contrasts: where Truffaut's style grew out of his theme, Richardson's looks the result of a deliberate effort of will, so that the bits and pieces remain unassimilated.'[4]

Richardson's and Woodfall's trajectory reflects one of the significant shifts within the British film industry during the 1960s. With the exception of *Look Back in Anger*, which was backed by Warner Bros. and released through Associated British-Pathé, all of the Woodfall productions until 1962 were backed by the independent consortium Bryanston and released through British Lion. Most of the key new wave films were produced by independents outside the Rank/ABPC duopoly: *Room at the Top* by Romulus (John and James Woolf) and released by British Lion, *A Kind of Loving* and *Billy Liar* by Joseph Janni and released by Anglo-Amalgamated. Rank, which for a long time refused to show 'X' certificate films in its cinemas, finally gave in by distributing *This Sporting Life*, produced by Independent Artists (Julian Wintle), though it was a box-office failure, a fact that apparently pleased John Davis, who declared in 1963 that the 'public has clearly shown that it does not want the dreary kitchen sink dramas'.[5] Historically, the new wave represents a moment in the early 1960s when independents almost succeeded in breaking the stranglehold of the circuits. It was not to be. Bryanston's chairman Michael Balcon got cold feet over Richardson's next project, an adaptation of Henry Fielding's eighteenth-century novel *Tom Jones* (1963), with the result that Woodfall turned instead to an American company, United Artists. *Tom Jones* went on to become a critical and commercial triumph, winning four Academy Awards (Best Film, Best Director, Best Screenplay for John Osborne and Best Music for John Addison). The loss of Woodfall marked the beginning of the end for Bryanston, which was wound up in 1965. 'I can only say that if I had had the courage to pawn everything I possessed and risk it on *Tom Jones* it would have been a wise decision', Balcon lamented in his autobiography.[6] Henceforth, it would be American companies to whom British film-makers would turn for financial support. The economic balance of power in the industry had shifted decisively: by 1967 over 90 per cent of production finance was American.[7]

Variety recognised that '*Tom Jones* marks a watershed for British cinema, creating an extravagant world perfectly in tune with that of "Swinging London"'.[8] The film reinterprets its source material for the permissive society: Tom, exuberantly played by Albert Finney, is an orphan who grows up to enjoy a liberated lifestyle of sexual and social adventures. It is a bawdy, sexy costume romp that harks back to the heyday of the Gainsborough melodramas but no longer with the moral necessity of punishing transgressive behaviour. Thus, Tom is free to enjoy the pleasures of a local wench and an aristocratic older woman and still succeeds in his ambition to marry his true love. His promiscuous lifestyle is celebrated rather than condemned – 'The whole world loves Tom Jones!' posters declared – and in this regard the character has been seen as a sort of eighteenth-century James Bond. At the same time, however, Richardson's and Osborne's interest in social critique is not lost: the stag-hunting scene near the beginning of the film exposes the cruelty and barbarism of the period and the attempt of his love-rival to frame Tom for murder reveals its social hypocrisy. Where *Tom Jones* is undeniably a cultural artefact of the 1960s is in its dazzling use of visual style. Richardson felt that if the sets and costumes were 'correct' in period then the style of the film could be thoroughly modern. To this end, cinematographer Walter Lassally shot it in muted pastel shades using a gauze over the camera (reportedly the silk veil from a lady's hat), while Richardson indulged his bag of directorial tricks, including devices such as captions, asides to the camera and speeded-up motion.[9] Overall, *Tom Jones* is a film of remarkable cultural confidence and stylistic virtuosity. It was also a film that proved impossible to repeat. Neither *The Amorous Adventures of Moll Flanders* (dir. Terence Young, 1964), loosely adapted from the novel by Daniel Defoe, nor *Lock Up Your Daughters* (dir. Peter Coe, 1969), from the play by Bernard Miles based on Fielding's *Rape upon Rape*, came close to matching its success.

The success of *Tom Jones* gave Richardson virtual *carte blanche* to develop whatever films he liked. In his posthumously published 'memoir', *Long Distance Runner*, Richardson revealed that he had long harboured 'a big plan to do a new and truthful version of the charge of the Light Brigade' and that the film 'had been in the works a long time'.[10] He started working on this project in the mid-1960s, in collaboration with Osborne, who was to write the script, filling in the time by directing other films. He made an adaptation of Evelyn Waugh's *The Loved One* (1965) for MGM – a satire of Americana that was billed as 'the motion picture with something to offend everybody' – followed by two films starring Jeanne Moreau, darling of the French *Nouvelle Vague* – *Mademoiselle* (1966) and *The Sailor from Gibraltar* (1967) – none of which did much to enhance his reputation. When he finally began shooting *The Charge of the Light Brigade* in 1967, therefore, Richardson was in need of a hit. United Artists backed the production to the tune of $6.5 million, at the time one of the highest ever budgets for a British film.

In setting out to make a 'truthful version' of the Charge of the Light Brigade – though its accuracy would inevitably be contested by historians – Richardson was reacting against a process of mythologisation that had been set in train immediately after the event itself. Most historians now agree that the infamous Charge of the Light Brigade, which occurred during the Battle of Balaclava on 25 October 1854 in the Crimean War, was one of the greatest military blunders in British history: a highly courageous but tactically futile manœuvre that arose because of misunderstandings in the chain of command and resulted in the death or injury of 247 of the 673 cavalrymen involved. This was not the way it was commemorated at the time. The mythologisation of the event into an act of heroic sacrifice was evident in the reports of the battle by William Russell, special correspondent of *The Times* – the Crimea was the first 'media war' in which the press published dispatches from the front – and most famously in the verse of the Victorian Poet Laureate Alfred, Lord Tennyson, whose tribute to the 'Gallant Six Hundred' remains on the English school curriculum to this day. As Orwell wryly remarked in *The Lion and the Unicorn*: 'English literature, like other literatures, is full of battle-poems, but it is worth noticing that the ones that have won themselves a kind of popularity are always a tale of disasters and retreats... The most stirring battle-poem in English is about a brigade of cavalry who charged in the wrong direction.'[11] Tennyson's poem of 'one of the most distinguished events in history conspicuous for sheer valour' is bizarrely credited as the inspiration for the 1936 Warner Bros. film *The Charge of the Light Brigade*, which even more bizarrely suggests that the Charge itself was a quixotic mission to settle a score with a treacherous Indian potentate. Starring Errol Flynn and Olivia de Havilland and with a supporting cast drawn mostly from the 'Hollywood British' colony (C. Aubrey Smith, David Niven, Patric Knowles, Donald Crisp, Henry Stephenson, Nigel Bruce), *The Charge of the Light Brigade* was one of a cycle of Northwest Frontier epics produced in Hollywood in the 1930s that also included *Lives of a Bengal Lancer*, *Wee Willie Winkie* and *Gunga Din*. The action occurs mostly in India and switches to the Crimea only for the climax, wherein the 27th Lancers (a fictional British regiment) find that their sworn enemy, Surat Khan, responsible for the massacre of British and Indian women, has joined the Russians. Directed with great panache and a complete disregard of historical fact by Michael Curtiz, the 1936 *Charge* was precisely the sort of mythologisation that Richardson was reacting against. The production discourse of the 1968 film claimed that it 'presents a strictly realistic version of the tragic cavalry charge which has unfortunately been glorified in contemporary and subsequent accounts'.[12]

The production history of *The Charge of the Light Brigade* was long and tortuous. As early as August 1965, the press reported that the Russian government had refused to allow permission to film in the Crimea itself. A Woodfall spokesman suggested mischievously that the reason 'was something to do with Russia not winning the Crimean War'.[13] John Osborne was already working on a script by this time, assisted in the historical details by John Mollo, and had a script ready by the autumn of 1965. However, his script did not satisfy Richardson, who later said that it 'had many splendid and poetic things in it – especially in its evocation of English society before the Crimean War – but it still needed a lot of work'.[14] Nevertheless, Osborne's script was still being used during the pre-production stages of the film one year later. Richardson appended a memorandum to its front:

> This script is intended to be, not so much in any sense a finished script, but as an interim report of how far we have got up to this moment...It is not intended to be gospel about every detail, and above all it is not intended to be a great stick to beat the director with. It is a guide to the sort of way we are going and to be interpreted freely and imaginatively.[15]

How much of Osborne's script made it into the finished film? In its basic structure and even in many small points of detail and dialogue, the Osborne script is very similar to the film. It features the same characters and many of the scenes from the film are recognisable in whole or in part. Its main protagonist is Captain Nolan, who joins Lord Cardigan's regiment in England after serving in India. (Nolan is a composite of two historical individuals: Captain John Reynolds of the infamous 'black bottle' incident and the actual Captain Nolan of the 15th Hussars who delivered the fateful order at Balaclava.) The script describes Nolan as 'an impressive-looking man' who 'has the look of a romantic but the intelligence of a self-divided [sic] and complex personality'. Cardigan takes an instant dislike to Nolan, who has a reputation as an expert on cavalry training. At a dinner in the officers' mess, Cardigan takes umbrage when he believes that Nolan is drinking porter ('I will not have porter or any other beer drunk in my mess. I've said so before. It's a drink for farmers and labouring men'), when in fact Nolan has a bottle of Moselle in a black bottle that has not been decanted. Refusing to listen to Nolan's protestations, Cardigan has him put under arrest. He also punishes Nolan by making Nolan's troop pay for their new uniforms, when Cardigan himself has bought the uniforms for the rest of the regiment. Cardigan is characterised as an extreme disciplinarian: a prisoner is flogged for an unspecified offence and Cardigan himself threatens to horsewhip a newspaper editor who has criticised him publicly for his harsh regime. (The script makes rather more of the criticism of Cardigan in the press than does the finished film.) When a British army is sent to the Crimea, Nolan is attached to the staff of the commander-in-chief, Lord Raglan. There is animosity between Cardigan, commanding the Light Brigade, and Lord Lucan, his immediate superior and brother-in-law. Lucan complains that Cardigan does not follow orders. In the meantime, Cardigan seduces Mrs Duberly, the wife of one of his officers. At Balaclava, a confused order from Raglan, delivered to

Lucan by Nolan, is the cause of the disastrous charge during which Nolan and many others perish.

In essence, therefore, the Osborne script is identifiable as the structural and, to a large extent, the ideological template for the film. There are some differences, however. Osborne included several of what he described as 'Méliès sequences' – a reference to the early film pioneer Georges Méliès – 'with painted sets, lunettes but with live actors in heightened costumes'. The script begins with such a scene at the Church of the Holy Sepulchre in Jerusalem featuring a violent clash between rival factions of Catholic and Orthodox monks. This suggests that Osborne was attempting, in a stylised way, to explain the origin of the Crimean War in a dispute over access to the Holy Places. Later, another scene shows the Czar of Russia seizing a map of Turkey. In the finished film, of course, the 'Méliès sequences' were replaced by animated interludes. Osborne's script also contains a marvellous scene near the end where, following the Charge, Cardigan finds himself surrounded by Russian lancers. 'It is quite impossible for a general to fight among common soldiers', Cardigan declares and trots back to his own line with the 'Russians staring after him in disbelief'.[16]

The situation regarding Osborne's script was complicated, however, by a legal action brought against Woodfall early in 1967, in which it was alleged that Osborne had based his script on Mrs Cecil Woodham-Smith's 1953 book *The Reason Why* that had exposed many of the myths about the Charge of the Light Brigade. In particular, *The Reason Why* had argued that the animosity between Lord Cardigan and Lord Lucan was a contributory factor in the disaster. The case was brought on behalf of the actor Laurence Harvey, who, through his company Harman Pictures, owned the film rights to *The Reason Why*. The author herself was of the opinion 'that Mr Osborne used my work as the basis of his screenplay and copied a substantial part'. Osborne replied to the effect that 'Mrs Woodham-Smith appears to have become deluded that only she has access to all the relevant historical information'.[17] Woodfall's defence was that they had undertaken their own research and that the historical facts were 'in the public domain'. Osborne also pointed out that his screenplay differed from the book in so far as he had invented a subplot involving a romance between Captain Nolan and a fictitious character called Clarissa, the wife of one of Nolan's fellow officers. This defence did not persuade the court. Mr Justice Goff was 'impressed by the marked similarity of the choice of incidents and by the juxtaposition of ideas' between script and book, and issued a temporary injunction against Woodfall preventing them from using the script.[18]

With the production unit set to start shooting in Turkey in April 1967, the ruling was a huge blow for Woodfall. In his autobiography Richardson laid the blame at Osborne's door: 'He had used the book; he was in breach of his writing contract with Woodfall; and Woodfall, of which he was a director, was clearly in breach of its contract with United Artists.'[19] An out-of-court settlement was reached whereby United Artists bought the rights to *The Reason Why* and Woodfall gave Laurence Harvey a part in the film. Richardson later claimed this was the reason for his falling-out with Osborne:

> There was nothing for him [Harvey], but then I thought of a one-day scene – an incident among incidents before the charge, when Prince Radziwill, a peacock-uniformed Polish dandy attached to the French and British forces, is surrounded by a group of wild Cossacks but by his dash escapes them. Originally John was to have played the role, but replacing him seemed a small price to pay to avoid the threatened prosecution. Not to John. He accused me of betrayal, and it led to a total breach between us.[20]

In the event, Woodfall won a sort of pyrrhic victory: Harvey's cameo, for which he was paid a reported £60,000, ended up on the cutting room floor.[21]

However, it is clear that Richardson's dissatisfaction with Osborne's script originated long before the court case. Indeed, even as the case was being heard, Richardson announced that another script had been commissioned from Charles Wood. Wood was a young writer who had worked on the screenplays for Richard Lester's *The Knack* (1965) and *How I Won the War* (1967) – the former produced by Woodfall – and who had, coincidentally, done his National Service in the 17th/21st Lancers, a unit that had been part of the Light Brigade, and so was steeped in regimental history. Wood later claimed that his first draft was 'wildly surreal, anachronistic, savage, over-written, pornographic, crammed with art student polemic, optimistically ironic, bitter about class and privilege' and that he threw in 'everything I felt about the British Empire, the British army, [and]

England under Queen Victoria'.[22] This may be so, but the script that he delivered on 3 March 1967, while the court case was being heard, and which was used as the basis of the production script, was not all that dissimilar from the discarded Osborne script. In essence, Wood used the same structure and characters, but he expanded the role of Clarissa (which Richardson had in mind for his wife Vanessa Redgrave) and omitted the prologue of fighting monks. It was Wood who introduced the idea that Lord Raglan, the aged commander-in-chief, thought he was fighting the French ('I think the French have been asking for it for some time, ever since they had my arm'). The sequence leading up to the Charge itself is much the same as in Osborne's script, though Wood added two scenes after the Charge – Cardigan and Lucan arguing on Cardigan's yacht, Raglan and Brigadier Airey surveying the corpse-strewn battlefield – that did not make it into the film.[23]

The Charge of the Light Brigade was shot between May and September 1967, first on location in Turkey, using some 4,000 Turkish troops as extras, and then back in England. The Charge itself was filmed in the Turkish province of Angolia where the production team had found two intersecting valleys with a hill between them that was geographically similar to the terrain at Balaclava itself. Richardson assembled a stellar cast that encompassed two entirely different generations of British screen acting. Elder statesmen Trevor Howard, Harry Andrews and Sir John Gielgud took the roles of, respectively, Cardigan, Lucan and Raglan, while, in addition to Vanessa Redgrave, the younger actors included David Hemmings as Nolan and Jill Bennett as Mrs Duberly. Richardson edited the film in conjunction with Kevin Brownlow, cutting entire sequences, including the expensively filmed Charge of the Heavy Brigade. To devise the animated sequences that were to serve as a framing device in the film, Richardson turned to Canadian-born animator Richard Williams, who reportedly was still working on the film 'right up to the day of the première'.[24]

The Charge of the Light Brigade was premièred at the Odeon, Leicester Square, on 10 April 1968 in the presence of the Duke of Edinburgh – the royal patronage illustrating once again the cultural prestige attached to the historical film in British cinema. However, another controversy was already brewing before the film had been seen. Richardson had refused the traditional press show, declaring that if the critics wanted to see the film they could pay to see it along with members of the public. He explained his decision in a long and, it must be said, inflammatory letter to *The Times*. It amounted to nothing less than a broadside against the national critics whom Richardson decried as 'the most personal, the most superficial and with the least good will in the world'. At the heart of Richardson's complaint was that most critics 'consider their work well done if they can write some light rubbish which amuses their readers' and failed to appreciate that the 'role of a critic...must be subordinated to what he is writing about, and to the society he is living in. He is good only in so far as he helps better films to be made or appreciated.' He compared film critics to 'spoilt and demanding children' and, in one widely quoted phrase, labelled them 'a group of acidulated, intellectual eunuchs hugging their prejudices like feather boas'.[25]

Richardson's outburst was characteristic of his unpredictable temperament. It is hard to determine how sincere it was: whether he had a genuine belief in the social responsibility of the critic, whether he was venting his frustration at the poor notices for his recent films, or whether it was merely a publicity stunt intended to generate interest in the film. Whatever his intention, the consequences were predictable. Much of Fleet Street was roused to indignation and Richardson's statement was condemned as 'hysterical and prejudiced'.[26] The Critics' Circle issued a statement deploring Richardson's stance but refusing to sanction a boycott of the film: 'While wholeheartedly condemning this restricted attitude which denies all fundamental principles of free speech, we have decided that each editor must act in the way he thinks best and decide the best means with which he wishes to deal with the film.'[27] His former Free Cinema colleague Lindsay Anderson came to Richardson's defence, however, averring that 'I am quite sure that most of those who fight for a serious and authentic British cinema would back Tony Richardson' and echoed Richardson in lambasting the national critics for their 'smart-alec demonstrations of intellectual superiority'.[28] (It is perhaps worth remembering that Anderson himself had been a critic for *Sequence* and *Sight and Sound*.)

If the critics had been as personal and superficial as Richardson alleged, it might have been expected that they would unleash their prejudices against the film. In fact, and to their credit, 'the critics were remarkably measured and careful in their responses'.[29] Few rubbished it completely and a good number found much to admire. The consensus was that it was 'uneven'. Dilys Powell described it as 'uneven but often brilliant'.[30] Margaret Hinxman called it 'an audacious triumph, but also a deeply dispiriting triumph'.[31] The *Observer* found it 'a highly sophisticated picture: exquisite to look at, superbly acted, harsh, bitter, funny', though added a caveat that 'the whole is less than the parts'.[32] Several critics expressed their admiration of Richardson's satirical use of history for social commentary. Alexander Walker hailed it as 'a brilliant period reconstruction, with a devastating running comment on the class system and military castes of Victorian England'.[33] Nina Hibbin, who described it as an 'anti-heroic epic', proclaimed Richardson as 'not only one of our most important and gifted directors but also a pioneer of progressive film trends'. She added, however, that 'he has boobed badly in denying critics the courtesy of a Press show for his new film, and by attacking them so viciously in the correspondence columns of *The Times*'.[34]

The main criticisms made of the film were that it was 'muddled' and 'confusing' as a narrative. This was particularly so with the Charge itself, presumed to be the film's climax. Patrick Gibbs in the *Daily Telegraph* felt that 'with the action moving from England to the Crimea the film seems to find itself in difficulties of exposition to which the parodies of political cartoons of the period introduced at this stage draw attention rather than provide a solution'.[35] John Coleman in the *New Statesman* complained that the ending 'leaves us almost as muddled as the men below as to what went on'.[36] Penelope Houston echoed this in the *Spectator*: '[The] charge, when it finally comes, seems less a climax than an incident: the threads have not been pulled together, and the film's slightly sullen and unforgiving mood imposes its detachment.'[37] The *Monthly Film Bulletin* published a long and largely negative review that called it 'a well-nigh intolerable mess, meandering, fidgety and indeterminate, trying with frequent signs of panic to reduce its subject matter nearer to manageable size by scurrilously simplifying and belittling the characters and the events of the Crimean War'. It drew attention to the director's 'customary array of alternative and conflicting styles' and complained that 'Richardson has become little more than an amorphous catalytic agent in a melee of wildly disparate elements'. 'Yet the irony of this monumental chaos from the critical point of view', it added, 'is that a bungled film about a bungled subject turns out in the last resort to be not entirely inappropriate.'[38] The tone of the review would tend to lend weight to Lindsay Anderson's complaint about 'the irresponsible snobbery of younger "intellectual" critics, who facilely denigrate any signs of promise among young British directors'. The eclectic use of style that the *Monthly Film Bulletin* found so off-putting in *The Charge of the Light Brigade* never seemed such a stumbling block when it came to reviewing the films of European 'art cinema' directors whose work was much admired within the intellectual film culture of which the *Bulletin* itself was a part.

Films and Filming – pointing out that 'Tony Richardson has been in the film industry long enough to know that apart from long-hair magazines like *Sight and Sound* and ourselves, film criticism is a highly organised aspect of film selling and promotion' – refused to review *The Charge* on the grounds that '[we] try never to go where we are not invited', but instead invited its readers to send in their own reviews.[39] The sample of readers' letters published in the magazine is valuable as evidence of the qualitative popular reception of the film, though with the caveats that the sample is small and that readers of *Films and Filming* were likely to be among the more discriminating cinema-goers. In general, they echoed the national critics in finding the film interesting but flawed. Anthony J. Ray of London felt that 'this is arguably Richardson's finest film to date, and certainly his most versatile … The more pity, then, that this in many ways accomplished work should be so disappointing.' 'It's a maddening film; one to go back to again and again', wrote Linda J. Triegel from Connecticut, USA. Brian Daves of Bristol was evidently not amongst Richardson's greatest admirers: 'After lending his name to two such undisputed disasters as *Mademoiselle* and *The Sailor from Gibraltar*, he must have guts – or maybe just sheer hard-boiled arrogance – to continue making pictures at all.' In contrast to Mr Ray, he felt that *The Charge* 'is probably his least satisfactory film, largely because it's so continuously and offensively pretentious'. 'The most riling aspect of the whole dismal enterprise', he concluded, 'is that Richardson and Wood clearly imagine that they're saying something new, invigorating and important on the subjects of war, social mores and the Victorians, when all they've got to offer is a lacklustre collection of lies, half-truths and clichés.'[40] It is ironic that one of the most damning reviews of *The Charge* came not from the national press but from one of the ordinary cinema-goers whom Richardson felt were being misled by the critics.

The American critical reception of *The Charge* in large measure mirrored the British in ranging from admiration to incomprehension. Hollis Alpert thought it 'a wonderfully ferocious and refreshing film that, for once, takes the silly glory and glamour out of war and substitutes something closer to the bitter truth'.[41] Vincent Canby found it 'a scathing, cryptic, sometimes brilliantly detailed caricature'. 'The actual events leading up to the final charge are likely to be as confusing to the moviegoer as they are to the participants, but they are visually stunning', he concluded, 'and the final impression of the movie – the silence on the body-littered battlefield broken by the buzzing of flies – is suddenly very personal, sad and even relevant.'[42] *Time*, however, was critical of Richardson's 'facile juxtapositions' between rich and poor and complained that Wood 'overloads the script with totally unsubtle pacifist propaganda'.[43] As a barometer of conservative Middle American opinion, *Time*'s disapproval of the film's 'pacifist propaganda' is hardly surprising. In contrast, *Variety* felt that 'as a protest against war…[it] is worth a flock of World War II pix that have tried to put over their anti-war messages'.[44]

While critics were divided about the efficacy of the anti-war theme of *The Charge of the Light Brigade*, British military historians were in no doubt that it distorted historical facts for its own ideological ends. John Terraine – who, as one of the writers of the acclaimed BBC series *The Great War* (1964), was no stranger to historical controversy, having clashed with Sir Basil Liddell Hart over an episode on the Battle of the Somme – complained that the film left out the Heavy Brigade, who during the same battle carried out 'one of the most brilliant cavalry actions on record'. 'They were a product of the same society, officered by the same class, formed in the same mould', Terraine averred. 'Their only sin, punished by oblivion, would seem to have been complete success.'[45] A correspondent in the *Listener*, however, felt that such criticisms were misplaced: 'Tony Richardson's film seems to have attracted more of this sort of criticism than any other since *Lawrence of Arabia*; and, as it happens, both of these take warfare at less than its usual value.'[46]

In analysing the style and content of *The Charge of the Light Brigade*, it is instructive to compare the film with *Zulu*, made only four years earlier. The two films have several themes in common, particularly as regards the representation of class, masculinity and militarism. It is a sign of the rapid shifts occurring in British film culture and British society at large during the 1960s, however, that *The Charge of the Light Brigade* could offer, in each instance, a quite radically different ideological stance towards those themes. Thus, for example, where *Zulu* ultimately resolves class differences between its initially antagonistic officers, in *The Charge* there is no such resolution. *Zulu* includes some pointed asides about social privilege in the British Army but settles into an action-oriented narrative of heroism and spectacle, whereas *The Charge* lays bare the social divisions of mid-Victorian Britain and suggests that these are responsible for the military blundering that culminates in the Charge itself. *Zulu* celebrates the heroism of British soldiers; *The Charge* is a savage lampoon of the values and attitudes of the military caste. There are also significant differences in narrative structure and style. *Zulu* focuses solely on the battle itself, but *The Charge* covers a much broader canvas that takes in the whole spectrum of British society. And, finally, where *Zulu* is a traditionally classical narrative, *The Charge* displays the eclectic use of style that critics found so problematic. One critic, for example, complained that it 'is confusingly inconsistent in style, as if frames from "Li'l Abner" were mixed in with "Prince Valiant"'.[47]

At a formal level, certainly, *The Charge of the Light Brigade* is a mixture of different styles that do not always fit comfortably together. Thus, on the one hand, an authentic sense of period is established by the deliberately archaic dialogue (Wood based characters' speech patterns on Carlyle and Thackeray) and by the costumes of David Walker that were modelled on authentic uniforms of the time. Lila di Nobili, who had worked with Luchino Visconti on the director's visually authentic nineteenth-century drama *The Leopard* (1963), was hired as 'colour and period consultant'. Like *Tom Jones*, the cinematography of *The Charge* – on this occasion by David Watkin – was intended to be 'in period'. Thus Watkin shoots it in a soft, naturalistic style using older camera lenses that provided less sharp picture definition. The result is that edges and backgrounds of images are sometimes blurred, resembling the 'look' of contemporary photographs of the Crimean War.[48] Yet, on the other hand, these stylistic devices, intended to create an authentic sense of period, were alienating to modern audiences. The dialogue verges on parody ('Who, Sir?' 'You, Sir!' 'Me, Sir?') and the cinematography was criticised by some for its murkiness. Eric Rhode, for example, complained that 'the whole movie looks as though it had been shot through a greasy lens'.[49]

The most unusual stylistic device used here – and greeted with 'unanimous praise' by the critics – are the animated sequences by Richard Williams.[50] Williams modelled the cartoon sequences on the style of contemporary satirical cartoons in magazines such as *Punch* and the *Illustrated London News*. At the same time, however, they also stand comparison with the surreal and zany animations of Terry Gilliam in the television comedy series *Monty Python's Flying Circus* (1969–74). The purpose of the animations is to provide historical context and to further the narrative. As a device they serve the purpose usually fulfilled in historical films by voice-overs or explanatory texts. Thus the opening of the film establishes the geopolitical background to the Crimean War through a sequence which has the Great Powers represented as animals. The Russian Bear menaces Turkey; the Austrian Peacock and French Cockerel look west to the sleeping British Lion; the Lion awakes and puts on a policeman's helmet. It is a highly imaginative and unorthodox means of establishing the historical background to the narrative that makes a more lasting impression than a conventional voice-over (the lengthy and convoluted introduction to *The Iron Duke*, for example) and also hints at the satirical tone of the film. In the opening title sequence Williams then uses a series of cartoon sketches to show the industrial power and imperial splendour of mid-Victorian Britain. There is also a motif of 'two nations' that will be a dominant theme of the film. Images of factories, smoke-belching chimneys, power looms and mine shafts establish the idea of Britain as the 'workshop of the world' but also expose the dreadful conditions of the workers. There then follow images of the leisured classes at the Great Exhibition of 1851 and representatives of the British Empire paying homage to Queen Victoria. In a remarkably succinct and effective way, the title sequence provides the sort of contextualisation that critics so often alleged was lacking in the historical film, alluding to the wider social and economic historical processes and dispensing with the need for clumsy voice-overs or rolling captions.

The use of satirical and surreal animated sequences clearly indicates that *The Charge of the Light Brigade* is an unconventional historical film. The animations are an integral part of the overall design of the film. They are cleverly and wholly integrated with the narrative. The popular war fever of 1854, for example, is depicted through crowds mouthing 'War, war, war'; but every face in the crowd has the same grotesque features, suggesting the uniformity of the mob and the absence of individual thought or conscience when war fever takes hold. As the film progresses the cartoons become more and more surreal: the British fleet is shown leaving from beneath Queen Victoria's skirts; the Czar of Russia puts his head in the British Lion's mouth and promptly has it bitten off; and Victoria and Albert are shown celebrating victory at the Battle of Alma by eating a cake in the design of the Winter Palace. Far from being mere inserts, the cartoons are used for ironic and satirical effect through their juxtaposition with the main narrative. The triumphant progress of the British fleet through the Mediterranean is contrasted with harrowing images from below decks of a ship caught in a vicious storm, while the premature newspaper announcement of the fall of Sebastopol is followed immediately by a cut to the trenches outside Sebastopol.

At the level of narrative, the main preoccupation of *The Charge of the Light Brigade*, especially in its first half, is the theme of class. The film establishes the social *milieu* of mid-Victorian Britain through a series of vignettes, cutting, for example, between the society wedding of Captain Morris to Clarissa (filmed in delicate pastel shades and brightly lit) and a poor urban environment (filmed in dark, grim, grainy colours and under-lit). The social structure is mapped onto social relations within the army, where there is division between the older, aristocratic officers who have purchased their commissions and a younger generation of more meritocratic officers exemplified by Nolan. Lord Raglan justifies the principle of aristocratic privilege within the army by quoting the Duke of Wellington: 'When there is danger it is the persons with a stake in the country – land, position, wealth – that are best able to defend it.' All professional soldiers hold the lower classes in contempt: 'Swab the scum clean' orders a recruiting sergeant when a group of new recruits are brought into barracks. The army offers a life of privilege for the officers, but is tough and brutal for the lower ranks, who are subjected to a regime of harsh discipline.

The Charge of the Light Brigade is scathing about the 'old brigade' who continue to hold positions of authority. Senior officers are held up to ridicule as hidebound by tradition: they reminisce about Waterloo (a battle fought almost 40 years earlier) and Lord Raglan, the commander-in-chief, lives under Wellington's shadow (quite literally,

16. A Colonel Blimp for the 1960s: the aged Lord Raglan (John Gielgud) pointing out 'the pretty valley' to Mrs Duberly (Jill Bennett) in *The Charge of the Light Brigade*.

as a huge statue of the Duke stands outside his office window and is kept in shot in several scenes that take place there). The character of Nolan represents a challenge to this traditional, old-fashioned army. He is a professional soldier who has seen active service in India and who has written books on the training of cavalry horses. Nolan is impatient with what he perceives as amateurism in the army ('I will not be patient to the noble amateurs who are so sick of their soldiering they would go home under the ridiculous supposition that war is an aid to civilisation') and argues for a more professional approach to warfare ('The solution to war is that it is best fought and when fought it is best fought to the death'). Both Cardigan and Raglan take an instinctive dislike to Nolan, whom they regard as an upstart. 'That young man, Nolan, I don't really like him. He rides too well', Raglan remarks, adding: 'It will be a sad day, Airey, when England has her armies officered by men who know too well what they are doing.' Raglan himself is portrayed as a waspish imbecile who is too old to command, a Colonel Blimp for the 1960s. He keeps referring to the French as the enemy ('The cavalry will advance on the French – er, the Russians – immediately') and issues comically bizarre commands ('Form the infantry nicely for the assault'). In the midst of directing a battle he lapses into incoherence when explaining tactics to Mrs Duberly ('Young ladies should concern themselves with what is pretty. England is pretty, babies are pretty, some table linen can be very pretty.') If Raglan is held up to ridicule, Cardigan is characterised as a grotesque, boorish reactionary. He is more concerned with the appearance of his troops (whom he refers to proudly as 'my cherrybums' on account of their red breeches) than with their training. He is also petulant and resentful that he has to serve under Lord Lucan who is married to his sister ('Lucan could not make himself fit to command a tent – command an escort – not fit to command a troop of knackered tailors on a stump donkey').

The film's attack on class and privilege was very much a preoccupation of the 1960s. This had been a prominent theme of new wave cinema and was still evident in films of the late 1960s such as *Accident* (dir. Joseph Losey, 1967) and *If...* (dir. Lindsay Anderson, 1968). Class was also a favourite target of television satire, such as *That Was The Week That Was* (in sketches like 'What is a northerner?') and *The Frost Report* ('I know my place'). Much of the legislative agenda of the Labour government of 1964–70 indicated, in principle at least, a commitment to social equality and the ending of privilege: the extension of social services, the introduction of comprehensive education and the expansion of the university sector. At the same time, however, many felt that the old élites remained in charge, and the traditional bastions of privilege – the public schools and Oxbridge – retained a considerable degree of social exclusion. The British Army had long ceased to be a bastion of privilege, but the military structure that outwardly resembled the class system made it an obvious target for the likes of Richardson (who had not been accepted for National Service due to being medically unfit) and Wood (who had reached the dizzy heights of 'acting unpaid lance corporal').

Another preoccupation of *The Charge of the Light Brigade* is sex. In contrast to the permissiveness of *Tom Jones*, however, *The Charge* has a more ambiguous attitude towards sex and sexuality. It presents Victorian sexual morality as repressive and inhibiting individual freedom, but subverts expectations by showing the younger generation as more prurient in their observation of sexual conventions than their elders. This is the purpose of the character of Clarissa. Clarissa is the epitome of bourgeois respectability, but is locked in a passionless marriage to Captain Morris. She is attracted to and falls in love with Nolan, their affair being represented, however, as an idealised romantic love rather than a purely sexual desire. Clarissa is associated throughout the film with the countryside: she appears in pastoral landscapes (gardens and river banks) that are shot through filters and lit naturally so as to achieve a dream-like quality. The affair between Clarissa and Nolan, in which they behave with much the same restrained passion as Laura Jesson and Alec Harvey in *Brief Encounter*, is a rural idyll reminiscent of European 'art' films such as *Elvira Madigan* (dir. Bo Widerberg, 1967). Whether the affair is consummated is ambiguous; Clarissa becomes pregnant and tells Nolan that she wishes the child was his. The chaste, romantic love between Clarissa and Nolan is contrasted with the voracious carnal appetite of Cardigan, who sees women as sexual objects and compares the sex act to riding a horse ('I like saddles, get on your back'). He makes an obvious pass at Clarissa that is politely rebuffed, but finds a willing partner in Fanny, the flirtatious wife of Paymaster Duberly whom Cardigan regards with contempt ('That ain't a rank, it's a trade'). Mrs Duberly makes clear her attraction to Cardigan ('You have the mane of a lion') and Cardigan dismisses Duberly from dinner on his yacht so that he can be alone with Fanny. The seduction parodies the famous eating scene from *Tom Jones* and is played for comic effect as they both remove their outer clothing to reveal corsets beneath.

In its critique of Victorian sexual morality, *The Charge of the Light Brigade* was again responding to the contemporary social climate. It was during the 1960s that Britain decisively broke free from the prurient sexual morality that had, depending upon one's point of view, acted as either a straight-jacket or a safety-valve since Victorian times. The decade began with the obscenity trial of Penguin Books for publishing D.H. Lawrence's *Lady Chatterly's Lover*; the court's decision in favour of the defendants – an example of what Arthur Marwick has termed the 'measured judgement' of the 1960s in which the authorities showed evidence of liberal and progressive tendencies[51] – opened the door to the publication of other books containing explicit sexual material. The year in which *The Charge of the Light Brigade* was shot, 1967, was a watershed for liberalising legislation in respect of sexual behaviour with the legalisation of abortion and homosexuality.

The cumulative effect of this legislation was to raise people's awareness of their own sexual freedom – a freedom further enhanced by the increasing availability of the contraceptive pill for women.

If class and sex are prominent themes of *The Charge of the Light Brigade*, however, it reserves its most savage polemic for the ideology of militarism. For all the social differences between Nolan and Cardigan, they are both members of a military caste that endorses war as the ultimate test of masculinity and courage. Nolan believes that war is 'the stuff we are all waiting for'. The film exposes the absurdity of the notion of war as a glorious enterprise. It shows British soldiers drowning at Calamita Bay and dying from cholera before they have even gone into battle. Heavy casualties are sustained at the Battle of Alma as the infantry advance at a walk into volleys of enemy fire. In the aftermath, the battlefield is littered with the bodies of dead and dying soldiers; Nolan is sickened by the sight. He shoots a Russian soldier who is looting the dead. Nolan's revulsion at the sight of the casualties is short-lived, however, for at Balaclava he volunteers to convey Raglan's order to Lord Lucan so that he can ride with the Light Brigade. Nolan clearly finds war an exhilarating experience.

The Charge itself is presented as a calamitous blunder rather than a heroic spectacle. Critics who complained that it was confusing had a point, but judging from the various drafts of the script this had always been the intention. Raglan, from his command post atop the hill, sees some British guns in the south valley being carried away by the Russians and wants the Light Brigade to advance into 'the pretty valley' in order to restore the guns 'to their rightful owners'. He makes it clear that Cardigan must avoid the north valley – 'that nasty valley with half the Russian army in it'. Raglan dictates his order to Brigadier Airey and it is conveyed to Lucan by Nolan. Lucan, unable to see the south valley from his position, hesitates to act on the order as he cannot see the enemy. Nolan points and yells 'There is your enemy, there are your guns', while a camera pan reveals that from Lucan's and Cardigan's point of view he is pointing at the north valley. Lucan, with obvious reluctance, sends the Light Brigade to attack the main Russian position believing that is Raglan's order. Cardigan leads the Light Brigade at a trot towards the opening of the two valleys. Nolan, riding with the Brigade, realises too late that Cardigan is heading into the wrong valley and rides to the front of the column, waving his sword to point them in the right direction, but is killed when the first cannon shell explodes above his head. The Light Brigade advance in the face of heavy gunfire and finally break into a charge that sees them overrun the Russian position, but at great loss.

Filmically, the sequence of the Charge is perhaps best described as anti-spectacle rather than spectacle. In contrast to, say, *Henry V* or *Zulu*, which use aspects of film form (rhythmic editing, montage, music) to impose a clarity of structure and meaning onto their battle sequences, the battle in *The Charge of the Light Brigade* lacks a clear formal structure. Partly this is due to scenes having been cut (the Laurence Harvey cameo, for example), though it also conveys the chaos and confusion of battle. Richardson uses a series of rapid cuts to show troopers falling from their horses; the effect is not dissimilar to Peter Watkins's *Culloden*. The scenes of carnage are intercut with Raglan and his staff watching the battle from the hill ('I don't know, I

17. *The Charge of the Light Brigade*: Captain Nolan (David Hemmings) is about to realise that the Brigade is advancing into the wrong valley.

don't know. It isn't done'). The end comes quickly. The survivors of
the Light Brigade stumble back, bloodied, battered, mostly without
horses. Cardigan seems oblivious to the decimation of the Brigade but
is furious with Nolan's apparent breach of military protocol ('How
dare he ride before the General of the Brigade like that?') until he is
told 'My lord, you have just ridden over his dead body'. Cardigan
addresses the survivors and asserts that the blunder was not his ('Men,
it was a mad-brained thing, but it was no fault of mine'). The film ends
with bitter recriminations between the senior British officers:
Cardigan blames Lucan, Lucan blames Raglan, Raglan blames Airey.
The credits roll over the image of a dead horse. The contrast between
this and the ending of *Zulu* could not be more pronounced.

There is no question that *The Charge of the Light Brigade* is an
explicitly anti-war and anti-militarist film. Again it was responding to
issues that were current in the late 1960s. Although Britain was not at
war itself, there was probably a greater anti-war feeling in the country
than at any time since the early 1930s, especially among the young.
The first major protests about the Vietnam War in Britain occurred in
1967, led by university students, culminating in the so-called 'Battle of
Grosvenor Square' (17 March 1968), when an estimated 25,000
protestors converged on the American Embassy and had to be
dispersed by a baton-charge of mounted police. Nina Hibbin
suggested that a scene in *The Charge* where Cardigan and his troopers
break up an anti-war demonstration in London was 'one of the film's
hints at parallels with the 1960s'.[52] The idea that *The Charge* is 'about'
Vietnam has been advanced by subsequent critics such as Andy
Medhurst, who describes it as 'a protest march of a film, with Vietnam
a structuring, unspoken presence'.[53] Wood, however, denied that it had
anything specifically to do with Vietnam, claiming instead that it was
against all war in principle: 'In those days almost everything about war
was excused and justified by being "about Vietnam really", and
sometimes it was politic to suggest so in order to get the money and
the attention. It wasn't, of course – it was/is as much about the
Falklands and the Gulf, and as little about the Crimea.'[54] This is, of
course, a reading that could be laid onto the film only in hindsight.

The Charge of the Light Brigade can be placed within a cycle of
anti-war films in British cinema during the late 1960s. It is comparable
to two other films released a year each side of Richardson's film. *How
I Won the War*, written by Wood and shot by David Watkin, was

adapted from a novel by Patrick Ryan and directed by Richard Lester. The film tells the story of a British platoon in North Africa during the Second World War which is sent on a mission to play a cricket match behind enemy lines in order to impress an American general. It can be seen as a parody of 'special mission' war films (*Cockleshell Heroes*, *The Guns of Navarone*, *Operation Crossbow*) and anticipates *The Charge* in two particular respects. First, the narrative lays bare social differences between officers and men whose relationship is one of mutual antagonism rather than the respect and comradeship of the traditional war film. The officers, personified by Lieutenant Goodbody (Michael Crawford) and Colonel Grapple (Michael Hordern), are, respectively, an egomaniac and an upper-class twit who thinks he is Lawrence of Arabia, while the men, such as Privates Clapper (Roy Kinnear) and Gripweed (an absurdly cast John Lennon), are self-interested and cynical. And second, Lester makes an even more eclectic use of style than Richardson, alternating between comedy and violence, humour and horror, realism and surrealism. Neil Sinyard describes *How I Won the War* as a 'thesis on the difference between the romantic images and the actual reality of war'.[55] It was released to critical hostility and audience apathy, ironically losing out at the box office to *The Dirty Dozen* (dir. Robert Aldrich, 1967), a violent but exciting example of the sort of 'special mission' narrative that *How I Won the War* set out to debunk.

Oh! What A Lovely War (dir. Richard Attenborough, 1969) is an even more heavily stylised film than either *How I Won the War* or *The Charge of the Light Brigade*. Adapted by Len Deighton from the play by Joan Littlewood, first performed at the Stratford East Theatre in 1963, *Oh! What A Lovely War* is a part-historical, part-musical, part-satirical imagining of the First World War as a spectacular musical hall pantomime staged on Brighton Pier and interspersed with popular songs of the period. It goes far further than *The Charge* in abandoning conventional narrative structure and presenting the war as a series of linked sketches. Its principal theme is once again the difference between the image and the reality of war and it is preoccupied with exposing the patriotic hubris that caused hundreds of thousands of men to flock to the colours. Thus General Haig (John Mills) sells tickets to the neon-lit extravaganza of 'World War One – Battles, Songs And A Few Jokes' and young men are shown being seduced into joining the army by a glamorous and sexually alluring actress

(Maggie Smith). Attenborough pulls off some bravura touches – including a 180-degree camera pan from a fairground shooting booth to the trenches and a final, haunting aerial shot revealing hundreds of white crosses fixed in the ground – though, like *The Charge*, it is a film of great moments rather than a great film. *Oh! What A Lovely War* was part of a revival of interest in the First World War, coinciding with the fiftieth anniversary, that also included Alan Clark's influential book *The Donkeys* (1961), the *Great War* television series and films such as *King and Country* (dir. Joseph Losey, 1964), which, taken together, created the popular image of the First World War as one of inhuman slaughter in which the enlisted men suffered as much from the incompetence of their own generals as from the enemy. The critical reception of *Oh! What A Lovely War* was similar to *The Charge* – a mixture of praise for its visual imagination and unease about its satirical attitude towards war.[56]

Yet, despite the anti-war popular demonstrations of the late 1960s, anti-war films did not fare especially well at the box office. Audiences seemed to prefer the comic-book certainties of war adventure films such as *Where Eagles Dare* (dir. Brian G. Hutton, 1969) and *Kelly's Heroes* (dir. Brian G. Hutton, 1970). There is only sketchy evidence to indicate how *The Charge of the Light Brigade* fared at the box office, though by all accounts it was something of a disappointment. It was ranked among the top ten British attractions by *Kine Weekly*, though there is no record of its actual grosses and the British market alone was not big enough to recover the production cost. It fared less well in America where its box-office returns were variously described as 'mild', 'slim', 'modest' and 'tame'. United Artists was able to absorb the losses – in 1968 it recorded pre-tax profits of $20 million – and continued to have sufficient faith in Richardson to back his film *Ned Kelly* (1970), in which Mick Jagger was improbably cast as the notorious Australian outlaw.[57]

'It is extraordinary', writes Murphy, 'that the three waves of ambitious, prestigious film making in Britain – 1933–37, 1944–49, 1963–69 – should all founder amidst a welter of expensive costume dramas.'[58] *The Charge of the Light Brigade* was not the only film that failed to live up to expectations. *Far From the Madding Crowd* – another example of a former new wave director (John Schlesinger) turning to the classic novel (Thomas Hardy) – was respectfully received by critics but its length (167 minutes) and slow pace meant that it fared

badly at the box office. *Alfred the Great*, backed by MGM and directed
by another British film-maker who came to prominence in the 1960s
(Clive Donner), was an imaginative attempt at a 'youth epic' that
featured an intense performance by David Hemmings as the young
Saxon king torn between his religious beliefs and his earthly desires.
Like *The Charge*, it is a revisionist film (there is no scene of Alfred
burning the cakes) that was probably too intelligent to appeal to a wide
audience. MGM's expensive British-produced musical remake of
Goodbye Mr Chips similarly failed to set the box office alight, despite a
fine performance from Peter O'Toole as the old schoolmaster: its
themes of duty, loyalty and the public school ethos were out of touch
with the popular mood at the end of the 1960s. United Artists backed
Harry Saltzman and Benjamin Fisz's production *Battle of Britain* (dir.
Guy Hamilton, 1969), a historically authentic, dramatically old-
fashioned all-star war epic in the tradition of Darryl F. Zanuck's *The
Longest Day* (1962). Its subject matter made it a hit in Britain, but it still
failed to recover its production cost of $12 million. None of these films
was bad, but they were too expensive to stand much chance of going
into profit, especially when the continuing decline of cinema audiences
is taken into account. Alexander Walker summarised the problem of
escalating costs in the late 1960s:

> All these films, and more, had been vastly more expensive than
> they had any warrant to be; but they had been caught up on the
> production escalator, operating in Britain in the last few years of
> the 1960s boom, which dragged films up to and past the floor
> where their makers should have prudently called a halt or got
> off.[59]

The Charge of the Light Brigade was one of the films caught on this
escalator. United Artists had expected a hit that would repeat the
success of *Tom Jones* and were prepared to spend 20 times as much on
The Charge as they had on the earlier film. This can be explained only
partly in terms of inflation. By the late 1960s, Hollywood was locked
into a blockbuster mentality, believing that only big-budget films with
expensive production values and stellar casts could return the scale of
profits on which the industry depended. The corollary of that logic –
that big films were also capable of incurring big losses – was rudely
demonstrated by the failure of films like *The Charge of the Light*

Brigade. The reason for its failure is probably best summed up by Mark Connelly: 'History provided a lesson and a parable for the present in *The Charge of the Light Brigade*...Unfortunately for Woodfall and United Artists, the cinema-going public was not in the mood for such a strange sermon.'[60]

11

The Conscience of the King:
Henry VIII and His Six Wives
(1972)

*H*ENRY VIII and His Six Wives, directed by Waris Hussein for
EMI, represents a return to a more conventional style of
historical film following the forays into the genre by the former new
wave film-makers in the late 1960s. It was part of a cycle of
handsomely mounted historical costume dramas in the early 1970s
that also included *Anne of the Thousand Days* (dir. Charles Jarrott,
1969) – released in Britain in 1970 – *Cromwell* (dir. Ken Hughes,
1970), *Nicholas and Alexandra* (dir. Franklin Schaffner, 1971), *Mary,
Queen of Scots* (dir. Charles Jarrott, 1971), *Young Winston* (dir.
Richard Attenborough, 1972) and *A Bequest to the Nation* (dir.
James Cellan Jones, 1973). These are all films notable for their
cultural and aesthetic conservatism: respectable, literate, wordy
scripts and a sober visual style of sensitive colour cinematography
and predominantly frontal staging. Filmically, their model was *A
Man for All Seasons* (dir. Fred Zinnemann, 1966), the successful
adaptation of the play by Robert Bolt, which won five Academy
Awards (including Best Film, Best Director and Best Actor for Paul
Scofield as Sir Thomas More). They also owed something to the
tradition of costume drama on British television: *Henry VIII and
His Six Wives* was inspired by the BBC serial *The Six Wives of
Henry VIII*. In content and tone the film is very different indeed
from *The Private Life of Henry VIII*, demonstrating yet again how
the same historical material is moulded to fit different production,
cultural and ideological contexts.[1]

The 1970s are generally regarded as the nadir of British cinema, described variously as 'the lowest point in British film making' and a period of 'penury and cultural decline' following the vigorous and exciting film culture of the 1960s.[2] Cinema attendances reached their lowest recorded level since statistics began to be compiled and film production was in a parlous state. The industry was afflicted by a chronic shortage of finance, brought about by the withdrawal of American capital. The Hollywood majors, hit by escalating production costs and declining cinema attendances, fell back on a strategy of economy and retrenchment that involved curtailing their overseas production arms. American investment in the British production sector fell from a high of £31.3 million in 1968 to a low of £2.9 million by 1974.[3] MGM closed its Borehamwood Studios in 1970 and the 'big three' British studios (Elstree, Pinewood and Shepperton) were forced to lay off workers when they could not fill their stages. This economic situation was exacerbated by the Conservative government elected in 1970, which drastically reduced the amount of subsidy paid to the film industry through the National Film Finance Corporation.[4] Paradoxically, the number of British-produced feature films actually increased in the first half of the 1970s, to between 80 and 90 per year, though this was due in large measure to the proliferation of cheaply made sex comedies that added nudity to the smutty humour popularised by the 'Carry On' films and their ilk.

All the evidence points toward an increasing fragmentation and compartmentalisation of the exhibition sector in the 1970s. The increased number of 'X'-certificate films suggests that the industry saw adults-only fare as a response to declining attendances. There were two distinct types of 'X'-certificate film that catered for different audiences: on the one hand, sex, horror and exploitation films for the 'dirty overcoat' brigade; on the other hand, serious films destined for the 'art house' crowd by *auteur* directors, such as Sam Peckinpah (*Straw Dogs*), Stanley Kubrick (*A Clockwork Orange*) and Ken Russell (*The Devils*), that took advantage of a relaxation in censorship to include more explicit violence, often sexual in nature. At the same time, however, some of the most popular films of the early 1970s were family-oriented, notably the vogue for big-screen versions of television comedies such as *Dad's Army*, *On the Buses*, *Bless This House* and *Love Thy Neighbour*. The recourse to tried-and-trusted formulae (albeit that film spin-offs of television sitcoms tended to open up their narratives, usually to their detriment) is another indicator of the economic and cultural penury of the British film industry at this time. The conventional wisdom seems to have been that if a series had been successful on television then audiences would pay to see it again in the cinema. So it was with *Henry VIII and His Six Wives*: the trade press identified 'the tremendous success of the TV series' as the reason why the film 'is expected to attract capacity business'.[5]

The costume drama, usually in the form of serialised adaptations of classic novels by authors such as Jane Austen, Charles Dickens and William Thackeray, has been a staple genre of British television, and especially of the BBC, since the 1950s. The arrival of colour broadcasting at the end of the 1960s opened up new possibilities for the genre and one of the significant production trends over the next decade was the 'historical play' (as it was known), exemplified by *The First Churchills* (1969), *The Six Wives of Henry VIII* (1970), *Elizabeth R* (1971) and *I, Claudius* (1976). *The Six Wives of Henry VIII* was produced by Ronald Travers and Mark Shivas and, according to its credits, was 'based on an idea by Maurice Cowan'. It was in effect a series of single plays as each of the six 90-minute episodes focused on one of Henry's wives and was by a different writer (in order Rosemary Anne Sisson, Nick McCady, Ian Thorne, Jean Morris, Beverley Cross and John Prebble). Henry was played throughout by Australian-born actor Keith Michell, who had been 'discovered' by Laurence Olivier and had been playing Henry on stage for the Young Vic since the early 1950s. The series was shown first on BBC2, starting on New Year's Day 1970, and was so successful that it was repeated a year later on BBC1.[6] It was sold to countries as diverse as Japan, Australia, Canada, Sweden, Finland, Belgium and West Germany, and was bought by the CBS network which broadcast it on American television. The decision to show it in a primetime slot (Sunday evenings at 9.30 p.m.) was 'a calculated risk' by the network, as previous imported British dramas, such as *The Forsyte Saga* and *Masterpiece Theatre*, had been shown through Public Service Broadcasting rather than on the main networks.[7] Michell's performance as Henry won him the best actor award of 1970 from the Society of Film and Television Arts.

The Six Wives of Henry VIII was admired for its attention to historical detail and for its *mise-en-scène*. Nancy Banks-Smith in the *Guardian* thought it 'very true to recorded history' and 'lovely to look at'.[8] For George Melly in the *Observer* it was 'beautiful to look at' and 'nearly avoided the dangers of modern historical dialogue'.[9] Stewart Lane in the *Morning Star* (successor to the *Daily Worker* as mouthpiece of the Communist Party of Great Britain) described it as 'splendidly produced, wonderfully acted and gorgeously costumed'.[10] In short, it exhibited all the hallmarks of 'quality' television: high production values, literate scripts, sensitive acting. This was a point made forcefully by Mary Malone in the *Daily Mirror*, asserting that 'this IS the real national theatre' and preferring it to 'the Wednesday Plagues [*sic*], dilettante half-hour dramas and Saturday Night soporifics'.[11]

Henry VIII and His Six Wives was conceived as a film adaptation of *The Six Wives of Henry VIII*. There was continuity in the personnel involved: television co-producer Mark Shivas was executive producer of the film, Ian Thorne who had written the Jane Seymour episode for television scripted the film and Keith Michell again played Henry. The film version was directed by a former BBC drama director, Indian-born Waris Hussein, who had ventured into feature films in the late 1960s. It does not seem appropriate to attribute any particular auteurist input to Hussein, whose feature films have been a mixed bag, including a social problem drama (*A Touch of Love*, 1969), a whimsical comedy (*Quackser Fortune Has a Cousin in the Bronx*, 1970) and an occult thriller (*The Possession of Joel Delaney*, 1971). Historical themes feature prominently in his television work, including an early *Doctor Who* serial ('Marco Polo') and the mini-series *Edward and Mrs Simpson* (1978). A comparison of the finished film and the shooting script, however, reveals, as with *A Night to Remember*, that the director's role was essentially that of translating the written word onto the screen.[12]

Henry VIII and His Six Wives was produced by Roy Baird for Anglo-EMI. Electrical and Musical Industries (EMI) was a British showbusiness corporation which acquired control of the ailing Associated British Picture Corporation in 1969. This paralleled developments in the US film industry in the late 1960s whereby large conglomerates whose primary interest was not in film took over most of the major studios, including Paramount (Gulf & Western), United Artists (Transamerica Corporation) and Warner Bros. (Kinney National Services). (In 1973 British Lion was bought by a property development corporation which promptly sold off most of its assets.) In 1970 EMI agreed a co-production arrangement with MGM and the actor-writer-producer Bryan Forbes was appointed Head of Production. Forbes resigned after two years, after insisting on a no-redundancy policy, and was replaced by Nat Cohen, co-founder of the producer-distributor Anglo-Amalgamated which had also been absorbed by EMI. Anglo-EMI, as the film subsidiary of EMI was known, was the leading British producer of the 1970s, with a balanced production programme that included television spin-offs for the domestic market (*Steptoe and Son*, *Are You Being Served?*), sex comedies (*Percy's Progress*), artistic films from *auteur* directors such as Joseph Losey (*The Go-Between*) and two sumptuously mounted, all-star adaptations of Agatha Christie mysteries (*Murder on the Orient Express*, *Death on the Nile*) that were successful in the international market. Cohen saw *Henry VIII and His Six Wives* as part of his international production strategy, inspired no doubt by the successful overseas sales of the BBC series. 'I was determined to bring this highly successful television series to the big screen', he remarked. 'We have what I believe will be a subject for the world market.'[13]

Henry VIII and His Six Wives was described by its producer as a 'medium budget' film (no precise amount was cited) and costs were kept down by drawing upon the research already undertaken for the television series. Thus, while the film did not use the same costumes as the television series (they were being exhibited on a tour at the time), it employed the same costume designer, John Bloomfield. It was shot at Elstree Studios in the autumn of 1971, with exteriors at Hatfield House, Allington Castle and Woburn Abbey. As usual, the film's production discourse emphasised attention to authenticity, with the music, for example, being composed by David Munro, a specialist in medieval chamber music, and performed by the Early Music Consort of London. Baird claimed that it was the most psychologically accurate portrait of Henry VIII to date:

> We try and show just what made Henry 'tick' and just why he did the things he did. We will also get inside Henry and show the complex inner conflicts of his mind, his desperate yearning for a son, his loves, and what led to his later and finally fatal illness. We hope the result will be the most complete and detailed portrait of a King ever seen on the cinema screen.[14]

The film would suffer in comparison to the television series, however, in so far as it had to compress nine hours of drama into two. In the process, one of the most important explanatory scenes was lost. The shooting script attributes Henry's deteriorating health in his later years (he suffered from severe headaches) to an accident during a joust when he was hit in the face by a lance because his visor stuck. However, the finished film omits this scene, and with it any explanation for Henry's headaches.

The film was released in the summer of 1972 to mixed reviews. Most critics found it less satisfying than the television series and complained that the narrative was too episodic to make entirely successful drama. 'The adaptation makes little effort to recast the material for the screen: episode follows truncated episode; turgid passages of television dialogue are interspersed with apologetic bits of crowd scene and action', wrote David Robinson.[15] John Russell Taylor concurred: 'The production seems a trifle impoverished. It is structured so that each ten minutes of flat television-style narrative, rather dully covering most of the necessary facts, is followed by maybe a minute of Cinema, usually a bloody execution or a royal rout and revel.'[16] Patrick Gibbs 'found its elementary history pretty indigestible, however much it may have been reconceived and re-written'.[17] George Melly thought that it 'seems both superficial and yet overlong'.[18] Nina Hibbin made her familiar complaint about the absence of any 'enriched social background...Ian Thorne's script scarcely hints at the many-sidedness of the gifted autocrat's character, or at the wide-ranging innovations of his reign.'[19] There were some more favourable opinions. Ian Christie, for example, believed that 'Waris Hussein has knotted the complex events together to form a satisfactory whole'.[20] And Derek Prouse felt that Hussein 'manages his handsome production with fluent authority'.[21]

The film journals were similarly lukewarm. Alex Stuart in *Films and Filming* called it 'a confused film, unsure as to whether it's a costume drama, an historical investigation, a romance, or an epic'.[22] Colin Ford in the *Monthly Film Bulletin* thought it 'more efficiently written, acted and filmed than most of the products of EMI since it entered the film business, though it shares with them its apparent *raison d'être*: after a successful television series and in the middle of a vogue for things Elizabethan and Tudor, it seems calculated to be a commercial success'.[23] Marjorie Bilbow of the trade paper *CinemaTV Today*, however, was less certain about its commercial prospects, suggesting that 'we must face the possibility that audiences have had a bellyful of Tudors in the past couple of years... It is a good, colourful, enjoyable film: my reservations about its popular appeal are not related to its quality as entertainment.'[24] The film was released only a few months after Hal B. Wallis's production of *Mary, Queen of Scots*, in which Glenda Jackson had repeated her acclaimed portrayal of Queen Elizabeth I from the television series *Elizabeth R*, opposite Vanessa Redgrave as Mary Stuart, while Wallis's film was itself a follow-up to his previous *Anne of the Thousand Days*, which had starred Richard Burton as Henry VIII and Genevieve Bujold as Anne Boleyn. The 'Carry On' series had also produced its own version of Henry VIII in 1971, with Sid James as the guffawing, skirt-chasing monarch. The view that British cinema-goers in the early 1970s had had a surfeit of Tudors was endorsed by a cinema manager in Cardiff, who reported that he was 'disappointed' in the box-office perform-ance of *Henry VIII and His Six Wives*, 'believing that the Tudor scene has, between cinema and television, been overdone'.[25]

Henry VIII and His Six Wives does not appear to have set the box office alight. It was given a limited initial release at selected London and provincial cinemas before its general release on the ABC circuit in January 1973, but it did not figure in the annual top 20 box-office attractions published by the trade press, unlike *Mary, Queen of Scots*, which came a respectable tenth in 1972.[26] *Mary, Queen of Scots*, however, benefited from the prestige of its selection for the Royal Film Performance of 1972 (*Anne of the Thousand Days* had been similarly honoured in 1970) and was shown at the Odeon, Leicester Square. *Henry VIII and His Six Wives* was not shown in any of the major showcase cinemas, opening at the relatively small (581 seats) ABC2 where it grossed £37,272 during a nine-week run. To put this in context, *Henry VIII*'s first-week gross of £5,403 made it a bigger box-office attraction than John Wayne in *The Cowboys*, which took only £696 in its first week at the ABC, Edgware Road, but paled in comparison to *The Godfather*, which took £12,814 in its first week at the ABC1 and £24,881 in its first week at the showcase Empire, Leicester Square.[27]

There is insufficient evidence to ascertain whether *Henry VIII and His Six Wives* ever went into profit, though at best it can be considered no more than a modest success. There is evidence to suggest that certain historical films did well as 'hard ticket specials' at showcase cinemas:

Mary, Queen of Scots took £64,543 in six weeks at the Odeon, Leicester Square, and *Young Winston* took £158,347 in 16 weeks at the same location.[28] It may reasonably be assumed from this that the audience for historical films comprised – or at least was held to comprise by distributors and exhibitors – mainly those cinema-goers who were prepared to pay higher ticket prices at the more prestigious locations. There is scant evidence of how the films performed on their regional release, though the report of EMI's distribution arm 'that although Grimsby was not noted for sophisticated audiences, *Henry VIII and His Six Wives* had achieved one of its best performances at the ABC' provides eloquent testimony that the film was not regarded as a guaranteed attraction for general audiences.[29]

In America, where it had a restricted release at selected cinemas, critical and popular reception was cool. The *Hollywood Reporter* found it no more than 'adequately entertaining' and felt that it 'seems pale, stale and less glossy' in comparison to recent Tudor films such as *A Man for All Seasons* and *Anne of the Thousand Days*.[30] Nora Sayre in the *New York Times* thought that 'it's a bit hard to be certain whom this movie was designed for', suggesting that it provided 'healthy popular entertainment for those who enjoy the lusher style of English classical acting', but concluding that it 'might make you yearn for urban grit and the most sarcastic jokes that our meanest streets can provide'.[31] In the 'New Hollywood' of the early 1970s where a new generation of directors had come to the fore on the back of critically acclaimed, gritty realist films – the likes of Bob Rafelson, Alan J. Pakula, John Cassavetes and Martin Scorsese – a traditional (in terms of both content and form) historical film such as *Henry VIII and His Six Wives* must have seemed rather old-fashioned fare.

Yet, for all that, *Henry VIII and His Six Wives* is as much a film of its time as any other. In this regard it is illuminating to compare the film with *The Private Life of Henry VIII* – a comparison that surprisingly few commentators at the time seem to have made – in order to see how the popular image of 'Bluff King Hal' in the 1970s differed from that of the 1930s. The most obvious difference is that unlike *The Private Life*, which had focused on the latter part of Henry's reign after the break from Rome, *Henry VIII and His Six Wives* covers almost the entirety of his reign. *The Private Life* had avoided any engagement with the religious and political upheavals of the English Reformation – largely, as we have seen, owing to censorship restrictions – but *Henry VIII and*

His Six Wives chronicles the tumultuous changes of the time and affords as much narrative space to the political background (albeit not as much as some critics would have preferred) as it does to Henry's marital escapades. Michell's performance as Henry is less showy than Laughton's but is more historically and psychologically accurate. His Henry is very much the Renaissance prince: he jousts, plays the lute, discusses theology and pays courtly love to Anne Boleyn. The film uses Henry's love letters to Anne ('Mine own sweetheart...I beseech you now to let me know your whole intention as to the love between us') as a linking device, portraying him as a romantic and affectionate lover. (This is in stark contrast to the two-part television drama *Henry VIII* of 2003, in which Ray Winstone's Henry controversially rapes Anne when she refuses to sleep with him.) One scene in *Henry VIII and His Six Wives* is virtually a direct riposte to the notorious banqueting scene in Korda's film that had so outraged the Earl of Cottenham: Michell's Henry uses cutlery to eat his food and wipes his mouth with a napkin.

Unusually, perhaps, *Henry VIII and His Six Wives* is preoccupied with the moral and legal justifications for Henry's actions. He is characterised at the outset as a devout Catholic prince who joins the alliance of Spain and the Holy Roman Empire against France – a war, as he sees it, 'to defend Christendom'. The script indicates that scenes of Henry taking Mass are 'very, very Catholic' and involve 'all the pomp and ceremony of the Roman Church'. If the popular view of Henry's breach with Rome is simply that he wanted to divorce Catherine of Aragon in order to marry Anne Boleyn, the film adopts a rather more nuanced position in accordance with developments in historical scholarship. In this interpretation, Henry becomes convinced that his marriage to Catherine of Aragon is illegal because she was the widow of his elder brother and that her failure to provide him with a male heir is God's judgement on their union. The film suggests that Henry was seeking papal authority for a divorce before he had set his sights on Anne Boleyn. When papal dispensation is not forthcoming, it is Thomas Cromwell, his machiavellian chief minister, who plants the seed that Henry should 'divorce the Pope'. The break with Rome is seen as an assertion of national independence rather than a doctrinal shift. Henry declares: 'Obedience to the Pope – the Bishop of Rome – is unmanly, unholy and is unEnglish!' The film remains faithful to the historical record in characterising Henry as an Anglo-Catholic and suggesting that he died 'in the religion of Christ'.

The film's emphasis on theology is unusual. To some extent this reflected the aim of making *Henry VIII and His Six Wives* a more authentic production. This had been evident in the television series, prompting one critic to complain that it 'was very true to recorded history and therefore a little prone to the sort of scene in which Henry is discovered debating theology'.[32] It is reminiscent of *A Man for All Seasons*, which dwelt at length on protracted discussions between Henry (Robert Shaw) and Sir Thomas More. How is the prominence of theological discourse in these film and television treatments of Henry VIII to be explained? A possible explanation is the emergence during the 1960s of new religious movements such as the Hare Krishna cult, the Children of God and the Church of Scientology. The significance of these movements lies not so much in their size (the number of active participants in Britain was probably not more than 10,000) but rather in their high media profile and their close association with popular culture (the Beatles and the Beach Boys declared themselves followers of the Indian 'guru' the Maharishi Mahesh Yogi, for example) which brought about wider public awareness of their beliefs than would otherwise probably have been the case. It would be misleading to suggest that the new religious movements were re-rehearsing the theological debates of the Reformation – they were responding to the concerns of the present and, in any case, a good number of them were influenced by non-western religious traditions – but there are, nevertheless, some quite direct parallels with the issues debated in films like *A Man for All Seasons* and *Henry VIII and His Six Wives*. To take just one example, the Jesus People insisted on a literal interpretation of the Bible in which scriptural quotation could be cited as proof of an argument. This has echoes in Henry's literal interpretation of the Book of Leviticus ('No union with a brother's wife may bear true issue') as the reason why his marriage to Catherine of Aragon is illegitimate. Scenes such as this are emblematic of a more intellectual representation of Henry VIII than the characterisation of Charles Laughton.

There are other areas, too, where *Henry VIII and His Six Wives* differs significantly in its ideological orientation from *The Private Life of Henry VIII*. The 1933 film had been concerned to promote consensus: it presented Henry's England as a socially and politically stable kingdom, while characterising Henry as an essentially decent ruler concerned for the welfare of his subjects. In contrast, however, the 1972 film presents Henry's England as a divided kingdom: divided between the 'old' and the 'new' religions and between rich and poor. There is a background of unrest: references to the Battle of Flodden and the Pilgrimage of Grace remind us of the internal dissent that had been entirely absent from Korda's version of Merrie England. The Dissolution of the Monasteries is depicted as an act of cultural vandalism: images of the burning of books inevitably take on other resonances since the acts of the Nazis in the 1930s. Henry's opponents are ruthlessly suppressed: monks are burned for opposing his religious reforms, Bishop Fisher is beheaded and Sir Thomas More is executed for refusing to recognise Henry's marriage to Anne Boleyn. More space is given to political intrigues at court than the 1933 film would permit: the Seymours are happy when the king turns his attention to their sister Jane as they seek to safeguard the Protestant faith,

18. Henry (Keith Michell) is beginning to tire of the exotic charms of Anne Boleyn (Charlotte Rampling) in *Henry VIII and His Six Wives*.

Cromwell's downfall follows the débâcle of the Anne of Cleves marriage, and the Howards plot to restore Catholicism by having the king marry their niece Catherine.

Henry VIII and His Six Wives, therefore, presents an England of factional strife and dissent rather than one based on consensus. To this extent it was very much a film of its time. There is no question that the Britain of the early 1970s was a much more divided society than it had been during the 1930s, the Jarrow march and the British Union of Fascists notwithstanding. It was a time of industrial unrest following the controversial new Industrial Relations Act of 1971 that provoked increased militancy on the part of some trade unions, culminating in the miners' strikes of 1972 and 1974 which were characterised by outbreaks of violence of a sort not witnessed since the troubled years before the First World War. There was violent disorder, too, in Northern Ireland where the escalation of sectarian strife in the late 1960s had led to British troops being sent to the province to help maintain order and to the resumption of terrorist activity by the Irish Republican Army (IRA), which had been relatively quiescent since the Second World War. The worst incident was the notorious 'Bloody Sunday' (30 January 1972) when troops fired on demonstrators in Londonderry resulting in the deaths of 13 civilians. In foreign affairs, the Conservative Prime Minister, Edward Heath, elected in the general election of June 1970, negotiated Britain's entry into the European Economic Community (EEC), or 'Common Market' – a decision that was steered through Parliament only with great difficulty and that won retrospective approval in a national referendum (in 1975) largely because the mass media sided overwhelmingly with the 'pro-European' camp.

The historical films of the early 1970s provide ample evidence of the thesis that their use of the past is influenced by the concerns of the present. It is interesting to note how many of them focus on internal dissent and division. The underrated *Cromwell*, produced by Irving Allen, was the first major historical film to focus on the English Civil War and Interregnum (as opposed to fictional films such as the swashbuckler *The Moonraker* and the cult historical horror film *Witchfinder General*): there were overtones of the 'Troubles' in Northern Ireland in the film's inclusion of Cromwell's ruthless suppression of the Irish Catholics. Similarly, *Mary, Queen of Scots* – released only two months after 'Bloody Sunday' – revolved around the competing claims to the English throne of the English Protestant Elizabeth Tudor and the Scottish Catholic Mary Stuart, prompting one reviewer to suggest that 'the script provides an unobtrusive counterpoint to the noble spectacle with its painfully topical undercurrent of Catholic–Protestant conflict'.[33] *Henry VIII and His Six Wives* similarly features dissent between Catholic and Protestant factions, though in this case none of the reviewers seems to have linked it to the contemporary situation in Northern Ireland.

However, a political subtext had been read into the television series by at least one critic. Philip Purser, television critic of the *Sunday Telegraph*, felt that in the Anne of Cleves episode it 'was hard not to see Henry's ill-fated League of Protestant Princes as a medieval EFTA in retaliation to the Common Market of the [Holy Roman] Empire'.[34] EFTA – the European Free Trade Association – was set up by countries which supported free trade but were wary of the political implications of the rival EEC; Britain was one of the founding members in 1959 but left in 1972 in order to join the EEC. It is only a coincidence that the Common Market was founded by the Treaty of Rome (25 March 1957) and that the film contains so many references to the break from Rome. It is also probably only a coincidence that all the scenes of Henry's campaigns in France in Thorne's script did not find their way into the finished film, at a time when Anglo-French relations were mellowing. France had been an implacable opponent of British membership of the Common Market during the 1960s when Charles De Gaulle had twice vetoed Britain's entry, but successful negotiations between Heath and new French President Georges Pompidou facilitated Britain's belated entry in 1973. Whether deliberately or not, the film reflects the issue of Britain's relations with her continental neighbours. Henry joins the Holy League in the war against France, but feels betrayed when the King of Spain makes a separate peace and promises to assist France against an English attack. Thereafter he becomes an isolationist who distrusts foreigners and is wary of European alliances. One incident recalls Korda's film as Henry commits himself to building up English sea power to protect his kingdom from foreign invasion, though there is even more emphasis on this in the shooting script as Henry tells Wolsey: 'We have a moat about us but it must be fortified. Ships and ships' ordnance, Wolsey, crews trained to fight with canon until we have built such a fleet as may not be destroyed.'

There is one other aspect in which *Henry VIII and His Six Wives* recalls Korda's film: the conservatism of its gender politics. Henry's wives are types rather than real people; there is little scope for individual characterisation. Their characters are represented in visual shorthand by their appearance and dress codes. Thus, Catherine of Aragon (Frances Cuka) is seen predominantly in dark, drab colours that signify dullness and barrenness; in contrast, the red and scarlet gowns of Anne Boleyn (Charlotte Rampling) indicate her passionate and wilful nature, while her exoticism is encapsulated through her performance in black face during a masquerade dance; Jane Seymour (Jane Asher) wears beige and cream which reflect her pale complexion and placid character. In this regard, the film differs somewhat from the television series which had made each wife the subject of a single play in her own right. The need for narrative compression in the film, however, meant that Henry's wives are less individually delineated than in the television series. Michell's Henry is far less a victim of feminine wiles than Laughton's had been. This is most apparent in the treatment of Catherine Howard: unlike the scheming, ambitious temptress of Korda's film, this Catherine (Lynne Frederick) is characterised as a naïve teenager who is out of her depth in the political intrigues of her relatives.

Henry VIII and His Six Wives exemplifies a middlebrow trend in British film culture during the 1970s. It was not an 'art' film for the intelligentsia, but nor was it lowbrow fare catering for the vulgar and the profane as so many films of the time were. This seems to have been the way in which it was received at the time. Derek Malcolm, for example, thought it 'an intelligent effort' that 'restores a bit of critical faith in that generally tasty genre'.[35] Yet it was a genre that was running out of cultural steam. The demand for traditional historical films had persisted into the early 1970s but did not last long thereafter as the cinema-going audience fragmented. The mid- and late 1970s would be a barren period for the genre. The only major costume film of any note was Stanley Kubrick's three-hour adaptation of William Thackeray's *Barry Lyndon* (1975), filmed on location in Ireland. Like *Tom Jones*, *Barry Lyndon* told the story of an eighteenth-century gentleman of fortune and his attempts to enter the aristocracy but, unlike *Tom Jones*, it charted the downfall of its protagonist with evident relish. *Barry Lyndon* is a difficult film to like: it is exquisite to look at (Ken Adam won an Academy Award for his meticulous production design and John Alcott for his muted, naturalistic cinematography), but tepid and slow-moving as a narrative. It has been claimed by one film theorist as 'a chilling theorem on the illusions of the Enlightenment and the ontological limits of the human condition'.[36] This may be so, but it went over the heads of cinema audiences. *Barry Lyndon* came joint twentieth at the box office with *Confessions of a Driving Instructor* – a sign of cultural penury indeed.

12

The British Are Coming:
Chariots of Fire (1981)

CHARIOTS of Fire, directed by Hugh Hudson and produced by David Puttnam, has a place in British cinema history not unlike *The Private Life of Henry VIII* almost 50 years earlier. Both films were about British historical subjects, both were made by ambitious independent producers and both seemed to herald a renaissance for the British film industry. *Chariots of Fire*, a modestly made film about British athletes competing at the VIIIth Olympiad in Paris in 1924, was the surprise success of the Academy Awards in March 1982, where it became the first British-produced film to win the Best Film Award since *Oliver!* (dir. Carol Reed, 1968). Screenwriter Colin Welland's famous and widely quoted remark upon collecting his own Academy Award ('The British are coming!') set the tone for the decade as British producers once again set their sights on the elusive American market. The case of *Chariots of Fire* demonstrates the fundamental importance of placing the production and reception of films in their historical contexts: released in April 1981 to a mixed reception from critics, it was initially a 'sleeper' but went on to achieve wider public acclaim when it was re-released a year later in the wake of its Oscar success and rode a wave of patriotic sentiment whipped up during the Falklands War. Uniquely, furthermore, *Chariots of Fire* has been claimed as both a pro- and an anti-Thatcherite text: as an endorsement of personal ambition and meritocracy on the one hand, as a critique of class and privilege on the other.[1]

'One of the paradoxes of the recent history of the cinema in the UK', the independent think-tank the Broadcasting Research Unit declared in 1987, 'is that the late 1970s and early 1980s was one of the most creative periods, and yet the cinema audience plummeted.'[2] In the late 1970s there had been a small upward trend in cinema attendances, on the back of the phenomenal success of blockbusters such as *Star Wars*, *Close Encounters of the Third Kind* and *Superman*, though this rise was short-lived as attendances fell from 112 million in 1979 to a low of 54 million in 1984.[3] This was the most precipitous decline since the late 1950s and can be attributed to a combination of several factors that were peculiar to the early 1980s. This was a period of economic recession aggravated by galloping inflation and rising unemployment: the official number of unemployed passed the two million mark – the highest level since 1935 – in August 1980 and reached three million 18 months later. Unemployment was most severe in traditional manufacturing industries such as steel and ship-building and among the young working classes, who hitherto had comprised the core of the cinema audience. The working classes and unemployed were less able to afford the increased cost of 'going to the pictures' (ticket prices doubled between 1977 and 1983), with the result that the cinema audience comprised a higher proportion of middle-class and white-collar workers than before. At the same time, the increasing ownership of home video recorders among the same social groups – half of British households had a VCR by the mid-1980s – also impacted on cinema-going habits. For many, cinema was no longer the preferred means of watching a film.

With Hollywood films dominating the box office to an ever greater degree, the British production sector contracted even further: 61 British features were produced in 1979, but this dropped to 31 in 1980 and 24 in 1981 (the leanest year for domestic production during the decade), before rising again to between 40 and 50 a year during the mid-1980s. A two-tier production sector had now emerged: a small indigenous film industry on the one hand, and, on the other, a service industry for Hollywood films which used British studio facilities for the production of special-effects blockbusters (the Superman films at Pinewood, *Star Wars* and the Indiana Jones films at Elstree). The demise of Thorn-EMI as an active producer early in the decade meant that the last remnants of the old studio system had finally disappeared; the ABC cinema circuit was sold to the Cannon Group, owned by Israeli entrepreneurs Menahem Golan and Yoram Globus, in 1986. The bulk of British production was now carried out by independent companies, of which the largest were Goldcrest Films (run by Canadian banker Jake Eberts), HandMade Films (backed by former Beatle George Harrison), Palace Pictures (which started out in video distribution before moving into film distribution and production) and Virgin Films (an offshoot of Virgin Records that mainly produced films with a musical cross-over interest). None of these companies, however, produced more than a handful of films. Channel 4, the new independent television channel which began broadcasting in 1982, backed a number of low-budget films, of which some were also accorded a theatrical release (including *The Ploughman's Lunch, My Beautiful Laundrette, Letter to Brezhnev* and *Sammy and Rosie Get Laid*). The economic instability of the film industry was further affected by the policies of Margaret Thatcher's Conservative government which, in line with its free-market, private-enterprise ethos, dismantled most of the legislation regulating the industry. Thus the exhibitors' quota for British films was suspended at the beginning of 1983 (it would never be reintroduced) and the Eady Levy was abolished in 1985. The NFFC, which had ceased to be a major investor in film production by this time, was replaced by the British Screen Finance Corporation, which had an annual grant of £1.5 million and would raise further capital through private investment. The government's decision in 1979 to make films eligible for capital tax allowances encouraged investment in the film industry from City institutions until this was removed in 1986, whereafter investment fell away.[4]

The troubled production history of *Chariots of Fire* illustrates the economic and cultural uncertainty of the British film industry at the beginning of the 1980s. Puttnam – who had made his name during the 1970s as producer of films by up-and-coming British directors Ridley Scott (*The Duellists*) and Alan Parker (*Bugsy Malone, Midnight Express*) – said that the idea for the film came to him when he read a book about the Olympics and 'came across a strange series of events regarding the Games of 1924, which I thought would be a good basis for a story. I was looking for a film not unlike *A Man for All Seasons* in terms of its moral position and its possibilities as an allegory.'[5] Puttnam had set up his own company, Enigma Productions, in 1976, but had no working capital of his own. The initial development money of £17,000 – necessary to pay for research leading to a script that could be presented to potential investors – was put up by Goldcrest, a company created by Canadian banker Jake Eberts in 1974. 'I was impressed by both the storyline and the eloquence with which David had presented it', Eberts said later, 'and, although he had not worked out in his own mind – still less with the proposed writer, Colin Welland – exactly how the film was going to be structured, I immediately agreed to provide development funds.'[6] This enabled Puttnam to commission a script from Welland, a film and television actor who had turned writer with the television mini-series *Yanks* (1979) about American airmen in Britain during the war.

The problems faced by independent producers in the post-studio era are demonstrated by the difficulties Puttnam encounted in raising finance for *Chariots of Fire*. The budget was estimated at $4 million, a very modest sum by Hollywood standards, but, even so, the film struggled to find a backer. Most companies rejected it on the grounds that it seemed an unlikely commercial prospect. The Rank Organisation expressed 'considerable reservations about the project'.[7] American producers were similarly unenthusiastic. Columbia turned it down because, they said, 'it has no viability at all in the American marketplace because of style and tone as well as subject matter'.[8] The lack of interest shown by the film industry was such that Puttnam also explored the possibility of making *Chariots of Fire* as a television mini-series, telling Michael Grade at London Weekend Television: 'As you know I did originally develop it as a feature, but I honestly believe it would be better for television.'[9] Whether this actually was Puttnam's intention is impossible to say, as his overtures to British television companies were no more successful than his approaches to film companies. Alasdair Milne, Director of Television at the BBC, agreed 'that the Colin Welland script is extremely fine', but reported 'that it would be far too expensive for us to make. Large crowd scenes, race meetings, railway stations in England and France and finally the Stade Colombes itself, put the project out of reach for us.'[10] One television company to show an interest was Euston Films, the film production arm of Thames Television, which was responsible for some of ITV's most successful series in the late 1970s and early 1980s such as *The Sweeney*, *Minder* and *Reilly – Ace of Spies*. Verity Lambert, Euston's Chief Executive, thought it 'an extremely good screenplay... It would be really terrific if we could produce this to put out in conjunction with the Olympic Games next year.'[11] Despite Lambert's interest, however, the television mini-series idea did not progress any further.

In the event, the backing for *Chariots of Fire* came from two sources, neither of which was British. Twentieth Century-Fox agreed to put up half of the production budget in return for distribution rights outside North America. The other major investor was Allied Stars, a producer-financier set up by Anglophile Egyptian shipping millionaire Mohammed Al Fayed and run by Fayed's son Dodi. The film went into production without a US distributor, although Fox had an option. It was evidently made against a background of distrust between the two backers – neither was prepared to put their share of the money into a joint production fund until the other did so first – and under conditions of severe budgetary restraints. On the last day of production Puttnam wrote to members of the unit: 'Today we've finished a picture that three months ago looked as if it would be impossible to make without our having to resort to crippling creative compromises and financial short-cuts.'[12] The eventual negative cost of *Chariots of Fire* was $5,891,000 (£4,032,859). It was only after it was completed that the US distribution rights were acquired by the Ladd Company – an independent producer set up by former Fox executive Alan Ladd Jr in 1979 – which distributed its films through Warner Bros. (which had, ironically, already turned down the distribution rights itself). The profits from the film – after the loans had been repaid to Fox and Allied Stars and after the distributors had deducted their fees and expenses – were to be shared between Fox, Allied and Enigma. Puttnam generously instituted a profit participation scheme, whereby Enigma's share of the profits was divided up between key production personnel and artistes.[13]

While Puttnam was negotiating the complex deals to secure financing for the project, Welland was busy shaping the historical material into a dramatically coherent narrative. It is clear that, from the beginning, Welland – a Labour Party activist who had once worked with avowedly socialist film-maker Ken Loach (on *Kes* in 1969) – wanted to use the story of Harold Abrahams and Eric Liddell (and, initially, Douglas Lowe, Britain's third athletics gold medallist in 1924) as a means of exploring themes of social exclusion and class privilege. His initial treatment and notes suggest that he saw the athletes as agents of social change:

Edwardian [*sic*] England was a model of Anglo-Saxon Protestant order – the King was on his throne, God was in his Heaven, and all, save the privileged few, were firmly in their place. But this postwar generation, at least some of it – enough

– is throwing down its gauntlet in every walk of life. Individuals are emerging determined to win through in their own right for what they, and they alone, believe is worthy.[14]

Welland envisaged that it would be 'primarily a film of three stories to be told both in parallel and interwoven – becoming progressively more interwoven as we move towards the climax in Paris'. His character notes portray the Jewish Abrahams and the Scottish Liddell as outsiders whose achievements on the athletics field are the expression of a desire for social acceptance (Abrahams) and of a deeply held religious faith (Liddell). In contrast, Lowe 'pursues Olympic honour not for the new order but for the old...Lowe is a gentleman first, a runner second. His path to his Olympic final is calculatedly off hand.' However, Lowe – winner of the 800 Metres and the last surviving member of Britain's gold medal triumvirate of 1924 – was entirely out of sympathy with the idea, telling Puttnam 'that your proposal...is not one with which I wish to be involved'.[15] He was, therefore, written out of the film.

Welland's first draft screenplay of April 1979 is structurally much the same as the finished film, beginning with the memorial service for Abrahams after his death in 1978, followed by a flashback to the famous scene of a group of young athletes on a training run along the beach at Broadstairs, Kent, in 1924.[16] There are differences in emphasis, however, that indicate Welland's ideological preoccupations. His first draft makes much more of the anti-semitism experienced by Abrahams on his arrival at Cambridge University in 1919 than the finished film and also displays a strong anti-American bias that is expressed through some obvious jokes ('Parlez-vous anglais, mademoiselle?'; 'I'm American'; 'Oh. Then you don't, do you!') and through scenes in the American training camp which characterise them as being obsessed with winning at all costs. (There is also one quite bizarre scene, fortunately dropped from the finished film, where the US athlete Paddock, blaming his poor showing in the 100 Metres on 'wet dreams', takes a highly unusual remedial action to prevent the same thing happening again.) It is evident that Welland was not committed to a strict doctrine of historical authenticity: he replaced Lowe with a fictional character called Lord Andrew Lindsay who wins the 400 Metres Hurdles (the character was partly based on Lord Burghley, who won the 110 Metres Hurdles in the 1928 Olympics) and invented a scene in which Liddell, who has refused to run in the heats of the 100 Metres because they are held on a Sunday, is summoned to a private meeting with the Prince of Wales who appeals to him to reconsider his decision.

The director, Hugh Hudson, an acclaimed television commercials director making his first feature film, advised Welland to 'make the Americans more sympathetic and thus alleviate the overall anti-American attitude'. He was also concerned that the character of Liddell's sister Jennie 'should not be quite so strict and Calvinistic'. It was Hudson, furthermore, who identified an explicit modern parallel in that the difference between Liddell and members of the Olympic Committee 'polarises a view that is so current at this moment: Moscow, etc'.[17] The production of *Chariots of Fire* coincided with the controversy brewing over the XXIInd Olympiad, to be held in Moscow in 1980, which had became the focus of a political crisis following the invasion of Afghanistan by the Soviet Union in 1979. The United States announced that it would boycott the Moscow Games; Britain did not, despite pressure from the newly elected Prime Minister, Margaret Thatcher, to do so.[18] The second draft of *Chariots of Fire* included a preface deploring the intrusion of politics into sport:

> These are sour days in Olympic history. The bureaucracies of big business and nation states have finally demanded more of the original slender ideal than it can possibly bear and it's fatally begun to crack. This year's Olympiad could possibly be the last.
>
> But it wasn't always so. Back beyond Moscow and Montreal, Bundage and the big brass bands, Hitler and the Zieg Heils, was a time when the young people who gathered under the five rings and flame did so of their own volition. They were fired by their own purpose, inspired by their own dreams and seeking only to test themselves, on their *own* behalf, against the fastest, the strongest, the highest on earth.
>
> Such men were Eric Liddell and Harold Abrahams. The one the son of a Scots missionary destined to follow in his father's footsteps and to die in Japanese hands in 1945. The other the son of a German Jew [*sic*] who battled against prejudice and the might of the English Protestant Establishment to become the last Englishman and the only Jew to win the Blue Riband of the Games – the 100 metres...

They both reach Gold, but on their own terms. Riding their 'Chariots of Fire' they fight against and eventually sweep aside those newly emerging Goliaths, nationalism and political expedience, those same monsters which today have resurfaced in the probable demise of the whole magnificent ideal.[19]

To make the point even more explicit, the revised screenplay opens with television images of 'a triumphant, manufactured trio' of East German athletes parading their medals (a reference, presumably, to revelations that Eastern bloc athletes were trained using steroids to enhance their levels of physical performance) and introduces a scene where the Duke of Sutherland, President of the British Olympic Association, laments the show of nationalism at the opening ceremony of the Games. He remarks: 'I'm not here for flags and anthems, but honest human endeavour – man against man... Nations have their teeth into our innocent ideal. Our games were conceived by athletes for athletes. Now they're floundering under the bullheaded priorities of a thing called the state.' Both the East Germans and Sutherland's remarks were dropped for the finished film. The other significant ideological change from the first draft was that Lindsay, the aristocratic amateur, now wins silver rather than gold in his event.

The shooting of *Chariots of Fire* took place over ten weeks between 15 April and 21 June 1980. It was shot entirely in Britain, with the Bebington Sports Arena on the Wirral in Merseyside standing in for the Stades de Colombes in Paris. Cambridge University refused permission to film in the college grounds because, Puttnam alleged, the governing bodies of the university 'objected to the tone of the script in so far as it suggested anti-semitism was rife in the 1920s, and even after we proved that our facts were correct they refused to budge from the position of non co-operation on the grounds that "it did no good" for the whole thing to be dragged up again sixty years later'.[20] The dash around the courtyard of Trinity College where Abrahams beats Lindsay and the college clock was staged at Eton College, Windsor. This incident was another invention of Welland's – the first athlete to 'beat the clock' in the twentieth century was Lord Burghley in 1927 and there was no other runner involved – and illustrates again that the film-makers were prepared to take some liberties with the historical record. Hudson claimed that the film was '75 per cent true; we've had to change some things to heighten the drama'.[21] Puttnam

19. The race that never occurred: Harold Abrahams (Ben Cross, *left*) and Lord Lindsay (Nigel Havers) run against the clock and each other in *Chariots of Fire*.

even went so far as to say on one occasion that it 'is a fictional tale based on some simple but amazing athletics facts'.[22] The production team consulted veterans of the 1924 Olympics, including Jackson Scholz (winner of the 200 Metres and runner-up to Abrahams in the 100 Metres) and Lord Noel-Baker (the non-playing British team captain). They also negotiated with relatives of Abrahams and Liddell, including Liddell's sister, Jennie, though it is abundantly clear from production records that the dramatic requirements of the story the film-makers wanted to tell took precedence. As Hudson told Welland in a revealing memorandum: 'Should there be problems with the actual Jennie then we invent an elder sister who could carry out the role we want.'[23]

The editing and post-production of *Chariots of Fire* was completed during the late summer and autumn of 1980. There were already indications that it was the type of film that would find favour within the British film establishment. Sir Richard Attenborough, who saw a rough cut of the film courtesy of editor Terry Rawlings, told Hudson that he 'thought it was absolutely magnificent. Its whole style and credibility, together with a group of quite famous performances, will, I am certain, make it not only a phenomenally successful film critically, but also at the box office'.[24] The prestige of the film was enhanced when it was selected for the Royal Film Performance (held at the Odeon, Leicester Square, on 30 March 1981 in the presence of Princess Margaret and the Queen Mother) and as the official British entry for the Cannes Film Festival (the coveted Palme d'Or that year went to the Polish film *Man of Iron*). *Chariots of Fire* was the first British-produced film chosen for the Royal Film Performance since *The Slipper and the Rose* in 1976 – another indication of the cultural penury of British cinema in the late 1970s – but must have seemed a natural choice for 'that most bizarre of British show business institutions'. 'The keynote to the selection of the Royal Film seems to be "taste", whatever that may mean in the eyes of the selectors, and "fittingness" above all else', one critic remarked. 'In that respect *Chariots of Fire* is a worthy choice.'[25]

There was an overwhelmingly positive response to *Chariots of Fire* from within the film industry. The veteran producer Sir John Woolf thought it 'a magnificent achievement...I do hope you have all the success you deserve – it's a real shot in the arm for the British film industry at a time when it is very badly needed.'[26] The British-based American film-maker Stanley Kubrick called it 'a splendid achievement on any account but particularly so in view of the time and money constraints under which you had to work'.[27] And Ken Green, a marketing executive for the distributor CIC International, sounded a patriotic note: 'It's nice to see that the *British* film industry is still alive and kicking at least once a year.'[28]

The Britishness of *Chariots of Fire* was prominent in the critical response to the film. While most reviewers mentioned that it was funded entirely by non-British sources, this fact did not strike the national critics as being incompatible with claiming it as an achievement for the British film industry – suggesting that they saw the film's Britishness as residing in its cultural capital rather than its financial backing. David Robinson acclaimed it as 'the kind of picture for which we have been looking to the British cinema, in vain, for many years...It is proudly and uncompromisingly British in theme and temperament, with no debilitating concessions to chimeric notions of an "international" style.'[29] Alexander Walker similarly remarked that *Chariots* 'is the kind of film that I'd almost given up hope of ever seeing made in Britain again. It shows they do still make them like they used to, only better.'[30] And Freda Bruce Lockhart found *Chariots* 'an exhilarating experience in British movies'.[31]

For other critics, however, *Chariots* was a good film, without necessarily representing the major landmark for British cinema that some of its admirers claimed. Derek Malcolm, for example, wrote: 'While it is certainly a well-made movie many people are going to enjoy – and that's a resounding triumph in the circumstances – it isn't exactly the birth of a New Wave.'[32] Patrick Gibbs concurred: 'While the chance may have been missed to make that elusive article, the memorable film, we have, instead, a very amiable one, with the period nostalgically caught.'[33] Jo Imeson, writing in the *Monthly Film Bulletin*, complained that 'the film seems stronger atmospherically than dramatically' and disliked 'the aggressively piecemeal style imported by Hugh Hudson, here making his first feature, from his television background'. 'The whole contradictory bundle is watchable', her review concluded, 'though bets are still wide open as to whether this cross-fertilisation of talent and entrepreneurial skills can inaugurate a new era for British commercial cinema.'[34] There were some critics, therefore, who poured cold water on the suggestion that *Chariots* heralded a renaissance or revival for the British film industry.

If opinions differed about the significance of *Chariots of Fire* for the film industry, so too did assessments of its ideological import. On the one hand, there were those critics who saw it as an essentially conservative film that endorsed traditional values of morality, decency and sportsmanship. Nigel Andrew noted its 'mythic nostalgia' and detected evidence of 'a wilful, almost wild unfashionableness'. 'A province of British history hitherto annexed by Pythonesque parody has been reclaimed as a rightful protectorate of British culture,' he wrote, 'its odd inflections of patriotism and idealism now mined not just for mirth but for meaning and a mirroring light on the present.'[35] One charge levelled against the film at the time – and one that has been repeated by some film studies academicians – is that any social critique the narrative may have possessed was lost beneath the surface attention to visual authenticity. Philip French, for example, remarked that 'the producers of *Chariots of Fire* are too deeply in love with the period trappings, and their graceful, innocent heroes, truly to confront the way in which the British amateur tradition rested on gross social inequality, or to accept that the corruption of values their film, by implication, records was the inevitable consequence of the democratisation of sport'. He conceded, nevertheless, that it was 'an immensely attractive, oddly moving and immaculately acted picture'.[36] Alan Brien similarly felt that the film displayed 'tell-tale signs of an ambiguous attitude to its social and historical implications concealing what could be a failure of nerve'. 'Often where we might have expected some critical comment,' he went on, 'the scenario takes refuge, as in the freshman club-recruiting scene, in what is almost D'Oyly Carte staginess, or, as during the Olympic Committee meeting, in revue-sketch crosstalk.'[37]

On the other hand, however, there were some critics who felt that the film's concerns with social exclusion and privilege did come through strongly. Interestingly, given the debate that has since emerged over its contested status regarding the social politics of Thatcherism, there were voices from both the right and the left of the political spectrum who detected – and approved of – what they saw as its critique of the elitism and snobbery of the world of the 1920s. 'This remarkable and confidently realised British film is about class, about prejudice, about false nationalism and – most of all – about principle', wrote David Castell in the *Sunday Telegraph*.[38] And Virginia Dignam of the *Morning Star* identified 'a story of class consciousness, racial prejudice and bigotry', though, in contrast to Philip French, she felt this atmosphere was 'captured with understanding and understatement'.[39]

What of the popular reception of the film? The instincts of the veteran trade reviewer Marjorie Bilbow were to prove accurate: 'Potentially good to very good in selected cinemas; but, not being an impulse buyer's movie, needing time for word-of-mouth recommendations to do the necessary.'[40] *Chariots of Fire* opened at selected cinemas in London's West End – in contrast to sure-fire blockbusters such as the Bond films that opened across the country – and enjoyed long runs at certain locations, including the Odeon Haymarket (where it ran for 23 consecutive weeks) and the Odeon Kensington (18 consecutive weeks). In contrast to most films, which are usually expected to show a falling-off in popularity after the first week, the weekly grosses of *Chariots of Fire* in the West End actually increased, suggesting that it did indeed benefit from word-of-mouth recommendations.[41] A similar pattern is evident in the provinces. *Chariots* was released in selected cinemas in the larger metropolitan centres (Manchester, Liverpool, Leeds, Sheffield, Nottingham,

Edinburgh, Glasgow) where initially it was 'somewhat slower in drawing audiences' but then showed evidence 'that it is growing in popularity with the public'.[42] At the year's end it was the twelfth most successful film of 1981 at the box office and the fifth most successful on the Odeon-Gaumont cinema chain, behind the Bond film *For Your Eyes Only*, a reissue of Walt Disney's perennially popular *Snow White and the Seven Dwarfs*, the Brooke Shields vehicle *The Blue Lagoon* and Roman Polanski's *Tess*. 'For the UK film industry in 1981', declared *Screen International*, 'the silver lining was the performance of British films in the Top 20 moneymaking chart.' 'The clouds', it added, however, 'are that this past 12 months is on course to register an all-time low in cinema admissions as well as being the worst ever year for indigenous production.'[43]

Outside Britain, however, *Chariots* fared less well, with *Variety* reporting that it 'appears to have flunked its initial tests in the foreign language markets'.[44] An executive of Twentieth Century-Fox's Continental Division told Puttnam: 'I shall never forgive the French audiences for ignoring the picture.'[45] This is perhaps not too difficult to understand, given its peculiarly British subject matter; its unpopularity in France in all likelihood had something to do with lines such as Lord Birkenhead's comment 'They're not a very principled lot, the Frogs'. It seems to have done better in the English-speaking markets, however, and it was reported that '*Chariots of Fire* continues its strong overseas box office performance in its most recent openings in Australia, Ireland and South Africa'.[46]

In the most important overseas market, the United States, all the evidence points to *Chariots* having been a significant success. A Warner Bros. executive reported 'that *Chariots of Fire* has opened in the US to lyrical views from the press across the board. This acclaim has been matched at the box office to an extent almost unprecedented for a British film.'[47] It is a statement that requires some qualification: as ever, the reception of British films in the United States needs to be put in context. There were some good notices, but they were hardly 'across the board' and they tended to see *Chariots* as a film destined for minority-interest 'art house' cinemas rather than as a mainstream success. This was already suggested by the fact that it was chosen to open the New York Film Festival, a showcase for independent and foreign films. Thus the critic David Denby thought it was 'precisely what art-house audiences want at the moment – a cautious, "distinguished", slightly boring good movie'. He also felt that it was an old-fashioned type of film 'imbued with the kind of low-key pride and patriotism that shone from British movies of the forties and fifties'.[48] The outspoken Pauline Kael, rarely a fan of British films, described it as 'retrograde moviemaking, presented with fake bravura'. She compared it to the Australian period films of the 1970s (such as Peter Weir's *Picnic at Hanging Rock* and Gillian Armstrong's *My Brilliant Career* – films notable for their languorous visual style) with her back-handed compliment that 'it's probably the best Australian film ever made in England'.[49] Richard Shickel called it 'a thinking man's *Rocky*' and thought it a 'lovely work... strangely evocative and moving'.[50] Most American critics seem to have regarded it as a nostalgic film, though Andrew Sarris saw 'an implied commentary on the present' in its extolling of the virtues of sportsmanship (which he compared – unfavourably – with the antics of US tennis star John McEnroe, winner of the 1981 Open Championships at Wimbledon).[51] A correspondent of the weekly periodical *Voice* – moved to protest about the 'diatribe' against *Chariots* – was in no doubt that it was relevant to the present day: 'Perhaps the reason this film is popular is due to the fact that Abrahams and Liddell represent modern (and not, as your reviewers suggest, antiquated and elitist) values: the desire to win and ruggedly individualistic faith.'[52]

The popular reception of *Chariots* in America seems to have followed the pattern set in Britain: it exhibited the characteristics of a 'sleeper' hit in so far as it was shown initially at selected cinemas in New York and grew in popularity as a result of good word-of-mouth recommendations.[53] Its box-office performance was enhanced by the clutch of awards that it garnered, including being nominated one of the top ten films of 1981 by the National Board of Review and receiving the Golden Globe as Best Foreign Film from the Hollywood Foreign Press Association. The distributor, Warner Bros., responded to the latter award by pointing out that *Chariots* was not a foreign-language film and was therefore eligible for the regular Academy Awards.[54] It was duly nominated for seven Academy Awards and, against most expectations, won in four categories: Best Film, Best Screenplay, Best Music (Vangelis Papathanassiou) and Best Costume Design (Milera Canonero) – the award for Best Director, however, went to Warren Beatty for *Reds*. There is no doubt that the nomination and award of the coveted Best Film 'Oscar' enhanced the appeal of *Chariots of Fire* in the

American market. In the six months until the end of March 1982 (the month in which the Academy Awards were held), *Chariots* had earned North American theatrical rentals of $10,873,321, but over the next three months its rentals more than doubled so that by the end of June they stood at a cumulative total of $26,343,726.[55] Its rentals eventually totalled $36 million (representing a total box-office gross of around $80 million) which set a new record for a 'foreign' film in the American market.[56] To put this in context, while it was only a fraction of the rentals of super-blockbusters such as *E.T.: The Extra-Terrestrial* ($209.9 million), *Star Wars* ($193.5 million) or *Raiders of the Lost Ark* ($115.5 million), it was on a par with the Bond movies *For Your Eyes Only* ($26.6 million) and *Octopussy* ($34 million).[57] Moreover, *Chariots* did not have anything like the saturation release or extensive advertising campaigns invested in the major studio summer releases. Judged by these criteria, the US box-office performance of *Chariots* may indeed be considered a major success.

The Oscar success of *Chariots of Fire* also gave the film a second wind in Britain. It was reissued – initially as part of a double-bill with Bill Forsyth's *Gregory's Girl* – in April 1982, following the Academy Awards. *Chariots* is a rare example of a film that was more successful on its reissue than on its initial release, ending the year as the leading British film and as second overall to the Dudley Moore comedy *Arthur* (with the caveat that 1982 was a year without either a Bond movie or a big George Lucas–Steven Spielberg production; Spielberg's *E.T.* was released at Christmas, too late to make an impression on the annual chart).[58] For all its very considerable commercial success, however, the complexities of the dual distribution arrangements and the division of profits was such that it took some time for any monies to filter through to Puttnam and his colleagues.[59] There were suspicions of irregularities in Fox's accounts, as the distributor had recently changed its accounting practices. Welland's agent wrote 'to express both my and Colin's disgust...that our September [1982] profit statement would yield no money at all'. 'I presume Fox think they are being tremendously clever in standing on their rights and holding up payment of the money', he went on, 'but it yet again emphasises the impossibility of doing any sort of sensible deal with an American major company.'[60] It was only at the beginning of December 1982 that Puttnam could report that 'the impasse seems to have been broken between Fox and Allied Stars and *Chariots*' profits will begin to flow next week'.[61]

Qualitative evidence of the popular reception of *Chariots of Fire* – both in Britain and overseas – would seem to endorse Marjorie Bilbow's prediction that it would appeal in large measure to 'discriminating' cinema-goers and to 'those middle-of-the-roaders who belong to the silent majority that still clings to the golden rules'. Puttnam received over 100 letters of congratulation from ordinary cinema-goers, many of which thanked him for a film that was widely described in terms such as 'inspiring' and 'uplifting'. One respondent, who evidently was acquainted with Puttnam, told him that 'I left the theatre feeling completely uplifted, proud of having been to Cambridge, of being British and of knowing you...In an age of cynicism and cheap thrills your beautiful film was truly inspirational to me.' [62] Another, from Massachusetts, claimed that it 'reinforced my quiet pride in my English background'.[63] The film seems particularly to have struck a chord among the Christian community for its portrayal of Liddell's quiet sincerity and faith. The Payne family of Swindon urged Puttnam: 'Please make more like it, we know they cost money, but take a tip from God Himself, "I will supply all your needs". He meant it then, and it still holds true.'[64] And the general-secretary of the Lord's Day League of New England wrote earnestly: 'We thank you so very much for your award winning film, *Chariots of Fire*, especially for its accent on keeping the Lord's Day holy...Your film has helped once more to bring this needed emphasis back into remembrance.'[65] It would seem, therefore, that the response to *Chariots of Fire* was more favourable from the public than from the critics and that cinema-goers responded to what they saw as its emphasis on traditional values. There were dissenting voices, but these were a minority. A correspondent to *Screen International*, for example, felt 'that *Chariots of Fire* was made, not with cinema audiences in mind, but as a David Puttnam exercise in "fine film making"'. He feared that, having risen to a position of influence in the British film industry, Puttnam 'intends to fritter it all away on films that are little more than dramatised Hovis adverts' and urged him instead 'to face up to his responsibilities, and make films for today's young, racially integrated audiences'.[66] (This was prompted by an annoucement that, as their next project, Puttnam and Hudson were planning a film of Sir Ernest Shackleton and the *Endurance* expedition.)

This criticism – brought by a distributor who claimed to be speaking for his Wardour Street colleagues – probably contained an element of

sour grapes on the part of a British film industry that had declined to
back *Chariots of Fire*. The popular success of *Chariots* suggests that it
was not as out of touch with what audiences – or, rather, a certain type
of audience – wanted. There was also considerable political interest in
the film. In the wake of its Academy Award success – *Chariots* also won
Best Film from the British Film and Television Academy – a group of
Labour MPs sponsored a motion 'that retention and development of
the British film industry is an important artistic and industrial priority'
and 'that the outstanding success of *Chariots of Fire* ... demonstrates
the continuing potential of this medium to make a significant
contribution to the nation's balance of payments'.[67] The conclusion that
the Thatcher government drew from the success of *Chariots*, however,
seems to have been that private investment rather than government
subsidy was the way forward for the film industry and that good
quality films could stand on their own feet in the market place.

Within a month of its triumph at the Academy Awards, furthermore, *Chariots of Fire* was to become – quite by chance – a point of
reference in a major international crisis. It was on 2 April 1982 that an
Argentinian invasion force seized the British colony of the Falkland
Islands in the South Atlantic. The British tabloid press responded to
this act of territorial aggression with a patriotic fervour that recalled the
age of high imperialism a century ago. The British government
responded with a determined show of military force by assembling a
task force of warships and troops to retake the islands. As efforts to find
a peaceful solution to the crisis faltered, the British task force sailed for
the South Atlantic. On 23 April, two days before the recapture of the
dependency of South Georgia, the *Daily Mail* reported that the prime
minister 'will take two hours off from the worsening Falklands crisis to
watch a special screening of *Chariots of Fire* at Chequers over the
weekend'.[68] Ironically, at the same time, the film was showing to great
popular acclaim in one cinema in Buenos Aires.[69] In America,
meanwhile, where the British government lobbied for assistance short
of actual military aid, *Chariots of Fire* seems to have been adopted as
part of a cultural offensive to win American hearts and minds in support
of the British cause. At the height of the crisis Puttnam was in
correspondence with the British ambassador in Washington:

> I am delighted with the success of the film and particularly for
> any benefit it might have brought to Anglo-US relations ... I

really do believe that the response not only to my film, but also *Nicholas Nickleby*, *Brideshead Revisited* and a number of other cultural events during the past twelve months has a genuine significance. I hope, and believe, that Her Majesty's Government have taken note of the very real benefit that these cultural successes bring to the area of international relations.[70]

Alexander Walker attributed the popular succcess of *Chariots of Fire* in America to the 'Falklands factor': 'There was a definite pro-British feeling in America at the time – the Brits were not going to be pushed around the way the Americans had in Vietnam. The untarnished glory of Britain's air and sea armada rubbed off on everything British – even to the revival of the long baggy running shorts worn by Ian Charleson and Ben Cross.'[71]

The Thatcher government was quick to associate itself with the success of films like *Chariots of Fire* and *Gandhi* (dir. Richard Attenborough, 1982), which achieved even greater recognition in winning eight Academy Awards including Best Film and Best Director. Yet the great irony of *Chariots of Fire* becoming a platform of patriotic and, by implication, pro-Thatcherite rhetoric is that this was a reading that was surely never intended by those who had made it. Welland and Hudson were both Labour Party stalwarts, while Puttnam joined the Social Democratic Party (SDP) in the early 1980s.[72] Puttnam later explained that he was deeply uncomfortable about the appropriation of *Chariots* by the political right:

> What was interesting...was the way in which the Tories – to my fury – managed to ride the surf of *Chariots* and almost give the impression that it was an enormous British triumph, that it signified a British resurgence in film making and that somehow or other it was a Tory-inspired success...What really upset me was that the film in terms of its content is extremely anti-establishment. It's about, if you like, the corruption of the establishment. And somehow or other that message got completely washed to one side in this notion that it was a flag-waving triumph.[73]

Hudson also reacted against those critics – on the left as well as the

right – who 'saw the film as flag-waving for Thatcherite policies...
Those policies and the values we are talking about probably created
the Falklands [sic] and they are certainly not supported by the film.'[74]
How, then, did a film that was certainly never intended as an endorsement of Thatcherism become, in the words of one commentator,
'tantamount to a Thatcherist parable'?[75]

Whether one reads *Chariots of Fire* as a 'right' or a 'left' film
depends largely on the perspective of the critic. On the one hand, for
the right, *Chariots* is a celebration of national greatness expressed
through the allegory of sporting achievement. The trailer described it
as 'a British film about British heroes' and traditional patriotic
symbols (the Union Jack, the National Anthem) are displayed
prominently. On the other hand, for the left, *Chariots* represents a
narrative of heroic struggle against social injustice. In this context, the
use of the hymn 'Jerusalem' – both in the film itself, during the
memorial service for Abrahams that frames the narrative, and as the
source of the title ('Bring me my bow of burning gold, bring me my
arrows of desire; bring me my spear, O clouds unfold, bring me my
chariot of fire') – explicitly links the film to the Labour movement.
William Blake's exhortational poem, which was set to music written
by Hubert Parry in 1916, has been sung at Labour Party conferences
since the 1920s.[76]

A close analysis of *Chariots of Fire* reveals a complex and at times
contradictory set of narrative ideologies relating to the themes of
nationhood, ethnicity and class. On one level, for example, the film
represents a Britain in which regional, ethnic and social differences are
minimised. The Olympic team becomes a metaphor for national unity
and social cohesion, in the same way as the ship in *A Night to
Remember* or the army platoon in *The Way Ahead*: it comprises
people from different social backgrounds (Lindsay an aristocrat,
Abrahams a Jew, Liddell a lower middle-class Scot, Aubrey Montague
a middle-class boy whose parents have implicitly made some financial
sacrifice to send him to Cambridge) who come together to represent
Great Britain. Abrahams and Liddell are initially cast as rivals –
Abrahams is bitterly disappointed when Liddell beats him in a
domestic event – but become team-mates ('rivals under the same flag')
and each is seen celebrating the other's victory in the Games. The
esprit de corps is established in the famous scene of the team together
on a training run along the beach that is used behind the opening titles

and is reprised at the end behind the cast credits: thus *Chariots* begins and ends on an image of team spirit and comradeship.

The images of national identity mobilised in the film are characteristic of what was to become known as the 'heritage film'. England is represented predominantly by Cambridge, stately homes and Gilbert & Sullivan: all recognisable as traditional signifiers of Englishness that would be identified by audiences at home and abroad. Scotland is represented in equally romanticised terms as a land of glens and valleys and churches, thus locating the film within the 'kailyard' tradition that has dominated cultural representations of rural Scotland and is best exemplified by *Whisky Galore!* and *The Tales of Para Handy*.[77] Liddell, albeit 'oriental born', nevertheless waxes lyrical about 'the heather on the hills'. The Scottishness of Liddell is, curiously, first asserted ('I am and will be whilst I breathe – a Scot') and then forgotten as he runs in the Olympics for Great Britain. Grant Jarvie argues, persuasively, that the film 'undoubtedly

20. Eric Liddell faces the Olympic Committee and his conscience in another dramatic scene invented for *Chariots of Fire*. *Left to right*: the Duke of Sutherland (Peter Egan), Liddell (Ian Charleson), Lord Birkenhead (Nigel Davenport), the Prince of Wales (David Yelland) and Lord Cadogan (Patrick Magee).

reflects a unionist interpretation of British culture' and 'reproduces a low-key strand of nationalism and patriotism through celebrating [the] Union Jack'.[78]

Yet, at the same time, *Chariots of Fire* is acutely aware of the complexities of national allegiance. The Englishness of Abrahams is problematised: he is the son of a Lithuanian Jew ('He worships this country. From nothing he built what he believed was enough to make true Englishmen of his sons') whose desire to succeed in athletics is, he says, 'a weapon [against] being Jewish'. Abrahams longs to be accepted as English, evidenced through his passion for Gilbert & Sullivan and the repeated motif of 'For he is an Englishman' (from *HMS Pinafore*) that he performs with gusto and which accompanies montages of him training and competing in athletics meetings. Liddell, for his part, is an evangelical Christian who believes in God first and country second. This is exemplified in the key scene where the Prince of Wales asks Liddell to reconsider his decision to withdraw from the 100 Metres heats:

Liddell: God made countries and God makes kings – and the laws by which they function. Those laws say the Sabbath is His and I for one intend to keep it His and His alone.
Prince of Wales: Mr Liddell, you're a child of your race, as am I. We share a common heritage – a common bond – a common loyalty. There are times when we're asked to make sacrifices in the name of that loyalty. Without them our allegiance is worthless. As I see it, for you this is such a time.
Liddell: Sir, God knows I love my country, but I love God more. I cannot sacrifice Him, not even for her.

In a film that is so preoccupied with the idea of belonging – belonging to the team and belonging to the nation – it is significant that the main protagonists are characterised as outsiders because of their social, ethnic or religious backgrounds. Liddell faces opposition from his sister Jennie who believes that his dedication to running is inspired by a desire for personal glory rather than the service of God. Liddell defends his decision to delay following his father as a missionary to China in order run in the Olympics by suggesting that his athletic prowess reflects God's will: 'I believe that God made me for a purpose – for China. But He also made me fast. And when I run

I feel His pleasure.' Abrahams and his coach Sam Mussabini are outsiders on account of their ethnicity: Abrahams a Jew, Mussabini half-Italian and half-Arab. Both feel excluded from the England that Abrahams describes as 'Christian and Anglo-Saxon'. When Abrahams wins the 100 Metres, Mussabini tells him: 'Do you know who you won for out there today? Us – you and old Sam Mussabini. I've waited thirty bloody years for this.' Two particular scenes enforce their outsider status. The first is the scene of the raising of the Union Jack and the playing of the National Anthem following the 100 Metres final. This is seen from Mussabini's perspective as he watches from the window of his dingy hotel room: he is excluded from the celebration in the stadium and has to participate by proxy in the victory he made possible. The second scene is the British team's homecoming. Abrahams does not join the others as they mount a car and wave to the crowds, but remains on the train, emerging only when the crowds have gone for a touching, private reunion with his girlfriend Sybil. A newspaper advertisement declares 'Abrahams the toast of England', but Abrahams himself remains apart from the celebrations.

A prominent theme of the film is the anti-semitism of the English establishment, represented by the university authorities. There are several small incidents: the head porter's overheard remark when Abrahams arrives at Caius College ('With a name like Abrahams he won't be singing in the chapel choir') and the Master of Trinity's comment to the Master of Caius after Abrahams has refused their advice not to use a professional coach ('There goes your Semite, Hugh – a different God, a different mountain top'). The original script contained more incidents of this sort, including a crippled war veteran who carries Abrahams's luggage ('Mine was a Yid, Harry. That's what we fought the bloody war for. To give all the Jew boys a good education') and one of the Americans referring to Abrahams as 'this guy Moses'. Yet even the reduced incidents in the film were exaggerated, according to Abrahams's family, one of whom told Puttnam: 'Jews are notoriously sensitive about anti-semitism and often encounter it, but, though occasionally hurt, none of our family has suffered significantly and particularly not at Cambridge...So I have said that the emphasis of the film is awry, but none the less it is a very fine story, well acted, directed and produced.'[79] It is a revealing anecdote that provides further evidence that the film-makers had a clear ideological agenda of their own and were selective in their treatment of the historical facts.

It would probably be fair to say that Abrahams's sense of exclusion and prejudice in the film is not matched by the attitude of other characters towards him: he is accepted by those who are themselves part of the establishment, including the aristocratic Lindsay and the socially connected actress Sybil Gordon who becomes his girlfriend. (Another instance of the film's use of dramatic licence is that Harold did not meet Sybil Evers until a decade after the Paris Olympics; they married in 1936 following Sybil's divorce from her first husband.) Even the attitude of the university authorities is motivated less by their anti-semitism ('Perhaps they really are God's chosen people after all', the Master of Trinity remarks ruefully when Abrahams completes the college dash) than it is by their dislike of the professional training methods, including the use of a coach, that Abrahams has adopted. It is here that the film is at its most ideological. It contrasts two different attitudes towards sport: on the one hand, the amateur ethos of playing the game for its own sake, and on the other hand, the professional ethic of playing to win and being single-minded in the pursuit of success. These differences are mapped onto the film's representation of class: Lindsay reflects the amateur code with its gentlemanly and Corinthian values (brilliantly exemplified in one of the film's most memorable images as he practises hurdling in the grounds of his stately home, a glass of champagne balanced on each hurdle), whereas Abrahams adopts the professional route, using a coach and undertaking a strict and disciplined training programme in preparation for the Games. Lindsay competes for sheer enjoyment ('To me the whole thing's fun') whereas Abrahams wants only to win (even saying at one point 'If I can't win I won't race').

While the different attitudes towards sport are an accurate reflection of competitive sport in Britain during the interwar years, in *Chariots of Fire* they become part of a discourse on class and modernisation that has clear contemporary overtones. This is apparent in the scene of the meeting between Abrahams and the Masters of Caius and Trinity. The Master of Trinity begins by extolling the virtues of sport 'in helping to complete the education of an Englishman' and in fostering 'an unassailable spirit of loyalty, comradeship and mutual responsibility', but goes on to suggest that Abrahams has 'lost sight of these ideals' and that he has 'concentrated wholly on developing your own technique and the pursuit...of individual glory'. This is, says the master, 'not a policy very conducive to the fostering of *esprit de corps*'. The class politics involved become evident:

> *Abrahams:* Perhaps you would prefer I played the gentleman and lost?
> *Master of Caius:* To playing the tradesman, yes.
> *Master of Trinity:* My dear boy, your approach has been, if I may say so, a little too plebeian. You are the elite, and are therefore expected to behave as such.

The film therefore suggests that the difference between amateurism and professionalism is also a difference of class. The masters believe that 'the way of the amateur is the only one to provide satisfactory results' – the irresistible implication being that 'satisfactory results' would be the preservation of elitism and social privilege. Abrahams's reply is to accuse the masters of clinging to 'the archaic values of the prep-school playground' and to tell them: 'I believe in the pursuit of excellence, and I'll carry the future with me.'

This is perhaps the most ideologically charged moment of the film – even more so than Liddell's meeting with the Prince of Wales – and one that is invariably cited by those commentators who interpret *Chariots of Fire* as an endorsement of Thatcherism. Abrahams's belief in 'the pursuit of excellence' has echoes in the rhetoric of the Thatcher government, while his running foul of the university establishment may be seen as a reflection of Mrs Thatcher's own battles with the grandees of the Conservative Party. Mrs Thatcher had become leader in 1975 in what MP Julian Critchley described as a 'peasants' revolt' against the patrician Edward Heath.[80] The new Tory leader came from the lower middle class (a grocer's daughter from Grantham) and her approach to politics might easily be described (to echo the Master of Trinity) as plebeian: forthright, plain-speaking, determined. Her belief in private enterprise, entrepreneurship and individualism would seem to be in tune with Abrahams's attitude towards sport.

This interpretation is appealing to some extent, though on closer inspection it is rather problematic. For one thing, *Chariots of Fire* was made before the full impact of what came to be known as Thatcherism had been felt. In her memoirs Margaret Thatcher described herself as 'an instinctive Conservative', but then said that, at the time she came to power in 1979, 'I had failed to develop these instincts either into a coherent framework of ideas or into a set of practical policies for government'.[81] The first term of the Thatcher government (1979–83) was dominated by rising unemployment and by race riots in inner-city areas like Brixton and Toxteth where social deprivation was most severe. There were, however, signs of what was to come in the adoption of a monetarist economic policy, the drive to curb public expenditure and measures such as the sale of council houses to their tenants. It was not until the second term (1983–87) that a distinctively Thatcherite ideology was fully implemented: privatisation of previously publicly owned industries and utilities, and reforms of the stock market, trade unions and local government. To interpret *Chariots of Fire* as 'a Thatcherist parable' is to read back into the film knowledge of what Thatcherism was to become by the mid-1980s. For example, the rhetoric of national greatness that came to be so indelibly associated with the Thatcher government was very much a product of the Falklands War and was much less in evidence before 1982. It was as much the (accidental) timing of *Chariots of Fire* as any intent on the part of the film-makers that allowed it to be appropriated by the right.

Furthermore, there are some aspects of the film that do not easily fit the Thatcherite paradigm. It seeks to distance itself from any mood of national belligerence, exemplified by the early scene of the freshman's dinner where the Master of Caius pays tribute to 'the flower of a generation' lost during the war ('I take the War List and I run down it. Name after name which I cannot read, and which we, who are older than you, cannot hear without emotion'). And, for all that Abrahams is critical of the 'archaic values' of the university establishment, it is an establishment to which he yearns to belong. The visual style of the film displays a sense of nostalgia for the past: the *mise-en-scène* dwells lovingly on the architectural grandeur of the buildings and on the sumptuously appointed interiors of college and chapel (one of Hudson's favourite devices is to begin a scene with a close shot and then have the camera pull back and away to reveal the splendour of the surroundings). It is elements such as these that lead John Hill to conclude his carefully nuanced reading of *Chariots* by suggesting that 'while the film shares with Thatcherism a certain nostalgia for English "greatness", it also reveals a certain tension between the culture of individual enterprise, on the one hand, and a cultural fascination with the aristocratic *ancien régime*, on the other'.[82]

It will be clear from this discussion that *Chariots of Fire* is an ideologically complex film, to a far greater extent than any reductionist reading of it as a pro- or anti-Thatcherite text would allow. This complexity is most apparent in the film's treatment of Lindsay, a fictional character who serves an intriguing ideological purpose. Lindsay (referred to in various drafts of the script as Lindsey, Andy and the Earl of Cumbria) was invented to take the place of the third gold medallist of 1924, Douglas Lowe, who had refused to have any involvement with the film. Described in the script as 'being born with a whole canteen of silver cutlery in his mouth', Lindsay was, Puttnam admitted to one correspondent, inspired by Lord Burghley, later the Marquis of Exeter.[83] In the script, he is not quite the 'Carefree Corinthian' as portrayed in the film: he trains so hard that his legs are described as being 'scarred and bloody' from hitting the hurdles and his efforts are duly rewarded with a gold medal in the 400 Metres Hurdles. In the film, his training routine is more off-hand and he comes second. As Lindsay's character was fictitious to begin with there would seem to be no reason why in the film he should win silver rather than gold other than an ideological one: the privileged aristocrat simply cannot win, as it would represent a triumph for those 'archaic values' of which the film, through Abrahams, is so critical. There is yet a further twist, however, in so far as it only through the intervention of Lindsay that Liddell is able to compete at all. Lindsay solves Liddell's dilemma of running (or rather not running) in the Sunday heat of the 100 Metres by generously withdrawing from the 400 Metres and allowing Liddell to take his place. Lindsay's simple rationale ('I've got my medal') represents all that is best about the amateur ethos and provides an eloquent contrast with the obsessive single-mindedness of Liddell and Abrahams. To this extent there is much truth in Sheila Johnston's description of *Chariots* as 'Janus-faced': it looks forward to the emergence of a classless meritocracy (one of the projects of Thatcherism according to its supporters) but also harks back to a lost age of chivalry and sportsmanship that was no longer evident in the win-at-all-costs modern age.[84]

There is another way, Johnston suggests, in which *Chariots of Fire* is Janus-faced, in so far as 'it can be both hailed as the vanguard of a "new" British cinema and, in Puttnam's little trailer, quietly take its place in the "Great Tradition" of that cinema's glorious past'. It is traditional in so far as it exemplifies the pictorialist cinematography that characterises so many British period films, though at the same time Hudson's use of non-standard narrational techniques (slow motion, repeating the races from different camera positions) would seem to suggest that he had 'artistic' aspirations in a manner not dissimilar to the new wave directors. The most famous scene in *Chariots* is the title sequence: the slow-motion sequence of clean-limbed young men running along the beach captures their athletic grace in a way that harks back to Eadweard Muybridge's pioneering photography of bodies in motion in the nineteenth century. At the same time, the music is very modern, Vangelis reflecting contemporary trends in pop by using a synthesiser rather than instruments for his uplifting main 'Runners' theme. The (limited) formal experimentation of *Chariots* was not, however, to be a characteristic of the 'heritage' cinema that followed later in the decade.

Chariots of Fire has sometimes been seen as marking the beginning of the heritage cinema of the 1980s and 1990s. This is a style rather than a genre of British film-making that privileges pictorialist *mise-en-scène*, focuses on narratives of predominantly upper-class life, and is temporally set (usually) in the first half of the twentieth century. The cycle of heritage films includes, but is not limited to, *Heat and Dust* (dir. James Ivory, 1982), *A Passage to India* (dir. David Lean, 1984), *A Room With A View* (dir. James Ivory, 1986), *A Handful of Dust* (dir. Charles Sturridge, 1987), *Maurice* (dir. James Ivory, 1987), *Howards End* (dir. James Ivory, 1992), *The Remains of the Day* (dir. James Ivory, 1993) and *Shadowlands* (dir. Richard Attenborough, 1993). It is significant that most of these films are adapted from novels (especially E.M. Forster) and in one sense the heritage film is simply another term for the quality literary adaptation that has been a feature of British cinema since the silent era. In this sense, *Chariots of Fire* does not really belong to the heritage cycle as it is a historical film based on actual people and events (as, indeed, was *Shadowlands*, though that film was also adapted from a play). Nevertheless, the academic debate over the heritage film (a term, incidentally, that has little or no currency in the film industry itself) is similar to that around *Chariots*. Most commentators on the heritage film discuss them in relation to the cultural and political manifestations of Thatcherism which produced the 'heritage industry' in the 1980s, but while some critics have seen them as innately conservative in their uncritical view of the past, others have argued that they provide a critique of social and sexual repression.[85]

None of the key people involved in the production of *Chariots of Fire*, however, was closely involved in the heritage cycle. Puttnam enjoyed further success as an independent producer with the whimsical Ealing-esque comedy *Local Hero* (dir. Bill Forsyth, 1983) and a harrowing account of the genocide in Cambodia, *The Killing Fields* (dir. Roland Joffe, 1984) – based on a true story – though had a less happy time during his ill-advised and short-lived term as Chief Executive of Columbia Pictures later in the decade. Hudson followed *Chariots* with a revisionist interpretation of the Tarzan myth in *Greystoke: The Legend of Tarzan, Lord of the Apes* (1984) which used the story of Edgar Rice Burroughs's noble savage as a means of exploring the hypocrisy and corruption of the establishment. However, his next film, *Revolution* (1985), was an unmitigated disaster: a costly would-be epic of the American War of Independence let down by an incoherent narrative, suggesting that, for all his undoubted pictorial sense, Hudson was a poor director without a good script.

Perhaps the main beneficiary of the success of *Chariots* – but also, in the long term, the main loser too – was Goldcrest. Eberts's investment of £17,000 returned £1 million with his share in the profit-participation scheme. It was Goldcrest, too, which put up development money that allowed Richard Attenborough to realise his 20-year ambition of making a biopic of Mahatma Gandhi. Following the critical and commercial success of these films, the next logical stop for Goldcrest was to move into direct financing and production. Eberts was astute enough not to put all his eggs in one basket and spread his risks by backing films in partnership with other investors, including *The Killing Fields*, *Local Hero*, *The Ploughman's Lunch* and *Another Country*. However, when Eberts left the company in 1984, his successor, James Lee, embarked upon a more ambitious production strategy, simultaneously backing three expensive films: *Revolution* (£19 million), *The Mission* (£17 million) – ironically produced by Puttnam – and *Absolute Beginners* (£8 million). The films all performed badly at the box office and collectively lost Goldcrest about £15 million. Goldcrest announced that it was withdrawing from film production in 1985, which, with a rather bitter irony, had been designated 'British Film Year' in an attempt to raise the economic and cultural profile of the British film industry. The collapse of Goldcrest was, in certain respects, a re-run of Korda's fate in the 1930s: one major critical and commercial success leading to a more ambitious and expensive production programme which failed to repeat the original success and precipitated a collapse. There are further parallels. *Chariots of Fire*, like *The Private Life of Henry VIII*, had earned most of its profits from the American market, where its British subject matter had given it a certain novelty value. Both films, however, proved to be one-offs. The lessons to be learned in the 1980s were not very different from those that should have been learned in the 1930s: that while the British film industry was capable of producing occasional international successes, these films were exceptional and unrepeatable. The failure of British producers to recognise this simple fact goes a long way towards explaining the cyclical boom-and-bust nature of the British film industry.

13

Queen and Country:
Elizabeth (1998)

ELIZABETH, directed by Shekhar Kapur for Working Title Films, marked a significant change of direction for the British historical film in the 1990s. It was part of a short production trend that revived the royal biopic, dormant since the 1970s, the other films in the cycle being *The Madness of King George* (dir. Nicholas Hytner, 1995) and *Mrs Brown* (dir. John Madden, 1997). Unlike earlier examples of the genre, however, *Elizabeth* remoulded the conventions of the biopic in startling and at times radical ways. It was far less bound by the discourse of historical authenticity than most biopics – thus provoking controversy within the historical community – and instead interpreted the early years of the reign of Queen Elizabeth I as part political melodrama and part Grand Guignol thriller. *Elizabeth* is a film of remarkable cultural confidence and visual power – characteristics widely attributed to its Indian director, making his first English-language film – that represents a departure from the restrained and sober style of the heritage cinema of the previous decade. In contrast to what is often referred to as the Merchant-Ivory style of film-making, with its literary pedigree and overriding theme of emotional repression, *Elizabeth* is notable for its highly 'filmic' style and for its daring representation of Elizabethan England as a hotbed of political intrigue and sexual passion. It was a critical and commercial success that, like *The Private Life of Henry VIII* six decades earlier, brought both economic and cultural prestige to the British film industry.[1]

Elizabeth is paradigmatic of economic and cultural developments in the British film industry during the 1990s. Its production history exemplifies the extent to which the structure and political economy of the film industry had changed in line with wider developments in the media and entertainment industries. *Elizabeth* was made by a production company with an impressive track record of turning out commercially successful films on an economical basis. Working Title Films had been set up by Sarah Radclyffe and Tim Bevan in 1984, and had focused initially on low-budget dramas such as *My Beautiful Laundrette, Sammy and Rosie Get Laid* and *Wish You Were Here*. In the early 1990s, however, Working Title came within the orbit of PolyGram Filmed Entertainment (PFE), itself a subsidiary of Dutch electronics giant Phillips. PolyGram was the leading investor in British film production during the 1990s and Working Title was by far the most successful production organisation, responsible for hit films including *Four Weddings And A Funeral, Trainspotting, Bean, SpiceWorld: The Movie* and *Notting Hill*. There were failures, too, but as PolyGram was part of a large multi-national entertainments conglomerate it was able to absorb its losses by investing profits from one division (music) into another (film production). In this respect PolyGram was similar to the major Hollywood studios which, since the late 1980s, had been absorbed by global conglomerates (Universal by Matsushita of Japan, Columbia by the Sony Corporation and Warner Bros. first by Time Inc. and then again by the Internet giant AOL). Indeed, PolyGram was regarded as 'Europe's only serious answer to the Hollywood studio system'.[2] Crucially, PolyGram had access to the American market through its co-ownership of an independent US distributor, Gramercy. It was only the guarantee of distribution in the United States that made the production of a film on the lavish scale of *Elizabeth* viable.

With a budget of £13 million ($25 million), *Elizabeth* was squarely in the higher-cost bracket of British film production. The average budget of a British film in the late 1990s was £2.6 million.[3] While the lion's share of the budget was provided by PolyGram, *Elizabeth* was also supported by Channel 4 and by the MEDIA Programme of the European Union, which put up the initial script development money.[4] It therefore exemplifies both the increasingly close relationship between the film and television industries – Channel 4's investment also secured an early terrestrial television première on 8 May 2000 – and closer ties between the

British and other European film industries. In the mid-1990s approximately one-third of British feature films involved co-production with European partners, particularly the films of *auteur* directors such as Ken Loach (*Land and Freedom, Carla's Song*), Peter Greenaway (*Prospero's Books, The Pillow Book*) and Sally Potter (*Orlando*).[5] *Elizabeth* was not strictly a co-production as such, but its stylistic features exhibited a certain 'European' influence and its international cast included two French actors (Fanny Ardant as Mary of Guise and footballer Eric Cantona as the French ambassador to Elizabeth's court).

Elizabeth was made at a time of apparent economic buoyancy and optimism for the British film industry. Cinema attendances were increasing, attributable largely to the boom in multiplex cinemas, and there was an upward trend in film production too, after the doldrums of the 1980s, peaking in 1996 when 128 films were made with some level of British financial involvement. The film industry was on the crest of a wave of confidence in the wake of the success of the romantic comedy *Four Weddings And A Funeral* (dir. Mike Newell, 1994), which had broken box-office records for a British film with a worldwide gross in excess of $200 million.[6] Upon closer inspection, however, this picture disguised underlying structural problems. American films comprised over 70 per cent of those shown on British screens and accounted for 80 per cent of box-office revenues, while over half the British films made, particularly those at the lower end of the cost range (78 of the 128 films made in 1996 cost less than £3 million), failed to secure a theatrical release. This situation can be blamed on the dominance of the distribution and exhibition sectors by American interests: Rank, the last British distributor, wound down early in the decade following its sale to Carlton Television, while most of the new multiplex cinemas were American-owned. A government report into the film industry, entitled, apparently without irony, *A Bigger Picture*, described the British production sector as a 'cottage industry' and warned that 'at the moment our success is precarious'.[7]

In so far as the only certainty in the film business is the uncertainty of success, then a £13 million historical drama certainly represented a considerable economic risk. As with *The Private Life of Henry VIII* in 1933, the British market alone was insufficient even to recoup the cost of production. *Elizabeth* would be dependent upon overseas markets, and inevitably, as is invariably the case, eyes would be fixed on the American market. To this extent the film can be seen as a calculated risk on the part of PolyGram. They would have noted the success in America of British-made heritage films such as *Howards End* ($18 million), *Much Ado About Nothing* ($23 million), *The Remains of the Day* ($19 million) and *The Madness of King George* ($15 million).[8] The film that seems to have been most influential was Nicholas Hytner's luscious adaptation of Alan Bennett's play *The Madness of King George III* (shorn of its numeral for the screen, allegedly to avoid confusion with sequels to *Lethal Weapon* or *The Karate Kid*). PolyGram executive Julia Short said that 'we did a great deal of research into previous costume dramas, and we took *The Madness of King George* as our ruler'.[9]

If *Elizabeth* was a calculated economic risk, the choice of Shekhar Kapur to direct it showed that Working Title was also prepared to take aesthetic risks. It was an unusual choice to say the least. Kapur, born in Lahore shortly before Partition, was an actor-director working in the Bombay-based Hindi film industry who had recently provoked controversy with *Bandit Queen* (1994), based on the true story of Phoolan Devi who became modern India's most notorious outlaw. With its graphic scenes of sexual violence and its coarse, rough-edged visual style, *Bandit Queen* was about as far removed from the fantasy world of 'Bollywood' films as can be imagined. It was banned by the Indian Board of Censors, but it was shown at the Cannes Film Festival. *Bandit Queen* had, in fact, been financed by Channel 4, which had commissioned it originally as a television docu-drama, and this may have had some influence on the choice of Kapur to direct *Elizabeth*. Scriptwriter Michael Hirst approved the decision:

> The idea of an Indian directing a quintessentially English subject must have surprised some – but it delighted me...He brought with him no preconceptions about Elizabeth. Without perhaps even being conscious of it, many English people are protective about the image – and virginity – of Elizabeth I; after all, she remains one of the greatest icons in our history. But the last thing the film needed was a reverential camera.[10]

Kapur, for his part, thought it 'an audacious offer'. He admitted that he had little prior knowledge of the subject: 'To ask an Indian who knows nothing about British history to make a film about a British icon. It was such a mad thing, I just had to do it.'[11] Yet perhaps an

Indian directing a film about Elizabeth I was no more 'mad' than a British director making a film of the life of Mahatma Gandhi; Kapur, no doubt aware of the irony, invited Lord Attenborough to play Sir William Cecil.

Elizabeth was in fact a very international production in terms of personnel. As well as Kapur, these included composer David Hirschfelder and editor Jill Bilcock (both Australian) and cinematographer Remi Adefarasin (English-Nigerian). The principal cast also included two Australians, Geoffrey Rush as Sir Francis Walsingham and newcomer Cate Blanchett, controversially preferred to home-grown talent (Emily Watson and Kate Winslet were both mentioned in connection with the film) for the title role.[12] Yet the involvement of so many overseas artistes was no more unusual for a British film of the 1990s than the presence of the European émigrés had been in the 1930s. As the veteran British director Lewis Gilbert remarked in 1999: 'You should be able to define a British film in the same way you can define a British Premier League football team – one where 60% of the players are foreign.'[13] It is a singular fact that so many of the most quintessentially 'English' films of the 1980s and 1990s have been made by outsiders. The Merchant-Ivory brand that became synonymous with heritage cinema comprised an Indian producer (Ismail Merchant), an American director (James Ivory) and a Polish-Jewish writer (Ruth Prawer Jhabvala), while other directors who contributed to the Anglo-American heritage cycle included New Zealander Jane Campion (*The Portrait of a Lady*) and Taiwanese Ang Lee (*Sense and Sensibility*).

The shooting of *Elizabeth* began at Shepperton Studios, Surrey, on 1 September 1997, followed by 12 'period' locations (including Durham Cathedral, York Minster, St Albans Church in Middlesex, Haddon Hall in Derbyshire and six castles in Northumberland – Aydon, Alnwick, Bamburgh, Chillingham, Raby and Warkworth).[14] A number of scenes, such as the coronation in Westminster Abbey (actually shot in York Minster) and the battlefield scene, were enhanced by 'invisible effects' (crowd enhancement and two-dimensional composites) in order 'to create and sustain its period setting'.[15] In this way *Elizabeth* exemplifies one of the trends that had become increasingly apparent in films during the late 1990s: the use of technological artifice to create an impression of authenticity. This was played down, however, in the production discourse, which did not draw attention to the computer-enhanced imagery. *Elizabeth*, therefore, was being differentiated from Hollywood blockbusters such as *Titanic*, which tended to use the special effects as one of the major selling points.[16]

How did *Elizabeth* fare commercially? *Screen International* summed up its box-office prospects thus: 'The *Armageddon* crowd will not go to see this, but, with some energetic marketing, overseas prospects look rosy.'[17] In other words, it predicted that *Elizabeth* would not compete with Hollywood blockbusters in the multiplexes, but that it had the hallmarks of 'quality' British production that tended to do well in foreign markets. This was to prove an accurate prediction. Released in Britain in the first week of October 1998 and in the United States one month later, by the end of the calendar year *Elizabeth* had grossed £4,411,181 in Britain and $14,620,584 in the United States. It eventually grossed $30 million in the United States and a further $34 million throughout the rest of the world by September 1999.[18] On one level, of course, these figures are small in comparison with the major studio releases of 1998, *Armageddon* (with a North American gross of $201 million) and *Saving Private Ryan* ($190 million), and minuscule put alongside the super-blockbuster *Titanic*, released towards the end of 1997, which had grossed $600 million in North America by November 1998.[19] To put this in context, however, *Elizabeth* received nothing like the saturation release of those films. Indeed, considering that it was a British film with neither any well-known stars nor a 'name' director, the box-office perform-ance of *Elizabeth* represents a considerable success. In Britain it was the third most successful British film of 1998 (behind the romantic comedy *Sliding Doors* and the gangster film *Lock, Stock and Two Smoking Barrels*, the latter released by PolyGram at the same time as *Elizabeth*), while in the United States it was the fourth most successful non-American English-language film of the year (behind *Sliding Doors*, *The Borrowers* and *SpiceWorld: The Movie*).[20]

The box-office success of *Elizabeth* can be attributed, in some measure at least, to PolyGram's canny release strategy. In Britain it was given a 'platform release', opening on 14 screens in London (including the Odeon, Leicester Square) before going on wider national release after four weeks. The rationale was explained by PolyGram executive Chris Bailey: 'With these more specialist titles, a platform release can raise the awareness of a film outside London. It builds up heat and is a hotter film when you open it regionally.'[21] A similar strategy was adopted in America, where it opened on just nine screens in New York, Chicago and Los Angeles, before going on a wider release (516 screens) after three weeks. In this way, *Elizabeth* followed an entirely opposite trajectory to the typical blockbuster: its opening was relatively low-key but it gathered momentum following good notices and word-of-mouth recommendations.

The box-office revenues of *Elizabeth* suggest that, while it was no blockbuster, it did nevertheless appeal beyond the usual audience for 'art house' fare. *Elizabeth* was an example of the 'cross over' film that bridges mainstream and art house audiences. On the one hand, it exhibited all the characteristics of quality middlebrow film production: a literate and intelligent script, attention to period detail and sumptuous visuals. Thus Richard Williams, in the *Guardian*, described *Elizabeth* as 'the very model of a successful historical drama – imposingly beautiful, persuasively resonant, unfailingly entertaining'.[22] On the other hand it also included certain 'box-office' elements (sex and violence) that are not typical of the genre. Its promotional discourse sought to assert its difference from the more familiar style of British period film-making. Producer Tim Bevan, for example, remarked: 'We wanted to do a period movie, but one that wasn't in the recent tradition of what I call "frock flicks". We wanted to avoid, as it were, the Merchant Ivory approach.'[23]

The idea that *Elizabeth* represented a different style of historical film informed the critical response, with many reviewers implicitly regarding this as a good thing. Philip French wrote that it 'is far removed from the colourful pageant of most British historical movies'.[24] Tom Charity similarly thought it 'a far cry from traditional British masterpiece theater [*sic*] filmmaking' and predicted that it would appeal to a wider audience 'who like their period costume dramas defrocked of aristocratic poise'.[25] Stella Bruzzi in *Sight and Sound* saw it as a 'far cry from the sterility of British heritage movies', which, by implication, referred to the Merchant-Ivory films.[26] And the Asian film magazine *Cinemaya* declared: 'The operatic flourishes, the emotional pitch, the heightened sense of melodrama take this film out of the realm of historical period dramas which are generally textbook perfect.'[27]

While most critics approved of its attempt to ring the changes, however, the British Asian newspaper *Asian Age* found it 'too self-conscious in its desire to leave most English costume dramas, well, in the closet'.[28] Opinions were divided on Kapur's style of direction, which Gerald Kaufman described as 'a curious mixture of the conventional and the outré'.[29] Quentin Curtis acknowledged Kapur's 'visual flair', but felt that, on occasion, 'the bouncy, kinetic flow of images and the shafts of light that too artfully pierce through the shrouded chambers of various castles resemble a pop video'.[30] Other critics felt that the film was let down by a weak script. Alexander Walker admired the 'rich, darkly melodramatic' style but felt that 'panache is not quite enough to pull the episodic script smoothly together'.[31] And Matthew Sweet similarly admired the 'lavish, sinister energy' of the direction, but averred that 'the disjunction between the film's luscious monumentalist pictures and its ho-hum dialogue is sometimes painfully obvious. The final scene of the film, for instance, has a visual magnificence rarely seen in British cinema. But Kapur has allowed Hirst to top it with a closing line of equally rare redundancy.'[32] This is a not unusual reaction for British critics, who are generally more comfortable talking about narrative (script) than visual style.

Certainly, it is through its formal qualities and its visual style that *Elizabeth* asserts its difference from the typical British historical/costume drama. The heritage cinema of the 1980s and 1990s tended to be characterised by a leisurely narrative pace, slow editing tempo and a preponderance of long shots and tableaux compositions. *Elizabeth*, however, exhibits a radically different aesthetic. There is nothing at all leisurely about the narrative: the editing is on a par with an action movie and the narrative itself moves from one event to another with breathless rapidity. The camerawork, furthermore, is far removed from the unobtrusive, reverential style of the Merchant-Ivory films. Kapur makes full use of the mobile camera, tracking the movements of his protagonists around the on-screen space rather than filming in tableaux, and deploys an array of unusual angles. Two recurring motifs are the overhead shot, which has the effect of making people appear tiny in relation to the vast stone edifices around them, and shots through curtains, drapes or gauze. For his critics, Kapur's direction represents style for style's sake as his camera placements and movements draw attention to his authorship rather than furthering the narrative. However, this can also be seen as a formal strategy to use shots for symbolic effect. The diagonal shafts of light that illuminate the scene of Elizabeth's coronation, for example, might be seen to represent the end of the dark days of Mary Tudor's reign, all of Mary's scenes having taken place in gloomy interiors.

The film's visuals are sensuous and highly ornate. Again *Elizabeth* is at some pains to differentiate itself from the style of more traditional historical films where *mise-en-scène* is deployed in support of historical verisimilitude through period trappings and décor. This is evident at some points in *Elizabeth* – portraits by Nicholas Hilliard (the Coronation portrait of 1559) and Marcus Gheeraerts (the Ditchley portrait of 1592) provided visual references – but it is not the dominant motif. Costume designer Alexandra Byrne averred that Kapur 'didn't want us to be tied to the fact and reality of it'.[33] The costumes and set dressings are, again, symbolic rather than authentic. The colour scheme is dominated by golds and reds: colours of wealth and passion, but also of danger and violence. According to Remi Adefarasin: 'Shekhar had very clear ideas how he wanted the film to look: more Rembrandt than Vermeer.'[34] This would explain the prominence of chiaroscuro effects, highlighting contrasts between light and shade, and the diffusion of background detail, so that only soft colours are visible and the eye of the spectator is focused on the foreground action. The picture of Elizabethan England that *Elizabeth* creates is a filmic world rather than a real world: to this extent it merits comparison with the visual style of *film noir*, which similarly used chiaroscuro effects and expressionist lighting to create a stylised representation of a *milieu* rather than an authentic reconstruction of social reality.

Elizabeth is reminiscent of *The Charge of the Light Brigade* in its highly eclectic use of different styles. There are certainly similarities to other films. Several critics compared it with *La Reine Margot* (dir. Patrice Chereau, 1993), a lavish adaptation of a novel by Alexandre Dumas, which painted a vivid account of political power struggles in sixteenth-century France leading to the Massacre of St Bartholomew's Eve. *La Reine Margot* was notable for placing a strong woman at the centre of the narrative (Isabelle Adjani as Princess Marguerite) and for its striking, at times gory, visuals. Another comparison that was frequently made was with *The Godfather* (dir. Francis Ford Coppola, 1972), which had made compelling drama out of the bloody struggles between warring Mafia families. There are also similarities with the horror film: the opening scenes of Protestants burned at the stake ('You can almost smell the burning flesh', wrote French) and the later

21. *Elizabeth* attracted controversy for its depiction of a passionate
love affair between the young princess (Cate Blanchett) and Robert
Dudley (Joseph Fiennes).

torture of a prisoner by Walsingham might almost have strayed in
from *Witchfinder General* (dir. Michael Reeves, 1968). The style of
Elizabeth is perhaps best described as operatic: it is highly
melodramatic, full of passion and violence and featuring moments of
heightened emotionality and visual excess.

The film's irreverential attitude to period authenticity – which also
extended to the inclusion of anachronistic musical references such as
Mozart's *Requiem* and Elgar's *Enigma Variations* – was undoubtedly a
major factor in the controversy that erupted over *Elizabeth* in certain
sections of the press. Most reviewers accepted that the film took some
liberties with history, but what incensed the *Daily Telegraph*, in
particular, was the suggestion that Queen Elizabeth had a sexual
relationship with Robert Dudley, the Earl of Leicester. Prominent
Tudor historians such as David Starkey were duly trotted out to refute
the idea that Elizabeth and Dudley were lovers in a physical sense.[35]
This was the point in the reception of the film, as Andrew Higson
observes, where 'the tension between official history and filmic

narrative came into sharpest focus'.[36] It is worth emphasising 'official history' here: the representation of Elizabeth as the 'Virgin Queen' had been a matter of political necessity during her reign and had become as accepted a part of popular history as Alfred burning the cakes or Drake playing bowls as the Armada approached. There is, of course, no way that historians can be certain one way or the other whether or not Elizabeth was a virgin. However, the most curious thing about the outburst against the film is that *Elizabeth* was not the first film to show Elizabeth in a sexual relationship with Dudley. *Mary, Queen of Scots* had included a scene of Elizabeth and Dudley in bed together, but this had barely raised a murmur, either from the press or within the academy, whose complaints on that occasion had focused on two fictitious meetings between Elizabeth and Mary. Why, then, should there have been such controversy over Elizabeth and Dudley in the throes of passion in 1998 when a similar scene (if, perhaps, not quite so sexually explicit) had passed without censure in 1972?

The answer to this question can only be speculative, but a possible explanation is the public reaction to the death of the Princess of Wales. This had been the occasion of massive and unprecedented displays of public grief, in sharp contrast to the dignified mourning that followed the deaths of other revered national figures such as Sir Winston Churchill or the Queen Mother.[37] At the height of her fame and beauty, Princess Diana had been probably Elizabeth I's closest rival as a national heroine, loved and admired with the fervour of a film star. Several critics made direct parallels between Blanchett's Elizabeth and the Princess of Wales: Anne Billson, for example, saw the film as 'the story of how a Diana Spencer ingenue can turn into a media-manipulating Margaret Thatcher', while Philip French felt that 'comparisons with Princess Diana are encouraged by the casting of her mentor, Richard Attenborough, as Elizabeth's wise adviser, Sir William Cecil'.[38] The shooting of *Elizabeth* at Shepperton Studios had begun shortly after the Princess's death in a car crash in Paris on 31 August 1997 and the production discourse of the film had made a point of how the shadow of Diana loomed over the filming. Blanchett recalled: 'Last summer on the first day of filming, the first lines that were spoken were, "The Queen is dead, long live the Queen!" Princess Diana had died two days before. It was very eerie.'[39] Is it entirely too fanciful to suggest that the defence of Elizabeth's reputation in response to the film was also, in some way, a defence of the memory of Princess Diana?

The controversy around *Elizabeth* illustrates yet again the level of cultural investment in filmic representations of the kings and queens of England. Queen Elizabeth I is a figure of supreme importance in both popular and academic histories of England: the ruler who united a nation divided along both social and ideological lines, saved it from foreign conquest, laid the foundations of an empire and presided over a great era of cultural achievements in music, painting and literature. Furthermore, as Michael Dobson and Nicola Watson demonstrate in their study of the changing cultural representation of Elizabeth I from the sixteenth century to the present, the figure of Elizabeth has always been 'central to the making (and unmaking) of Anglo-British national identity and Anglo-British culture'.[40] From Edmund Spenser's *Faerie Queene* to Miranda Richardson's 'Queenie' of *Blackadder II*, the persona of Elizabeth I has been constructed as much by the cultural imperatives of the present as it has by the course of historical scholarship. Nowhere is this more apparent than in the filmic representations of 'Good Queen Bess', which have often had implicit or explicit connections with the state of the nation. Flora Robson's Elizabeth in *Fire Over England*, for example, had asserted the need for national preparedness in response to the rise of European dictators; Jean Simmons's Elizabeth in *Young Bess* was nothing if not a conscious attempt to mark the coronation of another Queen Elizabeth to whom Miss Simmons bore more than a passing resemblance; and Glenda Jackson's Elizabeth in *Elizabeth R* had been a tough-minded, feminist career-woman in response to the emergence of Women's Lib.

The promotional materials for *Elizabeth* described it as 'a film about a very English subject'. Some reviewers, certainly, saw it in much the same terms as representing an entirely unproblematic view of national identity. This response was most evident in an extraordinary review by Christopher Tookey in the *Daily Mail*, in the course of which he rhapsodised about the scenery ('England furnishes a wealth of wonderful, too-long neglected locations') and the cinematography ('revels in the Englishness of the settings') and averred that Kapur is 'more eager than most British directors would be to embrace a Queen as heroine'. Tookey went on to relate *Elizabeth* to a range of contemporary issues:

> The film avoids becoming a history lesson; yet its messages for the present are instructive. One is that the neat division of a

ruler's life between private and public is an impractical one. The public always takes precedence, whether one likes it or not. This is a lesson younger members of our Royal family, and those who feel called to high government, may do well to ponder. It has clearly come too late for President Clinton. The film's other lesson – which it shares with that otherwise dissimilar movie, *Saving Private Ryan* – is that it's admirable to serve one's country. Kapur sees that Elizabeth flourished by putting the national interest first. He portrays this as a fine thing, even over-embellishing the patriotic finale by bringing in some anachronistic Elgar music.[41]

Tookey felt that '*Elizabeth* is to be welcomed because it is high time that our film industry made more movies about Britain's heroes' and used it to launch a savage attack on the nature of British films which, he felt, were hidebound by political correctness:

It is ridiculous that only in wartime do the British produce films about their great commanders, such as Nelson, when the French and Americans make film after film about their national heroes. Why are there no halfway decent pictures about such fascinating figures as Wellington or Sir Francis Drake? Feminism, pacifism, Marxism and just plain cynicism have all contributed to British film-makers' habit of heckling our heroes, or simply ignoring them; but all around the world, vast numbers of people pay to see movies built around heroic individuals who embody our deepest aspirations and fix our eyes upon excellence.[42]

Tookey's review is symptomatic of much that passes for film criticism in the tabloid press, not least for its failure to engage in any sustained way with the film itself, though it provides a fascinating example of how popular journalism can not only claim a film but read it against the grain in order to promote a conservative view of national identity that accords with the editorial policy and readership of that particular newspaper.

More academic commentators, however, have problematised the representation of national identity in the film and drawn attention to its equivocal position towards its subject. Bruzzi, for example, argues that '*Elizabeth* is not a celebration of Englishness ... [It] is marked by its distance rather than veneration for its subject, a standpoint no doubt informed by its director's origins.'[43] Higson nuances this assessment: 'If the film is not a *celebration* of Englishness, it can certainly be read as an *exploration* of Englishness, a historical meditation on the making of modern England and the construction of a central icon of the national heritage, the image of the Virgin Queen.'[44] Indeed, *Elizabeth* can be seen as an exploration of the national heritage on two different levels: both as a historical narrative representing a particular moment in English history and as a cultural commodity packaging images of Englishness for audiences in the late 1990s. In this sense, the film belongs to the moment of so-called 'Cool Britannia': a label applied by the press to the sense of cultural renewal that seemed to feed off the election of the New Labour government in 1997. A feature of the first term of Tony Blair's government was the attempt to 'rebrand' Britain as a modern, dynamic society that was no longer hidebound by the stuffy conventions of the past. 'Cool Britannia' was the popular manifestation of this process and found expression in film, television and, most of all, pop music.

The England that *Elizabeth* represents, however, is much darker than that on display in tourist-friendly films such as *SpiceWorld*, *Sliding Doors* or *Notting Hill*. It is closer to the bleak visions of contemporary society in the work of directors such as Mike Leigh (*Naked*) and Ken Loach (*Riff-Raff*, *Raining Stones*). It is significant in this regard that the narrative of *Elizabeth* focuses on the early years of the reign, a time of political turmoil, factional strife and religious uncertainty, rather than on the later years of empire-building and cultural achievement in which most 'Elizabethan' films are set – including the postmodern costume romp *Shakespeare in Love* (dir. John Madden, 1998) released around the same time. *Elizabeth* begins in 1554, during the short and bloody reign of Elizabeth's half-sister Mary Tudor, with the burning of 'Protestant heretics'; Elizabeth herself is accused of treachery, incarcerated in the Tower of London and only narrowly escapes death when the dying Mary cannot bring herself to sign her death warrant. Elizabeth is crowned queen, but spends most of the rest of the film under threat from various external and internal enemies. Mary of Guise raises an army in Scotland and threatens to invade England; the Duke of Norfolk covets the throne for himself and leads a Catholic faction at court that plots against the queen; and Elizabeth herself survives two assassination attempts.

The representation of Elizabethan England as a world of court intrigues and political violence clearly differentiates it from the cosy world of *Shakespeare in Love*. It exhibits all the characteristics of the thriller: paranoia, deception and the notion that society might at any time be plunged into a world of chaos and disorder. Indeed, this aspect of the film was emphasised by the promotional strategy in an attempt to market it to an audience other than that usually associated with 'frock flicks'. *Elizabeth*, furthermore, is a commentary on the nature of political power. Elizabeth's throne is insecure and, in order to safeguard it, and her own life, she has to condone the ruthless tactics of her secret service chief Walsingham, who acts as 'enforcer' in much the same way as Michael Corleone (Al Pacino) in *The Godfather*. Walsingham is amoral and entirely unscrupulous: he calmly slits the throat of a would-be assassin and seduces Mary of Guise in order to get into her bed and murder her (an incident that was one of the film's inventions but did not seem to raise any protest from historians). The climax of the film makes what seems like a conscious homage to *The*

22. *Elizabeth* was notable for its highly expressive visual style: note how Elizabeth alone is illuminated as she imposes her will upon her parliament.

Godfather as Walsingham orchestrates a Tudor 'Night of the Long Knives': the plotters are systematically rounded up and summarily executed to the strains of Thomas Tallis's *Te Deum*.

To some extent *Elizabeth* follows the narrative trajectory of other royal biopics such as *Victoria the Great*: in both films a politically naïve young woman succeeds to the throne of a divided kingdom and, through her leadership, succeeds in uniting the nation and becomes a much-loved and reverered national figure. However, Blanchett's Elizabeth does not take as naturally to the throne as Anna Neagle's Victoria. She is timid and uncertain in the beginning, for example in the scene where she follows the advice of her Privy Council to send an army to fight Mary of Guise against her own better judgement ('I do not like wars. They have uncertain outcomes'). (That Elizabeth's judgement was correct is vividly illustrated in a scene of the battlefield strewn with the dead bodies of her soldiers, a stream running red with their blood.) Elizabeth determines to resolve religious strife between Catholics and Protestants by introducing the Act of Uniformity. The film shows her rehearsing her speech and growing in confidence and stature during her address to her parliament as she falls back on a combination of patriotism ('This is common sense, which is a most English virtue') and coquetry ('How can I force Your Grace? I am a woman') to persuade the reluctant bishops to accept the Act (though she is also aided by the fact that Walsingham has prevented her most trenchant opponents from attending the debate). Thereafter Elizabeth asserts her authority both over her ministers and over her lover Dudley, whom she is determined will not be raised to the status of an over-mighty subject ('I am not your Elizabeth. I am no man's Elizabeth. And if you think to rule me you are mistaken').

Elizabeth has been interpreted as a narrative of female empowerment. Several critics linked the film to the discourse of 'Girl Power' popularised by the success of the Spice Girls, a loud mouthed and short-lived all-girl pop band of the late 1990s. Certainly, there are aspects of the film, including Elizabeth's assertion of her authority ('I will have one mistress here – and no master'), that would tend to support such a reading. At the same time, however, this empowerment is not without its price: Elizabeth casts aside her lover Dudley and sacrifices her own personal happiness to ensure the security and stability of her kingdom. On this point the film rehearses familiar motifs regarding the personal and public lives of the monarch. This is best expressed by Sir William Cecil as he tries to persuade Elizabeth to marry in order to secure an alliance with either France or Spain: 'Her Majesty's body and person are no longer her own property. They belong the state.' Elizabeth, however, refuses to marry. The final scenes of the film are highly symbolic: Elizabeth cuts her luscious hair (a symbolic act undertaken before enterting into holy orders), paints her face white ('I have become a virgin') and declares her allegiance to her country ('Observe, Lord Burghley, I am married – to England'). In this sense *Elizabeth* is about the 'making' of a queen: Elizabeth the woman adopts the persona of the 'Virgin Queen' and represents herself as symbol of the nation.

While the emphasis on the private and public faces of monarchy has been a feature of the royal biopic ever since *The Private Life of Henry VIII*, it possessed particular significance in the 1990s, at a time when the British Royal Family was coming under greater public scrutiny than at any time in its recent history. The 1990s had not been a happy time for the House of Windsor: mounting public criticism of the behaviour of certain younger members of the Royal Family, divorces and subsequent revelations of infidelities, and what appeared to be, to all intents and purposes, an undeclared media war between the Prince and Princess of Wales and their friends to put each side's case to the public. While the institution of monarchy was never seriously threatened – opinion polls have consistently shown no more than 20 per cent of the British public in favour its abolition[45] – there was, nevertheless, a sense during the 1990s that the monarchy was in crisis. It is significant in this regard that the royal biopics of the 1990s were concerned with moments of instability for the monarchy. *The Madness of King George* – which suggested that the king's illness was the result of the hereditary condition of porphyria, a medical complaint not understood in the eighteenth century – focused on the attempt of the Whig party to have the king declared insane and thus establish the Prince of Wales as Regent. As one reviewer remarked: 'Satirical pot-shots at the dismal state of the current monarchy are clearly intentional and generally hit the mark.'[46] *Mrs Brown*, produced by BBC Scotland but given a theatrical release, focused on Queen Victoria's close friendship with her Scottish ghillie, John Brown, following the death of Prince Albert – a relationship that in its day caused a degree of scandal and that had clear echoes in the 1990s. Both these films were concerned with eroding the public face of the monarchy to reveal embarrassing secrets that went to the heart of the institution. In *The Madness of King George* the king is stripped of his dignity, both literally and metaphorically, while in *Mrs Brown* there is a strong implication (without any historical foundation) that the queen has an inappropriate relationship with her servant. In *Elizabeth*, the revelation that Dudley is already married prompts Elizabeth to end to their affair. The deteriorating relationship between the two lovers is exemplified visually in two scenes where they dance a *volta*: in the first scene their bodies and movements are in harmony with each other, but in the second scene their dancing is stilted and lacks the physical intimacy of the first sequence. In this case it is surely not too speculative to draw a parallel with photographs of the Prince and Princess of Wales, particularly during an official visit to South Korea in 1992, where their uncomfortable body language betrayed the growing estrangement between the royal couple.

Higson attributes the success of *Elizabeth* to its generic hybridity: part historical film, part conspiracy thriller and part romance, it contained elements 'that appealed to different audience groups and interests'.[47] However, while this is certainly correct, the hybrid nature of *Elizabeth* alone is insufficient as an explanation of its success. No amount of clever niche marketing can induce audiences to see a film they have no interest in seeing. It would seem appropriate to explain the success of *Elizabeth* in terms of the historical circumstances of its production and reception. There were four contextual factors unique to the late 1990s which all, to a greater or a lesser degree, probably had some bearing on the success of the film. First, the rise in cinema attendances during the decade meant that the audience for all films was larger than it had been at any time since the 1970s. Second, the cultural phenomenon of 'Cool Britannia' helped to sustain interest in British films both in Britain and in America for a short period during the late 1990s. Third, *Elizabeth* coincided with a revival of popular interest in the Tudor period, unfashionable for many years but coming back into vogue, as the success of David Starkey's Channel 4 documentary series on Elizabeth I (2001) and Henry VIII (2002) demonstrated. Fourth, and perhaps most significantly, *Elizabeth* had acquired an unexpected and entirely accidental significance following the death of the Princess of Wales, when its narrative of a young princess struggling with the pressures of royal life had uncanny contemporary echoes. To this extent *Elizabeth* has so far proved to be what the veteran Hollywood screenwriter William Goldman has called 'a non-recurring phenomenon'.[48] It did not give rise to a cycle of similar films and there have been no attempts to repeat its mixture of historical narrative and political thriller in British cinema. That critical and popular success in the cinema remains uncertain was demonstrated by the fact that Shekhar Kapur's next film, a revisionist version of *The Four Feathers* (2002), met with an extremely lukewarm critical reception and sank without trace at the box office.

Elizabeth also benefited from the fact that it had a powerful distributor behind it. The importance of distribution is demonstrated by the relatively poor showing of two historical films made either side of *Elizabeth* that did not achieve anything like its impact. Ken Loach's *Land and Freedom* (1995) was a characteristically passionate account of the Spanish Civil War that critics compared to Orwell's *Homage to Catalonia*. Loach and scriptwriter Jim Allen used the story of a British Communist fighting on the Republican side to draw parallels with the fragmentation of the British left during the 1980s. The message is laid on thick: just as internecine strife on the Republican side handed victory to the Fascists in the 1930s, so the divisions within the British Labour Party during the 1980s allowed Thatcherism to succeed. *Land and Freedom* was an Anglo-German-Spanish co-production made on a much smaller budget than *Elizabeth* (£3 million), but, despite winning the International Critics' Prize and the Ecumenical Prize at the Cannes Film Festival in 1995, it had only a limited release in Britain, where it was handled by the independent distributor Artifical Eye which concentrated on a small number of art house cinemas. Loach was furious and complained loudly. Artificial Eye claimed that 'it boils down to economics' and averred that multiplex cinemas were reluctant to book the film.[49] However, the multiplex chain United Cinema International (UCI) replied that 'our customers would have liked to see *Land and Freedom*. Unfortunately Artificial Eye, not the exhibitor, prevented them.'[50] *Land and Freedom* was belatedly shown in multiplexes in Aberdeen and York, though it never secured an extensive release.

A similar situation occurred with *To Kill A King* (dir. Mike Barker, 2003), an Anglo-German co-production that had an even more troubled history than *Land and Freedom*. This film, focusing on the relationship between Oliver Cromwell and Sir Thomas Fairfax, had run out of money during production and failed to find a major distributor. It was eventually put out by Pathé Distribution, another independent, and failed to secure more than an extremely limited release. It seems unusual that *To Kill A King* should have fared as badly as it did, for, unlike *Land and Freedom*, it had a recognisable 'name' cast, including Tim Roth as Cromwell, Dougray Scott as Fairfax and Rupert Everett as Charles I. One critic felt that it 'bids fair to be the first intelligent movie treatment of British history for many a year, while avoiding the staginess and gloss of, say, *A Man for All Seasons* or *The Lion in Winter*'.[51]

There are two general similarities between *Land and Freedom* and *To Kill A King* that may explain their failure in comparison with *Elizabeth*. First, both are relatively cerebral films, featuring extended scenes in which their protagonists discuss politics – something that *Elizabeth* for the most part avoided. Second, both films are about uncomfortable subjects: the Spanish Civil War and the English Civil War. *Land and Freedom* is an explicitly left-wing film from an avowedly socialist director; *To Kill A King* is perhaps less directly political, but nevertheless deals with the consequences of regicide and revolt against legitimate authority (the equivalent, perhaps, of *Elizabeth* being told from the Duke of Norfolk's point of view). Both films are studies in the failure of revolutionary movements. Their stories do not lend themselves to narratives of national greatness. And, perhaps, the general public has little interest in Communist revolutionaries or parliamentary generals in comparison with royalty. In any event, it seems that audiences – and distributors – were not attracted by these more radical and challenging narratives. If *Elizabeth* demonstrated anything, it was that history must be both popular and accessible if it is to be turned successfully into a mainstream feature film. This was the lesson that Korda had learned in the 1930s when *Rembrandt* failed where *The Private Life of Henry VIII* had succeeded. In this respect, at least, little had changed.

Conclusion

THIS book set out to explore a particular thesis: that historical films are as much about the present in which they are made as they are about past in which they are set. While this is far from being a new idea, it has tended, hitherto, to be taken as a self-evident truth. However, we must always be alert to the danger of reading films simply to prove our own preconceived theories or of making film-makers agents in a historical process of which they themselves were completely unaware. Only by close, empirically based investigation of the historical contexts of production and reception is it possible to establish what were the intentions of film-makers and the extent to which the meanings in the films that may now seem obvious to us were identified by contemporaries. What I hope this study has demonstrated is not only that film-makers have been very conscious of the possibilities of the historical film as a vehicle for responding to the issues and concerns of the present but also that critics (and, in those cases where sufficient evidence exists, audiences) have been alert to these meanings. In some cases, the imparting of contemporary meaning into films has been so explicit that it is inscribed directly into the texts (*Henry V*), while in other instances we have to rely on contextual evidence to support our reading (the 'Victoria' films, *The Charge of the Light Brigade*, *Chariots of Fire*). Elsewhere, the imparting of contemporary meaning may not have been intentional on the part of the film-makers but did nevertheless inform the reception of the films (*A Night to Remember, Zulu, Elizabeth*). It would be disingenuous to claim that every historical film has been made consciously as a commentary on the times in which it was made and there are some films which have proved more resistant to such readings (*Beau Brummell*, for example). Yet, even if the historical theme of a film does not immediately or obviously speak for the present, all films are products of their own times and cannot escape being informed by their own social, cultural and industrial circumstances.

If one overriding theme has emerged from this book, it is that the historical film has proved highly flexible as a vehicle for exploring political and social concerns. In the 1930s, for example, historical films were used towards numerous different ideological ends, whether endorsing consensus (*The Private Life of Henry VIII*), validating the institution of monarchy (*Victoria the Great*), promoting the foreign policy of appeasement (*The Iron Duke*) or urging the need for national preparedness (*Fire Over England, Sixty Glorious Years*). The fact that such an explicitly anti-appeasement film as *Sixty Glorious Years* could be made only four years after the equally explicit pro-appeasement *The Iron Duke* demonstrates that the politics of the genre were subject to radical change over short periods of time. This is a characteristic of all film genres, of course: genres are not static entities that remain fixed over many decades (this is a weakness of structuralist approaches to genre) but, instead, should be seen as variable and shifting structures that are in a constant state of flux as they are shaped by and respond to various external determinants. As with all historical processes, the reasons for these changes are highly complex. To some extent, of course, the differences between *The Iron Duke* and *Sixty Glorious Years* reflect changes in the political climate as attitudes towards Germany in the late 1930s hardened from the more tolerant view that had prevailed earlier in the decade. Yet the differences are also due to agency: *The Iron Duke* represents George Arliss's belief in 'honourable dealings between nations' as much as *Sixty Glorious Years* was shaped by Sir Robert Vansittart's anti-appeasement views.

It was during the Second World War that the historical film was put to its most direct propagandist use, as film-makers projected a version of British history that accorded with the official directives of the MOI.

Thus there was a cycle of films dramatising narratives of British resistance to tyrants and foreign powers (*This England*, *The Prime Minister*, *The Young Mr Pitt*, *Henry V*). Arguably, the most radical of these was also the least successful (*This England*), largely because it failed to find an adequate formula for dramatising complex motifs of history and heritage. The most successful, aesthetically as well as commercially, resorted to a 345-year-old play for its inspiration. The production history of *Henry V* reveals just how far the film-makers were prepared to go in adapting Shakespeare's text to fit the contemporary ideological climate and illustrates the consonance between the economic and cultural imperatives of the film industry, on the one hand, and the requirements of official propaganda agencies on the other.

The post-war period was characterised by historical films that engaged with questions of class, masculinity and national decline. It was during this period that the British historical film most fully embraced the aesthetic of historical verisimilitude and the ethos of stoical and undemonstrative masculinity (*Scott of the Antarctic*, *A Night to Remember*). These films fitted the prevailing critical discourse of realism and emotional restraint that was valued not only as the preferred style of British film-making but also as being representative of the British character in times of adversity. And they again demonstrate the importance of agency: these films were perfectly in line with the production ideologies of Ealing Studios and the Rank Organisation. It is significant that a film that tried to do something different, by playing down the discourse of historical verisimilitude in favour of a more sumptuous visual style and a display of male emotionality, was greeted with almost universal hostility by British critics, despite its high production values and star names. *Beau Brummell* exhibited characteristics that were 'unBritish' – visual flair and melodrama – and did not therefore fit into the accepted criteria for critical approval. Yet, for all its stylistic differences, *Beau Brummell* was as much a film of its times as the others, exploring social change and meritocracy in the new Britain of the 1950s (for which the Regency period was a particularly apposite choice).

During the 1960s, the historical film underwent a radical transformation. *Zulu* is a key transitional film: simultaneously the last of the old-fashioned imperial adventure epics and the first of the new historical films that offered a more sceptical view of British history. Its combination of heroic spectacle and ambivalence towards militarism and imperialism was successful with audiences at a time when cinema-going was no longer the pre-eminent social pastime it had been in previous decades. In the late 1960s and early 1970s, the historical film fractured into different lineages: while *The Charge of the Light Brigade* and *Alfred the Great* attempted to remould the genre to fit the tastes of younger audiences (an attempt that, it must be said, was largely unsuccessful), the persistence of the traditional formula was illustrated by middlebrow films, such as *A Man for All Seasons*, *Anne of the Thousand Days*, *Mary, Queen of Scots* and *Henry VIII and His Six Wives*, that seem to have been made with an older audience in mind. This was the first sign of the fragmentation of audiences that would see the historical film, from the 1970s, shift away from the mainstream of film culture.

Since the mid-1970s, furthermore, the historical film has only an occasional presence in British cinema. This helps to explain the cultural and economic significance attached to both *Chariots of Fire* and *Elizabeth*. Yet again, the histories of production and reception are instructive in revealing the contemporary parallels that were consciously intended in the one instance (*Chariots of Fire*) and implicit in the other (*Elizabeth*). The contested meanings of *Chariots of Fire* further expose a tension between the intent of the film-makers and the views of academic commentators who have read the film as an endorsement of the social politics of Thatcherism in quite the opposite way to which it was intended. Both these films, moreover, demonstrate the importance of historical context in influencing the reception of films. They drew much of their cultural significance from events that were coincidental to the films but which, nevertheless, had a major bearing on the ways in which they were understood, namely the Falklands War (*Chariots of Fire*) and the death of the Princess of Wales (*Elizabeth*). Here the film-makers had no control over events but saw their films acquire symbolic meaning over and above what was intended.

While the relationship between past and present in the historical film has been the main theme of this study, various other issues have been highlighted along the way. The first of these is the existence of different discourses of reception. The historical film is unique in so far as it has to contend not just with the aesthetic prejudices of critics and the fickle tastes of audiences, but also with the rants of professional historians. The controversy that erupted over *Elizabeth* was merely the most recent example of a recurring debate concerning the historical accuracy, or otherwise, of the historical film. *The Private Life of Henry VIII*, *Zulu*, *The Charge of the Light Brigade*, *Chariots of Fire* and *Elizabeth* were all charged with the crime of being 'false' history. Interestingly, perhaps the least historically accurate film in this study, *Beau Brummell*, does not seem to have provoked any outcry from historians, suggesting that it was seen in the same terms as historical novels – as being essentially a work of fiction that happened to be set against a historical background. Historians particularly take issue when film-makers adapt the past to meet their own ideological ends (*The Charge of the Light Brigade*, *Chariots of Fire*). (However, *Henry V*, in which the historical past was very systematically adapted for ideological needs, escaped this sort of censure, perhaps because of its special cultural status. In any event Shakespeare's own use of history was, to say the least, highly imaginative.)

As far as the critics are concerned, there are consistent themes in the reception of the historical film. The right-wing press takes offence at films that do anything to undermine the popular image of national icons (*The Private Life of Henry VIII*, *Elizabeth*). The left-wing press dislikes films that ignore the wider social context of the past (*The Private Life of Henry VIII*, *Victoria the Great*, *A Night to Remember*). The film industry trade press prefers those films deemed to have populist appeal (*The Private Life of Henry VIII*) and qualities of spectacle and narrative excitement (*Zulu*), and is more reserved about those with a narrower appeal (*Henry VIII and His Six Wives*). The middlebrow film critics admire films that meet the criteria of 'art' (*Henry V*) or realism (*Scott of the Antarctic*, *A Night to Remember*) and denigrate those that are overly melodramatic (*Beau Brummell*). And the intellectual film critics prefer a 'filmic' use of form and visual style (*Henry V*, *Elizabeth*) to conventional realistic treatment (*A Night to Remember*) – except in the case of Tony Richardson, who, after *Tom Jones*, could do nothing right. Popular taste, in terms of which films were successful at the box office, accords most closely with the trade press. This is perhaps only to be expected, given that the primary objective of reviews in the trade press is to assess the popular appeal and commercial potential of films. That said, however, where qualitative evidence of popular reception exists – such as the Mass-Observation respondents on *Victoria the Great*, the readers' reviews of *The Charge of the Light Brigade* published in *Films and Filming* and David Puttnam's correspondents concerning *Chariots of Fire* – there is evidence of a consonance between the views of cinema-goers (albeit, in all likelihood, the more discerning ones) and the critical response to those films. While the evidence is fragmentary, there is enough to suggest, albeit tentatively, that there is less difference between the critical and popular reception of the historical film than there is between the critical and popular reception of other genres such as the horror film, the costume melodrama and the James Bond films.

Another issue that has arisen repeatedly in the course of this study is the extent to which the historical film is a vehicle for the economic and cultural export of Britishness. It is highly significant in this regard that the historical film has been at the forefront of attempts to open the American market for British films: Korda, Balcon and Wilcox in the 1930s, Rank in the 1940s and 1950s, Woodfall in the 1960s, Goldcrest in the 1980s and PolyGram in the 1990s all attempted to break into the American market on the back of historical films. This is largely a matter of economic necessity as, even in the case of films that are very successful in Britain, such as *The Private Life of Henry VIII* and *Zulu*, the domestic market alone has been insufficient to return a profit on films that, by their nature, are often towards the higher-cost end of British film production. It would be fair to say that failures outnumber successes in this regard – American audiences on the whole seem to have been resistant to films about English kings and queens or battles that the British won – though it is apparent that certain films (*The Private Life of Henry VIII*, *Henry V*, *Chariots of Fire*, *Elizabeth*) have achieved significant success in niche markets. Even then, however, the cases of *Henry V* and *Chariots of Fire* demonstrate that the economics of distribution are such that record-breaking box-office grosses in America do not translate into large profits for British producers.

What of the future for the historical film? The commercial success of the historical film has always been uncertain: Korda spent much of the rest of his career trying to repeat the success of *The Private Life of Henry VIII*. For every historical film that succeeds (*Elizabeth*), there is another that fails (*To Kill A King*). The historical film has generally been among the most expensive British productions and is therefore dependent upon overseas markets for its ultimate profitability. The British production sector as it currently stands is too small and unstable to support the consistent production of large-scale historical films. For these reasons it seems likely that the genre will continue to have, at best, a marginal presence in the British cinema. Yet this could be an advantage. The fanfare surrounding films like *Chariots of Fire* and *Elizabeth* indicates their special status. The British historical film is now such a rarity that a new production represents an event of considerable cultural significance. This, in turn, helps to generate interest in British cinema in general and in the historical film in particular.

Moreover, the historical film continues to be present in a different form. One of the most visible production trends in the British television industry over the last few years has been the revival of the historical play. In the course of writing this book British television has produced handsomely mounted historical dramas about Anne Boleyn (*Anne Boleyn*, 2003), Henry VIII (*Henry VIII*, 2003) Charles II (*The Power and the Passion*, 2003) and James I (*Gunpowder, Treason and Plot*, 2004) These were notable for their high production values, sumptuous sets and costumes, and a 'filmic' style which differentiated them from the historical dramas of the 1970s. This production trend also coincided with a separate, though related cycle of docu-dramas about the Second Word War: *Dunkirk*, *D-Day* and the misleadingly titled *When Hitler Invaded Britain* (all 2004). It is too early to tell whether this represents the emergence of a new genre of historical 'films' for television, though the prominence of these dramas in the television schedules is testimony to the enduring fascination of British history for both cultural producers and audiences.

Notes

For the endnotes, books are cited by the edition used. Full publication details of all books consulted are provided in the Bibliography. Where film reviews or newspaper articles are cited without a page reference, the source is the British Film Institute's microfiche collection, which until recently does not include page numbers. Quotations from *Variety* and the *New York Times* are taken from the collected volumes of film reviews for those publications. I have used the following abbreviations for archival sources: BFI (British Film Institute); BL (British Library); PRO (Public Records Office).

Introduction

1. Interviewed for the BBC/Film Education programme *Screening Histories* (BBC2, 1998).

2. See Siegfried Kracauer, *From Caligari to Hitler: A Psychological History of the German Film* (Princeton, 1947). I have put the word 'reflect' in inverted commas to indicate that the metaphor is not unproblematic. Textualist critics regard this notion as too simplistic and prefer to understand films as 'constructions' that create their own representations of social reality through the specific codes and conventions of the medium. See, for example, Graeme Turner, *Film As Social Practice* (London, 1988). My own position on the 'reflectionist' debate is explained in *Cinemas of the World: Film and Society from 1895 to the Present* (London, 2003), pp.27–32.

3. Mark C. Carnes, 'Introduction', to *Past Imperfect: History According to the Movies* (London, 1996), p.10.

4. See, for example, Graham Roberts, *Forward Soviet! History and Non-fiction Film in the USSR* (London, 1999); Richard Taylor, *Film Propaganda: Soviet Russia*

and Nazi Germany (London, 1979); and David Welch, *Propaganda and the German Cinema 1933–1945* (Oxford, 1983).

5. See, for example, Michael Coyne, *The Crowded Prairie: American National Identity in the Hollywood Western* (London, 1997); Philip French, *Westerns: Aspects of a Movie Genre* (London, 1973); and Richard Slotkin, *Gunfighter Nation: The Myth of the Frontier in Twentieth-Century America* (New York, 1992).

6. For a historical mapping of the costume film, see Sue Harper, *Picturing the Past: The Rise and Fall of the British Costume Film* (London, 1994). Questions of generic categorisation are addressed in Andrew Higson, *English Heritage, English Cinema: Costume Drama Since 1980* (Oxford, 2003), pp.9–13, and in the editors' introduction to Claire Monk and Amy Sargeant (eds), *British Historical Cinema* (London, 2002), pp.1–14. The latter book contains several contributions focusing on films that are not strictly historical films within this definition, indicating that the terms are not fixed. See also the review article by Sue Harper, 'The taxonomy of a genre: historical, costume and "heritage" film', *Journal of British Cinema and Television*, vol. 1, no. 1 (2004), pp.131–6.

7. The distinction between 'history' and 'the past' is elucidated in E.H. Carr, *What Is History?* (Harmondsworth, 1964), pp.10–14, and by Arthur Marwick, *The Nature of History* (London, 3rd edn 1989), pp.1–14.

8. It is a moot point how far in the past a film has to be set in order to be categorised as historical. For example, films about the Second World War made after the event such as *The Dam Busters* (dir. Michael Anderson, 1955), *The Battle of the River Plate* (dir. Michael Powell, 1956) and *Battle of Britain* (dir. Guy Hamilton, 1969) tend to be classified as 'war films' – a genre that also, of course, includes fictional stories. The term 'retro-film' has been adopted by some commentators to describe films set in the more recent past such as *Dance With A Stranger* (dir. Mike Newell, 1985) and *Scandal* (dir. Michael Caton-Jones, 1989).

9. F.J.C. Hearnshaw and J.E. Neale, 'Fire Over England', *Sight and Sound*, vol.6, no.22 (Summer 1937), pp.98–9.

10. On the Gainsborough melodramas see Sue Aspinall and Robert Murphy (eds), *BFI Dossier 18: Gainsborough Melodrama* (London, 1983); Pam Cook, *Fashioning the Nation: Costume and Identity in British Cinema* (London, 1997); and Harper, *Picturing the Past*, pp.119–35.

11. Historical Association, *History Teaching Films* (London, 1937), p.18.

12. '*Chariots* short on facts', *Bulletin*, 13 August 1984.

13. 'Henry VIII on the Film: Vulgar Buffoon or Great King?', *Daily Telegraph*, 3 November 1933, p.12; letter from Bernard Van Thal, *Daily Telegraph*, 7 November 1933, p.11; 'Henry VIII on the Film: Producer's Reply to Lord Cottenham', *Daily Telegraph*, 6 November 1933, p.10.

14. 'Elizabeth *intacta*', *Daily Telegraph*, 9 March 1998, p.21; 'Film changes sexual history of Elizabeth I, the Virgin Queen', ibid, p.3.

15. BFI BBFC Scenario Reports 1946–47, 53a, *The Private Life of the Virgin Queen*, 25 February 1947. The script examiner 'MK' was Madge Kitchener, niece of Field Marshal Lord Kitchener.

16. A.J.P. Taylor, *English History 1914–1945* (Oxford, 1965), p.313.

17. Alan Lovell, 'The British Cinema: The Unknown Cinema', typescript of paper presented to the British Film Institute Education Department on 13 March

1969 (held by the BFI National Library), p.5. Lovell identified the historical film as one of six principal film genres 'created by the British entertainment cinema' alongside the war film, the Gothic film (including both horror and thrillers), literary adaptation, social documentary and comedy. Few scholars now would agree with his sweeping assertion that 'the first two genres (History and War) can safely be ignored as being of little intrinsic interest' (p.6). See also Lovell's 'The British Cinema: The Known Cinema?', in Robert Murphy (ed.), *The British Cinema Book* (London, 2nd edn 2001), pp.200–5, which reveals that Lovell is still inclined towards documentary and realism and is generally dismissive of the new film history that sets out to reclaim non-realist genres such as horror and melodrama.

18. Sue Harper, *Women in British Cinema: Mad, Bad and Dangerous to Know* (London, 2000), p.3.

19. John Sedgwick, *Popular Filmgoing in 1930s Britain: A Choice of Pleasures* (Exeter, 2000), *passim*. Sedgwick has developed a statistical index of film popularity known as 'POPSTAT' derived from the exhibition patterns of individual films. POPSTAT does not provide actual box-office grosses but rather allows the researcher to rank films in order of popularity based on the number and size of cinemas in which they were shown and the length of their run. It is based on a sample of between 81 and 92 cinemas in London and nine provincial cities for the period between 1 January 1932 and 31 March 1938. In the absence of any reliable box-office grosses for this period, POPSTAT is invaluable for comparing the relative popularity of individual films, albeit with the caveats that it is based on a small sample of cinemas, does not take account of reissues after the initial release, and provides only quantitative evidence of popularity. The mean POPSTAT index is usually around six, on a scale in which zero indicates a film with no bookings (primarily British 'quota' films and foreign-language films which failed to secure circulation within the sample set). The highest index for an individual film during this period is 92.89 for *Cavalcade* (dir. Frank Lloyd, 1933); the highest for a British film is 55.13 for *The Private Life of Henry VIII*. POPSTAT should be considered alongside, rather than as an alternative to, other sources such as *Kine Weekly*'s 'book of form' (which began in 1937) and Mass-Observation's survey of cinema-going in 'Worktown' (Bolton) in 1937–38.

20. I was taken to task for using the term 'narrative ideologies' in my books *Licence To Thrill: A Cultural History of the James Bond Films* (London, 1999) and *Saints and Avengers: British Adventure Series of the 1960s* (London, 2002) by one reviewer who found the idea 'awkward' and 'intellectually inadequate'. See the review article by Nannette Aldred in *Visual Culture in Britain*, vol. 4, no. 1 (2003), pp.119–22. No one can seriously dispute that films are ideological in the sense that they express, whether consciously or unconsciously, the values, beliefs, attitudes, assumptions and ideas of those who made them. The principal means by which ideology in film is expressed is through narrative (for example, what themes the film explores, what conflicts it sets up and how they are resolved). The notion of 'narrative ideologies', therefore, strikes me as a useful way of approaching the analysis of film texts – while always accepting, of course, that films also express meaning through other means than narrative (form and visual style, for example).

1. Merrie England: *The Private Life of Henry VIII* (1933)

1. For details of the production and reception histories of the film, see: Charles Drazin, *Korda: Britain's Only Movie Mogul* (London, 2002), pp.96–105; Sue Harper, *Picturing the Past: The Rise and Fall of the British Costume Film* (London, 1994), pp.20–3; Karol Kulik, *Alexander Korda: The Man Who Could Work Miracles* (London, 1975), pp.83–95; Marcia Landy, *British Genres: Cinema and Society, 1930–1960* (Princeton, 1991), pp.61–3; Rachael Low, *The History of the British Film 1929–1939: Film Making in 1930s Britain* (London, 1985), pp.167–9; Jeffrey Richards, *The Age of the Dream Palace: Cinema and Society in Britain 1930–1939* (London, 1984), pp.259–61; and Sarah Street, *Transatlantic Crossings: British Feature Films in the USA* (London, 2002), pp.47–55. The importance of *The Private Life of Henry VIII* has recently been affirmed by its inclusion in the I.B. Tauris 'British Film Guides' series: see Greg Walker, *The Private Life of Henry VIII* (London, 2003).

2. Roy Armes, *A Critical History of British Cinema* (London, 1978), p.116.

3. Harper, p.22.

4. Low, p.115.

5. Rachael Low, *The History of the British Film 1918–1929* (London, 1971), p.42.

6. Ibid., p.43.

7. Margaret Dickinson and Sarah Street, *Cinema and State: The Film Industry and the British Government 1927–84* (London, 1985), p.42.

8. Linda Wood (ed.), *British Films 1927–1939: BFI Reference Guide* (London, 1986), p.117.

9. Political and Economic Planning, *The British Film Industry: A report on its history and present organisation, with special reference to the economic problems of British feature film production* (London, 1952), p.50.

10. 'UA to Handle London Film Product', *Kinematograph Weekly*, 25 May 1933, p.1.

11. Kulik, p.85; Richards, p.260. The three-reel Laurel and Hardy comedy *Oliver the Eighth* (1934) – sometimes referred to as *The Private Life of Oliver the Eighth* – used the same idea as Hardy becomes the eighth husband of the Oliver-hating, throat-slitting Mae Busch.

12. Elsa Lanchester, *Elsa Lanchester Herself* (London, 1983), pp.111–12.

13. Michael Korda, *Charmed Lives: A Family Romance* (London, 1980), pp.100–1.

14. Ernest Betts, *The Private Life of Henry VIII* (London, 1934), p.xvi.

15. Linda Wood, 'Low-Budget British Films in the 1930s', in Robert Murphy (ed.), *The British Cinema Book* (London, 2nd edn 2001), p.59.

16. BFI LFP (London Film Productions Collection) Box 5 contains data on budgets and revenues for the company's 1930s films in a memorandum by production manager Sir David Cunynghame, 7 January 1946. Following *The Private Life of Henry VIII*, the films became more expensive: *Catherine the Great* (£127,868), *The Private Life of Don Juan* (£109,987), *The Scarlet Pimpernel* (£138,392), *Sanders of the River* (£144,161), *The Ghost Goes West* (£161,362), *Things to Come* (£256,028), *Rembrandt* (£140,236) and *Elephant Boy* (£149,882).

These figures are different from those in Box 2353 of the Prudential Archive used by Drazin, though the discrepancies are slight.

17. The title of the film was originally announced as *Royal Husband,* in *Kinematograph Weekly,* 18 May 1933, p.61. The course of the production was reported on the 'British Studio News' pages of *Kinematograph Weekly*: 'A Studio Feast', 8 June 1933, p.28; 'Henry's Gasper', 15 June 1933, p.27; 'Lighting for "Henry VIII"', 22 June 1933, p.43; 'Elsa Lanchester acquires German accent', 29 June 1933, p.33; 'A Queen's Execution', 6 July 1933, p.17; 'Side-lights on History in London Film Epic', 20 July 1933, p.28. The serialisation in *Film Weekly* was in four parts: 18 August 1933, p.11; 26 August 1933, p.11; 1 September 1933, p.11; 8 September 1933, p.14. The screenplay published with an introduction by Ernest Betts in 1934 differs in numerous details from the finished film – including the order of scenes as well as specific dialogue – and was probably based on a pre-production script. The BFI National Library holds a copy of the release script (S215), but not a shooting script.

18. Arthur Wimperis, 'Why Film Authors Are Not "Stars"', *Picturegoer Weekly,* 24 March 1934, p.11.

19. Drazin, p.98.

20. Quoted in 'Alexander Korda and the International Film', *Cinema Quarterly,* vol. 2, no. 1 (Autumn 1933), pp.13–14.

21. *Picturegoer Weekly,* 17 February 1934, p.24.

22. *Kinematograph Weekly,* 24 August 1933, p.17.

23. *Variety,* 17 October 1933.

24. BFI LFP Box 5: Memorandum of 7 January 1946.

25. 'Korda and the Big Time', *World Film News,* vol. 1, no. 9 (December 1936), p.3.

26. *Kinematograph Weekly,* 19 October 1933, p.1.

27. Street, p.49.

28. John Sedgwick, *Popular Filmgoing in 1930s Britain: A Choice of Pleasures* (Exeter, 2000), p.238.

29. *Monthly Film Bulletin,* vol.13, no.151 (July 1946), p.94.

30. Eric Rhode, *A History of the Cinema from its Origins to 1970* (Harmondsworth, 1978), p.349.

31. Betts, p.xvi.

32. *Observer,* 29 October 1933. Reprinted in Anthony Lejeune (ed.), *The C.A. Lejeune Film Reader* (Manchester, 1991), pp.89–90.

33. Paul Rotha, with Richard Griffith, *The Film Till Now: A Survey of World Cinema* (London, 1949 edn), p.546.

34. Kevin Gough-Yates, 'The British Feature Film as a European Concern: Britain and the Emigré Film-Maker, 1933–45', in Günter Berghaus (ed.), *Theatre and Film in Exile: German Artists in Britain, 1933–1945* (Oxford, 1989), p.135.

35. Ibid., p.136.

36. 'Foreigners in our midst', *World Film News,* vol. 1, no. 2 (May 1936), p.17.

37. Quoted in 'Alexander Korda and the International Film', pp.14–15.

38. Dilys Powell, 'The Private Life of Henry VIII', *The Movie,* no.3 (1979), p.56.

39. Betts, p.xvi.

40. *Variety,* 17 October 1933.

41. *Rob Wagner's Script,* 2 December 1933, p.8.

42. Andrew Higson, *Waving the Flag: Constructing a National Cinema in Britain* (Oxford, 1995), p.28.

43. Charles Shiro Tashiro, 'Fear and Loathing of British Cinema', *Spectator: The University of Southern California Journal of Film and Television Criticism*, vol.14, no.2 (Spring 1994), p.25.

44. *Kinematograph Weekly*, 15 June 1933, p.27; 29 June 1933, p.33.

45. Charles R. Beard, 'Why Get It Wrong?', *Sight and Sound*, vol. 2, no.8 (Winter 1934), p.124.

46. *The Times*, 25 October 1933, p.10.

47. *Daily Telegraph*, 25 October 1933, p.12.

48. *Manchester Guardian*, 25 October 1933, p.12.

49. *Tribune*, 19 July 1946.

50. *Kinematograph Weekly*, 24 August 1933, p.17.

51. Forsyth Hardy, 'Films of the Quarter', *Cinema Quarterly*, vol.2, no.1 (Autumn 1933), p.39.

52. F.D. Klingender, 'From Sarah Bernhardt to Flora Robson: The Cinema's Pageant of History', *World Film News*, vol. 1, no. 12 (March 1937), pp.8–11.

53. On the operation and policies of the BBFC, see Nicholas Pronay, 'The First Reality: Film Censorship in Liberal England', in K.R.M. Short (ed.), *Feature Films as History* (London, 1981), pp.113–37, and 'The political censorship of films in Britain between the wars', in Nicholas Pronay and D.W. Spring (eds), *Politics, Propaganda and Film, 1918–45* (London, 1982), pp.98–125; Jeffrey Richards, 'The British Board of Film Censors and content control in the 1930s (1): images of Britain', *Historical Journal of Film, Radio and Television*, vol. 1, no. 2 (1981), pp.95–119, and 'The British Board of Film Censors and content control in the 1930s (2): foreign affairs', *Historical Journal of Film, Radio and Television*, vol. 2, no. 1 (1982), pp.38–48; and James C. Robertson, *The British Board of Film Censors: Film Censorship in Britain 1896–1950* (London, 1985).

54. *BBFC Annual Report* (London, 1937), p.4.

55. BFI BBFC Scenario Reports 1933, No. 113, *The Private Life of Henry VIII* (JCH).

56. An 'A' certificate required that children under 16 must be accompanied by an adult, though there is anecdotal evidence to suggest this was not always rigorously enforced by some cinemas.

57. Richards, *The Age of the Dream Palace*, p.260.

58. The notion that British films of the 1930s endorsed political and social consensus is argued most cogently by Anthony Aldgate and Jeffrey Richards. See, especially, chapters 2 and 3 of their jointly authored book *Best of British: Cinema and Society from 1930 to the Present* (London, rev. edn 1999), pp.19–54; Aldgate, 'Ideological Consensus in British Feature Films, 1935–1947', in Short (ed.), *Feature Films as History*, pp.94–112; and Richards, *The Age of the Dream Palace*, *passim*. The existence of a 'cinema of consensus' is affirmed by more recent work such as Stephen C. Shafer, *British Popular Films 1929–1939: The Cinema of Reassurance* (London, 1997), which extends the coverage to some less familiar films but adds little new in terms of method or contextualisation.

59. Greg Walker, 'The Private Life of Henry VIII', *History Today*, vol. 51, no. 9 (September 2001), p.10.

60. Ibid., p.14.

61. Ibid., p.15.

62. Betts, pp.14–15.

63. Harper, pp.56–63.

64. George Orwell, *The Lion and the Unicorn: Socialism and the English Genius* (Harmondsworth, 1982 edn), p.40.

65. 'The titters that greet this repeated encroachment on the privacy of a dead King of England, and the queues in the streets outside the theatre, seem to indicate, too, that the end justifies the means – when the end is a matter of pounds, shillings and pence; and they also afford a sad commentary on our time', *Daily Telegraph*, 3 November 1933, p.12.

66. Betts, p.6.

67. Orwell, p.49.

68. Walker, p.12.

69. Stephen Constantine, *Unemployment in Britain between the Wars* (Harlow, 1980), p.3.

70. *Variety*, 17 October 1933.

71. Forsyth Hardy, 'Films of the Quarter', *Cinema Quarterly*, vol. 2, no. 3 (Spring 1934), p.179.

72. Klingender, p.9.

73. 'The Private Life of Alexander the Great', *Picturegoer Weekly*, 18 January 1936, p.13.

74. 'Denham Gets on with the Job', *World Film News*, vol. 1, no. 4 (July 1936), p.6.

75. For a detailed account of Korda's relations with his financial backers and his part in the crisis of the late 1930s, see Sarah Street, 'Alexander Korda, Prudential Assurance and British Film Finance in the 1930s', *Historical Journal of Film, Radio and Television*, vol.6, no.2 (1986), pp.161–79.

76. Graham Greene, 'The Middlebrow Film', in David Parkinson (ed.), *The Graham Greene Film Reader: Mornings in the Dark* (Manchester, 1993), p.401.

77. Quoted in Harper, p.24.

78. Sue Harper, *Women in British Cinema: Mad, Bad and Dangerous to Know* (London, 2000), pp.169–70.

79. Graham Greene, 'Rembrandt', *The Graham Greene Film Reader*, p.159.

80. *Picturegoer Weekly*, 16 March 1935, p.6; *World Film News*, vol.1, no.1 (April 1936), p.5.

81. Gore Vidal, *Screening History* (London, 1992), pp.45–6.

82. See the essay by editor Rudy Behlmer, 'The Heroic Virtues', in the Warner Bros./University of Wisconsin published screenplay series, *The Sea Hawk* (Madison, 1982), pp.11–44.

83. See Jeffrey Richards, '"Patriotism with Profit": British Imperial Cinema in the 1930s', in James Curran and Vincent Porter (eds), *British Cinema History* (London, 1983), pp.245–56.

84. Martin Gilbert (ed.), *Winston S. Churchill, Volume V: Companion – Part 2* (London, 1985), Korda to Churchill, 6 October 1934, p.881.

85. Ibid, pp.989–1031.

86. See Jeffrey Richards and Jeffrey Hulbert, 'Censorship in action: the case of *Lawrence of Arabia*', *Journal of Contemporary History*, vol. 19, no. 1 (January 1984), pp.153–70. The screenplay of the aborted film is reproduced, with

supporting documentation, in Andrew Kelly, Jeffrey Richards and James Pepper, *Filming T.E. Lawrence: Korda's Lost Epics* (London, 1997).

87. PRO INF 1/867: Minutes of the Co-ordination Committee of the Ministry of Information, 23 November 1939.

88. On British propaganda in the United States see, especially, Nicholas John Cull, *Selling War: The British Propaganda Campaign Against American 'Neutrality' in World War II* (New York, 1995) and Susan A. Brewer, *To Win the Peace: British Propaganda in the United States During World War II* (Ithaca, 1997). Accounts of Korda's intelligence work are inevitably highly speculative, for example Thomas E. Mahl, *Desperate Deception: British Covert Operations in the United States, 1939–44* (Washington, 1998), pp.67–8.

89. H. Mark Glancy, *When Hollywood loved Britain: The Hollywood 'British' film 1939–45* (Manchester, 1999), p.110. See also K.R.M. Short, 'That Hamilton Woman (1941): propaganda, feminism and the production code', *Historical Journal of Film, Radio and Television*, vol.11, no.1 (1991), pp.3–19.

90. Winston S. Churchill, *The Second World War, Volume III: The Grand Alliance* (London, 1985 edn), p.382. On Churchill's film interests, see D.J. Wenden and K.R.M. Short, 'Winston S. Churchill: film fan', *Historical Journal of Film, Radio and Television*, vol.11, no.3 (1991), pp.197–214.

2. Age of Appeasement: *The Iron Duke* (1935)

1. In contrast to *The Private Life of Henry VIII* there is relatively little commentary on *The Iron Duke*. Secondary sources are limited in the main to Sue Harper, *Picturing the Past: The Rise and Fall of the British Costume Film* (London, 1994), pp.32–3; Marcia Landy, *British Genres: Cinema and Society, 1930–1960* (Princeton, 1991), pp.70–2; and Jeffrey Richards, *The Age of the Dream Palace: Cinema and Society in Britain 1930–1939* (London, 1984), pp.274–5.

2. Rachael Low, *The History of the British Film 1929–1939: Film Making in 1930s Britain* (London, 1985), p.136.

3. Michael Balcon, 'G.B. Goes International', *World Film News*, vol.1, no.3 (June 1936), p.6.

4. Victor Saville, 'My Ideal Film', *Picturegoer Weekly*, 9 December 1933, p.12.

5. Saville has been afforded scant attention, the only critical study being the slim National Film Theatre booklet *Victor Saville* (London, 1972). For an illuminating discussion of Saville's earlier work in relation to other British film-makers of the time, see Charles Barr, 'Desperate Yearnings: Victor Saville and Gainsborough', in Pam Cook (ed.), *Gainsborough Pictures* (London, 1997), pp.47–59.

6. *Victor Saville*, p.5.

7. Ibid.

8. Roy Moseley, *Evergreen: Victor Saville in His Own Words* (Carbondale, 2000), p.81. This is a published version of the manuscript autobiography held by the BFI Special Collections Unit in their Victor Saville Collection (VS 1).

9. Ibid., p.83.

10. *Cinema Quarterly*, vol. 3, no. 2 (Winter 1935), p.114. Leslie Halliwell added his own variation on a familiar anecdote when he remarked that going to the cinema 'gave me an idea of what happened in history, admittedly a hazy one since Disraeli and Voltaire and Richelieu and Rothschild all seemed to look like George Arliss', *Seats In All Parts: Half A Lifetime at the Movies* (London, 1985), p.10.

11. Richards, p.274.

12. George Arliss, *George Arliss By Himself* (London, 1940), pp.187–8. Balcon was moved to respond to a *Picturegoer* correspondent who had questioned the choice of Arliss to assert that 'Mr Arliss is pre-eminently a master of the craft of efficiently portraying the character and personality of his biographical subject… I do feel that the right time to say that a picture is handicapping the star or that it travesties history is when it has been finished and presented, and not conscionably before', *Picturegoer Weekly*, 28 July 1934, p.7.

13. Arliss, p.189.

14. See the *Kinematograph Weekly* reports on the production, including: 'George Arliss Begins as Wellington', 6 September 1934, p.25; 'War over Welwyn', 20 September 1934, p.35; 'Arliss re-enacts history', 27 September 1934, p.35; '"The Iron Duke" in Production', 4 October 1934, p.25; 'Arliss's Last Shot', 11 October 1934, p.37. Some indication of the nature of the director's role at this time as a 'hired hand' is that Saville finished his work on *The Iron Duke* on Tuesday, 9 October and the following day began directing *The Dictator* for independent producer Ludovico Toeplitz at Ealing Studios, taking over from American director Al Santell. See 'Victor Saville takes over "The Dictator"', *Kinematograph Weekly*, 11 October 1934, pp.3 and 5.

15. The BFI National Library holds Saville's own bound copy of the shooting script of *The Iron Duke* (S7669). This is close to the finished film, with minor differences in dialogue.

16. Harper, p.33.

17. British press book for *The Iron Duke*, held by the BFI National Library.

18. *Daily Film Renter*, 3 December 1934, p.4; *Kinematograph Weekly*, 6 December 1934, p.21.

19. *Picturegoer Weekly*, 22 December 1934, p.20.

20. *Cinema Quarterly*, vol. 3, no. 2 (Winter 1935), p.114.

21. *Monthly Film Bulletin*, vol. 1, no. 12 (January 1935), p.115.

22. *Variety*, 18 December 1934.

23. *Variety*, 29 January 1935.

24. US press book for *The Iron Duke*, held by the BFI National Library.

25. *Photoplay*, April 1935, p.52.

26. *New York Times*, 25 January 1935, p.27.

27. John Sedgwick, *Popular Filmgoing in 1930s Britain: A Choice of Pleasures* (Exeter, 2000), p.269.

28. Moseley, p.83.

29. 'G-B's Success in America', *Daily Film Renter*, 4 December 1934, p.7.

30. Sarah Street, *Transatlantic Crossings: British Feature Films in the USA* (London, 2002), p.77.

31. *Variety*, 29 January 1935.

32. Arliss, p.187.

33. *New York Times*, 25 January 1935, p.27.

34. Arliss, p.187.

35. On the Treaty of Versailles and its consequences, see Anthony Lentin, *Guilt at Versailles: Lloyd George and the Pre-History of Appeasement* (London, 1985), and Alan Sharp, *The Versailles Settlement: Peacemaking in Paris, 1919* (London, 1991).

36. Landy, p.72.

37. A.J.P. Taylor, *The Origins of the Second World War* (London, 1961), p.189.

38. *Cinema Quarterly*, vol. 3, no. 2 (Winter 1935), p.114.

39. Sir John Woolf, 'Foreword' to Moseley, p.xiv.

40. Harper, p.33.

41. Arliss, p.222.

42. *Kinematograph Weekly*, 21 April 1938, p.9.

3. Monarchy and Empire: *Victoria the Great* (1937) and *Sixty Glorious Years* (1938)

1. On the 'Victoria' films see the 'usual suspects': Sue Harper, *Picturing the Past: The Rise and Fall of the British Costume Film* (London, 1994), pp.53–5; Marcia Landy, *British Genres: Cinema and Society, 1930–1960* (Princeton, 1991), pp.68–70; Rachael Low, *The History of the British Film 1929–1939: Film Making in 1930s Britain* (London, 1985), pp.249–50; and Jeffrey Richards, *The Age of the Dream Palace: Cinema and Society in Britain 1930–1939* (London, 1984), pp.264–9.

2. See Sarah Street, *Transatlantic Crossings: British Feature Films in the USA* (London, 2002), pp.22–31.

3. For details of the censorship of *Nell Gwyn*, see Anthony Slide, *'Banned in the USA': British Films in the United States and their Censorship, 1933–1960* (London, 1998), pp.107–10.

4. Low, pp.147–8.

5. *Today's Cinema*, 15 April 1937, p.2.

6. Herbert Wilcox, *Twenty-Five Thousand Sunsets: The Autobiography of Herbert Wilcox* (New York, 1967), pp.111–12.

7. Ibid., p.111.

8. Jeffrey Richards, 'The British Board of Film Censors and Content Control in the 1930s: images of Britain', *Historical Journal of Film, Radio and Television*, vol.1, no.2 (1981), p.109.

9. As usual the filming of *Victoria the Great* was reported in *Kinematograph Weekly*: 'Technicolor for Wilcox film', 1 April 1937, p.3; 'Victoria the Great', 15 April 1937, p.35; 'Anna as Queen', 22 April 1937, p.37; 'Coronation ceremony for "Victoria the Great"', 6 May 1937, p.35; 'Impressive scenes filmed for "Victoria the Great"', 13 May 1937, p.31; 'Victoria the Great', 27 May 1937, p.50; 'New Wilcox record', 3 June 1937, p.39.

10. Herbert Wilcox, 'How we made "Victoria"', *Film Weekly*, 25 December 1937, p.20.

11. Wilcox, *Twenty-Five Thousand Sunsets*, p.115.

12. Wilcox, 'How we made "Victoria"', p.20.

13. *New Yorker*, 23 October 1937.

14. *Kinematograph Weekly*, 23 September 1937, p.24.

15. *Film Weekly*, 25 September 1937, p.7

16. *Monthly Film Bulletin*, vol.4, no.45 (September 1937), p.192.

17. 'Anna Neagle – Victoria Victorious', *Picturegoer Weekly*, 18 September 1937, p.10.

18. *The Times*, 17 September 1937, p.10.

19. *Picturegoer Weekly*, 1 January 1938, p.9.

20. *Film Weekly*, 25 September 1937, pp.27–8.

21. *Monthly Film Bulletin*, vol.4, no.45 (September 1937), pp.191–2.

22. F.J.C. Hearnshaw, 'Victoria the Great', *Sight and Sound*, vol.6, no.24 (Winter 1937-38), p.205.

23. *Spectator*, 24 September 1937, p.499.

24. *New Statesman*, 25 September 1937.

25. *Daily Film Renter*, 22 December 1938, p.4.

26. John Sedgwick, *Popular Filmgoing in 1930s Britain: A Choice of Pleasures* (London, 2000), p.274.

27. Jeffrey Richards and Dorothy Sheridan (eds), *Mass-Observation at the Movies* (London, 1987), pp.32–136.

28. Leslie Halliwell, *Seats In All Parts: Half A Lifetime at the Movies* (London, 1985), p.61.

29. Wilcox, *Twenty-Five Thousand Sunsets*, p.116.

30. *New York Times*, 29 October 1937, p.19.

31. *Hollywood Spectator*, 20 November 1937, p.7.

32. *Rob Wagner's Script*, 20 November 1937, p.20.

33. See John M. MacKenzie, *Propaganda and Empire: The manipulation of British public opinion, 1880–1960* (Manchester, 1984), p.92.

34. Wilcox, 'How we made "Victoria"', p.20.

35. Wilcox, *Twenty-Five Thousand Sunsets*, p.115.

36. The heyday of historical research into the newsreels was in the 1970s, exemplified by Anthony Aldgate, *Cinema and History: British Newsreels and the Spanish Civil War* (London, 1979); Nicholas Pronay, 'British Newsreels in the 1930s: 1. Audience and Producers', *History*, vol. 56 (October 1971), pp.411–18; and Pronay, 'British Newsreels in the 1930s: 2. Their Policies and Impact', *History*, vol. 57 (February 1972), pp.63–72.

37. Richards, *The Age of the Dream Palace*, p.264.

38. Wilcox, *Twenty-Five Thousand Sunsets*, p.120.

39. *Kinematograph Weekly*, 21 April 1938, p.19.

40. *Kinematograph Weekly*, 28 April 1938, p.31.

41. The production was again reported in *Kinematograph Weekly*: '"Victoria" weds at Denham', 2 June 1938, p.25; 'Aubrey Smith watches Victorian cricket', 16 June 1938, p.29; 'Wilcox's Two Large Scale Productions', 23 June 1938, p.36; 'Wilcox concludes studio sequences', 30 June 1938, p.48; 'Wilcox to film at royal palaces', 7 July 1938, p.31; 'Wilcox shoots Braemar gathering', 28 July 1938, p.30; 'Wilcox gets permission to shoot at Osborne', 18 August 1938, p.25.

42. Wilcox, *Twenty-Five Thousand Sunsets*, p.120.

43. Ibid.

44. Michael Powell, *A Life in Movies: An Autobiography* (London, 1986), p.298. See also Sue Harper, 'A note on Basil Dean, Sir Robert Vansittart and

British Historical Films of the 1930s', *Historical Journal of Film, Radio and Television*, vol. 10, no. 1 (1990), pp.81–7.

45. *The Times*, 14 October 1938, p.2.

46. *Sunday Times*, 16 October 1938.

47. *Film Weekly*, 22 October 1938, p.27.

48. *New York Times*, 18 November 1938, p.25.

49. *Spectator*, 4 November 1938.

50. *New Statesman*, 22 October 1938.

51. *World Film News*, vol.3, no.7 (November 1938), p.295.

52. *Today's Cinema*, 14 October 1938, p.4.

53. *Observer*, 16 October 1938. Reprinted in Anthony Lejeune (ed.), *The C.A. Lejeune Film Reader* (Manchester, 1991), pp.136–40.

54. Harper, *Picturing the Past*, p.54.

55. For broadly sympathetic and critical views of Chamberlain in the late 1930s, see, respectively, John Charmley, *Chamberlain and Lost Peace* (London, 1989), and R.A.C. Parker, *Chamberlain and Appeasement: British Policy and the Coming of the Second World War* (London, 1993).

56. *Rob Wagner's Script*, 9 November 1940, p.16.

57. Harper, p.54.

58. *Daily Film Renter*, 22 December 1938, p.1.

59. Wilcox, *Twenty-Five Thousand Sunsets*, pp.122–3.

60. Anna Neagle, *There's Always Tomorrow* (London, 1974), p.115.

61. Wilcox, *Twenty-Five Thousand Sunsets*, p.125.

62. For the production and reception histories of *Forever and A Day*, see H. Mark Glancy, *When Hollywood loved Britain: The Hollywood 'British' film 1939–45* (Manchester, 1999), pp.170–80.

63. Quoted in Alan A. Coulson, 'Anna Neagle', *Films in Review*, vol.18, no.3 (March 1967), p.157.

64. PRO BT 64/4493: 'British first features released through British Lion Film Corporation Ltd. during 30 months to 30 June 1949'. This file contains documents relating to the production costs and domestic revenues of films released by British Lion (including *The Courtneys of Curzon Street* and *Spring in Park Lane*) until April 1950. Wilcox claimed in his autobiography – probably with some exaggeration – that *Spring in Park Lane* 'took £1,600,00 at the box office in this market alone, and still holds the attendance record for any British film', *Twenty-Five Thousand Sunsets*, p.202.

65. Wilcox, *Twenty-Five Thousand Sunsets*, p.168.

66. Ibid., p.193.

67. Ephraim Katz, *The Macmillan International Film Encyclopedia* (London, 1994), p.997.

68. *Films and Filming*, vol.21, no.4 (January 1975), p.39.

4. Class and Nation: *This England* (1941)

1. *This England* tends to be glossed over in histories of British cinema. See James Chapman, *The British at War: Cinema, State and Propaganda, 1939–1945*

(London, 1998), pp.233–5; Sue Harper, *Picturing the Past: The Rise and Fall of the British Costume Film* (London, 1994), pp.103–4; Robert Murphy, *Realism and Tinsel: Cinema and Society in Britain 1939–48* (London, 1989), pp.29–30; and Jeffrey Richards, 'Mobilizing the Past: *The Young Mr Pitt*', in Anthony Aldgate and Jeffrey Richards, *Britain Can Take It: The British Cinema in the Second World War* (Edinburgh, 2nd edn 1994), pp.138–40.

2. Leslie Halliwell, *Seats in All Parts: Half A Lifetime at the Movies* (London, 1985), p.93.

3. Charles Barr, 'Introduction: Amnesia and Schizophrenia', in Barr (ed.), *All Our Yesterdays: 90 Years of British Cinema* (London, 1986), p.12.

4. Anthony Aldgate, 'The British Cinema during the Second World War', in Aldgate and Richards, *Britain Can Take It*, p.3.

5. Roger Manvell, *Film* (Harmondsworth, 1946 edn), pp.133–6.

6. Ibid., p.136.

7. *Spectator*, 3 November 1939.

8. *Documentary News Letter*, vol. 2, no. 12 (December 1941), p.225.

9. Ibid., p.221.

10. Rachael Low, *The History of the British Film 1929–1939: Film Making in 1930s Britain* (London, 1985), p.211. The studio that British National bought was Rock Studios at Elstree, formerly Leslie Fuller Studios, formerly Ideal Studios. This small studio was situated close to the larger Elstree Studios owned by ABPC, which, confusingly, had once been called British National Studios.

11. Michael Powell, *A Life in Movies: An Autobiography* (London, 1986), p.340.

12. John Corfield, 'Don't Promote Films: Make Them', *Daily Film Renter*, 1 January 1940, p.7.

13. 'British History in New Corfield Film', *Today's Cinema*, 25 June 1940, p.1.

14. 'Production Record in Air Blitz', *Kinematograph Weekly*, 13 February 1941, p.1. This would have meant an average production cost of £18,750. It seems reasonable to assume that some films, such as *Gaslight* or the Leslie Howard vehicle *Pimpernel Smith* (1941), would have cost more, while others, such as *Old Mother Riley Cleans Up* (1941), would have cost less. The Board of Trade file on *Contraband* (PRO BT 64/114) reveals that British National were 'desirous of claiming Double Quota for the film' which meant that it would have to cost £40,000, though this was complicated by deferred payments to Michael Powell and Conrad Veidt which meant that it did not strictly qualify.

15. Richard Findlater, *Emlyn Williams: Theatre World Monograph No. 8* (London, 1956), p.61.

16. The quotation is from John of Gaunt's deathbed speech in *Richard II*, Act II, Scene 1; the most famous lines are 40 to 50:

> This royal throne of kings, this scepter'd isle,
> This earth of majesty, seat of Mars,
> This other Eden, demi-Paradise;
> This fortress built by Nature for herself
> Against infection and the hand of war;
> This happy breed of men, this little world;
> This precious stone set in a silver sea,
> Which serves it in the office of a wall,

Or as a moat defensive to a house,
Against the envy of less happier lands;
This blessed plot, this earth, this realm, this England.

The version recited by Clements/Rookeby in *This England* omits lines 47–49. An abbreviated version of the speech is quoted by Basil Rathbone (as Sherlock Holmes) at the end of *Sherlock Holmes and the Secret Weapon* (1942) – 'This fortress built by nature for herself...this blessed plot, this earth, this realm, this England' – in line with the Universal Pictures Sherlock Holmes series' convention of concluding on a patriotic note. The first film in the series, *Sherlock Holmes and the Voice of Terror* (1942) had used Holmes's words from 'His Last Bow' ('There's an east wind coming, Watson').

17. 'Anglo-American's Programme of Hits from British National', *Kinematograph Weekly*, 9 Januuary 1941, p.38B.

18. C.A. Lejeune, *Chestnuts in Her Lap 1936–1946* (London, 1947), p.57.

19. *Monthly Film Bulletin*, vol. 8, no. 86 (February 1941), p.14.

20. *New Statesman*, 24 May 1941.

21. *Motion Picture Herald*, 8 March 1941, p.36.

22. *New York Times*, 18 November 1941, p.33.

23. Quoted in James Harding, *Emlyn Williams: A Life* (London, 1993), p.116.

24. Harper, p.103; Richards, p.139.

25. Cecil Day-Lewis, 'The English Village', *Picture Post*, 3 January 1942, p.4.

26. Anthony Armstrong, *Village at War* (London, 1941), p.254.

27. Angus Calder, *The People's War: Britain 1939–45* (London, 1969), p.416.

28. *Time and Tide*, 31 May 1941.

29. The classic historical account of the shift to the left is Paul Addison, *The Road to 1945: British Politics and the Second World War* (London, 1975). The most recent assessment of the importance of 1940 is Malcolm Smith, *Britain and 1940: History, myth and popular memory* (London, 2000).

30. Murphy, p.30.

31. George Orwell, *The Lion and the Unicorn: Socialism and the English Genius* (Harmondsworth, 1982 edn), pp.52–4.

32. Ibid., pp.47–8.

33. J.B. Priestley, *Postscripts* (London, 1940), p.36.

34. Addison, p.17.

35. For a characteristically close reading of the film and its ideology of 'conservative populism', see Andrew Higson, *Waving the Flag: Constructing a National Cinema in Britain* (Oxford, 1995), pp.243–62.

36. For a sympathetic contextual history of the film, see Jeffrey Richards, 'The Englishman's Englishman: *Pimpernel Smith*', in Aldgate and Richards, *Britain Can Take It*, pp.43–75.

37. Quoted in David Badder, 'Powell and Pressburger: The War Years', *Sight and Sound*, vol. 48, no. 1 (Winter 1978–79), p.11.

38. See Jeffrey Richards, 'Why We Fight: *A Canterbury Tale*', in Anthony Aldgate and Jeffrey Richards, *Best of British: Cinema and Society from 1930 to the Present* (London, rev. edn 1999), pp.57–76.

5. Cry God for Larry, England and St George: *Henry V* (1944)

1. *Henry V* has been the subject of extensive critical and historical commentary, including, but not limited to: Dudley Andrew, *Film in the Aura of Art* (Princeton, 1984), pp.131–51; James Chapman, *The British at War: Cinema, State and Propaganda, 1939–1945* (London, 1998), pp.244–8; Clive Coultass, *Images for Battle: British Film and the Second World War, 1939–45* (London, 1989), pp.167–8; Harry M. Geduld, *Filmguide to Henry V* (Bloomington, 1973); Sue Harper, *Picturing the Past: The Rise and Fall of the British Costume Film* (London, 1994), pp.86–8; John G. Nichols, 'The Atomic Agincourt: *Henry V* and the Filmic Making of Postwar Anglo-American Cultural Relations', *Film and History*, vol.27, nos 1–4 (1997), pp.88–94; Peter Nichols, 'A classy tale', *Sight and Sound*, New Series, vol.1, no.6 (October 1991), p.33; Dale Silviria, *Laurence Olivier and the Art of Film Making* (London, 1985), pp.75–141; and Sarah Street, *Transatlantic Crossings: British Feature Films in the USA* (London, 2002), pp.96–106. Accounts of the making of the film can be found in John Cottrell, *Laurence Olivier* (London, 1975), pp.187–200; Roger Lewis, *The Real Life of Laurence Olivier* (London, 1996), pp.201–6; and Donald Spoto, *Laurence Olivier: A Biography* (London, 1991), pp.140–8. Critics writing about the film as a Shakespearean adaptation include Graham Holderness, *Visual Shakespeare: Essays in Film and Television* (Hertfordshire, 2002), pp.91–123; Marsha McCreadie, '*Henry V*: Onstage and On Film', *Literature/Film Quarterly*, vol.5, no.4 (1977), pp.316–21; and Michael Manheim, 'Olivier's *Henry V* and the Elizabethan World Picture', *Literature/Film Quarterly*, vol.11, no.3 (1983), pp.179–84.

2. This dedication does not appear on the version released on DVD by Carlton Video (VFA10646) in their 'Silver Collection', which is evidently a much later print (the titles include a copyright renewal notice by Rank Film Distributors dated 1978). The previous video release by Rank Home Video in the 'Rank Classic Collection' (0010) is from an original print that includes both the dedication and the credits for Eagle-Lion and Two Cities, also missing from the DVD release.

3. On the Rank Organisation, see Geoffrey Macnab, *J. Arthur Rank and the British Film Industry* (London, 1993) and Alan Wood, *Mr Rank: A Study of J. Arthur Rank and British Films* (London, 1952).

4. Rachael Low, *The History of the British Film 1929–1939: Film Making in 1930s Britain* (London, 1985), p.214.

5. Macnab, p.32.

6. Political and Economic Planning, *The British Film Industry: A report on its history and present organisation, with special reference to the economic problems of British feature film production* (London, 1952), p.81.

7. On the Palache Report, see Margaret Dickinson and Sarah Street, *Cinema and State: The Film Industry and the British Government 1927–84* (London, 1985), pp.139–49.

8. David Lean, 'Brief Encounter', *Penguin Film Review*, no. 4 (October 1947), pp.34–5.

9. On the (sometimes opposing) attitudes of the different propaganda agencies towards history, see chapter 6 of Harper, pp.77–94.

10. PRO INF 1/724: 'International Propaganda and Broadcasting Enquiry', 21 June 1939.

11. PRO INF 1/867: 'Programme for Film Propaganda', 29 January 1940.

12. Minutes of the British Film Producers Association, 13 March 1942.

13. For the production and reception histories of *The Prime Minister*, see Jeffrey Richards, *Thorold Dickinson: The Man and His Films* (London, 1986), pp.84–93.

14. 'When Britain fought Europe', *Picture Post*, 8 November 1941, p.12.

15. *Today's Cinema*, 17 June 1942, p.4.

16. Jeffrey Richards, 'Mobilizing the Past: *The Young Mr Pitt*', in Anthony Aldgate and Jeffrey Richards, *Britain Can Take It: The British Cinema in the Second World War* (Edinburgh, 2nd edn, 1994), p.151.

17. See James Chapman, '*The Life and Death of Colonel Blimp* (1943) Reconsidered', *Historical Journal of Film, Radio and Television*, vol. 15, no. 1 (March 1995), pp.19–54.

18. Laurence Olivier, *Confessions of an Actor* (London, 1987 edn), pp.130–1.

19. PRO INF 1/224: Filippo Del Giudice to Jack Beddington, 7 November 1942.

20. BL LOA (Laurence Olivier Archive) Films 3/2/1: Del Giudice to Beddington, 1 January 1943.

21. BL LOA Films 3/1: 'Synopsis of the projected film of Shakespeare's "Henry the Fifth" prepared by Alan Dent', n.d., p.1.

22. Spoto, pp.95–6.

23. Olivier, p.133. For more about Bower's role in the production of the film, see Brian McFarlane, 'Dallas Bower: The Man Behind Olivier's *Henry V*', *Shakespeare Bulletin: A Journal of Performance Criticism and Scholarship*, vol. 12, no. 1 (Winter 1994), pp.45–6.

24. BL LOA Films 3/2/1: Dallas Bower to Laurence Olivier, 28 October 1942.

25. Ibid. Contract between Laurence Olivier and Two Cities Films Ltd, 12 September 1943. A letter from Phil C. Samuel to Del Giudice (12 February 1945) reveals that, in addition to the £15,000 for not appearing in another film for 18 months, Olivier was also given an interest-free loan of £10,000 to be repaid from his share of the profits of any other films he might make for Two Cities.

26. Laurence Olivier, 'The Making of *Henry V*', *Masterworks of the British Cinema: The Lady Vanishes, Brief Encounter, Henry V* (London, 1990), pp.193–4.

27. BL LOA Films 3/1: 'Synopsis of the projected film of Shakespeare's "Henry the Fifth"', p.1.

28. While the textual changes may have enraged the Shakespearean purists, few film critics seem to have been aware of them in anything more than a very general sense. An honourable exception was Edgar Anstey, whose review in the *Spectator* (1 December 1944) was unusual for the detailed knowledge it demonstrated of the play. Interestingly, Anstey was of the view that, far from rendering the film more effective as propaganda, the omissions had the opposite effect:

> From all Shakespeare's plays *Henry V* was chosen because of its supposed topicality. The assumption was that the great mass of people, both here and overseas, would find in it some timely message relevant to the British tradition and the British spirit. What will the great mass of people in fact carry away from *Henry V*? They will first notice that it begins with the formulation of a British case for the invasion of France which is so tortuous and incomprehensible that the film's makers have felt bound to

present it in terms of comedy. But the legal justification is nevertheless used to provide a sort of Hitlerite justification for an attack upon the incompetent and effeminate French...Some of the film's omissions are curious. The scene in the play in which traitors give a perfect demonstration of a Fifth Column of the period has been omitted in spite of its topicality. And the battlefield atrocities of the day become somewhat one-sided, for although the French attack on the British camp-servants is shown, the King's order to kill the French prisoners has been omitted.

29. The wording of the dedication appears to have been suggested by Major-General Roy Urquhart, who had commanded the British 1st Airborne Division at Arnhem, and Chief of Combined Operations Major-General R.E. Laycock. Olivier reacted angrily to a suggestion that the dedication should be changed when *Henry V* was released in America, telling Rank: 'I didn't ever see Del about it, and I would not have complied with any suggestion of approaching Generals Urquhart and Laycock as I would not have liked them to feel that we felt their dedication to be inadequate or that there was any reason at all to change it' (BL LOA Films 3/4/1: Olivier to J. Arthur Rank, 7 January 1946).

30. BL LOA Films 3/1: 'Some suggested points for exploitation of "Henry V"', by Alan Dent, n.d.

31. See Vincent Porter and Chaim Litewski, '*The Way Ahead*: Case history of a propaganda film', *Sight and Sound*, vol.50, no.2 (Spring 1981), pp.110–16.

32. BL LOA Films 3/1: 'Synopsis of the projected film of Shakespeare's "Henry the Fifth"', p.3.

33. 'How Henry V was designed', *Picture Post*, 24 February 1945, p.23.

34. 'Eire location for "Henry V"', *Kinematograph Weekly*, 22 April 1943, p.35.

35. BL LOA Films 3/3: Cutting from the *Irish Press*, 29 March 1943.

36. 'Agincourt Front', *New Statesman*, 5 June 1943.

37. BL LOA Films 3/3: Éamonn de Valéra to Olivier, 29 July 1943.

38. The production of the film was reported extensively in *Kinematograph Weekly*: 'Film location sought in Eire', 8 April 1943, p.34; 'Agincourt refought in Eire', 3 June 1943, p.34; 'Camp site in Eire for "Henry V"', 1 July 1943, p.29; 'Palace sequence of "Henry V"', 19 August 1943, p.26; 'Two periods in English history', 2 September 1943, p.57; 'Medieval camp scenes reconstructed', 9 September 1943, p.21; 'British camp sequences in Two Cities' "Henry V"', 23 September 1943, p.24; 'Harfleur sequence at Denham', 30 September 1943, p.20; '"Henry V": Opening scenes filmed', 28 October 1943, p.45; 'Final "Henry V" sequences', 13 January 1944, p.25. See also C. Clayton Hutton, *The Making of Henry V* (London, 1945), for factual information about the film.

39. The 'certified cost of production' of *Henry V* was £474,888 (BL LOA Films 3/1: GFD Royalty Statement, 30 August 1947). The BFI Library microfiche on *Henry V* includes a set of notes written to accompany a screening for the Sittingbourne Film Society on 9 October 1965 which suggest the total cost was slightly higher at £475,708 and include a breakdown of costs, indicating that a great deal was spent on sets (£109,864) and wardrobe (£39,641). Actors' fees accounted for £65,124 and the Irish location expenses amounted to £50,946. The source of these figures is, however, unstated.

40. BL LOA Films 3/2/1: 'Memorandum', dated April 1946, summarising financial arrangements between Two Cities and GFD in respect of *Henry V*.

41. BL LOA Films 3/4/1: Del Giudice to Olivier, 24 October 1946.

42. BL LOA Films 3/2/1: J. Arthur Rank to Del Giudice, 6 September 1945.

43. 'I showed him the film with 40 minutes cut', Olivier said 22 years later. 'As I remember, it cut all the Pistol scenes, the Four Captains, the Four Dukes, etc. etc., in fact practically everything out of the film except the main scenes immediately relative to the central character of Henry V. After seeing it, though he knew it was going to cost him money, make distribution difficult and some releases impossible, he had to admit to me – which he did with a fairly good grace, I must say – that not only was the film quite boring now, seeing practically no other characters in it but Henry V, but it also seemed much longer', BL LOA Films 3/5: Olivier to Cecil Tennant, 18 November 1966.

44. BL LOA Films 3/3: E.T. Carr to Olivier, 24 July 1944.

45. Ibid.: Clayton Hutton to Olivier, 23 March 1945.

46. *The Times*, 23 November 1944.

47. *Manchester Guardian*, 5 September 1945.

48. *Monthly Film Bulletin*, vol.11, no.132 (December 1944), p.182.

49. J.P. Mayer, *British Cinemas and their Audiences: Sociological studies* (London, 1948), p.178.

50. Ibid., p.214.

51. 'School Interest in "Henry V"', exhibitors' campaign book for *Henry V*, BFI National Library.

52. F.W. Wilkinson, 'Henry V', *Sight and Sound*, vol.13, no.52 (Winter 1944–45), pp.85–6.

53. *Sunday Times*, 26 November 1944.

54. *Observer*, 26 November 1944.

55. Roger Manvell, *Film* (Harmondsworth, 1946 edn), p.99.

56. *News Chronicle*, 25 November 1944.

57. *New Statesman*, 2 December 1944.

58. *Evening Standard*, 25 November 1944.

59. BL LOA Films 3/3: Clayton Hutton to Olivier, 26 May 1945.

60. BL LOA Films 3/4/1: Phil C. Samuel, 11 September 1945; Maurice Cranston, 'The Pre-Fabricated Daydream', *Penguin Film Review*, no.9 (May 1949), p.30; Leslie Halliwell, *Halliwell's Hundred: A nostalgic selection of films from the golden age* (London, 1982), p.127.

61. BL LOA Films 3/2/1: GFD Royalty Statement, 30 August 1947.

62. Mayer, p.236.

63. BL LOA 3/4/1: Olivier to Del Giudice, 7 October 1946.

64. BL LOA 3/3: Olivier to Del Giudice, 6 December 1944.

65. Ibid.: 'Some Observations and Suggestions on the Exploitation of *Henry V*, arising out of the visit to Dublin', n.d.

66. John Ellis, 'The Quality Film Adventure: British Critics and the Cinema 1942–1948', in Andrew Higson (ed.), *Dissolving Views: Key Writings on British Cinema* (London, 1996), pp.66–93. This is a substantially revised version of Ellis's seminal article 'Art, Culture and Quality: Terms for a Cinema in the Forties and Seventies', *Screen*, vol. 19, no. 3 (Autumn 1978), pp.9–49.

67. BL LOA Films 3/5: F.S. Gillie to Olivier, 26 July 1946.

68. Ibid.: Olivier to George Macy, 7 February 1951.

69. Quoted in Winston S. Churchill, *The Second World War, Volume IV: The*

Hinge of Fate (London, 1985 edn), p.675.

70. Quoted in Jan G. Swynnoe, *The Best Years of British Film Music, 1936–1958* (Woodbridge, 2002), p.115.

71. BL LOA Films 3/3: Del Giudice to Olivier, 4 December 1944.

72. John W. Young, '*Henry V*, the Quai d'Orsay, and the well-being of the Franco-British Alliance, 1947', *Historical Journal of Film, Radio and Television*, vol. 7, no. 3 (1987), pp.319–21.

73. Olivier wrote to the distributor: 'I understand there is certain feeling aroused by the characters of the French King and the Dauphin, but more particularly by the attitude of the English towards the French throughout the film. These things, of course, it was almost impossible to eliminate. If, however, there are certain lines or certain small speeches which by their elimination would not damage the film, and would ease the Anglo-French situation, I would be more than happy to co-operate in every way I can', BL LOA Films 3/4/1: Olivier to Air Commodore Fred West, 2 January 1947.

74. BL LOA Films 3/1: 'Synopsis of the projected film of Shakespeare's "Henry the Fifth"', p.3.

75. BL LOA Films 3/5: E.T. Carr to Arthur W. Kelly, 24 July 1944.

76. *New York Times*, 18 July 1946, p.30.

77. *Hollywood Review*, 23 April 1946, p.1.

78. *Time*, 8 April 1946.

79. *Nation*, 20 July 1946.

80. *Variety*, 24 April 1946.

81. Street, p.99.

82. BL LOA Films 3/6: 'Notes on American release of "Henry V"', n.d.

83. Ibid.: Jerry Dale to Olivier, 19 December 1946.

84. Ibid.: Dale to Olivier, 17 March 1947.

85. The success of *Henry V* was extensively reported in both the trade and general press: '"Henry V" Opens Door to British Films in U.S.', *Kinematograph Weekly*, 20 June 1946, p.1; '"Henry V" Stuns New York', *Daily Sketch*, 19 June 1946; *Daily Film Renter*, 27 September 1948, p.1.

86. BL LOA Films 3/2/1: 'Summary of gross revenues and deductions in respect of USA', included with letter from Josef Somlo of Two Cities to Olivier's agent Cecil Tennant, 5 September 1947.

87. A long correspondence between Olivier's solicitors and John Davis of the Rank Organisation (BL LOA Films 3/2/1–3) ended with Davis agreeing to pay Olivier ten per cent of the net profits of *Henry V* (Del Giudice had promised him 20 per cent). However, Davis went to labyrinthine lengths first to show that *Henry V* had not gone into profit and then to minimise the amount payable. Olivier's solicitors felt 'there is no doubt we are being twisted' (Frederic Burgis to Tennant, 8 October 1948). For example, Davis would deduct from the profits any sundry charges that he could find, including the catering for the première and the £2,000 charitable donation made to the Airborne Commandos Fund. Davis's highly questionable accounting practices meant that by June 1957 *Henry V* showed a profit of only £100,131 19s 0d. Even then Davis was up to his usual tricks, charging £20,000 for the cost of advertising a Superscope reissue of the film in America against the monies already paid. This meant that, technically, Olivier then owed the Rank Organisation money!

88. Street, pp.106–9.

89. Quoted in John Walker (ed.), *Halliwell's Film & Video Guide* (London, 13th edn, 1999), p.349.

90. Critical commentary includes, but is not limited to, Jill Forbes, 'Henry V', *Sight and Sound*, vol.58, no.4 (Autumn 1989), pp.266–7; James Quinn and Jane Kingsley-Smith, 'Kenneth Branagh's *Henry V* (1989): Genre and interpretation', in Claire Monk and Amy Sargeant (eds), *British Historical Cinema*, pp.163–75; Michael Pursell, 'Playing the Game: Branagh's *Henry V*', *Literature/Film Quarterly*, vol.20, no.4 (1992), pp.268–75; William P. Shaw, 'Textual Ambiguities and Cinematic Certainties in *Henry V*', *Literature/Film Quarterly*, vol. 22, no. 2 (1994), pp.117–27; and 'BW', 'Branagh's *Henry V*: Allusion and Illusion', *Shakespeare on Film Newsletter*, vol. 14, no. 1 (December 1989), pp.1–10.

6. The Dunkirk Spirit: *Scott of the Antarctic* (1948)

1. See Charles Barr, *Ealing Studios* (London, 1977), pp.77–9; Sue Harper, *Picturing the Past: The Rise and Fall of the British Costume Film* (London, 1994), pp.114–15; Lawrence Kardish, 'Michael Balcon and the Idea of a National Cinema', in Geoff Brown and Lawrence Kardish, *Michael Balcon: The Pursuit of British Cinema* (New York, 1984), p.68; and Jeffrey Richards, *Films and British National Identity: From Dickens to 'Dad's Army'* (Manchester, 1997), pp.52–5.

2. Jean Quéval, 'Le chef-d'œuvre du cinéma scott', *Cahiers du Cinéma*, vol. 3, no.13 (June 1952), p.75.

3. Ken Russell, *Fire Over England: The British Cinema Comes Under Friendly Fire* (London, 1993), p.19.

4. Michael Balcon, *Michael Balcon presents... A Lifetime of Films* (London, 1969), p.120.

5. Still the definitive study of the studio and its films is Barr: see pp.39–49 for his characteristically perspicacious discussion of the Ealing 'team'.

6. Balcon, p.48.

7. Michael Balcon, 'Rationalise!', *Sight and Sound*, vol.9, no.36 (Winter 1940–41), p.62.

8. Michael Balcon, 'The British Film during the War', *Penguin Film Review*, no. 1 (August 1946), p.69.

9. See, for example, the entry on 'Ealing comedies' in Ephraim Katz, *The Macmillan International Film Encyclopedia* (London, 1994), p.401: 'A cluster of sophisticated satirical films produced in the late 40s and early 50s at England's Ealing Studios under the leadership of Sir Michael Balcon. Typically British in their irreverent, self-deprecating, understated humor, these comedies enjoyed universal success.'

10. 'Let British Films Be Ambassadors to the World', *Kinematograph Weekly*, 11 January 1945, p.163.

11. Quoted in Sue Harper, *Women in British Cinema: Mad, Bad and Dangerous to Know* (London, 2000), p.53.

12. Margaret Dickinson and Sarah Street, *Cinema and State: The Film Industry and the British Government 1927–84* (London, 1985), pp.170–7.

13. Peter King (ed.), *Scott's Last Journey* (London, 1999), pp.153–78.

14. For an account of Ponting's role as photographer for the Scott expedition, see Dennis Lynch, 'The Worst Journey in the World: Herbert G. Ponting in the Antarctic, 1910–1912', *Film History*, vol. 3, no. 4 (1989), pp.291–306.

15. Balcon, *A Lifetime of Films*, p.171.

16. BFI MEB (Michael and Aileen Balcon Collection) G/79: Balcon to Martin Lindsay, MP, 11 November 1946.

17. BFI IM (Ivor Montagu Collection) 247 contains Montagu's research notes and his preliminary outline (written by hand on the back of a typescript about elections in Soviet Russia!).

18. Ibid.: Sidney Cole to Montagu, 8 November 1947.

19. A full account of the making of the film can be found in David James, *Scott of the Antarctic: The Film and its Production* (London, 1948). James, who joined the Royal Navy Volunteer Reserve in 1939, had been involved in the evacuation of Dunkirk, as, too, had Scott's son, Peter. See also the four-page typescript 'The Story Behind "Scott of the Antarctic"' on the BFI microfiche for the film, and Sir Michael Balcon, 'The Technical Problems of "Scott of the Antarctic"', *Sight and Sound*, vol. 17, no. 68 (Winter 1948–49), pp.153–5.

20. PRO BT 64/4491: 'Revenues and production costs of Ealing features to March, 1950'.

21. BFI MEB G/79: Balcon to John Mills, 22 October 1947.

22. James, p.14.

23. Ibid., p.107.

24. BFI IM 252: John Mills to Sidney Cole, 17 May 1948.

25. John Mills, *Up in the Clouds, Gentlemen Please* (London, 1980), pp.205–6.

26. Balcon, *A Lifetime of Films*, p.172.

27. BFI MEB G/80: Frank Debenham to Balcon, 30 November 1948.

28. Ibid.: Balcon to Debenham, 2 December 1948.

29. BFI BBFC Scenario Reports 1946–47, 81a, 15 August 1947 (MK).

30. BFI MEB G/80: Sir Henry French to Balcon, 18 October 1948.

31. Ibid.: J. Arthur Rank to Balcon, 5 December 1948.

32. Undated letter from the Rev. B. Gregory and the Rev. Canon R.E. Parsons, honorary secretaries of the Christian Cinema and Religious Film Society, on the BFI microfiche for *Scott of the Antarctic*.

33. *News of the World*, 2 January 1949.

34. *Daily Graphic*, 30 November 1948.

35. *Sunday Dispatch*, 5 December 1948.

36. *Sunday Times*, 5 December 1948.

37. *The Times*, 30 November 1948; 3 January 1949.

38. *Daily Worker*, 4 December 1948.

39. 'Reticent Epic', *Observer*, 5 December 1948.

40. 'In Memoriam', *Tribune*, 10 December 1948.

41. *Daily Telegraph*, 6 December 1948.

42. *Sunday Graphic*, 5 December 1948.

43. *Evening Standard*, 2 December 1948.

44. *Monthly Film Bulletin*, vol.16, no.181 (January 1949), p.4

45. Arthur Vesselo, 'The Quarter in Britain', *Sight and Sound*, vol.18, no.69 (Spring 1949), p.49.

46. Roger Manvell, 'Scott of the Antarctic', *Chichester Quarterly* (Spring 1949), p.12.

47. *Kinematograph Weekly*, 15 December 1949, p.13. The figure of £214,223 is from 'Revenues and production costs of Ealing features to March, 1950' (PRO BT 64/4491).

48. Balcon, p.174.

49. *New York Times*, 26 February 1951, p.20.

50. BFI MEB 81: Montagu to Balcon, 22 September 1949.

51. BFI IM 252: Notes on viewing 'Scott' by Walter Meade, 29 July 1948.

52. For an analysis of the music, see Richards, pp.312–19, and Jan G. Swynnoe, *The Best Years of British Film Music, 1936–1958* (Woodbridge, 2002), pp.175–6.

53. Barr, p.78.

54. Andrew Spicer, *Typical Men: The Representation of Masculinity in Popular British Cinema* (London, 2001), p.34.

55. Kenneth More, *More or Less* (London, 1979), p.132.

56. BFI IM 249: Final White Script, 28 November 1947.

57. BFI IM 252: Notes on viewing 'Scott' by Walter Meade, 29 July 1948.

58. Harper, *Picturing the Past*, p.115.

59. Barr, p.78.

60. J.B. Priestley, *Postscripts* (London, 1940), p.2.

61. Sue Harper and Vincent Porter, *British Cinema of the 1950s: The Decline of Deference* (Oxford, 2003), p.71.

62. Ibid., p.70.

63. Barr, p.179.

64. William Whitebait, 'Bombardment', *New Statesman*, 5 April 1958, p.432.

65. Barr, p.7.

7. Hollywood's England: *Beau Brummell* (1954)

1. There is precious little secondary source material on *Beau Brummell* beyond Sue Harper and Vincent Porter, *British Cinema of the 1950s: The Decline of Deference* (Oxford, 2003), pp.119–20, and Marcia Landy, *British Genres: Cinema and Society, 1930–1960* (Princeton, 1991), pp.92–4.

2. Linda Wood (ed.), *British Film Industry* (London, 1980), Leaflet A, n.p.

3. Leslie Halliwell, *Seats in All Parts: Half a Lifetime at the Movies* (London, 1985), p.130.

4. Arthur Marwick, *British Society Since 1945* (Harmondsworth, 3rd edn 1996), p.117.

5. Harper and Porter, p.114.

6. See H. Mark Glancy, 'Hollywood and Britain: MGM and the British "Quota" Legislation', in Jeffrey Richards (ed.), *The Unknown 1930s: An Alternative History of the British Cinema, 1929–1939* (London, 1998), pp.57–72.

7. *Kinematograph Weekly*, 30 December 1954, p.6.

8. Sue Harper, 'Bonnie Prince Charlie Revisited: British Costume Film in the 1950s', in Robert Murphy (ed.), *The British Cinema Book* (London, 2nd edn 2001), pp.127–36.

9. Jeffrey Richards, *Films and British National Identity: From Dickens to 'Dad's Army'* (Manchester, 1997), p.170.

10. James Morgan, 'Coronatiana USA', *Sight and Sound*, vol.23, no.1 (Summer 1953), p.43; 'With an Eye to the Coronation', *Theatre Arts*, vol. 37, no. 7 (July 1953), p.88.

11. The figure of $3 million is quoted in *Time*, 18 October 1954, and other contemporary reviews. A lower cost of $1,762,000 is cited in the Eddie Mannix Ledger, held by the Margaret Herrick Library at the Academy of Motion Picture Arts and Sciences, which records the costs and grosses of all MGM productions. However, the ledger also includes an additional figure of $1,050,000 in the cost column, which would bring the total to $2,812,000. See the table in Harper and Porter, p.119.

12. *Motion Picture Herald*, 9 October 1954, p.18.

13. *New York Times*, 21 October 1954, p.31.

14. *Today's Cinema*, 16 November 1954, Royal Film Supplement, p.3.

15. 'Royal Occasion', *Observer*, 21 November 1954.

16. *New Statesman*, 20 November 1954.

17. 'Buttons & Beaus', *Financial Times*, 22 November 1954.

18. '"Bore Brummell" is a better title', *Daily Mail*, 16 November 1954.

19. 'History Through a Yankee Lens', *Daily Worker*, 16 November 1954.

20. 'This is a very dull story to tell before the Queen', *News Chronicle*, 16 November 1954.

21. *Time and Tide*, 17 November 1954.

22. 'Dipping in English History', *Manchester Guardian*, 16 November 1954.

23. 'Was Beau Stewart such a good companion?', *Evening Standard*, 16 November 1954.

24. 'Beau Bloomer', *Daily Express*, 16 November 1954.

25. 'Decline & Fall', *Sunday Times*, 21 November 1954.

26. 'Bore Brummell', *Daily Mail*, 16 November 1954

27. *Kinematograph Weekly*, 30 September 1954, p.5.

28. *Daily Telegraph*, 17 November 1954.

29. See Andrew Spicer, 'Fit for a King? The Royal Film Performance', *Journal of British Cinema and Television*, vol. 2, no. 2 (forthcoming). I am grateful to Dr Spicer for showing me a copy of this article, originally written for the *Journal of Popular British Cinema*, in advance of publication.

30. 'Royal Occasion', *Observer*, 21 November 1954

31. *Time*, 18 October 1954.

32. Harper, p.131.

33. Ibid.

34. See the British press book for *Beau Brummell*, BFI National Library.

35. Harper and Porter, p.119.

36. The four Miss Marple films, all directed by George Pollock, were *Murder She Said* (1961), *Murder at the Gallop* (1963), *Murder Most Foul* (1964) and *Murder Ahoy* (1964).

8. Nearer, My God, To Thee: *A Night to Remember* (1958)

1. See Jeffrey Richards, *A Night to Remember: The Definitive Titanic Film* (London, 2003), for a comprehensive account of the production and reception histories of the film. Other secondary sources include articles by Richard Howells, 'Atlantic Crossings: Nation, Class and Identity in *Titanic* (1953) and *A Night to Remember* (1958)', *Historical Journal of Film, Radio and Television*, vol. 19, no. 4 (October 1999), pp.421–38; and Howard Maxford, 'Call Sheet: *A Night to Remember*', *Film Review*, no.592 (April 2000), pp.74–9. The cultural history/cultural studies interest in the *Titanic*, stimulated by James Cameron's 1997 film, is exemplified by Tim Bergfelder and Sarah Street (eds), *The Titanic in Myth and Memory: Representations in Visual and Literary Culture* (London, 2004).

2. Raymond Durgnat, *A Mirror for England: British Movies from Austerity to Affluence* (London, 1970), p.150.

3. John Hill, *Sex, Class and Realism: British Cinema 1956–1963* (London, 1986), p.38.

4. Michael Powell paints an amusing picture of 'the bourgeois tantrums of John Davis' in *Million Dollar Movie* (London, 1992), p.11. For a generally sympathetic account of Davis, see Charles Drazin, *The Finest Years: British Cinema of the 1940s* (London, 1998), pp.43–55.

5. Vincent Porter, 'Methodism versus the Market-Place: The Rank Organisation and British Cinema', in Robert Murphy (ed.), *The British Cinema Book* (London, 2nd edn 2001), p.89.

6. For a detailed history of the Rank Organisation and its production strategies during the 1950s, see Sue Harper and Vincent Porter, *British Cinema of the 1950s: The Decline of Deference* (Oxford, 2003), pp.35–56.

7. William MacQuitty, *A Life to Remember* (London, 1991), pp.5–6.

8. *Daily Film Renter*, 29 November 1956, p.4.

9. See Andrew Higson, 'Polyglot Films for an International Market: E.A. Dupont, the British Film Industry, and the Idea of a European Cinema, 1926–1930', in Andrew Higson and Richard Maltby (eds), *'Film Europe' and 'Film America': Cinema, Commerce and Cultural Exchange 1920–1939* (Exeter, 1999), pp.274–301.

10. See Robert Peck, 'The Banning of *Titanic* (1943): A Study in British Post-war Censorship in Germany', *Historical Journal of Film, Radio and Television*, vol.20, no.3 (August 2000), pp.122–32.

11. See Howells, 'Atlantic Crossings', pp.421–38.

12. Drazin, p.53.

13. *Kinematograph Weekly*, 15 December 1955, p.4.

14. Quoted in Harper and Porter, p.52.

15. *Kinematograph Weekly*, 18 December 1958, p.6. MacQuitty claimed that *A Night to Remember* was sold as a package of ten films and that Rank offset profits against the other films in the package. See Richards, p.98.

16. Roy Ward Baker, *The Director's Cut: A Memoir of 60 Years in Film and Television* (London, 2000), p.95.

17. Ephraim Katz, *The Macmillan International Film Encyclopedia* (London, 1994), p.76.

18. 'British Feature Directors: An Index to their Work', *Sight and Sound*, vol. 27, no. 4 (Autumn 1958), p.290. See also the generally dismissive entry – 'English mainstream, 50s vintage, which is to say that … he's made a couple of films that are worth seeing but by and large it's a case of the soft pedal and the muffled impact' – in *Film Dope*, no.2 (March 1973), p.29. For a critical reassessment of Baker's career, see Peter Hutchings, 'Authorship and British Cinema: The case of Roy Ward Baker', in Justine Ashby and Andrew Higson (eds), *British Cinema, Past and Present* (London, 2000), pp.179–89.

19. Richards, p.41.

20. Baker, p.94. On Baker's approach to film-making, see his article 'Discovering Where the Truth Lies', *Films and Filming*, vol. 7, no. 8 (May 1961), p.17.

21. Richards, p.77.

22. BFI S190 *A Night to Remember*: Shooting Script, August 1957. There was one significant error of fact in the shooting script: Herbert Lightoller's wife calls him 'Charlie'.

23. Baker, p.100; MacQuitty, pp.323–4.

24. Baker, p.100.

25. For a discussion of the competing claims of 'Autumn' and 'Nearer, My God, To Thee' – and, moreover, the different versions of the hymns – see Richards, pp.116–21.

26. Ibid., pp.28–58. See also the documentary featurette 'The Making of *A Night to Remember*' on the Carlton 'Rank Collection' DVD (VFC05996).

27. Baker, p.95.

28. Kenneth More, *More or Less* (London, 1979), p.173.

29. 'Stiff upper lip went down with the Titanic', *Reynolds News*, 6 July 1958.

30. 'I salute a film to remember', *News of the World*, 6 July 1958.

31. 'Tragedy at Sea', *The Times*, 2 July 1958.

32. 'A Night that Shook the World', *Daily Telegraph*, 5 July 1958.

33. 'What happened when the Titanic went down', *Manchester Guardian*, 5 July 1968.

34. 'The Cruel Sea', *Observer*, 6 July 1958.

35. 'Remembering the Titanic', *Sunday Times*, 6 July 1958.

36. *Financial Times*, 7 July 1968.

37. *New Statesman*, 12 July 1958.

38. 'The Titanic won't keep British films off the rocks', *Tribune*, 11 July 1958.

39. *Films and Filming*, vol. 4, no. 11 (August 1958), p.26.

40. *Monthly Film Bulletin*, vol. 25, no. 295 (August 1958), p.100.

41. *Film Daily*, 17 December 1958, p.6.

42. *Motion Picture Herald*, 20 December 1958, p.92.

43. *Saturday Review*, 18 December 1958.

44. *Saturday Review*, 20 September 1958.

45. Richards, p.27.

46. Ibid., p.74.

47. On the *Titanic* and the code of chivalry, see Mark Girouard, *The Return to Camelot: Chivalry and the English Gentleman* (New Haven, CT, 1981), pp.4–7.

48. Lindsay Anderson, 'Get Out and Push!', in Tom Maschler (ed.), *Declaration* (London, 1957), p.157.

49. Baker, p.104.

50. Harper and Porter, p.55.

9. Men of Harlech: *Zulu* (1964)

1. *Zulu* barely rates a mention in the standard histories of British cinema such as Armes and Street, and receives only scant attention even from Raymond Durgnat, *A Mirror for England: British Movies from Austerity to Affluence* (London, 1970), p.82. For contested readings of the film see Christopher Sharrett, '*Zulu*, or the Limits of Liberalism', *Cineaste*, vol. 25, no. 4 (2000), pp.28–33, and the ensuing correspondence in *Cineaste*, vol. 26, no. 2 (2001), pp.59–61. For a considered and nuanced assessment of the critical positions on the film, see Sheldon Hall, 'Monkey feathers: Defending *Zulu* (1964)', in Claire Monk and Amy Sargeant (eds), *British Historical Cinema* (London, 2002), pp.110–28. For an exhaustive production history, see Sheldon Hall, *Zulu: With Some Guts Behind It – The Making of the Epic Movie* (Sheffield, forthcoming).

2. Jeffrey Richards, *Films and British National Identity: From Dickens to 'Dad's Army'* (Manchester, 1997), p.147.

3. See Alexander Walker, *Hollywood, England: The British Film Industry in the Sixties* (London, 1974), *passim*.

4. *Kinematograph Weekly*, 19 December 1963, p.5.

5. *Kinematograph Weekly*, 17 December 1964, p.8.

6. This article, 'Slaughter in the Sun', was published under the pseudonym 'John Curtis' in *Lilliput* (April 1958), pp.56–60, 77. I am indebted to Dr Sheldon Hall for providing both the full reference to this article and a copy of Prebble's original text, which was substantially edited before publication. Interestingly, several of the deleted passages were used as episodes in the film, including the over-turning of the wagons and the company sergeants intoning 'Look to your front…Mark the orders…Mark your target when it comes.'

7. *Daily Cinema*, 5 November 1962, p.9.

8. Letter from Levine to Baker and Endfield, 24 July 1963, published in *Kinematograph Weekly*, 1 August 1963, p.12. The publication of a letter such as this, clearly written for consumption within the trade, can be seen as part of the publicity discourse to promote the film. Thus it begins: 'The shooting is over – the shouting begins! And there is so much to shout about, thanks to you.'

9. $3.5 million was the amount stated by Baker in the *Motion Picture Herald*, 18 September 1963, p.9. Sheldon Hall suggests that this figure was inflated for publicity purposes and marshals evidence that the direct cost of *Zulu* was $1.75 million. See Hall, *Zulu: With Some Guts Behind It*. The Levine quotation is from his published letter in *Kinematograph Weekly*, 1 August 1963, p.12.

10. Walker, pp.186 and 135; Clive Hirschhorn, *The Columbia Story* (London, 1989), p.248.

11. On Baker's career and screen image, see David Berry, *Wales and Cinema: The First Hundred Years* (Cardiff, 1994), pp.259–68; Andrew Spicer, *Typical Men: The Representation of Masculinity in Popular British Cinema* (London, 2001), pp.72–5; and Peter Stead, *Acting Wales: Stars of Stage and Screen* (Cardiff, 2002), pp.60–9.

12. 'The Story Behind *Zulu*', *Zulu* press book, BFI Library. In fact *Zulu* exaggerates the number of Welsh soldiers at Rorke's Drift.

13. Wayne Drew, 'Views of the Valleys: Images of Welsh Culture and History', NFT programme notes (17 March 1985) on the BFI microfiche for *Zulu*.

14. On Endfield's short Hollywood career, see Brian Neve, *Film and Politics in America: A Social Tradition* (London, 1992), pp.176–81. On HUAC and the blacklist, see Larry Ceplair and Steven Englund, *The Inquisition in Hollywood: Politics in the Film Community, 1930–60* (Urbana, IL, 2003 edn), pp.254–97.

15. For contemporary accounts of the production, see: '"Zulu" safari makes camp at Twickenham', *Kinematograph Weekly*, 18 July 1963, p.12; Stanley Baker, 'Meeting the Challenge of Producing an Epic As a First Picture', *Motion Picture Herald*, 18 September 1963, pp.9–11; 'Zulu', *ABC Film Review*, vol.14, no.4 (April 1964), pp.16–17; and the three-page typescript entitled 'Production Notes' on the BFI microfiche for *Zulu*. Secondary accounts can be found in Berry, *Wales and Cinema*, pp.266–7, and George Smith, 'Behind the Scenes: *Zulu*', *Movie Collector*, no.4 (March 1994), pp.11–15. See also the two-part documentary *The Making of Zulu*, featuring interviews with surviving members of cast and crew and with Baker's widow Ellen, Lady Baker, on the *Zulu* 'Special Edition' DVD (Paramount Pictures EN 103088).

16. *Motion Picture Herald*, 25 May 1964, pp.15–16.

17. *The Longest Day*, however, was made in black-and-white, a deliberate choice by producer Darryl F. Zanuck to emulate the realism associated with Second World War documentary film.

18. Hall, 'Monkey feathers', p.117.

19. Steve Neale, *Genre and Hollywood* (London, 2000), p.85.

20. Hall, p.113.

21. Ibid., p.117.

22. 'Imperialists', *Sunday Telegraph*, 26 January 1964.

23. *Kinematograph Weekly*, 23 January 1964, p.10.

24. *Variety*, 29 January 1964.

25. 'I'd like to give "Zulu" a VC of its own', *Evening News*, 23 January 1964.

26. 'A Savage Tale of Errol Flynnery', *Daily Mail*, 21 January 1964.

27. 'Documentary Saga', *Financial Times*, 24 January 1964.

28. *Films and Filming*, vol. 10, no. 5 (February 1964), p.30.

29. *Monthly Film Bulletin*, vol. 36, no. 361 (February 1964), pp.23–4.

30. *Spectator*, 31 January 1964.

31. *Observer*, 26 January 1964.

32. 'African Antics', *Daily Telegraph*, 24 January 1964.

33. 'A lovely war!', *Daily Worker*, 25 January 1964.

34. *Hollywood Reporter*, 3 February 1964, p.3.

35. *New York Times*, 8 July 1964, p.38.

36. Eighteen years later the *New York Times*, reviewing *Zulu Dawn*, attested that *Zulu* was 'a movie that presented white British troops slaughtering such staggering numbers of Africans that trouble sometimes broke out in theaters in which *Zulu* was shown' (11 July 1982, p.39).

37. Durgnat, p.82.

38. Jim Pines, 'Images of Empire: Colonial Surveillance', NFT programme notes (7 June 1986), on the BFI microfiche for *Zulu*.

39. Sharrett, p.29.

40. Ibid., p.31.

41. For a detailed history of the battle itself, see Ian Knight, *Nothing Remains But to Fight: The Defence of Rorke's Drift* (London, 1993).

42. Bromhead's great-nephew Sir Benjamin Bromhead complained that it 'is a pity that some of his [Prebble's] facts were not more carefully checked' and attested that at the time of Rorke's Drift his great-uncle 'was a man of 35, a mature man, unlike in character to the foppish youth shown in the film' (*Daily Telegraph*, 28 February 1964). James Booth mentions the complaints from Henry Hook's family in *The Making of Zulu*. The character whom *Zulu* most misrepresents is Commissary Dalton, who is portrayed in the film as a rather wimpish character but who has since been claimed as the 'real hero' of Rorke's Drift for persuading Chard and Bromhead to stay when they were prepared to leave the post. The reputations of Chard and Bromhead were challenged in the television documentary *Zulu: The True Story* (BBC2, 24 October 2003). See also Charlotte Edwardes, 'Wrong men given VCs at Rorke's Drift', *Sunday Telegraph*, 19 October 2003, p.16.

43. Sharrett, pp.29–30.

44. 'Men of Harlech' commemorates the defence of Harlech Castle (Gwynedd) in 1468 against the Earl of Pembroke. The music was first published in 1784; there are different versions of the lyrics, the most common English versions being by W.H. Baker (1860) and John Oxenford (1873), as well as in Welsh by 'Talhaiarn' and a German version by Heinrich Möller. The version sung in *Zulu* is peculiar to the film: 'Men of Harlech, stop your dreaming/Can't you see their spear points gleaming/See their warrior pennants streaming/To this battle field. Men of Harlech stand ye steady/It can not be ever said ye/For the battle were not ready/Welshmen never yield. From the hills rebounding/Hear their cry resounding/Summon all at Cambria's call/The mighty foe surrounding. Men of Harlech on to glory/This will ever be your story/Keep these burning words before ye/Welshmen will not yield.' One of the delightful quirks of the scene is that all the men know these non-standard lyrics and join in.

45. BFI S11701: *Zulu (The Battle of Rorke's Drift)*: Screenplay by John Prebble and Cy Endfield, Final Shooting Script, 25 February 1963.

46. For example, Nina Hibbin: 'The one point that is never even hinted at is that the land belonged to the Zulus and the British had no business to be there at all' (*Daily Worker*, 25 January 1964). And on the occasion of one of its frequent Christmas television screenings, one reviewer stated: 'In outline, this is traditional *Boy's Own* stuff, and the way the film concentrates on the tactics of attack and defence – convincingly and excitingly, as it happens – seems to be evading the issue of why the troops are there in the first place' (*Listener*, 20–27 December 1984, p.70).

47. The opening of the film contains a curious discrepancy in the date. An opening caption gives the date as 23 January 1879, whereas both Burton's narration and the dispatch (shown on screen as the camera moves in to a close up of the word 'ISANDHLWANA') state the battle as having occurred (correctly) on the morning of 22 January. To further confuse the matter, the date on the dispatch itself is 11 February 1879. Before reading the dispatch, Burton intones: 'The Secretary of State for War *has today* received the following

dispatch from Lord Chelmsford, Commander-in-Chief of Her Majesty's Forces in Natal Colony, South Africa' (my emphasis). It is unclear whether 'today' is meant to be 23 January as per the caption or 11 February as per the date on the document.

48. For an overview of these and other films see Jeffrey Richards, 'Imperial heroes for a post-imperial age: films and the end of empire', in Stuart Ward (ed.), *British Culture and the End of Empire* (Manchester, 2001), pp.128–44. For a case study of *North West Frontier*, see Steve Chibnall, *J. Lee Thompson* (Manchester, 2000), pp.203–27.

49. Sharrett, p.32.

50. Alexander Walker, for example, felt that Green's 'paternal colour-sergeant is right in character *and period*' (*Evening Standard*, 23 January 1964), while Ann Pacey wrote that his 'mutton-chop whiskers, bright blue eyes and tough but understanding attitude seem so absolutely right that one feels he has stepped out of the history books' (*Daily Herald*, 24 January 1964). Quigly averred that 'Stanley Baker, Michael Caine and (especially) Nigel Green are nicely in mood and period' (*Spectator*, 31 January 1964).

51. Sharrett, p.33.

52. See Edmund J. Yorke, 'Cultural myths and realities: the British Army, war and Empire as portrayed on film, 1900–90', in Ian Stewart and Susan L. Carruthers (eds), *War, Culture and the Media: Representations of the Military in 20th Century Britain* (Trowbridge, 1996), pp.91–100.

53. Nicholas J. Cull, 'Peter Watkins' *Culloden* and the alternative form in historical filmmaking', *Film International*, no.1 (2003), pp.48–53.

54. Ibid., p.51.

55. Robert A. Rosenstone, 'Introduction', in Rosenstone (ed.), *Revisioning History: Film and the Construction of a New Past* (Princeton, 1995), p.8.

56. Ibid., p.12.

57. *Monthly Film Bulletin*, vol.46, no.551 (December 1979), p.257.

58. *New York Times*, 11 July 1982, p.39.

59. Trevor Willsmer, 'Zulu' (video review), *Movie Collector*, no.4 (March 1994), p.31.

60. Stead, p.68.

10. Decline and Fall: *The Charge of the Light Brigade* (1968)

1. The most detailed account of the film is to be found in Mark Connelly, *The Charge of the Light Brigade* (London, 2003). For an astute contemporary commentary on the film, see John Craddock, '*The Charge of the Light Brigade* in perspective', *Film Society Review*, vol. 4, no. 7 (March 1969), pp.15–34. Tony Richardson's own account of the filming can be found in *Long Distance Runner: A Memoir* (London, 1993), pp.193–201.

2. 'The Man Behind an Angry Young Man', *Films and Filming*, vol. 5, no. 5 (February 1959), p.9.

3. Robert Murphy, *Sixties British Cinema* (London, 1992), p.16. The arch-auteurist Andrew Sarris similarly felt that 'Richardson's direction lacks any

genuinely unifying force or conviction', *The American Cinema: Directors and Directions 1929–1968* (New York, 1996 edn), p.199.

4. Penelope Houston, *The Contemporary Cinema* (Harmondsworth, 1963), p.121. For an account of Richardson's critical reputation at the end of the 1960s, see George Lellis, 'Recent Richardson – Cashing the Blank Cheque', *Sight and Sound*, vol. 38, no. 3 (Summer 1969), pp.130–3.

5. Quoted in Murphy, p.28.

6. Michael Balcon, *Michael Balcon presents...A Lifetime of Films* (London, 1969), p.198.

7. Alexander Walker, *Hollywood, England: The British Film Industry in the Sixties* (London, 1974), p.475.

8. *Variety*, 13 April 1964.

9. Duncan Petrie, *The British Cinematographer* (London, 1996), p.119.

10. Tony Richardson, *Long Distance Runner: A Memoir* (London, 1993), pp.165–6.

11. George Orwell, *The Lion and the Unicorn: Socialism and the English Genius* (Harmondsworth, 1982 edn), p.42.

12. 'Tony Richardson warns his unit against epic-itus', press release by Matthew West Associates Ltd, 16 May 1967, on the BFI microfiche for *The Charge of the Light Brigade*, p.2.

13. *Daily Sketch*, 25 August 1965.

14. Richardson, p.194.

15. BFI S8575: *The Charge of the Light Brigade*: Screenplay by John Osborne, 14 October 1965, revised 16 November 1965. Richardson's memorandum, dated 18 November 1966, is attached inside the front cover.

16. This sequence evidently was shot, as there are production stills of Trevor Howard as Cardigan surrounded by Russian horsemen with their lances pointing at him. This was also the scene for which Laurence Harvey filmed his cameo as Prince Radziwill that was cut from the film (see note 21 below).

17. *Guardian*, 22 February 1967.

18. *Daily Telegraph*, 21 March 1967.

19. Richardson, p.194.

20. Ibid., p.195.

21. David Lewin, 'The most expensive face on the cutting room floor', *Daily Mail*, 17 December 1967.

22. Charles Wood, 'Into the Valley', *Sight and Sound*, New Series, vol. 2, no. 1 (May 1992), p.26.

23. BFI S7043: *The Charge of the Light Brigade*: Screenplay by Charles Wood, 3 March 1967.

24. The location filming was widely reported in the press: David Lewin, 'The Farce of the Light Brigade', *Daily Mail*, 27 June 1967; 'The Shooting Begins at Balaclava', *Observer Magazine*, 30 June 1967; *Morning Star*, 19 August 1967. The BFI microfiche for the film contains two press releases: 'Tony Richardson warns his unit against epic-itus', 16 May 1967, and 'Filming completed on Woodfall's "The Charge of the Light Brigade"', 15 September 1967.

25. *The Times*, 9 April 1968.

26. 'Film director "bans" the critics', *Sun*, 9 April 1968.

27. *The Times*, 13 April 1968.

28. 'Ban on critics for Royal film show', *Evening News*, 8 April 1968.

29. Connelly, p.60.

30. 'Mostly history', *Sunday Times*, 14 April 1968.

31. 'Their glory fades', *Sunday Telegraph*, 14 April 1968.

32. *Observer*, 28 April 1968.

33. 'Into the valley of death', *Evening Standard*, 11 April 1968.

34. 'Anti-heroic epic of that heroic Charge', *Morning Star*, 13 April 1968.

35. '"Light Brigade" as a social disaster', *Daily Telegraph*, 13 April 1968.

36. 'Loose Rein', *New Statesman*, 19 April 1968.

37. 'Slight brigade', *Spectator*, 19 April 1968.

38. *Monthly Film Bulletin*, vol.35, no.414 (July 1968), pp.98–9.

39. *Films and Filming*, vol.14, no.9 (June 1968), p.18.

40. *Films and Filming*, vol.14, no.11 (August 1968), pp.57–8.

41. 'Into the Valley Again', *Saturday Review*, 12 October 1968.

42. *New York Times*, 7 October 1968, p.59.

43. 'The Reason Why', *Time*, 11 October 1968.

44. *Variety*, 17 April 1968.

45. Letter from John Terraine, 'Forgotten charge', *Sunday Telegraph*, 21 April 1968.

46. Letter from D.S. McGuffie, 'CND-ish', *Listener*, 9 May 1968.

47. Dan Wakefield, 'Cartoon Empires', *Atlantic Monthly*, January 1969, p.116.

48. Petrie, p.151.

49. 'The Talents of a Showman', *Listener*, 18 April 1968.

50. Connelly, p.61.

51. Arthur Marwick, *The Sixties: Cultural Revolution in Britain, France, Italy and the United States c.1958–c.1974* (Oxford, 1998), p.17.

52. 'Anti-heroic epic of that heroic Charge', *Morning Star*, 13 April 1968

53. Andy Medhurst, 'War Games', *Sight and Sound*, New Series, vol. 2, no. 1 (May 1992), p.28.

54. Wood, p.26.

55. Neil Sinyard, *The Films of Richard Lester* (London, 1985), p.49.

56. On *Oh! What A Lovely War*, see Alan Burton, 'Death or glory? The Great War in British film', in Claire Monk and Amy Sargeant (eds), *British Historical Cinema* (London, 2002), pp.38–9, and Michael Paris, 'Enduring Heroes: British Feature Films and the First World War, 1919–1997', in Paris (ed.), *The First World War and Popular Cinema: 1914 to the Present* (Edinburgh, 1999), pp.67–8.

57. Connelly, p.65.

58. Murphy, p.274.

59. Walker, p.443.

60. Connelly, p.79.

11. The Conscience of the King: *Henry VIII and His Six Wives* (1972)

1. There is scant commentary on this film, or indeed on any of the royal biopics of the early 1970s. The only passing reference I have come across is in

Sheldon Hall, 'The Wrong Sort of Cinema: Refashioning the Heritage Film Debate', in Robert Murphy (ed.), *The British Cinema Book* (London, 2nd edn, 2001), pp.193–4.

2. Alexander Walker, *National Heroes: British Cinema in the Seventies and Eighties* (London, 1985), p.135; Sue Harper, *Women in British Cinema: Mad, Bad and Dangerous to Know* (London, 2000), p.127. The 1970s is probably British cinema's least researched decade, the only secondary sources of note being Walker, *National Heroes*, and Andrew Higson, 'A diversity of film practices: renewing British cinema in the 1970s', in Bart Moore-Gilbert (ed.), *Cultural Closure? The Arts in the 1970s* (London, 1994), pp.216–39.

3. Margaret Dickinson and Sarah Street, *Cinema and State: The Film Industry and the British Government 1927–84* (London, 1985), p.240.

4. Ibid., p.241.

5. *CinemaTV Today*, 15 July 1972, p.2.

6. Asa Briggs, *The History of Broadcasting in the United Kingdom. Volume V: Competition 1955–1974* (Oxford, 1995), p.937.

7. *Variety*, 4 August 1971.

8. *Guardian*, 2 January 1970.

9. *Observer*, 11 January 1970.

10. *Morning Star*, 3 January 1970.

11. 'Our national theatre – for real', *Daily Mirror*, 4 February 1970.

12. BFI S7354: *Henry VIII Project* (title amended to 'Henry VIII and His Six Wives'). Shooting script by Ian Thorne, September 1971.

13. *Today's Cinema*, 27 October 1971, p.9.

14. Quoted in typescript press release on the BFI microfiche for *Henry VIII and His Six Wives*. The production of the film was reported in *Today's Cinema*, 12 October 1971, p.2, and *CinemaTV Today*, 20 November 1971, pp.10–11.

15. *Financial Times*, 14 July 1972.

16. *The Times*, 14 July 1972.

17. *Daily Telegraph*, 17 July 1972.

18. 'Hal in a rush', *Observer*, 16 July 1972.

19. *Morning Star*, 14 July 1972.

20. *Daily Express*, 12 July 1972.

21. *Sunday Times*, 16 July 1972.

22. *Films and Filming*, vol. 19, no. 1 (October 1972), p.51.

23. *Monthly Film Bulletin*, vol. 39, no. 462 (July 1972), p.140.

24. *CinemaTV Today*, 8 July 1972, p.22.

25. *CinemaTV Today*, 16 September 1972, p.2.

26. *CinemaTV Today*, 30 December 1972, p.1.

27. *CinemaTV Today*, 22 July 1972, p.2; *CinemaTV Today*, 2 September 1972, p.2.

28. *CinemaTV Today*, 29 April 1972, p.2; *CinemaTV Today*, 23 September 1972 p.2 .

29. *CinemaTV Today*, 16 September 1972, p.3.

30. *Hollywood Reporter*, 19 March 1974, p.3.

31. *New York Times*, 14 December 1972, p.57.

32. *Guardian*, 2 January 1970 (Nancy Banks-Smith).

33. Cecil Wilson, 'It's Queen Glenda…by a head', *Daily Mail*, 28 March 1972.

34. *Sunday Times*, 1 February 1970.

35. *Guardian*, 12 July 1972.

36. Paolo Cherchi Usai, 'Stanley Kubrick', in Geoffrey Nowell-Smith (ed.), *The Oxford History of World Cinema* (Oxford, 1996), p.459.

12. The British Are Coming: *Chariots of Fire* (1981)

1. The most nuanced discussion of the themes of *Chariots of Fire* and its (ambiguous) relationship with Thatcherism is from John Hill, *British Cinema in the 1980s: Issues and Themes* (Oxford, 1999), pp.20–8. Elsewhere there is a significant body of critical literature on the film, including Ed Carter, '*Chariots of Fire*: Traditional Values/False History', *Jump Cut*, no.28 (1988), pp.15–20; Sheila Johnston, 'Charioteers and Ploughmen', in Martyn Auty and Nick Roddick (eds), *British Cinema Now* (London, 1985), pp.99–110; and Steve Neale, '"Chariots of Fire", Images of Men', *Screen*, vol.23, nos 3/4 (September–October 1982), pp.47–53. Among the commentators who read the film as a broadly pro-Thatcherite text are Thomas Elsaesser, 'Images for Sale: The "New" British Cinema', in Lester Friedman (ed.), *British Cinema and Thatcherism: Fires Were Started* (London, 1993), pp.52–69, and Leonard Quart, 'The Religion of the Market: Thatcherite Politics and the British Film of the 1980s', also in Friedman, *British Cinema and Thatcherism*, pp.15–34. For details of the film's production see Andrew Yule, *Enigma: David Puttnam – The Story So Far...* (Edinburgh, 1988), pp.159–89, and Alexander Walker, *National Heroes: British Cinema in the Seventies and Eighties* (London, 1985), pp.173–81.

2. David Docherty, David Morrison and Michael Tracey, *The Last Picture Show? Britain's changing film audiences* (London, 1987), p.1.

3. Hill, p.48.

4. Ibid., p.37.

5. 'Interview with David Puttnam', information booklet for *Chariots of Fire* on the BFI Library's microfiche for the film.

6. Jake Eberts and Terry Ilott, *My Indecision Is Final: The Rise and Fall of Goldcrest Films* (London, 1990), p.31.

7. BFI DP (David Puttnam Collection) 17: Anthony Williams to Puttnam, 21 August 1979.

8. Ibid.: Tim Vignoles to Puttnam, 4 September 1979.

9. Ibid.: Puttnam to Michael Grade, 29 June 1979.

10. Ibid.: Alasdair Milne to Puttnam, 20 August 1979.

11. Ibid.: Verity Lambert to Muir Sutherland (c.c. Puttnam), 8 August 1979.

12. BFI DP 68(a): Letter from Puttnam to members of the Profit Participation Fund, 21 June 1980.

13. BFI DP 68(b) includes details of the Profit Participation Fund for *Chariots of Fire*. Puttnam, through Enigma Productions, received the largest share on a downwards sliding scale: 20.5% on the first $1 million profits, with phased reductions to 15.5% on profits over $3 million. Goldcrest received a flat rate of 7.5%, director Hugh Hudson and writer Colin Welland received 5% each, and production personnel including James Crawford (associate producer), Lynda

Smith (production assistant), Terry Rawlings (editor) and David Watkin (cinematographer) received 1% each. The principal cast members Ian Charleson, Ben Cross, Nigel Havers and Ian Holm were on a sliding scale up to 2% for profits over $2 million. The Fund trustees, Norman Swindell and Joyce Herlihy, each received 2.5%, with Herlihy receiving an additional 1% for her role as production manager.

14. BFI DP 1: '1924 Runners, by Colin Welland. A treatment for a film – July 1978', handwritten notes, p.2. Typed copies of this treatment, with minor alterations, can be found in DP 3, 4, 5 and 6.

15. BFI DP 17: Douglas Lowe to Puttnam, 29 June 1978.

16. BFI S7969: *Chariots of Fire*. A film by Colin Welland. First draft, April 1979.

17. BFI DP 16: Hugh Hudson to Colin Welland, 4 January 1980.

18. Margaret Thatcher, *The Downing Street Years* (London, 1993), p.88.

19. BFI S18578: *Chariots of Fire*. A film by Colin Welland. Second draft, 13 February 1980. This text appears also in the brochure for the Royal Film Performance of *Chariots of Fire* at the Odeon, Leicester Square, on 30 March 1981, suggesting that it represents the 'preferred reading' of the film on the part of its makers.

20. BFI DP 33: Puttnam to Sid Correll, 7 May 1982.

21. Quoted in Quentin Falk, 'Cutting a dash against time', *Screen International*, 28 June 1980. p.15.

22. BFI DP 17: Puttnam to the Earl of Lindsey, 11 April 1980.

23. BFI DP 16: Hudson to Welland, 4 January 1980.

24. BFI DP 52: Sir Richard Attenborough to Hudson, 29 October 1980.

25. Tony Sloman, '"Chariots of Fire": Royal film', *What's On*, 27 March 1981.

26. BFI DP 52: Sir John Woolf to Puttnam, 31 March 1981.

27. Ibid.: Stanley Kubrick to Puttnam, 16 April 1981.

28. Ibid.: Ken Green to Puttnam, 27 March 1981.

29. 'The kind of picture we have looked for in vain', *The Times*, 3 April 1981.

30. 'Britain back on the tracks', *Evening Standard*, 2 April 1981.

31. *Catholic Herald*, 17 April 1981.

32. 'Dash of inspiration', *Guardian*, 2 April 1981.

33. 'Golden runners of roaring epoch', *Daily Telegraph*, 31 March 1981.

34. *Monthly Film Bulletin*, vol.48, no.568 (May 1981), p.90.

35. 'Running for Britain', *Financial Times*, 3 April 1981.

36. 'Wizard Olympic champions', *Observer*, 5 April 1981.

37. 'Why did Harold run?', *Sunday Times*, 5 April 1981.

38. 'Track record', *Sunday Telegraph*, 5 April 1981.

39. 'Actors pull own chariots', *Morning Star*, 3 April 1981.

40. *Screen International*, 11 April 1981, p.19.

41. The film's London box-office history can be tracked through *Screen International*. *Chariots* took £21,091 (net) in its first week at the Odeon, Haymarket, £16,727 in its second week, £19,250 in its third week, £21,604 in its fourth week and £18,363 in its fifth week. In its sixth week it opened at another two Odeons (Kensington and Westbourne Grove) and took £24,780 at all three cinemas, rising to £29,340 in the seventh week. Thereafter there is a steady, though not precipitous, downward trend. *Chariots* remained in the London top ten for 23 consecutive weeks from 11 April until 12 September.

42. *Screen International*, 6 June 1981, p.18.

43. *Screen International*, 26 December 1981, p.1.

44. '"Chariots of Fire" Scores in Britain; O'Seas is in Doubt', *Variety*, 24 June 1981.

45. BFI DP 53: Elisabeth Gaganie to Puttnam, 30 October 1981.

46. *Screen International*, 31 October 1981, p.8.

47. BFI DP 33: Julian Senior to Puttnam, 4 December 1981.

48. *New York*, 5 October 1982.

49. *New Yorker*, 24 October 1981.

50. 'Winning Race', *Time*, 21 September 1981.

51. 'Chariots of Mixed Feelings', *Voice*, 7 October 1981.

52. Letter from James Mackay, 'Running Commentary', *Voice*, 18 November 1981.

53. '"Chariots": Slow & Steady Will Win the Race', *Variety*, 25 November 1981.

54. Aljean Harmetz, 'Sometimes a Movie Makes a Studio Proud', *New York Times*, 10 February 1982.

55. BFI DP 70: Warner Bros. 'Chariots of Fire Participation Report No.2' (to 31 March 1982); 'Chariots of Fire Participation Report No.3' (to 30 June 1982).

56. Eberts, p.35. See also reports in *The Times* ('Chariots of gold') and *Daily Telegraph* ('Box office record') on 15 July 1982.

57. Sarah Street, *Transatlantic Crossings: British Feature Films in the USA* (London, 2002), p.195; Patrick Robertson (ed.), *The Guinness Book of Film Facts and Feats* (London, 1985), p.37.

58. *Screen International*, 27 December 1982, p.1.

59. BFI DP 68 contains a convoluted paper trail of documentation relating to the rental income of *Chariots of Fire*. Twentieth Century-Fox's 'Foreign Distribution Statement' to 31 December 1983 reveals that Fox had total receipts of $13,769,497 from theatrical rentals of *Chariots* in the United Kingdom, Continental Europe and other 'international' territories. From this amount, however, was deducted Fox's distribution fee ($5,066,063), distribution expenses relating to shipping, duties, payments to trade associations, advertising, dubbing etc. ($4,587,061), the original advance made to the producers ($3,024,699), interest on the advance ($1,445,026) and a mysterious 'supervisory fee' ($50,000). When all incidentals were deducted from the receipts, Fox's accounting managed to show a deficit of $403,322. It was not until *Chariots* passed $15 million in rentals (over twice that amount in actual box-office grosses) in 1984 that Fox paid a sum of $782,963 into the common fund – from which, of course, Fox took a share along with Allied and Enigma.

60. BFI DP 16: Anthony Jones to Puttnam, 10 August 1982.

61. BFI DP 70: Puttnam to John Chambers, 3 December 1982.

62. BFI DP 52: 'Frank' to Puttnam, 30 August 1981.

63. Ibid.: Arthur B. Needham to Puttnam, 24 June 1982.

64. Ibid.: 'The Payne family' to Puttnam, 23 October 1981.

65. BFI DP 53(b): Rev. J. Grant Swank Jr to Puttnam, 11 May 1982.

66. *Screen International*, 2 May 1981, p.4.

67. Notices of Questions and Motions: 31 March 1982, No.89, on the BFI Library microfiche for *Chariots of Fire*. The motion was proposed by Bob Cryer

and supported by Gerald Kaufman, Jack Dormand, Clinton Davis, Frank Haynes and Don Dixon.

68. 'And Chequers of Fire', *Daily Mail*, 23 April 1982.

69. This was reported in, of all places, the *Morning Star* (23 April 1982): 'Queues in Buenos Aires wait patiently to get inside, applaud scenes when the British national anthem is played and even sell their ticket stubs outside to unfortunates who cannot get in, but then boast about their prestige by showing friends their "ticket" in order to join in the general enthusiasm.' The *Evening Standard* (24 April 1982) also noted the 'incredible' popular reception of *Chariots* in Buenos Aires.

70. BFI DP 53(b): Puttnam to Sir Nicholas Henderson, 29 April 1982.

71. Walker, p.179.

72. Yule, p.242.

73. Speaking on *Maggie's Cultural Revolution*, Part 1 (BBC Radio 2, 11 May 2004).

74. 'Hugh Hudson' (interviewed by Tom Ryan), *Cinema Papers*, no.47 (August 1984), p.252.

75. Geoff Eley, '*Distant Voices, Still Lives*. The Family is a Dangerous Place: Memory, Gender and the Image of the Working Class', in Robert A. Rosenstone (ed.), *Revisioning History: Film and the Construction of a New Past* (Princeton, 1995), p.23.

76. On the use of 'Jerusalem' in both *Chariots of Fire* and *The Loneliness of the Long Distance Runner*, see Sophia D. Blades, 'Blake's "Jerusalem" and Popular Culture', *Literature/Film Quarterly*, vol. 11, no. 4 (1983), pp.211–14.

77. Hostile and sympathetic discussions of the 'kailyard' tradition can be found in, respectively, the editor's introduction to Colin McArthur (ed.), *Scotch Reels: Scotland in Film and Television* (London, 1982), pp.1–6, and Jeffrey Richards, *Films and British National Identity: From Dickens to 'Dad's Army'* (Manchester, 1997), pp.191–8.

78. Grant Jarvie, '*Chariots of Fire*, Culture and the Sports Media Complex', *Cencrastus*, no. 40 (Spring 1990), p.13.

79. BFI DP 53: Anthony Abrahams to Puttnam, 7 April 1981.

80. Kenneth O. Morgan, *The People's Peace: British History 1945–1990* (Oxford, 1990), p.441.

81. Thatcher, p.14.

82. Hill, p.28.

83. BFI DP 53 (b): Lynda Smith to Theresa Zapotacky (of Tucson, Arizona), 28 April 1982: 'Lord Andrew Lindsay was based on two characters who typified the aristocratic classes at the time – one of whom was as you surmise quite rightly – Lord Burghley.' The characterisation of Lindsay was evidently close enough to Burghley that the sports historian Richard Holt, in his book *Sport and the British: A Modern History* (Oxford, 1989), writes of the film: 'Harold Abrahams is criticized by his Cambridge tutors for being too Semitic in his single-minded pursuit of victory in contrast to the young Lord Burghley's casualness' (p.275).

84. Johnston, p.104.

85. The best summary of the 'heritage film' debate is Sheldon Hall, 'The Wrong Sort of Cinema: Refashioning the Heritage Film Debate', in Robert Murphy (ed.), *The British Cinema Book* (London, 2nd edn, 2001), pp.191–9. See

also Cairns Craig, 'Rooms Without A View', *Sight and Sound*, New Series, vol. 1, no. 6 (June 1991), pp.10–13; Claire Monk, 'Sexuality and the Heritage', *Sight and Sound*, New Series, vol. 5, no. 10 (October 1995), pp.32–4; Claire Monk, 'The British heritage-film debate revisited', in Claire Monk and Amy Sargeant (eds), *British Historical Cinema* (London, 2002), pp.176–98; and Amy Sargeant, 'Making and selling heritage culture: Style and authenticity in historical films on film and television', in Justine Ashby and Andrew Higson (eds), *British Cinema, Past and Present* (London, 2000), pp.301–15. The most sustained academic engagement with the heritage film has come from Andrew Higson, whose developing ideas can be tracked through 'Re-presenting the National Past: Nostalgia and Pastiche in the Heritage Film', in Friedman (ed.), *British Cinema and Thatcherism*, pp.109–29; 'The Heritage Film and British Cinema', in Higson (ed.), *Dissolving Views: Key Writings on British Cinema* (London, 1996), pp.232–48; and Higson, *English Heritage, English Cinema: Costume Drama Since 1980* (Oxford, 2003), pp.9–45.

13. Queen and Country: *Elizabeth* (1998)

1. *Elizabeth* has been the focus of much critical commentary that locates it in the context of debates around 'heritage' and 'post-heritage' film: Pamela Church Gibson, 'From Dancing Queen to Plaster Virgin: *Elizabeth* and the end of English heritage?', *Journal of Popular British Cinema*, no.5 (2002), pp.133–41; Andrew Higson, *English Heritage, English Cinema: Costume Drama Since 1980* (Oxford, 2003), pp.194–256; Kara McKechnie, 'Taking liberties with the monarch: The royal bio-pic in the 1990s', in Claire Monk and Amy Sargeant (eds), *British Historical Cinema* (London, 2002), pp.217–36; and Julianne Pidduck, '*Elizabeth* and *Shakespeare in Love*: Screening the Elizabethans', in Ginette Vincendeau (ed.), *Film/Literature/Heritage: A Sight and Sound Reader* (London, 2001), pp.130–5.

2. 'A Price Worth Paying', *Screen International*, 16 October 1998, p.12.

3. 'Gunning for glory', *Screen International*, 22 January 1998, p.13.

4. Eddie Dyja (ed.), *BFI Film and Television Handbook 1999* (London, 1998), p.18.

5. Ian Christie, 'As Others See Us: British Film-making and Europe in the 90s', in Robert Murphy (ed.), *British Cinema of the 90s* (London, 2000), pp.68–79.

6. Nick Roddick, 'Four Weddings and a Final Reckoning', *Sight and Sound*, New Series, vol. 5, no. 1 (January 1995), p.15.

7. Department of Culture, Media and Sport, *A Bigger Picture: The Report of the Film Policy Review Group* (London, 1998), p.10.

8. Sarah Street, *Transatlantic Crossings: British Feature Films in the USA* (London, 2002), p.202.

9. Quoted Roddick, p.13.

10. Michael Hirst, 'Introduction', *The Script of Elizabeth* (London, 1998), p.10.

11. Quoted in 'For Shekhar Kapur, Elizabeth was another Indira', *Asian Age*, 12 January 1999, pp.1–2.

12. 'From Bandit Queen to Queen Elizabeth', *Cinemaya: The Asian Film Quarterly*, no.36 (Summer 1997), p.64; Alison Boshoff, 'Hunt for star to play Virgin Queen', *Daily Telegraph*, 13 May 1997, p.5.

13. *Screen International*, 8 January 1999, p.32.

14. Production reports appeared in *Screen International*, 29 August 1997, p.25; *British Film and Television Facilities Journal*, Cannes Special Issue (Spring 1998), p.43; and Hilary Macaskill, 'A Castle Fit for a Celluloid Queen', *Independent on Sunday*, Travel Section, 15 October 1998, p.7.

15. *Broadcast Supplement B+*, 9 October 1998, p.S-18.

16. Higson, p.248.

17. *Screen International*, 18 September 1998, p.28.

18. Internet Movie Database: Business Data page for *Elizabeth* (www.imdb.com/title/tt0127536/ business), accessed 28 May 2004.

19. *Screen International*, 11 December 1998, p.30.

20. *Screen International*, 18 December 1998, p.25.

21. *Screen International*, 9 October 1998, p.27.

22. 'Liz the lionheart', *Guardian*, 2 October 1998, p.6.

23. Quoted in Higson, p.197.

24. 'Another fine Bess', *Observer Review*, 4 October 1998, p.6.

25. 'Royal flush', *Time Out*, 14–21 October 1998, p.87.

26. *Sight and Sound*, New Series, vol. 8, no. 11 (November 1998), p.48.

27. *Cinemaya: The Asian Film Quarterly*, no. 43 (Spring 1999), pp.29–30.

28. Matt Wolf, 'Make way for the Tudor twins', *Asian Age*, 17 November 1998, p.14.

29. 'Royal flush', *New Statesman*, 2 October 1998, p.36.

30. 'Good Queen Bess as a born-again virgin', *Daily Telegraph*, 2 October 1998, p.23.

31. 'Ruff justice', *Evening Standard*, 1 October 1998, p.17.

32. *Independent on Sunday*, 4 October 1998.

33. Quoted in Higson, p.249.

34. Quoted in Monica Baker, 'Interview with Remi Adefarasin', *Black Film Maker*, vol. 2, no. 5 (1999), p.13.

35. 'Elizabeth intacta', *Daily Telegraph*, 9 March 1998, p.21. See also Danae Brook, 'Elizabeth I is known as the Virgin Queen. So why does a new film show her having sex with a courtier?', *Mail on Sunday*, 13 September 1998, pp.52–3. David Starkey called the film 'a rattling good yarn', 'The drama queen', *Sunday Times*, 20 September 1998, p.5.

36. Higson, p.243.

37. See Jeffrey Richards, Scott Wilson and Linda Woodhead (eds), *Diana: The Making of a Media Saint* (London, 1999), *passim*.

38. 'It's like The Godfather with frocks', *Sunday Telegraph Review*, 4 October 1998, p.7; 'Another fine Bess', *Observer Review*, 4 October 1998, p.6.

39. Quoted in Sheila Johnston, 'G'day to you Queen Bess', *Sunday Telegraph Review*, 20 September 1998, p.5.

40. Michael Dobson and Nicola Watson, *England's Elizabeth: An Afterlife in Fame and Fantasy* (Oxford, 2002), p.4.

41. 'Tonic for heroine addicts', *Daily Mail*, 2 October 1998, p.44.

42. Ibid., p.45.

43. *Sight and Sound*, New Series, vol.8, no.11 (November 1998), p.48.

44. Higson, p.198.

45. Jeffrey Richards, 'The Hollywoodisation of Diana', in Richards, Wilson and Woodhead (eds), *Diana: The Making of a Media Saint*, p.72.

46. *Sight and Sound*, New Series, vol.5, no.12 (December 1995), p.56.

47. Higson, p.256.

48. William Goldman, *Adventures in the Screen Trade: A Personal View of Hollywood and Screenwriting* (London, 1984), p.49.

49. Louise Brealey, 'Freedom Fighter', *Premiere*, vol. 3, no. 12 (January 1996), p.20.

50. Letter from Steve Knibbs, 'UK film misses wider audience', *Evening Standard*, 14 November 1995, p.53.

51. Philip Kemp, 'Love of the common people', *Sight and Sound*, New Series, vol.13, no.6 (June 2003), p.36.

Bibliography

Archival and Unpublished Document Sources

British Film Institute Special Collections
Aileen and Michael Balcon Collection (MEB); British Board of Film Censors Scenario Reports (BBFC); Sir David Cunynghame Collection (DC); Filippo Del Giudice Collection (FDG); London Film Productions Collection (LFP); Ivor Montagu Collection (IM); David Puttnam Collection (DP); Victor Saville Collection (VS).

British Film Institute unpublished scripts

Chariots of Fire. A film by Colin Welland. First draft, April 1979 (S7969)
Chariots of Fire. A film by Colin Welland. Second draft, 13 February 1980 (S18578)
The Charge of the Light Brigade. Screenplay by John Osborne, 14 October 1965, revised 16 November 1965 (S8757)
The Charge of the Light Brigade. Screenplay by Charles Wood, 3 March 1967 (S7043)
Henry the Fifth. Shooting script, n.d. (S106)
Henry VIII and His Six Wives. Shooting script by Ian Thorne, September 1971 (S7354)
The Iron Duke. Pre-production script, n.d. (S7669)
A Night to Remember. Shooting script, August 1957 (S190)
The Private Life of Henry VIII. Release script, n.d. (S215)
Scott of the Antarctic. Final White Script, 28 November 1947 (IM Collection 249)
Zulu (The Battle of Rorke's Drift). Screenplay by John Prebble and Cy Endfield. Final Shooting Script, 25 February 1963 (S11701)

British Library Department of Manuscripts
Laurence Olivier Archive, Films 3: papers relating to the production and distribition of *Henry V*, 1943–82.

Public Records Office, Kew, London
BT 64: Board of Trade Manufactures Department, including records of the Cinematograph Films Council.
INF 1: General records, correspondence and memoranda of the Ministry of Information, including the Films Division, 1939–45.

Newspapers and Periodicals

Sources of reviews and contemporary articles can be traced through my endnotes. Most film reviews are taken from the British Film Institute Library's microfiche collection and include the *Asian Age, Daily Express, Daily Graphic, Daily Herald, Daily Mail, Daily Sketch, Daily Telegraph, Daily Worker, Evening News, Evening Standard, Financial Times, Guardian, Independent, Independent on Sunday, Mail on Sunday, Manchester Guardian, Morning Star, New Statesman, News Chronicle, News of the World, Observer, Picture Post, Reynolds News, Spectator, Sunday Dispatch, Sunday Graphic, Sunday Telegraph, Sunday Times, Time and Tide, Time Out, The Times* and *Tribune*. American newspaper sources include the *Nation, New York Times, New Yorker, Rob Wagner's Script, Saturday Review, Time, Village Voice* and *Voice*.

Trade Papers and Film Periodicals

Again sources can be traced through the endnotes. Production details and selected reviews have been collected from the following film industry trade journals, fan magazines and film periodicals: *American Cinematographer* (US), *Black Filmmaker* (GB), *British Film and TV Facilities Journal* (GB), *Broadcast* (GB), *Cahiers du Cinéma* (France), *Cineaste* (US), *Cinema Papers* (Australia), *Cinema Quarterly* (GB), *Cinemaya* (GB), *CinemaTV Today* (GB), *Daily Cinema* (US), *Daily Film Renter* (GB), *Documentary News Letter* (GB), *Eyepiece* (GB), *Film Comment* (US), *Film Daily* (US), *Film Dope* (US), *Film Review* (GB), *Film Weekly* (GB), *Films and Filming* (GB), *Films in Review* (US), *Hollywood Reporter* (US), *Hollywood Review* (US), *Hollywood Spectator* (US), *Kinematograph Weekly* (GB), *Listener* (GB), *Monthly Film Bulletin* (GB), *Motion Picture Herald* (US), *Motion Picture Product Digest* (US), *The Movie* (GB), *Movie Collector* (GB), *Penguin Film Review* (GB), *Photoplay* (US), *Picturegoer Weekly* (GB), *Premiere* (GB), *Screen International* (GB), *Sight and Sound* (GB), *Theatre Arts* (US), *Today's Cinema* (GB), *Variety* (US) and *World Film News* (GB).

Published Screenplays

Masterworks of the British Cinema: Brief Encounter, Henry V, The Lady Vanishes
(London: Faber and Faber, 1990)
The Private Life of Henry VIII, ed. Ernest Betts (London: Methuen, 1934)
The Sea Hawk, ed. Rudy Behlmer (Madison: University of Wisconsin Press, 1982)
The Script of Elizabeth, by Michael Hirst (London: Boxtree, 1998)
Three British Screen Plays: Brief Encounter, Odd Man Out, Scott of the Antarctic,
ed. Roger Manvell (London: Methuen, 1950)

Published Reports

A Bigger Picture: The Report of the Film Policy Review Group (London:
Department of Media, Culture and Sport, 1998)
*The British Film Industry: A report on its history and present organisation, with
special reference to the economic problems of British feature film production*
(London: Political and Economic Planning, 1952)
History Teaching Films (London: The Historical Association, 1937)

Memoirs and Autobiographies

Arliss, George, *George Arliss by Himself* (London: John Murray, 1940)
Baker, Roy Ward, *The Director's Cut: A Memoir of 60 Years in Film and Television*
(London: Reynolds & Hearn, 2000)
Balcon, Michael, *Michael Balcon Presents... A Lifetime of Films* (London:
Hutchinson, 1969)
Halliwell, Leslie, *Seats In All Parts: Half A Lifetime at the Movies* (London:
Granada, 1985)
Korda, Michael, *Charmed Lives: A Family Romance* (London: Allen Lane, 1980)
Lanchester, Elsa, *Elsa Lanchester Herself* (New York: St Martin's Press, 1983)
MacQuitty, William, *A Life to Remember* (London: Quartet, 1991)
Mills, John, *Up in the Clouds, Gentlemen Please* (London: Weidenfeld &
Nicolson, 1980)
More, Kenneth, *More or Less* (London: Hodder & Stoughton, 1978)
Moseley, Roy, *Evergreen: Victor Saville in His Own Words* (Carbondale: Southern
Illinois University Press, 2000)
Neagle, Anna, *There's Always Tomorrow* (London: W.H. Allen, 1974)
Olivier, Laurence, *Confessions of an Actor* (London: Weidenfeld & Nicolson,
1982)
Powell, Michael, *A Life in Movies: An Autobiography* (London: William
Heinemann, 1986)
Powell, Michael, *Million-Dollar Movie* (London: William Heinemann, 1992)
Richardson, Tony, *Long Distance Runner: A Memoir* (London: Faber & Faber,
1993)

Thatcher, Margaret, *The Downing Street Years* (London: HarperCollins, 1993)
Wilcox, Herbert, *Twenty-Five Thousand Sunsets: The Autobiography of Herbert Wilcox* (New York: A.S. Barnes, 1967)

Books

Addison, Paul, *The Road to 1945: British Politics and the Second World War* (London: Jonathan Cape, 1975)
Aldgate, Anthony, *Cinema and History: British Newsreels and the Spanish Civil War* (London: Scolar Press, 1979)
Aldgate, Anthony, and Jeffrey Richards, *Best of British: Cinema and Society from 1930 to the Present* (London: I.B. Tauris, rev. edn 1999)
Aldgate, Anthony, and Jeffrey Richards, *Britain Can Take It: The British Cinema in the Second World War* (Edinburgh: Edinburgh University Press, 2nd edn 1994)
Andrew, Dudley, *Film in the Aura of Art* (Princeton: Princeton University Press, 1984)
Armes, Roy, *A Critical History of British Cinema* (London: Secker & Warburg, 1978)
Armstrong, Anthony, *Village at War* (London: Collins, 1941)
Ashby, Justine, and Andrew Higson (eds), *British Cinema, Past and Present* (London: Routledge, 2000)
Aspinall, Sue, and Robert Murphy, *BFI Dossier 18: Gainsborough Melodrama* (London: British Film Institute, 1983)
Barr, Charles, *Ealing Studios* (London and Newton Abbot: Cameron & Tayleur, 1977)
Barr, Charles (ed.), *All Our Yesterdays: 90 Years of British Cinema* (London: British Film Institute, 1986)
Bergfelder, Tim, and Sarah Street (eds), *The Titanic in Myth and Memory: Representations in Visual and Literary Culture* (London: I.B. Tauris, 2004)
Berry, David, *Wales and Cinema: The First Hundred Years* (Cardiff: University of Wales Press, 1994)
Betts, Ernest, *The Film Business: A History of British Cinema 1896–1972* (London: George Allen & Unwin, 1973)
Brewer, Susan A., *To Win the Peace: British Propaganda in the United States during World War II* (Ithaca: Cornell University Press, 1997)
Briggs, Asa, *The History of Broadcasting in the United Kingdom, Volume V: Competition 1955–1974* (Oxford: Oxford University Press, 1995)
Brown, Geoff, and Lawrence Kardish, *Michael Balcon: The Pursuit of British Cinema* (New York: Museum of Modern Art, 1984)
Calder, Angus, *The People's War: Britain 1939–1945* (London: Jonathan Cape, 1989)
Callow, Simon, *Charles Laughton: A Difficult Actor* (London: Methuen, 1987)
Carnes, Mark C. (ed.), *Past Imperfect: History According to the Movies* (London: Cassell, 1996)
Carr, E.H., *What Is History?* (Harmondsworth: Penguin, 1964)

Ceplair, Larry, and Steven Englund, *The Inquisition in Hollywood: Politics in the Film Community, 1930–1960* (Urbana: University of Illinois Press, 2003)

Chapman, James, *The British at War: Cinema, State and Propaganda, 1939–1945* (London: I.B. Tauris, 1998)

Charmley, John, *Chamberlain and the Lost Peace* (London: Hodder & Stoughton, 1989)

Chibnall, Steve, *J. Lee Thompson* (Manchester: Manchester University Press, 2000)

Churchill, Winston S., *The Second World War, Volume III: The Grand Alliance* (London: Penguin, 1985; first published in 1950)

Churchill, Winston S., *The Second World War, Volume IV: The Hinge of Fate* (London: Penguin, 1985; first published in 1951)

Connelly, Mark, *The Charge of the Light Brigade* (London: I.B. Tauris, 2003)

Constantine, Stephen, *Unemployment in Britain Between the Wars* (Harlow: Longman, 1980)

Cook, Christopher (ed.), *The Dilys Powell Film Reader* (Manchester: Carcanet Press, 1991)

Cook, Pam, *Fashioning the Nation: Costume and Identity in British Cinema* (London: British Film Institute, 1997)

Cottrell, John, *Laurence Olivier* (London: Weidenfeld & Nicolson, 1975)

Coultass, Clive, *Images for Battle: British Film and the Second World War, 1939–1945* (London: Associated University Presses, 1989)

Cull, Nicholas John, *Selling War: The British Propaganda Campaign Against American Neutrality in World War II* (New York: Oxford University Press, 1995)

Curran, James, and Vincent Porter (eds), *British Cinema History* (London: Weidenfeld & Nicolson, 1983)

Dickinson, Margaret, and Sarah Street, *Cinema and State: The Film Industry and the British Government 1927–84* (London: British Film Institute, 1985)

Dobson, Michael, and Nicola J. Watson, *England's Elizabeth: An Afterlife in Fame and Fantasy* (Oxford: Oxford University Press, 2002)

Docherty, David, David Morrison and Michael Tracey, *The Last Picture Show? Britain's Changing Film Audience* (London: British Film Institute, 1987)

Drazin, Charles, *The Finest Years: British Cinema of the 1940s* (London: André Deutsch, 1998)

Drazin, Charles, *Korda: Britain's Only Movie Mogul* (London: Sidgwick & Jackson, 2002)

Durgnat, Raymond, *A Mirror for England: British Movies from Austerity to Affluence* (London: Faber & Faber, 1970)

Eberts, Jake, and Terry Ilott, *My Indecision is Final: The Rise and Fall of Goldcrest Films* (London: Faber & Faber, 1990)

Findlater, Richard, *Emlyn Williams: Theatre World Monograph No. 8* (London: Rockliff, 1956)

Friedman, Lester (ed.), *British Cinema and Thatcherism: Fires Were Started* (London: UCL Press, 1993)

Gilbert, Martin (ed.), *Winston S. Churchill, Volume V: Companion – Part 2* (London: William Heinemann, 1985)

Girouard, Mark, *The Return to Camelot: Chivalry and the English Gentleman*

(New Haven, CT: Yale University Press, 1981)

Glancy, H. Mark, *When Hollywood loved Britain: The Hollywood 'British' film, 1939–45* (Manchester: Manchester University Press, 1999)

Goldman, William, *Adventures in the Screen Trade: A Personal View of Hollywood and Screenwriting* (London: Macdonald, 1984)

Hall, Sheldon, *Zulu: With Some Guts Behind It – The Making of the Epic Movie* (Sheffield: Tomahawk Press, forthcoming)

Halliwell, Leslie, *Halliwell's Hundred: A nostalgic selection of films from the golden age* (London: Granada, 1982)

Harding, James, *Emlyn Williams: A Life* (London: Weidenfeld & Nicolson, 1993)

Harper, Sue, *Picturing the Past: The Rise and Fall of the British Costume Film* (London: British Film Institute, 1994)

Harper, Sue, *Women in British Cinema: Mad, Bad and Dangerous to Know* (London: Continuum, 2000)

Harper, Sue, and Vincent Porter, *British Cinema of the 1950s: The Decline of Deference* (Oxford: Oxford University Press, 2003)

Higson, Andrew, *Waving the Flag: Constructing a National Cinema in Britain* (Oxford: Clarendon Press, 1995)

Higson, Andrew, *English Heritage, English Cinema: Costume Drama Since 1980* (Oxford: Oxford University Press, 2003)

Higson, Andrew (ed.), *Dissolving Views: Key Writings on British Cinema* (London: Cassell, 1996)

Hill, John, *Sex, Class and Realism: British Cinema 1956–1963* (London: British Film Institute, 1986)

Hill, John, *British Cinema in the 1980s: Issues and Themes* (Oxford: Clarendon Press, 1999)

Hirschhorn, Clive, *The Columbia Story* (London: Octopus Books, 1989)

Holderness, Graham, *Visual Shakespeare: Essays in Film and Television* (Hatfield: University of Hertfordshire Press, 2002)

Holt, Richard, *Sport and the British: A Modern History* (Oxford: Clarendon Press, 1989)

Houston, Penelope, *The Contemporary Cinema* (Harmondsworth: Penguin, 1963)

Hutton, Clayton, *The Making of Henry V* (London: Ernest J. Day, 1945)

James, David, *Scott of the Antarctic: The Film and its Production* (London: Convoy Publications, 1948)

Katz, Ephraim, *The Macmillan International Film Encyclopedia* (London: Macmillan, 1994)

Kelly, Andrew, Jeffrey Richards and James Pepper, *Filming T.E. Lawrence: Korda's Lost Epics* (London: I.B. Tauris, 1997)

Kemp, Philip, *Lethal Innocence: The Cinema of Alexander Mackendrick* (London: Methuen, 1991)

King, Peter (ed.), *Scott's Last Journey* (London: Gerald Duckworth, 1999)

Knight, Ian, *Nothing Remains But To Fight: The Defence of Rorke's Drift* (London: Greenhill Books, 1993)

Knight, Ian, *The National Army Museum Book of the Zulu War* (London: Sidgwick & Jackson, 2003)

Kracauer, Siegfried, *From Caligari to Hitler: A Psychological History of the*

German Film (Princeton: Princeton University Press, 1947)

Kulik, Karol, *Alexander Korda: The Man Who Could Work Miracles* (London: W.H. Allen, 1975)

Landy, Marcia, *British Genres: Cinema and Society 1930–1960* (Princeton: Princeton University Press, 1991)

Landy, Marcia (ed.), *The Historical Film: History and memory in Media* (London: Athlone Press, 2001)

Lejeune, Anthony (ed.), *The C.A. Lejeune Film Reader* (Manchester: Carcanet Press, 1991)

Lejeune, C.A., *Chestnuts in Her Lap 1936–1946* (London: Phoenix House, 1947)

Lentin, Antony, *Guilt at Versailles: Lloyd George and the Pre-History of Appeasement* (London: Methuen, 1985)

Lewis, Roger, *The Real Life of Laurence Olivier* (London: Century Books, 1996)

Low, Rachael, *The History of the British Film 1918–1929* (London: George Allen & Unwin, 1971)

Low, Rachael, *The History of the British Film 1929–1939: Film Making in 1930s Britain* (London: George Allen & Unwin, 1985)

McArthur, Colin (ed.), *Scotch Reels: Scotland in Cinema and Television* (London: British Film Institute, 1982)

MacKenzie, John M., *Propaganda and Empire: The manipulation of British public opinion, 1880–1960* (Manchester: Manchester University Press, 1984)

Macnab, Geoffrey, *J. Arthur Rank and the British Film Industry* (London: Routledge, 1993)

Mahl, Thomas E., *Desperate Deception: British Covert Operations in the United States, 1939–44* (Washington: Brassey's, 1998)

Manvell, Roger, *Film* (Harmondsworth: Penguin, 1946 edn)

Marwick, Arthur, *The Nature of History* (London: Macmillan, 3rd edn, 1989)

Marwick, Arthur, *British Society Since 1945* (London: Penguin, 3rd edn, 1996)

Marwick, Arthur, *The Sixties: Cultural Revolution in Britain, France, Italy and the United States, c.1958–c.1974* (Oxford: Oxford University Press, 1998)

Mayer, J.P., *British Cinemas and their Audiences: Sociological Studies* (London: Dennis Dobson, 1948)

Monk, Claire, and Amy Sargeant (eds), *British Historical Cinema* (London: Routledge, 2002)

Morgan, Kenneth O., *The People's Peace: British History 1945–1990* (Oxford: Oxford University Press, 1992)

Murphy, Robert, *Realism and Tinsel: Cinema and Society in Britain 1939–49* (London: Routledge, 1989)

Murphy, Robert, *Sixties British Cinema* (London: Routledge, 1992)

Murphy, Robert (ed.), *British Cinema of the 90s* (London: British Film Institute, 2000)

Murphy, Robert (ed.), *The British Cinema Book* (London: British Film Institute, 2nd edn, 2001)

Neale, Steve, *Genre and Hollywood* (London: Routledge, 2000)

Neve, Brian, *Film and Politics in America: A Social Tradition* (London: Routledge, 1992)

Nowell-Smith, Geoffrey (ed.), *The Oxford History of World Cinema* (Oxford: Oxford University Press, 1996)

Orwell, George, *The Lion and the Unicorn: Socialism and the English Genius*, with an introduction by Bernard Crick (Harmondsworth: Penguin, 1982; originally published 1941)

Parker, R.A.C., *Chamberlain and Appeasement: British Policy and the Coming of the Second World War* (London: Macmillan, 1993)

Parkinson, David (ed.), *The Graham Greene Film Reader: Mornings in the Dark* (Manchester: Carcanet Press, 1993)

Petrie, Duncan, *The British Cinematographer* (London: British Film Institute, 1996)

Priestley, J.B., *Postscripts* (London: Victor Gollancz, 1940)

Rhode, Eric, *A History of the Cinema from its Origins to 1970* (London: Allen Lane, 1976)

Richards, Jeffrey, *Visions of Yesterday* (London: Routledge & Kegan Paul, 1973)

Richards, Jeffrey, *The Age of the Dream Palace: Cinema and Society in Britain 1930–1939* (London: Routledge & Kegan Paul, 1984)

Richards, Jeffrey, *Thorold Dickinson: The Man and His Films* (London: Croom Helm, 1986)

Richards, Jeffrey, *Films and British National Identity: From Dickens to 'Dad's Army'* (Manchester: Manchester University Press, 1997)

Richards, Jeffrey, *A Night to Remember: The Definitive Titanic Film* (London: I.B. Tauris, 2003)

Richards, Jeffrey, and Dorothy Sheridan (eds), *Mass-Observation at the Movies* (London: Routledge & Kegan Paul, 1987)

Richards, Jeffrey, Scott Wilson and Linda Woodhead (eds), *Diana: The Making of a Media Saint* (London: I.B. Tauris, 1999)

Robertson, James C., *The British Board of Film Censors: Film Censorship in Britain, 1896–1950* (London: Croom Helm, 1985)

Rollins, Cyril B., and Robert J. Wareing, *Victor Saville* (London: British Film Institute, 1972)

Rosenstone, Robert (ed.), *Revisioning History: Film and the Construction of a New Past* (Princeton: Princeton University Press, 1995)

Rotha, Paul, with Richard Griffith, *The Film Till Now: A Survey of World Cinema* (London: Spring Books, 1949; first published in 1930)

Russell, Ken, *Fire Over England: The British Cinema Comes Under Friendly Fire* (London: Hutchinson, 1993)

Sarris, Andrew, *The American Cinema: Directors and Directions, 1929–1968* (New York: Da Capo Press, 1996; first published in 1968)

Sedgwick, John, *Popular Filmgoing in 1930s Britain: A Choice of Pleasures* (Exeter: Exeter University Press, 2000)

Shafer, Stephen C., *British Popular Films 1929–1939: The Cinema of Reassurance* (London: Routledge, 1997)

Sharp, Alan, *The Versailles Settlement: Peacemaking in Paris, 1919* (London: Macmillan, 1991)

Short, K.R.M. (ed.), *Feature Films as History* (London: Croom Helm, 1981)

Silviria, Dale, *Laurence Olivier and the Art of Filmmaking* (London: Associated University Presses, 1985)

Sinyard, Neil, *The Films of Richard Lester* (London: Croom Helm, 1985)

Slide, Anthony, *'Banned in the USA': British Films in the United States and their*

Censorship 1933–1960 (London: I.B. Tauris, 1998)

Slide, Anthony (ed.), *Selected Film Criticism: Foreign Films 1930–1950* (Metuchen, NJ: The Scarecrow Press, 1984)

Smith, Malcolm, *Britain and 1940: History, myth and popular memory* (London: Routledge, 2000)

Sorlin, Pierre, *The Film in History: Restaging the Past* (Oxford: Basil Blackwell, 1980)

Spicer, Andrew, *Typical Men: The Representation of Masculinity in Popular British Cinema* (London: I.B. Tauris, 2001)

Spoto, Donald, *Laurence Olivier: A Biography* (London: HarperCollins, 1991)

Stead, Peter, *Acting Wales: Stars of Stage and Screen* (Cardiff: University of Wales Press, 2002)

Street, Sarah, *British National Cinema* (London: Routledge, 1997)

Street, Sarah, *Transatlantic Crossings: British Feature Films in the USA* (London: Continuum, 2002)

Swynnoe, Jan G., *The Best Years of British Film Music, 1936–1958* (Woodbridge: Boydell Press, 2002)

Taylor, A.J.P., *The Origins of the Second World War* (London: Hamish Hamilton, 1961)

Taylor, A.J.P., *English History 1914–1945* (Oxford: Clarendon Press, 1965)

Turner, Graeme, *Film As Social Practice* (London: Routledge, 1988)

Vidal, Gore, *Screening History* (London: André Deutsch, 1992)

Vincendeau, Ginette (ed.), *Film/Literature/Heritage: A Sight and Sound Reader* (London: British Film Institute, 2001)

Walker, Alexander, *Hollywood, England: The British Film Industry in the Sixties* (London: Michael Joseph, 1974)

Walker, Alexander, *National Heroes: British Cinema in the Seventies and Eighties* (London: Harrap, 1985)

Walker, Greg, *The Private Life of Henry VIII* (London: I.B. Tauris, 2003)

Walker, John (ed.), *Halliwell's Film & Video Guide* (London: HarperCollins, 13th edn, 1998)

Warren, Patricia, *British Film Studios: An Illustrated History* (London: B.T. Batsford, 1995)

Wood, Alan, *Mr Rank: A study of J. Arthur Rank and British Films* (London: Hodder & Stoughton, 1952)

Wood, Linda (ed.), *British Film Industry* (London: British Film Institute, 1980)

Wood, Linda (ed.), *British Films 1927–1939: BFI Reference Guide* (London: British Film Institute, 1986)

Yule, Andrew, *Enigma: David Puttnam – The Story So Far...* (Edinburgh: Mainstream Publishing, 1988)

Articles and Chapters

Anderson, Lindsay, 'Get Out and Push!', in Tom Maschler (ed.), *Declaration* (London: MacGibbon & Kee, 1957), pp.154–78.

Barr, Charles, 'Desperate Yearnings: Victor Saville and Gainsborough', in Pam

Cook (ed.), *Gainsborough Pictures* (London: Cassell, 1997), pp.47–59.

Carter, Ed, '*Chariots of Fire*: Traditional Values/False History', *Jump Cut*, no.28 (1988), pp.15–20.

Chapman, James, '*The Life and Death of Colonel Blimp* (1943) Revisited', *Historical Journal of Film, Radio and Television*, vol.15, no.1 (March 1995), pp.19–54.

Craddock, John, '*The Charge of the Light Brigade* in perspective', *Film Society Review*, vol.4, no.7 (March 1969), pp.15–34.

Cull, Nicholas J., 'Peter Watkins' *Culloden* and the alternative form in historical filmmaking', *Film International*, no.1 (2003), pp.48–53.

Curtis, John [John Prebble], 'Slaughter in the Sun', *Lilliput*, April 1958, pp.56–60, 77.

Ellis, John, 'Art, Culture, Quality: Terms for a Cinema in the Forties and Seventies', *Screen*, vol.19, no.3 (Autumn 1978), pp.9–49.

Ellis, John, 'The Quality Film Adventure: British Critics and the Cinema 1942–1948', in Andrew Higson (ed.), *Dissolving Views: Key Writings on British Cinema* (London: Cassell, 1996), pp.66–93.

Gibson, Pamela Church, 'From Dancing Queen to Plaster Virgin: *Elizabeth* and the end of English Heritage?', *Journal of Popular British Cinema*, no.5 (2002), pp.133–41.

Glancy, H. Mark, 'Hollywood and Britain: MGM and the British "Quota" Legislation', in Jeffrey Richards (ed.), *The Unknown 1930s: An Alternative History of the British Cinema, 1929–1939* (London: I.B. Tauris, 1998), pp.57–74.

Gough-Yates, Kevin, 'The British Feature Film as a European Concern: Britain and the Emigré Film-Maker, 1933–45', in Günter Berghaus (ed.), *Theatre and Film in Exile: German Artists in Britain, 1933–1945* (Oxford: Berg, 1989), pp.135–6.

Harper, Sue, 'A Note on Basil Dean, Sir Robert Vansittart and British Historical Films of the 1930s', *Historical Journal of Film, Radio and Television*, vol.10, no.1 (1990), pp.81–7.

Higson, Andrew, 'A diversity of film practices: renewing British cinema in the 1970s', in Bart Moore-Gilbert (ed.), *Cultural Closure? The Arts in the 1970s* (London: Routledge, 1994), pp.216–39.

Higson, Andrew, 'Polyglot Films for an International Market: E.A. Dupont, the British Film Industry, and the Idea of a European Cinema, 1926–1930', in Andrew Higson and Richard Maltby (eds), *'Film Europe' and 'Film America': Cinema, Commerce and Cultural Exchange 1920–1939* (Exeter: Exeter University Press, 1999), pp.274–301.

Howells, Richard, 'Atlantic Crossings: Nation, Class and Identity in *Titanic* (1953) and *A Night to Remember* (1958)', *Historical Journal of Film, Radio and Television*, vol.19, no.4 (October 1999), pp.421–38.

Johnston, Sheila, 'Charioteers and Ploughmen', in Martyn Auty and Nick Roddick (eds), *British Cinema Now* (London: British Film Institute, 1985), pp.99–110.

Lovell, Alan, 'The British Cinema: The Unknown Cinema', paper presented to the British Film Institute Education Department, 13 March 1969 (held by BFI National Library).

Lynch, Dennis, 'The Worst Location in the World: Herbert G. Ponting in the Antarctic, 1910–1912', *Film History*, vol.3, no.4 (1989), pp.291–306.

McCreadie, Marsha, '*Henry V*: Onstage and On Film', *Literature/Film Quarterly*, vol.5, no.4 (1977), pp.316–21.

McFarlane, Brian, 'Dallas Bower: The Man Behind Olivier's *Henry V*', *Shakespeare Bulletin: A Journal of Performance Criticism and Scholarship*, vol.12, no.1 (Winter 1994), pp.45–6.

Manheim, Michael, 'Olivier's *Henry V* and the Elizabethan World Picture', *Literature/Film Quarterly*, vol. 11, no. 3 (1983), pp.179–84.

Neale, Steve, '"Chariots of Fire", Images of Men', *Screen*, vol.23, nos 3/4 (September–October 1982), pp.47–53

Nichols, John G., 'The Atomic Agincourt: *Henry V* and the Filmic Making of Postwar Anglo-American Cultural Relations', *Film and History*, vol. 27, nos 1–4 (1997), pp.88–94.

Paris, Michael, 'Enduring Heroes: British Feature Films and the First World War, 1919–1997', in Michael Paris (ed.), *The First World War and Popular Cinema: 1914 to the Present* (Edinburgh: Edinburgh University Press, 1999), pp.51–73.

Peck, Robert, 'The Banning of *Titanic* (1943): A Study in British Post-war Censorship in Germany', *Historical Journal of Film, Radio and Television*, vol. 20, no.3 (August 2000), pp.122–32.

Porter, Vincent, and Chaim Litewski, '*The Way Ahead*: Case history of a propaganda film', *Sight and Sound*, vol.50, no.2 (Spring 1981), pp.110–16.

Pronay, Nicholas, 'British Newsreels in the 1930s: 1. Audience and Producers', *History*, vol. 56 (October 1971), pp.411–18.

Pronay, Nicholas, 'British Newsreels in the 1930s: 2. Their Policies and Impact', *History*, vol.57 (February 1972), pp.63–72.

Pronay, Nicholas, 'The Political Censorship of Films in Britain between the Wars', in Nicholas Pronay and D.W. Spring (eds), *Politics, Propaganda and Film, 1918–45* (London: Macmillan, 1982), pp.98–125.

Richards, Jeffrey, 'The British Board of Film Censors and Content Control in the 1930s (1): Images of Britain', *Historical Journal of Film, Radio and Television*, vol.1, no.2 (1981), pp.97–116.

Richards, Jeffrey, 'The British Board of Film Censors and Content Control in the 1930s (2): Foreign Affairs', *Historical Journal of Film, Radio and Television*, vol.2, no.1 (1982), pp.39–48.

Richards, Jeffrey, 'Imperial heroes for a post-imperial age: films and the end of empire', in Stuart Ward (ed.), *British culture and the end of empire* (Manchester: Manchester University Press, 2001), pp.128–44.

Richards, Jeffrey, and Jeffrey Hulbert, 'Censorship in Action: The case of *Lawrence of Arabia*', *Journal of Contemporary History*, vol. 19, no. 1 (January 1984), pp.153–69.

Sedgwick, John, 'Michael Balcon's close encounter with the American market, 1934–36', *Historical Journal of Film, Radio and Television*, vol.16, no.3 (August 1996), pp.333–48.

Sharrett, Christopher, '*Zulu*, or the Limits of Liberalism', *Cineaste*, vol.25, no.4 (2000), pp.28–33.

Short, K.R.M., '*That Hamilton Woman* (1941): Propaganda, Feminism and the Production Code', *Historical Journal of Film, Radio and Television*, vol.11, no.1 (1991), pp.3–19.

Spicer, Andrew, 'Fit for a King? The Royal Film Performance', *Journal of British Cinema and Television*, vol.2, no.2 (2005).

Street, Sarah, 'Alexander Korda, Prudential Assurance and British Film Finance in the 1930s', *Historical Journal of Film, Radio and Television*, vol.6, no.2 (1986), pp.161–79.

Tashiro, Charles Shiro, 'Fear and Loathing of British Cinema', *Spectator: The University of Southern California Journal of Film and Television Criticism*, vol.14, no.2 (Spring 1994), pp.23–37.

Walker, Greg, 'The Private Life of Henry VIII', *History Today*, vol.51 no.9 (September 2001), pp.10–15.

Wenden, D.J., and K.R.M. Short, 'Winston S. Churchill: film fan', *Historical Journal of Film, Radio and Television*, vol.11, no.3 (1991), pp.197–214.

Yorke, Edmund J., 'Cultural myths and realities: the British Army, war and Empire as portrayed on film, 1900–90', in Ian Stewart and Susan L. Carruthers (eds), *War, Culture and the Media: Representations of the Military in 20th Century Britain* (Trowbridge: Flicks Books, 1996), pp.91–100.

Young, John W., '*Henry V*, the Quai d'Orsay, and the Well-being of the Franco-British Alliance, 1947', *Historical Journal of Film, Radio and Television*, vol.7, no.3 (1987), pp.319–21.

Filmography

The Private Life of Henry VIII

London Film Productions. 1933.

Producer and director: Alexander Korda; *Story and dialogue:* Lajos Biro, Arthur Wimperis; *Director of photography:* Georges Perinal; *Set designer:* Vincent Korda; *Costumes:* John Armstrong; *Supervising editor:* Harold Young; *Music:* Kurt Schroeder; *Historical adviser:* Philip Lindsay; *Certificate:* A; *Running time:* 96 minutes (8,664 feet).

Cast: Charles Laughton (King Henry VIII), Robert Donat (Thomas Culpeper), Binnie Barnes (Catherine Howard), Elsa Lanchester (Anne of Cleves), Wendy Barrie (Jane Seymour), Merle Oberon (Anne Boleyn), Lady Tree (Nurse), Franklyn Dyall (Thomas Cromwell), John Loder (Thomas Peynell), Miles Mander (Wriothesley), Claud Allister (Cornell), Laurence Hanray (Archbishop Cranmer), William Austin (Duke of Cleves), Everly Gregg (Catherine Parr), John Turnbull (Holbein), Judy Kelly (Lady Rochford), Frederick Cully (Duke of Norfolk), Gibb McLaughlin (French executioner), Sam Livesey (English executioner).

Premières: Paris, Lord Byron Cinema, 1 October 1933; New York, Radio City Music Hall, 12 October 1933; London, Leicester Square Theatre, 24 October 1933.

The Iron Duke

Gaumont-British Picture Corporation. 1935.

Director: Victor Saville; *Producer:* Michael Balcon; *Original screenplay:* H.M. Harwood; *Director of photography:* Kurt Courant; *Art director:* Alfred Junge;

Costumes: Cathleen Mann, Herbert Norris; *Editor:* Ian Dalrymple; *Musical direction:* Louis Levy; *Period adviser:* Herbert Norris; *Military adviser:* Captain H. Oakes-Jones; *Certificate:* U; *Running time:* 88 mins (7,969 ft).

Cast: George Arliss (Sir Arthur Wellesley, Duke of Wellington), Gladys Cooper ('Madame', Duchesse d'Angouleme), Ellaine Terriss (Kitty, Duchess of Wellington), A.E. Matthews (Lord Hill), Emlyn Williams (Bates), Lesley Wareing (Lady Frances Webster), Felix Aylmer (Lord Uxbridge), Peter Gawthorne (Duke of Richmond), Norma Varden (Duchess of Richmond), Walter Sondes (Webster), Allan Aynesworth (King Louis XVIII), Gyles Isham (Castlereagh), Gibb McLaughlin (Talleyrand), Campbell Gullan (D'Artois), Franklyn Dyall (Blücher), Farren Souter (Metternich), Frederick Leister (King of Prussia), Gerald Lawrence (Czar of Russia), Edmund Willard (Marshal Ney), Annie Esmond (Denise).

Première: London, Tivoli Cinema, 30 November 1934.

Victoria the Great

Imperator Film Productions. 1937.

Producer and director: Herbert Wilcox; *Scenario and dialogue:* Miles Malleson, Charles de Grandcourt; *Director of photography:* Frederick A. Young; *Technicolor photography:* William V. Skall; *Colour director:* Natalie Kalmus; *Art director:* L.P. Williams; *Costumes:* Doris Zinkeisen, Tom Heslewood; *Supervising editor:* James Elmo Williams; *Music:* Anthony Collins; *Musical director:* Muir Mathieson; *Certificate:* U; *Running time:* 112 mins (10,152 ft).

Cast: Anna Neagle (Queen Victoria), Anton Walbrook (Prince Albert), H.B. Warner (Lord Melbourne), Walter Rilla (Prince Ernst), Mary Morris (Duchess of Kent), James Dale (Duke of Wellington), Felix Aylmer (Lord Melbourne), Charles Carson (Sir Robert Peel), C.V. France (Archbishop of Canterbury), Gordon McLeod (John Brown), Arthur Young (William Ewart Gladstone), Greta Wegener (Baroness Lehzen), Paul Leyssac (Baron Stockmar), Percy Parsons (Abraham Lincoln), Derrick de Marney (Benjamin Disraeli), Henry Hallatt (Joseph Chamberlain), Hugh Miller (Lord Beaconsfield), Wyndham Goldie (Cecil Rhodes), Miles Malleson (Physician), Tom Heslewood (Sir Francis Grant), Frank Birch (Charles Dilke), Ivor Barnard (Assassin).

Premières: Ottawa, 15 August 1937; London, Leicester Square Theatre, 17 September 1937; New York, Radio City Music Hall, 30 October 1937.

Sixty Glorious Years

Imperator Film Productions. 1938.

Producer and director: Herbert Wilcox; *Scenario and dialogue:* Miles Malleson, Sir Robert Vansittart; *Director of photography:* Frederick A. Young; *Colour director:*

Natalie Kalmus; *Art director:* L.P. Williams; *Costumes:* Doris Zinkeisen, Tom Heslewood; *Editor:* Jill Irving; *Music:* Anthony Collins; *Musical director:* Muir Mathieson; *Certificate:* U; *Running time:* 95 mins (8,575 ft).

Cast: Anna Neagle (Queen Victoria), Anton Walbrook (Prince Albert), C. Aubrey Smith (Duke of Wellington), H.B. Warner (Lord Melbourne), Walter Rilla (Prince Ernst), Greta Wegener (Baroness Lehzen), Felix Aylmer (Lord Palmerston), Lewis Casson (Lord John Russell), Charles Carson (Sir Robert Peel), Joyce Bland (Florence Nightingale), C.V. France (Archbishop of Canterbury), Derrick de Marney (Disraeli), Frank Cellier (Lord Derby), Malcolm Keen (Gladstone), Harvey Braban (Lord Salisbury), Henry Hallatt (Chamberlain), Aubrey Dexter (Prince of Wales), Wyndham Goldie (A.J. Balfour), Frederick Lister (H.H. Asquith), Olaf Olsen (Prince Frederick William of Prussia), Pamela Standish (Princess Royal), Marie Wright (Maggie), Stuart Robertson (Anson), Gordon McLeod (John Brown), Laidman Browne (General Gordon), Robert Eddison (Professor).

Première: London, Odeon, Leicester Square, 14 October 1938.

This England

British National Pictures. 1941.

Director: David Macdonald; *Producer:* John Corfield; *Original story and screenplay:* A.R. Rawlinson, Bridget Boland; *Dialogue:* Emlyn Williams; *Associate producer:* Richard Vernon; *Director of photography:* Mutz Greenbaum; *Settings:* Duncan Sutherland; *Music:* Richard Addinsell; *Musical director:* Muir Mathieson; *Certificate:* U; *Running time:* 82 mins (7,500 ft).

Cast: Emlyn Williams (Appleyard), John Clements (Rookeby), Constance Cummings (Ann), Frank Pettingell, Esmond Knight, Roland Culver, Morland Graham, Leslie French, Martin Walker, Ronald Ward, James Harcourt, Walter Fitzgerald, Dennis Wyndham, Charles Victor, Amy Vess, William Humphries, Roddy McDowall.

Trade show: London, Pheonix, 11 February 1941.

Henry V

Two Cities Films. 1944.

Producer and director: Laurence Olivier; *Screenplay:* Laurence Olivier and Reginald Beck; *Adaptation:* Alan Dent; *Associate producer:* Dallas Bower; *Director of photography:* Robert Krasker; *Art director:* Paul Sheriff, assisted by Carmen Dillon; *Scenic artist:* E. Lindgaard; *Costume designer:* Roger Furse, assisted by Margaret Furse; *Special effects:* Percy Day; *Editor:* Reginald Beck; *Music:* William Walton; *Conducted by:* Muir Mathieson; *Certificate:* U; *Running time:* 137 mins (12,296 ft).

Cast: Laurence Olivier (King Henry V), Leslie Banks (Chorus), Felix Aylmer (Archbishop of Canterbury), Robert Helpman (English herald), Gerald Case (Earl of Westmoreland), Griffith Jones (Earl of Salisbury), Morland Graham (Sir Thomas Erpingham), Nicholas Hannen (Duke of Exeter), Michael Warre (Duke of Gloucester), Ralph Truman (Mountjoy), Ernest Thesiger (Duc de Berri), Frederick Cooper (Corporal Nym), Roy Emerton (Bardolph), Robert Newton (Ancient Pistol), Freda Jackson (Mistress Quickly), George Cole (Boy), George Robey (Sir John Falstaff), Harcourt Williams (King Charles VI of France), Russell Thorndike (Duke of Bourbon), Leo Genn (Constable of France), Francis Lister (Duke of Orleans), Max Adrian (Dauphin), Esmond Knight (Captain Fluellen), Michael Shepley (Captain Gower), John Laurie (Captain Jamy), Niall MacGinnis (Captain Macmorris), Frank Tickle (Governor of Harfleur), Renee Asherson (Princess Katharine), Ivy St Helier (Lady Alice), Janet Burnell (Queen of France), Arthur Hambling (John Bates), Jimmy Hanley (Michael Williams), Ernest Hare (Priest), Valentine Dyall (Duke of Burgundy).

Premières: London, Carlton, Haymarket, 27 November 1944; Boston, Esquire Theatre, 3 April 1946.

Scott of the Antarctic

Ealing Studios. 1948.

Director: Charles Frend; *Producer:* Michael Balcon; *Screenplay:* Walter Meade, Ivor Montagu; *Additional dialogue:* Mary Haley Bell; *Associate producer:* Sidney Cole; *Directors of photography:* Jack Cardiff, Osmond Borradaile, Geoffrey Unsworth; *Art director:* Arne Akermark; *Editor:* Peter Tanner; *Music:* Ralph Vaughan Williams; *Special effects art director:* Jim Morahan; *Technical advisers:* Quintin Riley, David James; *Certificate:* U; *Running time:* 111 mins (9,886 ft).

Cast: John Mills (Captain Robert Falcon Scott), Diana Churchill (Kathleen Scott), Harold Warrender (Dr E.A. Wilson), Anne Firth (Oriana Wilson), Derek Bond (Captain L.E.G. Oates), Reginald Beckwith (Lieutenant H.R. Bowers), James Roberston Justice (Petty Officer 'Taff' Evans), Kenneth More (Lieutenant E.R.G.R. 'Teddy' Evans), Norman Williams (Chief Stoker W. Lashly), John Gregson (Petty Officer T. Crean), James McKechnie (Surgeon Lt. E.L. Atkinson), Barry Letts (Apsley Cherry-Garrard), Dennis Vance (Charles S. Wright), Larry Burns (Petty Officer P. Keohane), Edward Lisak (Dimitri), Melville Crawford (Cecil Meares), Christopher Lee (Bernard Day), John Owers (F.J. Hooper), Bruce Seton (Lieutenant H. Pennell), Clive Morton (Herbert Ponting), Sam Kydd (Leading Stoker E. McKenzie), Mary Merrett (Helen Field), Dandy Nichols (Caroline), Percy Walsh (Chairman of meeting).

Première: London, Empire, Leicester Square, 29 November 1948.

Beau Brummell

Metro-Goldwyn-Mayer. 1954.

Director: Curtis Bernhardt; *Producer:* Sam Zimbalist; *Screenplay:* Karl Tunberg; based on the play by Clyde Fitch; *Director of photography:* Oswald Morris; *Art director:* Alfred Junge; *Costume designer:* Elizabeth Haffenden; *Editor:* Frank Clarke; *Music:* Richard Addinsell; *Certificate:* U; *Running time:* 110 mins (10,028 ft).

Cast: Stewart Granger (George Bryan 'Beau' Brummell), Elizabeth Taylor (Lady Patricia), Peter Ustinov (Prince of Wales), Robert Morley (King George III), James Hayter (Mortimer), James Donald (Lord Edwin Mercer), Rosemary Harris (Mrs Maria Fitzherbert), Paul Rogers (William Pitt), Noel Willman (Lord Byron), Peter Bull (Charles James Fox), Peter Dyneley (Midger), Charles Carson (Sir Geoffrey Baker), Ernest Clark (Dr Warren), Mark Dignam (Burke), David Horne (Thurlow), Ralph Truman (Sir Ralph Sidley), Elwyn Brook-Jones (Tupp), George de Warfaz (Dr Dubois), Henry Oscar (Dr Willis), Desmond Roberts (Colonel), Harold Kasket (Mayor of Calais).

Première: London, Empire, Leicester Square, 15 November 1954.

A Night to Remember

Rank Organisation. 1958.

Director: Roy Baker; *Producer:* William MacQuitty; *Screenplay:* Eric Ambler; based on the book by Walter Lord; *Executive producer:* Earl St John; *Director of photography:* Geoffrey Unsworth; *Art director:* Alex Vetchinsky; *Costume designer:* Yvonne Caffin; *Editor:* Sidney Hayers; *Music:* William Alwyn; *Special effects:* Bill Warrington; *Certificate:* U; *Running time:* 123 mins (11,063 ft).

Cast: Kenneth More (Second Officer Herbert Lightoller), Ronald Allen (Clarke), Ronald Ayres (Major Arthur Peuchen), Honor Blackman (Mrs Lucas), Anthony Bushell (Captain Rostron), John Cairney (Murphy), Jill Dixon (Mrs Clarke), Jane Downs (Mrs Lightoller), James Dyrenforth (Colonel Gracie), Michael Goodliffe (Thomas Andrews), Kenneth Griffith (John Phillips), Harriette Johns (Lady Richard), Frank Lawton (The Chairman), Richard Leech (First Officer William Murdoch), David McCallum (Harold Bride), Alec McCowan (Cottam), Tucker McGuire (Molly Brown), John Merivale (Lucas), Ralph Michael (Yates), Laurence Naismith (Captain Smith), Russell Napier (Captain Lord), Redmond Phillips (Hoyle), George Rose (Joughin), Joseph Tomelty (Dr O'Laughlin), Patrick Waddington (Sir Richard), Jack Watling (Fourth Officer Joseph Boxhall).

Première: London, Odeon, Leicester Square, 3 July 1958.

Zulu

Paramount/Diamond Films. 1964.

Director: Cy Endfield; *Producers:* Stanley Baker, Cy Endfield; *Screenplay:* Cy Endfield, John Prebble; *Director of photography:* Stephen Dade; *Art director:* Ernest Archer; *Wardrobe supervisor:* Arthur Newman; *Editor:* John Jympson; *Music:* John Barry; *Certificate:* U; *Running time:* 138 mins (12,150 ft).

Cast: Stanley Baker (Lieutenant John Chard, R.E.), Jack Hawkins (Reverend Otto Witt), Ulla Jacobsson (Margareta Witt), James Booth (Private Henry Hook), Michael Caine (Lieutenant Gonville Bromhead), Nigel Green (Colour Sergeant Bourne), Patrick Magee (Surgeon Major Reynolds), Ivor Emmanuel (Private Owen), Paul Daneman (Sergeant Maxfield), Glynn Edwards (Corporal Allen), Neil McCarthy (Private Thomas), David Kernan (Private Hitch), Gary Bond (Private Cole), Peter Gill (Private 612 Williams), Richard Davies (Private 593 Jones), Dafydd Harvard (Gunner Howarth), Denys Graham (Private 716 Jones), Dickie Owen (Corporal Schiess), Larry Taylor (Hughes), Joe Powell (Sergeant Windridge), John Sullivan (Stephenson), Harvey Hall (Sick Man), Gert Van Den Bergh (Adendorf), Dennis Folbigge (Commissary Dalton), Kerry Jordan (Company cook), Ronald Hill (Bugler), Chief Buthelezi (Cetewayo), Daniel Tshabalala (Jacob), Ephraim Mbhele (Red Garters), Simon Sabela (Dance leader). Narration spoken by Richard Burton.

Première: London, ABC Plaza, 22 January 1964.

The Charge of the Light Brigade

United Artists/Woodfall Films. 1968.

Director: Tony Richardson; *Producer:* Neil Hartley; *Screenplay:* Charles Wood; *Director of photography:* David Watkin; *Period and colour consultant:* Lila de Nobili; *Historical research:* John Mollo; *Art director:* Edward Marshall; *Costume designer:* David Walker; *Supervising editor:* Kevin Brownlow; *Second unit director:* Christian de Chalonge; *Music:* John Addison; *Special effects:* Robert MacDonald, Paul Pollard; *Animation:* Richard Williams; *Certificate:* A; *Running time:* 132 mins (12,690 ft).

Cast: Trevor Howard (Lord Cardigan), David Hemmings (Captain Nolan), Vanessa Redgrave (Clarissa), John Gielgud (Lord Raglan), Harry Andrews (Lord Lucan), Jill Bennett (Mrs Duberly), Peter Bowles (Paymaster Duberly), Micky Baker (Trooper Metcalfe), Leo Britt (General Scarlet), Mark Burns (Captain Morris), John Carney (Trooper Mitchell), Helen Cherry (Lady Scarlett), Ambrose Coghill (Douglas), Chris Cunningham (Farrier), Mark Dignam (General Airey), Alan Dobie (Mogg), Georges Douking (Marshal St Anaud), Andrew Faulds (Quaker Preacher), Willoughby Goddard (Squire de Burgh), Ben Howard (Pridmore), Rachel Kempson (Mrs Codrington), T.P. McKenna (William Howard Russell), Howard Marion Crawford (Sir George Brown), Michael Miller (Major-General Sir Colin Campbell), Declan Mulholland (Farrier), Roger Mutton

(Codrington), Valerie Newman (Mrs Mitchell), Roy Patterson (Regimental Sergeant Major), Corin Redgrave (Featherstonehaugh), Norman Rossington (Sergeant Major Corbett), Dino Shafeek (Nolan's manservant), John Treneman (Sergeant Smith), Colin Vancao (Captain Charteris), Donald Wolfit ('Macbeth').

Première: London, Odeon, Leicester Square, 10 April 1968.

Henry VIII and His Six Wives

Anglo-EMI. 1972.

Director: Waris Hussein; *Producer:* Roy Baird; *Screenplay:* Ian Thorne; *Executive producer:* Mark Shivas; *Director of photography:* Peter Suschitzky; *Production designer:* Roy Stannard; *Costume designer:* John Bloomfield; *Editor:* John Bloom; *Music:* David Munro; *Certificate:* A; *Running time:* 125 mins (11,275 ft).

Cast: Keith Michell (King Henry VIII), Frances Cuka (Catherine of Aragon), Charlotte Rampling (Anne Boleyn), Jane Asher (Jane Seymour), Jenny Bos (Anne of Cleves), Lynne Frederick (Catherine Howard), Barbara Leigh-Hunt (Catherine Parr), Donald Pleasence (Thomas Cromwell), Michael Gough (Norfolk), Brian Blessed (Suffolk), Michael Goodliffe (Thomas More), Robin Sachs (Culpeper), Garfield Morgan (Gardiner), Michael Byrne (Edward Seymour), Peter Clay (Thomas Seymour), David Baillie (Norris), Clive Merrison (Weston), Mark York (Brereton), Nicholas Amer (Chapuys), Sarah Long (Mary), Peter Madden (Fisher), Damien Thomas (Smeaton), Simon Henderson (Prince Edward).

Première: ABC, Shaftesbury Avenue, 13 July 1972.

Chariots of Fire

Enigma Productions/Twentieth Century-Fox/Allied Stars. 1981.

Director: Hugh Hudson; *Producer:* David Puttnam; *Screenplay:* Colin Welland; *Executive producer:* Dodi Fayed; *Associate producer:* James Crawford; *Director of photography:* David Watkin; *Art director:* Roger Hall; *Costume designer:* Milena Canonero; *Editor:* Terry Rawlings; *Music composed, arranged and performed by:* Vangelis Papathanassiou; *Advisers:* Jennie Liddell, Jackson Scholz; *Certificate:* U; *Running time:* 120 mins (10,904 ft).

Cast: Ben Cross (Harold Abrahams), Ian Charleson (Eric Liddell), Ian Holm (Sam Mussabini), Nigel Havers (Lord Andrew Lindsay), Cheryl Campbell (Jennie Liddell), Alice Krige (Sybil Gordon), Nicholas Farrell (Aubrey Montague), Lindsay Anderson (Master of Caius College), Sir John Gielgud (Master of Trinity), Struan Rodger (Sandy McGrath), Nigel Davenport (Lord Birkenhead), Peter Egan (Duke of Sutherland), David Yelland (Prince of Wales), Patrick Magee (Lord Cadogan), Brad Davis (Jackson Scholz), Dennis Christopher (Charles Paddock), Daniel Gerroll (Henry Stallard), Yves Beneton (George Andre), John

Young (Reverend J.D. Liddell), Yvonne Gilan (Mrs Liddell), David John (Ernest Liddell), Benny Young (Rob Liddell), Gerry Slevin (Colonel Keddie), Philip O'Brien (American team coach), Richard Griffith (Caius head porter).

Première: London, Odeon, Leicester Square, 30 March 1981.

Elizabeth

Working Title Films/PolyGram Filmed Entertainment. 1998.

Director: Shekhar Kapur; *Producers:* Alison Owen, Eric Fellner, Tim Bevan; *Screenplay:* Michael Hirst; *Executive producer:* Jane Frazer; *Director of photography:* Remi Adefarasin; *Production designer:* John Myhre; *Costume designer:* Alexandra Byrne; *Editor:* Jill Bilcock; *Music:* David Hirschfelder; *Certificate:* 15; *Running time:* 123 mins (11,081 ft).

Cast: Cate Blanchett (Queen Elizabeth I), Geoffrey Rush (Sir Francis Walsingham), Joseph Fiennes (Robert Dudley, Earl of Leicester), Christopher Ecclestone (Duke of Norfolk), Richard Attenborough (Sir William Cecil), Fanny Ardant (Mary of Guise), Kathy Burke (Mary Tudor), Eric Cantona (Monsieur de Foix), James Frain (Alvaro de la Quadra), Vincent Cassel (Duc d'Anjou), Daniel Craig (John Ballard), Angus Deayton (Woad, Chancellor of the Exchequer), Edward Hardwicke (Earl of Arundel), Terence Rigby (Bishop Gardiner), John Gielgud (The Pope), Amanda Ryan (Lettice Howard), Kelly MacDonald (Isabel Knollys), Emily Mortimer (Kate Ashley), Rod Culbertson (Master Ridley), George Yiasoumi (King Philip II of Spain), Jamie Foreman (Earl of Essex), Wayne Sleep (Dance tutor).

Première: London, Odeon, Leicester Square, 29 September 1998.

Index

Note: Page numbers in **bold type** denote an illustration.